RENCONTRES
283

Série *Civilisation médiévale*
dirigée par Richard Trachsler et Estelle Doudet
24

La Permission et la Sanction

Actes des colloques « La permission et la sanction : théories légales et pratiques du théâtre (1400-1600) » et « Les conflits de juridiction (1400-1600) » organisés respectivement les 26 et 27 novembre 2009 et les 29 et 30 mars 2012 à l'université d'Amsterdam

La Permission et la Sanction

Théories légales et pratiques du théâtre (XIVe-XVIIe siècle)

Sous la direction de Marie Bouhaïk-Gironès,
Jelle Koopmans et Katell Lavéant

PARIS
CLASSIQUES GARNIER
2017

Marie Bouhaïk-Gironès est chargée de recherche au CNRS (centre Roland-Mousnier, université Paris-Sorbonne). Spécialiste de l'histoire des pratiques théâtrales (XIIe-XVIe siècle), elle a notamment publié *Les Clercs de la basoche et le théâtre comique (Paris, 1420-1550)* (Paris, 2007), et codirigé l'ouvrage collectif *Prédication et performance du XIIe au XVIe siècle* (Paris, 2013).

Jelle Koopmans enseigne la littérature française à l'université d'Amsterdam et est spécialiste du théâtre des XVe et XVIe siècles. Il a notamment publié des éditions critiques de textes de théâtre et nouvelles, et les cinquante-trois farces du *Recueil de Florence* (Orléans, 2011) et le premier volume du *Recueil des sotties françaises* (Paris, 2014).

Katell Lavéant, maître de conférences à l'université d'Utrecht (Pays-Bas), est spécialiste du théâtre dans les Pays-Bas méridionaux, notamment sous la Réforme. Elle a publié *Un théâtre des frontières. La culture dramatique dans les provinces du Nord aux XVe et XVIe siècles* (Orléans, 2011). Elle travaille actuellement sur la poésie bourguignonne et sur la culture joyeuse dans la société médiévale et renaissante.

ISBN 978-2-406-06382-7 (livre broché)
ISBN 978-2-406-06383-4 (livre relié)
ISSN 2103-5636

INTRODUCTION

La littérature dans ses rapports avec le droit et la loi a fait l'objet de recherches neuves depuis une vingtaine d'années[1]. Cependant, le lien spécifique entre le théâtre et la loi reste encore largement à explorer, en particulier pour la période allant du XIVe au XVIIe siècle. En effet, il est important de saisir des continuités qui dépassent une périodisation traditionnelle entre le Moyen Âge et le début de l'époque moderne, dans la mesure où le phénomène théâtral se caractérise par une absence de rupture dans les pratiques. Outre une forme de subvention de la part de l'Église et des autorités laïques, on observe tout au long de la période un mouvement de contrôle, voire de censure, ainsi qu'un grand nombre d'interdictions, d'événements à caractère dramatique, ou de situations que nous qualifierons globalement de « théâtre », mais dont nous n'excluons pas certaines circonstances ludiques (A. Rizzi), des festivités telles que le carnaval (H. Greco-Kaufmann ; D. Reid), ou des cas de mise en scène de la justice (F. Camphuijsen). En ce sens, la proposition de Christian Biet de parler de "séance théâtrale" résume notre approche large du phénomène, dans ce qu'il présente de problématique pour des autorités ayant parfois autant de mal à le contrôler que (comme nous aujourd'hui) à en déterminer la nature exacte. Cette nature floue participe justement de l'impossibilité de déterminer des limites clairement établies sur le plan juridique à ces situations mouvantes, sans oublier que ce qui est autorisé ou toléré dans une juridiction ou à un moment précis peut faire l'objet de sanctions dans d'autres.

Utiliser le nouveau medium, le contrôler, le surveiller : tels semblent bien être les enjeux de ces différentes autorités qui se voient confrontées à une expression efficace au sein d'une opinion publique en train de se constituer. Il s'agit dans cet ouvrage de scruter les rapports entre la

---

1 Voir entre autres, Ch. Biet, *Droit et littérature sous l'Ancien Régime. Le Jeu de la valeur et de la loi*, Paris, Champion, 2002 ; plus récemment, *Écrivains juristes et juristes écrivains, du Moyen Âge au Siècle des Lumières*, Bruno Méniel (dir.), Paris, Classiques Garnier, 2015.

législation et la pratique théâtrale dans leurs différents aspects : de la conceptualisation légale du fait théâtral à l'entrecroisement des jeux dramatiques et de la formation rhétorique des étudiants (M. Ferrand), de la propagande orchestrée par le pouvoir aux sanctions des différentes autorités (A. van Dixhoorn ; A.-L van Bruaene), de la collaboration harmonieuse aux conflits de juridiction (O. Spina ; A. Sanchez Jimenez). C'est en partie l'histoire d'une conceptualisation : comment la loi et la législation arrivent-ils à définir le fait théâtral ? C'est également une confrontation à la pratique : de la régulation à la censure et même à l'interdiction. C'est finalement une histoire des gens de théâtre et de leur formation ainsi que des milieux intellectuels où le théâtre se fait et se définit. L'analyse de cette question coïncide avec un nouvel intérêt des historiens pour l'investissement de l'espace public à la fin du Moyen Âge[2]. Il permet également une interrogation autre des sources et un retour sur la place problématique du phénomène au sein d'une société à la découverte de son théâtre.

Parmi les lignes directrices qui se dessinèrent lors de deux colloques tenus à Amsterdam en 2009 et 2012, plusieurs méritent d'être soulignées ici, pour tenter de cerner, sinon de répondre, à une chaîne de questionnement : qui contrôle quoi, où et comment, et avec quels effets ? Si, comme nous l'avons souligné plus haut, il est bien difficile de cerner le *quoi*, cet objet performatif protéiforme, il s'avère tout aussi compliqué d'approcher de manière univoque le *qui*. Qui encadre, qui contrôle ? La dichotomie autorités religieuses / autorités civiles ne doit pas faire oublier que dans chacune de ces catégories, de nombreuses parties sont engagées, parfois de façon conflictuelle[3]. Pour ne prendre qu'un exemple, dans les cas de poursuites judiciaires de représentations polémiques dans les espaces des Pays-Bas au milieu du XVIe siècle, lors

2 P. Boucheron et N. Offenstadt, *L'espace public au Moyen Âge. Débats autour de Jürgen Habermas*, Paris, PUF, 2011.

3 Sur les conflits de juridiction entre les juridictions ecclésiastiques et les juridictions royales, voir par exemple le cas de l'affaire Poncelet : les plaidoiries du procureur du roi et de l'évêque de Paris lors d'un conflit de juridiction qui les oppose en 1416 devant le Parlement de Paris autour du cas de Poncelet de Montchauvet, clerc criminel ayant exercé une activité du spectacle, nous éclairent sur les processus de construction empirique des normes en matière de statut du théâtre et de ses acteurs. M. Bouhaïk-Gironès, « Le statut de l'acteur face aux pratiques du droit : l'exemple de l'affaire Poncelet au Parlement de Paris (1416) », *Droit et pratiques théâtrales (12e-16e s.), Cahiers de Recherches Médiévales et Humanistes*, 23, juin 2012, p. 127-140.

de la montée des idées de la Réforme, il ne s'agissait pas seulement de déterminer si les personnes poursuivies relevaient des autorités civiles ou religieuses, mais de savoir si l'autorité compétente était l'autorité ecclésiastique locale ou l'Inquisition (A.-L. Van Bruaene). Les conflits de juridiction pouvaient ainsi rendre le contrôle et la sanction plus difficiles, et dans beaucoup de cas, les acteurs et les organisateurs d'une représentation avaient la possibilité de faire appel auprès d'une autre institution que celle qui avait émis une première interdiction. Pourquoi ces conflits de juridictions se révèlent aussi nombreux, d'après les sources ? Les structures pouvaient se recouper, les autorités se croiser, les pratiques anciennes de contrôle ne pas être immédiatement supplantées par de nouvelles régulations (A. Rizzi ; H. Greco-Kaufmann) – l'étude des sources met ainsi clairement en évidence qu'un contrôle local a existé bien avant la mise en place d'un système plus centralisé au plan régional ou national, notamment lors de la multiplication de représentations polémiques au XVIe siècle. Mais ce flou sur le champ des juridictions fait aussi écho à la difficulté à cerner l'objet mis en cause.

Où l'on en revient au *quoi et à ses acteurs*. Quelles personnes peuvent être tenues responsables d'une représentation polémique ? Les joueurs ou les organisateurs de la représentation ? Ceux qui laissent jouer la pièce, ou ceux qui l'ont écrite, imprimée, diffusée[4] ? Et quels objets sont visés par le contrôle et la sanction, ou pour mieux dire : de quel texte s'agit-il ? La performance théâtrale a ceci de particulier que la parole jouée sur scène a un statut particulièrement ambigu quand il s'agit de censurer un texte. Il y a toujours un décalage possible entre le texte proposé pour la représentation et contrôlé auparavant d'une part, et celui qui est effectivement prononcé sur scène d'autre part. La reconstitution de ce texte après une représentation est tout aussi problématique[5]. De plus, il faut tenir compte d'un troisième écart possible, entre ce qui est dit sur la scène et ce qui est ressenti (ou compris) par

4 K. Lavéant, « Le théâtre du Nord et la Réforme : un procès d'acteurs dans la région de Lille en 1563 », *European Medieval Drama*, 11 (2007), p. 59-77 ; K. Lavéant, « Une scène incontrôlable ? L'encadrement juridique des pratiques théâtrales à Lille et dans sa région à l'époque de la Réforme », *Tangence*, 104 (2014), p. 11-26.

5 M. Bouhaïk-Gironès, « À qui profite l'auteur ? Théâtre, responsabilité de la parole et fonction-auteur à la fin du Moyen Âge », Revue *Parlement(s). Revue d'histoire politique*, hors-série n° 8, *Scènes politiques*, dir. C. Legoy, 2012, p. 27-37.

le public. Il est en ce sens nécessaire de considérer non pas uniquement le temps de la performance, mais également ce qui se passe avant et après, pour comprendre comment ce phénomène dans son ensemble est pris en compte dans les enquêtes. Une constante apparaît dans les cas étudiés : une irréductible incontrôlabilité du théâtre, car les instruments de la censure sont difficilement adaptables à la représentation spectaculaire. Il est très complexe d'établir les responsabilités. Retenons ici qu'en fin de compte, dans les situations analysées, la loi et la justice s'occupent bien des hommes et des pratiques, et non pas du concept général du théâtre.

Qui et *quoi* apparaissant comme problématiques, *où* l'est peut-être moins, mais là encore, il faut tenir compte de la diversité des cadres de représentation, et ne pas oublier l'auberge, les maisons des particuliers, la "chambre"[6] (W. Prevenier), face aux lieux plus attendus de la rue, de la place publique, de la scène ouverte (mieux balisés par l'historiographie comme espaces performatifs), sans oublier de considérer l'apparition des théâtres modernes tels qu'ils se constituent au XVIe siècle (A. Sanchez Jimenez ; O. Spina). Jusqu'à quel point faut-il penser, pour la période étudiée, qu'il existe des différences fondamentales dans la législation et la vision du contrôle du théâtre entre l'espace public et l'espace "privé" ou considéré comme tel dans les sources ? Là aussi, on constate une grande variété des lieux utilisés par l'activité dramatique, malgré les tentatives de limiter cet envahissement par la performance des différents espaces dans la ville, ou du moins de circonscrire ces lieux.

Reste la question de la manière dont les autorités régulent ou tentent de réguler ces performances, autrement dit la question du *comment*. Il faut d'abord rappeler qu'il existe une organisation du contrôle du texte avant la représentation. On le voit apparaître dans les sources de la pratique et il est repérable dans les documents d'archives dès la première moitié du XVe siècle. Ce contrôle repose sur une pratique localisée, car la législation régionale, royale ou impériale n'est pas encore formalisée à cette époque. Ces situations méritent d'être davantage étudiées, car

6 K. Lavéant, « Le théâtre à l'auberge : l'hôtellerie, lieu de représentations dramatiques dans les villes du Nord aux XVe et XVIe siècles », *Drama, Performance and Spectacle in the Medieval City – Mélanges en hommage à Alan Hindley*, dir. C. Emerson, M. Longtin et A. Tudor, Louvain, Peeters, 2010, p. 149-162.

si l'on peut observer un certain système dans ce contrôle (notamment dans une répartition possible des rôles entre autorités civiles et ecclésiastiques), les cas que nous avons conservés laissent aussi apparaître des zones d'ombre et des incertitudes sur la manière dont cette censure pouvait effectivement s'appliquer. Au XVIe siècle, notamment du fait de l'apparition de la Réforme, on constate dans ces certains espaces européens la naissance d'une législation plus large. Ainsi, dans les Pays-Bas sous la domination des empereurs Habsbourg, cette législation, qui touche d'abord la diffusion des textes écrits à partir de 1520, vise progressivement la parole publique et finalement le théâtre ainsi que le chant, bien qu'il faille attendre 1560 pour qu'une ordonnance de Philippe II d'Espagne pose un cadre précis pour le contrôle du contenu religieux des textes dramatiques – sans pour autant interdire le théâtre dans son ensemble, ni même le théâtre moral et religieux. Cependant, il faut également prendre en compte le fait que le théâtre est régulé ou se régule d'autres manières à partir du XVIe siècle, par une ramification du contrôle au niveau local, qui passe désormais par de plus nombreuses instances. C'est par exemple par l'institutionnalisation des spectacles des étudiants – en intégrant pleinement le théâtre aux moyens pédagogiques – que les autorités universitaires parisiennes tentent d'intervenir, elles que le mode de production collectif ne cesse d'inquiéter (M. Ferrand). Dans la capitale anglaise, ce sont les paroisses londoniennes qui se voient confier un rôle clé dans le contrôle des spectacles au cours du XVIe siècle (O. Spina).

En fin de compte, quels sont les effets de la censure ? Dans certains cas évoqués ici ou pour d'autres qu'il faudrait étudier précisément, on peut se demander quels sont les dispositifs de défense mis en place par les acteurs pour y échapper ou pour s'y conformer. Le problème du contrôle est à double tranchant : la censure exacerbe le désir de transgression et attire l'attention sur ce que l'on voudrait passer sous silence ou minimiser. Transgresser la loi par le biais du théâtre permet en effet d'agrandir les effets du discours proposé. C'est sans doute pourquoi les autorités sont très prudentes quand il s'agit d'engager des poursuites et hésitent à faire passer devant la justice les acteurs fauteurs de trouble, car elles savent qu'un procès pourrait leur servir de chambre d'écho. La figure du censeur ou du défenseur est d'ailleurs présente sur la scène. Dans les mystères, celle de l'Inquisiteur donne corps à l'image d'une société chrétienne unifiée et répressive à l'encontre de tous les détracteurs de la foi (C. Salatko-Petryszcze) ; quant à la Vierge Marie, c'est dans son rôle d'avocate du genre humain qu'elle est figurée sur la scène (D. Hüe). Par ailleurs, dans les moralités, la prise de parole publique est interrogée à travers la mise en scène du personnage de Justice, qu'il représente la loi, la permission ou la sanction (E. Doudet). Autrement dit, dans les textes de théâtre eux-mêmes, on voit émerger un discours réflexif qui témoigne de l'importance des notions de permission et de sanction pour la compréhension du phénomène performatif de la fin du Moyen Âge au XVIIe siècle.

Cet ouvrage collectif marque l'aboutissement d'un projet financé par l'Organisation pour la Recherche Néerlandaise (NWO) : *Law and Drama : How Theatrical Practices are defined by, with, and against the Law in France & French-speaking regions (13th-16th centuries)*, dont l'ancrage institutionnel se trouvait à l'Université d'Amsterdam pour la période 2008-2013. Sous la direction de Jelle Koopmans, ce projet a associé deux chercheuses en post-doctorat, Marie Bouhaïk-Gironès et Katell Lavéant, et un doctorant, Simon Gabay, autour des questions liées au statut juridique du théâtre pendant la période médiévale, dans une approche combinant une réflexion sur les pratiques et les textes théâtraux, et sur les sources de législation, de régulation et de censure portant sur ces situations performatives[7].

Les articles ici rassemblés sont le fruit de deux colloques tenus à l'Université d'Amsterdam en 2009 et 2012 dans le cadre de ce projet. Ils ont été l'occasion de faire se rencontrer et dialoguer des spécialistes de domaines linguistiques et géographiques très variés, permettant de croiser une réflexion sur des situations du domaine francophone avec d'autres sur des lieux aussi divers que Venise, Londres, Lucerne et les espaces des Pays-Bas, sur une période allant de la fin du Moyen Âge au début de l'époque moderne. Loin de disperser les approches, la diversité

7 Parmi les résultats de ce projet, on citera notamment les travaux suivants, fruit de la collaboration au sein de cette équipe : M. Bouhaïk-Gironès, S. Gabay, J. Koopmans et K. Lavéant, « Legal theory, legal practice, and drama (1200-1600) », *Law and Humanities, 5/1 : Law and Literature* (2011), p. 75-95 ; « Droit et pratiques théâtrales (12e-16e s.) », dossier thématique de la revue *Cahiers de Recherches Médiévales et Humanistes*, n° 23, 2012 ; *Recueil des sotties françaises, tome 1*, dir. M. Bouhaïk-Gironès, J. Koopmans & K. Lavéant, Paris, Classiques Garnier, 2014.

des cas étudiés a au contraire constamment mis en lumière des points de convergence autour de quelques notions centrales, que les articles de ce volume éclairent.

Marie BOUHAÏK-GIRONÈS,
Jelle KOOPMANS
et Katell LAVÉANT

Outre les contributeurs à ce volume, il nous faut également remercier Matthieu Bonicel, Charles-Antoine Chamay et Tjeerd Schiphof de leur participation à ces rencontres et de leurs contributions particulièrement éclairantes sur, respectivement : les sources réglementaires des performances en France, le théâtre à Genève pendant la Réforme et la réglementation sur le théâtre en Angleterre et aux Pays-Bas. De même, nous remercions Simon Gabay pour avoir alors proposé une réflexion stimulante sur le théâtre dans les conciles (de Bâle à Trente) et participé à l'organisation du second colloque.

PREMIÈRE PARTIE

LÉGISLATIONS ET JURIDICTIONS RÉGIONALES

THE LAW, JUSTICE, GOVERNANCE, AND THEATRICAL KNOWLEDGE

in the Sixteenth-Century Dutch-speaking Low Countries[1]

INTRODUCTION

In the study of literary culture and the related problem of freedom of expression, the impact of political and judicial authorities is often interpreted as an obstructive element of constraint. Instead, this essay will focus on the positive role of the law and censorship measures as an affirmative, creative, and formative contribution to the development of theatrical cultures in the early modern Low Countries.

In the fifteenth century, the authorities warranted the institutionalization of the rhetorical-theatrical paradigm, a culture of experts and their interpretation of the literary performance as a form of public speech (rhetoric). In the wake of the Reformations of the sixteenth century however, governmental, judicial, intellectual and religious authorities would contribute to the separation of the theatre and other forms of public speech, and the creation of a new theatrical paradigm.

Acts of government and the practice of justice always cause intended and unintended effects on institutions, groups, and individuals. Prudent authorities will therefore likely base their decisions on estimates of their effects. Such estimates will be grounded in some sort of understanding (whether true or false, whether local or universal, whether explicit or implicit) of the social and cultural phenomena that the authorities aim to extirpate, regulate, stimulate, or empower.

1 With thanks to Susie Speakman Sutch (Ghent University) for critical comments and corrections. The essay was written with a postdoctoral grant of the Belgian Research Foundation-Flanders (FWO).

Authorities, then, must have had some understanding of the phenomena they sought to influence. They needed names, categories and taxonomies of social phenomena (i.e. knowledge), in order to make laws covering many cases or to apply the law prudently in a particular case. Their knowledge, and the expertise of others that they accepted, was institutionalized as authoritative as a result of their power. In short, authorities did not only make use of knowledge created and provided by others (experts, informants) but were themselves positive sources of knowledge on all sorts of political, social, and cultural phenomena. These forms of public knowledge were negotiated results of legal principles, daily experiences, and controversies.

The theatrical (role-playing, performance, and all sorts of foregrounded action and speech in front of a live audience) was omnipresent in early modern public life; and the authorities played a defining role in the institutionalization of theatrical knowledge in the Dutch-speaking Low Countries of the sixteenth-century, together with local and regional networks of experts and informants[2]. This knowledge was turned into law and governmental measures, and practiced in courts of justice. This essay will explore the problem that the institutionalized theatrical knowledge of the early modern period cannot simply be compared to our category of the theatre. Instead, it will be argued that the latter was the combined result of the religious policies of late-sixteenth century Europe, and the rise of the classicizing interpretation of the theatrical culture of antiquity or of its early Christian critics.

In an attempt to understand the juridical and epistemological status of the theatrical in the sixteenth-century Dutch-speaking Low Countries, this essay will probe the transformation of the theatrical paradigm in the well-documented case of Holland, and examine the juridical status

2 My views on the theatrical and theatricality have been influenced by Cl. Geertz, *Negara: The Theatre State in Nineteenth-Century Bali*, Princeton, Princeton University Press, 1980; S. Greenblatt, *Renaissance Self-fashioning. From More to Shakespeare*, Chicago/London, University of Chicago Press, 1980; E. Fischer-Lichte, "Wahrnehmung und Medialität", in: E. Fischer-Lichte, C. Horn and S. Umathum (eds), *Wahrnehmung und Medialität*, Tübingen/Basel, Francke, 2001, p. 11–27; A. Kotte, "The transformation of a ceremony of penance into a play", *Theatrical Events: Borders Dynamics Frames*, V. A. Cremona, P. Eversmann, H. van Maanen, W. Sauter and J. Tulloch (dir.), Amsterdam/New York, Rodopi, 2004, p. 53–68; P. Eversmann, "Introduction to part two", V. A. Cremona et al., op. cit., p. 133–138; J. McGavin, *Theatricality and Narrative in Medieval and Early Modern Scotland*, Ashgate, Aldershot, 2007.

of the theatrical through the lens of the successful reference work on the practice of criminal justice by the Flemish-born lawyer Joos de Damhoudere. The resulting epistemology of the theatrical will be compared to the status of the theatrical in a court of law in the cases the Antwerp sheriff brought against a local printer and two rhetoricians in the 1540s.

Since parts of this essay will deal with the positive (creative) role of censorship in the institutionalization of theatrical knowledge, a preliminary remark on the principles of sixteenth-century governance and justice in the Low Countries seems in order. The combined evidence from criminal proceedings on local and regional levels[3]; letters from the central government in Brussels on the execution and effective implementation of laws[4]; legal treatises published in the 1550s[5], and judgments by historians underline the role of knowledge in governance and justice[6].

An important part of governance and legal practices was to establish a trustworthy version of the relevant facts. The guiding principle was to govern and judge with reason and clemency, and only to be unforgiving if absolutely necessary. The establishment of the truth and the use of reason in making and applying laws were not self-evident, and this was well-known in government circles and beyond.

The epistemological difficulty was that decisions were always grounded in the opinions provided by witnesses, judges, councils of government and their advisors, and local experts and informants, and only seldom in undisputable facts. This made the act of governing and judging a delicate matter. The authorities were always in danger of punishing the wrong people, enforcing bad measures, producing unwanted effects, and endangering the peace, which required the highest caution.

3 See the cases in this essay and also M. Vrolijk, *Recht door gratie: gratie bij doodslagen en andere delicten in Vlaanderen, Holland en Zeeland (1531–1567)*, Hilversum, Verloren, 2004.

4 See for this attitude for example the letters by the governess Parma to cities of Holland and Zealand in: Archives Générales du Royaume, Brussels, Papiers d'État et de l'Audience, inv. no. 327–330.

5 A. Perneder, *Een tractaet van criminele saken, ghesedt by maniere van een judiciele practica van saken die dlijf aengaen*, Antwerpen, Hans de Laet, 1550; J. De Damhoudere, *Practycke ende handbouck in criminele zaeken, verchiert met zommeghe schoone figuren ende beilden ter materie dienende* [...], Leuven, Steven Wouters and Ian Bathen, 1555.

6 See for example, H. van Nierop, *Treason in the Northern Quarter: war, terror, and the rule of law in the Dutch revolt*, Princeton, N.J., Princeton University Press, 2009 (translated by J. C. Grayson).

The fundamental problem of society and government was, in the philosophy of the Bruges rhetorician Eduard de Dene, for example, that opinions rule the world, while society is in terrible need of reason and truth. The truth however, educated people were warned, could not easily be established by humans, since *quot homines, tot sententiae*; so many people, so many opinions[7]. The solution recommended in legal treatises of the 1550s included prayer and good intentions, and also to refrain from self-interest, to try one's very best, and to take advice from others[8].

In short, governing and legal authorities interested in continuity had to make decisions that took the nature of specific phenomena into account, in order to understand (un)intended effects and make rulings that would augment rather than diminish their reputation. This is why the role of knowledge should be preliminary to any effort to understand the interplay between the law and the theatrical.

TRANSFORMING THE THEATRICAL PARADIGM

What, then, was the epistemological status of the theatrical? With what sort of juridical-technical framework did contemporaries describe, define, analyze and solve issues concerning the theatrical, and what institutions, groups, and networks were involved in negotiating and consolidating these conceptualizations?

Unlike the culture of professional performers (often travelling companies of entertainers), the urban theatrical world grew to prominence as part of a public and private festive calendar, with the active support and engagement of persons and institutions of the local, regional, and central governments. Craft guilds, confraternities, neighborhoods, and

---

7 E. de Dene, "Refereyn. [*incipit*:] De Weerelt zynde gheel nv int quaede ghestelt", from his manuscript book *Testament rhetoricael*, W. Waterschoot, D. Coigneau et al, *Jaarboek De Fonteine* 26, 28, and 30 (1976–1980). Edition Digitale Bibliotheek der Nederlandse Letterkunde (DBNL) 2003, p. 81–83.

8 See, "Dlof ende officium van goede richters ende justiciers", in: Perneder, op. cit., f. 50-f. 54ro. See also the dedication of De Damhoudere, op. cit.; and the dedication to the Prince of Orange of the French edition, *Practique judiciaire es causes criminelles*, Antwerp, Jean Bellere, 1564.

other urban institutions patronized, sponsored and organized literary performances, contests, and festivals[9].

Local governments in particular increasingly invested substantial financial resources in support of this community-based theatrical culture. From the francophone court to the local councils the government also increasingly valued the theatrical expertise of individuals, such as the professional *rhétoriqueurs* of the Burgundian court and from the 1450s onwards the city *retorisienen*, who were paid individuals or groups from the local community associated with the corporate bodies that quickly monopolized the role of experts in theatrical civic culture[10].

Those corporate bodies, the so-called chambers of rhetoric, were a mid-fifteenth-century synthesis of Dutch pedagogical and learned vernacular traditions and the francophone model of the *seconde rhétorique.* Influenced by this paradigm, the chambers of rhetoric claimed their culture of performative literature (songs, poems, plays) to be part of the rhetorical tradition, stressing the relations with the world of learning, in particular the seven liberal arts. Their claim to expertise in theatrical culture was soon acknowledged and protected by the government at the local and regional level predominantly. Many chambers or individual rhetoricians gained rights in the organization of local theatrical culture and chambers of important cities acquired or usurped the privilege to induct other corporations into the local or regional network of chambers[11].

---

9 See P. Arnade, *Realms of Ritual: Burgundian Ceremony and Civic Life in Late Medieval Ghent*, Ithaca/London, Cornell University Press, 1996; K. Ashley and W. Hüsken (dir.), *Moving Subjects: Processional Performance in the Middle Ages and the Renaissance*, Amsterdam, Rodopi, 2001.

10 See E. Lecuppre-Desjardin, *La ville des ceremonies: Essai sur la communication politique dans les anciens Pays-Bas bourguignons.* Turnhout, Brepols, 2004; E. Doudet, *Poétique de Georges Chastelain (1415–1475): "Un cristal mucié en un coffre"*, Paris, Champion, 2005; A.-L. Van Bruaene, *Om beters wille: Rederijkerskamers en de stedelijke cultuur in de Zuidelijke Nederlanden (1400–1650)*, Amsterdam, Amsterdam University Press, 2008; A. van Dixhoorn, *Lustige geesten: Rederijkers in de Noordelijke Nederlanden (1480–1650)*, Amsterdam, Amsterdam University Press, 2009.

11 A.-L. Van Bruaene, "A wonderful triumfe, for the wynnyng of a pryse": Guilds, Ritual, Theater, and the Urban Network in the Southern Low Countries, ca. 1450–1650", *Renaissance Quarterly*, 65 (2006), p. 374–405; A. van Dixhoorn, "Chambers of Rhetoric: Performative Culture and Literary Sociability in the Early Modern Northern Netherlands", *The Reach of the Republic of Letters: Literary and Learned Societies in Late Medieval and Early Modern Europe*, A. van Dixhoorn and S. Speakman Sutch (dir.), Leiden, Brill, 2008, p. 119–158.

An attempt by the government of Philip the Fair in 1493 to establish a sovereign chamber that would execute these privileges on a national level failed[12]. However, it attests to the crucial role of the government in the acceptance and increasing institutionalization of these local bodies of community-based vernacular experts and their interpretation of theatrical culture. Ultimately, the chambers of rhetoric were considered vital elements of any town and city. In many places they gained precedence in the representation of the community, with the militia guilds[13].

By 1500, the chambers and their leading members, these true *retorisienen*, had acquired a role as teachers of the public, protected by law against competitors, as foundational institutions of society. Crucial to their community service was the use of public spaces, such as market squares, churches, and other public buildings granted by the authorities, at local events or rhetorical festivals.

This formalization and protection of rhetorician culture by law rested on theatrical knowledge, a coalition and cultural consensus shared between chambers of rhetoric and institutions that were potential competitors in the field: most of the secular and (segments of the) religious clergy, schools, networks of humanists, and intellectual professionals (musicians, clerks, jurists, etc.) held together by active engagement of the members of these groups in the chambers of rhetoric. This coalition solidified the protection of rhetorical culture by law, but as all coalitions, it remained by no means unchallenged; and already it became seriously threatened by proponents of the protestant Reformations of the sixteenth century[14].

At first this threat was the result of a new consensus that was being worked out among circles of government and networks of Catholic reformers. This consensus was grounded in views on the relation between the community, the sacred and the prerogatives of the Roman Church to interpret, criticize and purify religious ceremonies, institutions, customs and traditions. The effect was that chambers of rhetoric, but other groups from the local community as well, had to re-negotiate and reaffirm the role of theatrical culture in society, forced by the anti-heresy policies of

12 Van Bruaene, *Om beters wille*, p. 63–66.

13 Van Bruaene, op. cit., 91–96; Van Dixhoorn, *Lustige geesten*, p. 62–63, 131, 155–158.

14 Van Bruaene, op. cit.; Van Dixhoorn, op. cit.; cf. N. Moser, *De strijd voor rhetorica: poëtica en positie van rederijkers in Vlaanderen, Brabant, Zeeland en Holland tussen 1450 en 1620*, Amsterdam, Amsterdam University Press, 2001, p. 194–202.

local, regional and central governments. The classicist attacks on the rhetorical interpretation of theatrical culture only became prominent in the early seventeenth century and also forced the rhetoricians to redefine their relations to the field of learning and the other cultural authorities[15].

The new environment, in which chambers of rhetoric, within a century after their establishment, had to renegotiate their rhetorical-theatrical paradigm, can be observed in relative detail in the county of Holland. One of the core provinces of the Habsburg Low Countries, Holland also ranked as the third region in Dutch-speaking rhetorical culture from the 1480s onwards. Soon after the emergence of the first Protestant circles in the province in the 1520s, its rhetorical-theatrical culture came under attack from a coalition of Dominicans, Franciscans, and the Chapel of Our Lady and the Court of Holland in The Hague. This coalition was the engine of a regional reformist network of clergymen loyal to the Catholic Church and highly active in lobbying for a new relation between Church and community. This network emerged as the force that would eventually forge a new theatrical consensus[16].

From the early 1520s onwards, key figures such as Antoine de Lalaing, Count of Hoochstraten (stadtholder of Holland and very influential at the Habsburg Court) or mid-century, Wilhelmus Lindanus, dean of the Chapel of Our Lady in The Hague, tried to curtail the role of theatrical culture in treating the Scriptures and matters of religion[17]. This proved to be very difficult since the rhetorical-theatrical consensus remained more or less intact on local levels or was even reinforced. The chambers of rhetoric also reorganized and re-activated their regional network as a festival culture comparable to the festival cultures of Flanders and Brabant. This increased their visibility and re-enforced their claim to

15 Van Dixhoorn, op. cit., p. 185–190, 209–226; cf. Moser, op. cit., p. 194–202, and E. K. Grootes, "De ontwikkeling van de literaire organisatievormen tijdens de zeventiende eeuw in Noordnederland", *De zeventiende eeuw*, 8 (1992), p. 53–65.

16 Van Dixhoorn, op. cit., 210–214, 219–221; F. C. van Boheemen and Th. C. J. van der Heijden (ed.), *Retoricaal memoriaal. Bronnen voor de geschiedenis van de Hollandse rederijkerskamers van de middeleeuwen tot het begin van de achttiende eeuw*, Delft, Eburon, 1999, p. 677–678; P. Fredericq, "De inquisiteur Sonnius over de rederijkers (1551)", *Tijdschrift voor Nederlandse taal en letterkunde*, 10 (1891), p. 32.

17 Lalaing was certainly not against rhetorician culture as such, since he and his wife favored the establishment of a chamber of rhetoric in their town of Hoochstraten in 1534. Van Bruaene, op. cit., 95. Lindanus, who was influential at the court in Brussels, would become Bishop of Roermond in 1562 and Bishop of Ghent in 1588.

learned expertise through these competitions with the active support of local governments and institutions[18].

A series of investigations of "scandalous" performances in various cities and towns of Holland had raised increasing concerns on the regional level and forced a rather radical transformation in theatrical knowledge at the Court of Holland. The body of alarming information on suspect performances, which by the way, might just as well have been incriminating traditional practices previously not conceived to be heretical, was piling up in the Catholic reformist circles of Holland. The evidence, acquired from informants, from official investigations, and from the study of suspect scripts, showed that censorship (required by an imperial ordinance of 1528) had no effect[19]. The Court of Holland then proceeded to ban all plays mentioning "sacred matters" in the course of 1528 and 1529. This ban apparently had no effect either and in September 1539, while expecting a new imperial ordinance, the Court of Holland ordered the full stop of *all* performances, religious *and* secular[20].

The famous imperial ordinance of 1540 however overruled this radical approach and reinstituted an approbation policy, which meant that plays had to be approved by a local clergyman (an expert in theology) prior to performance[21]. The results (again) did not satisfy the Catholic reformists, one of whom submitted another radical proposal to the government in Brussels in 1551 (Holland had lost its edge in censorship policies after the death of Hoochstraten in 1540), to simply eradicate the chambers of rhetoric, which he believed to be the root of all heresy[22].

The government in Brussels, however, still not convinced that a radical change in the relation between Church, government, and community was needed, decided in favor of an experiment with censorship, and installed a provincial committee of doctors of theology. The members, all key figures of the Catholic reform in Holland, had the impossible task of checking every single play prior to performance[23]. The experiment came to nothing. Yet, the new insights developed by this network

18 Van Dixhoorn, op. cit., p. 209–226. The imperial ordinance was dated 18 January 1527 (O.S.) and was published in Holland 4 February 1527 (O.S.).

19 Ibid., p. 209–226.

20 Van Boheemen and Van der Heijden, *Retoricaal Memoriaal*, p. 10–11.

21 Ibid., p. 11–12.

22 Van Dixhoorn, op. cit., p. 212.

23 Ibid., p. 212; Fredericq, op. cit., p. 32.

might very well have been sanctioned and universalized by the royal ordinance of 1560[24].

In line with the prevailing rhetorical-theatrical paradigm, and the ordinance of 1540, the royal ordinance aimed at all performative literature, not just the theatre play[25]. The novelty introduced by this law was that matters of religion and the Church were reserved as the prerogative of experts in theology. This pushed Dutch communal theatrical culture (and its experts, the rhetoricians) back into the realm of the common laity, and disassociated (communal) theatrical expressions from the sophisticated and learned, privileging a trend among learned clergy and humanists to folklorize community theatre[26].

The dilemma's of government and the role of theatrical knowledge in the negotiations between rhetoricians, Catholic Reformers, the law, and justice are shown in more detail in a case revealed by an extensive report on the state of religion submitted to the Regent of the Low Countries, Margaret of Parma. April 1565, the Regent had forwarded a questionnaire to the Court in The Hague. The questions were derived from a letter by Wilhelmus Lindanus, who had expressed his concern about the state of religion in the provinces of Holland and Zealand. The investigation took the Court and its informants almost a year. The Regent received their rather optimistic report on January 10th, 1566 (1565 O.S.)[27].

One of the questions expressed concern that the Bishop of Middelburg, Nicolaus de Castro, having tried to punish "*quelques suspectez de la chambre*

24 The ordinance of 26 January, 1559 (O.S.) published in Van Boheemen and Van der Heijden, op. cit., 13–15. Parma asked the Court of Holland for advice in a letter dated 15 November 1559. Ibid., 13.

25 The ordinance of 1540 referred to the plays of the Ghent festival of 1539, and "vele onbehoirlicke spelen, liedikins, refereynen ende figuren scandaleux, dangereux ende suspect van ketterie"; and the 1560 ordinance targeted: "diversche spelen van sinne oft moraliteyt, camerspelen, batementen, rondeelkens, refereynen, baladen ende diergelijcke" disseminated, sung or performed in any way. The ordinance of 1528 was only directed at "batementen" or "diversche spelen" (various plays). See the editions published in Van Boheemen and Van der Heijden, op. cit., 10–14.

26 See also H. Pleij, "The despisers of rhetoric: origins and significance of attacks on the art of therhetoricians (rederijkers) in the sixteenth century", *Rhetoric, Rhétoriqueurs, Rederijkers. Proceedings of the colloquium, Amsterdam, 10–13 November 1993*, J. Koopmans et al. (dir.), Amsterdam, North Holland, 1995, p. 157–174.

27 J. Kleijntjes, "Verslag over den godsdienstigen toestand in Holland en Friesland", *Haarlemsche bijdragen*, 59 (1940/1941), p. 52–101.

de Rhétorique en Zeelande, qui avoient publicquement jeu une farse scandeleuse de la brage de Sainct Franchois", had been prevented from doing so. The Court's answer summarized the case and corrected some assumptions implicit in the question. The case against the chamber of rhetoric of the village of Kapelle had been initiated by an accusation from the *provisoer* and dean of Reimerswaal, a nearby city[28].

The complaint alleged that the rhetoricians had played a scandalous farce in 1563. The *provisoer* and dean had pressed charges before the Great Council of Malines but were referred to the Court of Holland. An officer of the Court then heard both parties extensively, and from his report, the Court concluded that a farce had been performed on Shrove-Tuesday with the formal consent of the dean of the Chapter of Our Lady in Kapelle and the deputy superintendent of the region, which was perfectly in accordance with the ordinance of 1560[29].

The Court had further concluded that the farce had not dealt with St Francis, and had featured the pants of Priapus instead. The play did not contain anything scandalous against the Catholic religion, although, the judges concluded, its obscene language could be considered indecent. In a letter to the Great Council in Malines (dated September 10, 1565), the Court of Holland clearly professed knowledge of the technical terms of rhetorical culture, calling the farce an "esbattement" and referring to the "prince" of the chamber. The letter stressed the innocent nature of the play; although indecent, it was not found indecent enough to bother the attorney-general. The Court finally mentioned two additional excuses: the play had been performed by people living in the countryside and during Shrove Tuesday[30].

Although it is perfectly possible that Priapus had been dressed as St Francis or a Franciscan, which would have made the performance less innocent than the script, but was difficult to prove, the case suggests that the dean of Reimerswaal had been pushing a reformist view, running the danger (at least from the Court's perspective) of criminalizing traditional farcical culture (with its legitimate topics, language, time, and place). Interestingly however, the folklorizing excuse in the Court's

28 Ibid., 57–58.

29 Ibid., 57–58.

30 J. Bijlo, *Kroniek van Kapelle-Biezelinge en Eversdijk*, Middelburg, Zeeuws Genootschap der Wetenschappen, 1923, p. 211–212 (bijlage 4).

letter suggests a distancing towards the same joyful culture from an esthetic point of view (and thus also attests to the newly controversial status of the rhetorical paradigm)[31].

The principle defined by the placard of 1560 would also become the corner stone of a radical anti-theatrical lobby of university-trained *Calvinist* ministers in the heartland of the Reformed Church in the south of Holland after 1572. They would gradually succeed in redefining the body of theatrical knowledge at the Court of Holland and the States of Zealand by continuously linking the community theatre play with all sorts of low brow and commercial entertainment. They contributed to the dissociation of community theatre from the culture of learning that had been the cornerstone of rhetorician culture. In most cities, towns and villages, or so it seems, this lobby forced theatrical culture, already damaged by the dismantling of most of the public festive infrastructure, away from the streets into controlled environments accessible to paying audiences only[32].

DE DAMHOUDERE AND THE LEGAL STATUS OF THE THEATRICAL

The law and day-to-day governmental measures were consolidating theatrical knowledge on local, regional, and central levels, and had thus been co-agents in the development of the rhetorical-theatrical paradigm. Local knowledge of theatrical culture was the result of engagements and negotiations between local networks and institutions. Local knowledge became universalized through the efforts of networks of lobbyists, informants, and men of government. The "universal" knowledge was codified in decisions and laws on the central levels of state and society, and in legal treatises that dealt more extensively with the legal status of theatrical phenomena, and again in their turn influenced local and regional levels.

31 "Kleijntjes, op. cit., 58 ("schurrile propoosten [...] die nyet wel dienden ter eerbaerheyt"); Bijlo, op. cit., 212 ("landluijden op een dorp").

32 Van Dixhoorn, *Lustige geesten*, 214–226.

In order to bring these elements into sharp focus, this essay will discuss the legal manual by Joos de Damhoudere. The Latin edition, *Praxis rerum criminalium* was published in Leuven in 1554. In 1555, De Damhoudere published an abbreviated Dutch edition, *Practycke ende handbouck in criminele zaeken* in Leuven and a *Practique judiciaire es causes criminelles* in Paris. The book went through 22 Latin, 11 Dutch, and many French and German editions[33].

This ambitious project was an appropriation of the late fifteenth-century legal manual *Corte instructie in materie criminele* by the Flemish lawyer Philip Wielant that must have circulated widely in three distinct manuscript families in the early sixteenth century and was printed in Antwerp in 1558[34]. The *Practycke* and the French and Latin translations were based on the second expanded version of the *Corte instructie* (written in 1515–1516). The book was intended for the education of young lawyers of the Court of Flanders. It was based on procedures that Wielant also wanted to be implemented in Flemish courts of aldermen and feudal courts[35].

De Damhoudere's *Practycke* closely follows the structure, argument, and wording of the *Corte Instructie*, adding legal knowledge created in the decades after 1516 and expanding sections that particularly interested De Damhoudere, such as the offence of injury. The *Corte Instructie* introduced a new genre in law literature hitherto dominated by Italian theorists; it pragmatically followed existing court proceedings of the Court of Flanders and vernacularized scholarly sources[36].

The sources of the *Corte Instructie* and by implication of the *Practycke* were the proceedings at the Court of Flanders, Roman and canon law, and the privileges of the Flemish cities, particularly Ghent[37]. The *Corte Instructie* thus universalized local knowledge by relating the proceedings of the Court of Flanders and the privileges of Flanders to the existing law literature and by recommending this knowledge not only to lawyers of

33 J. Dauwe and J. Monballyu (ed.), *J. De Damhouder, Practycke ende handbouck in criminele zaeken. Anastatische herdruk naar de editie Leuven 1555*, Roeselare, 1981. For this essay I have consulted the 1555 and 1561 Dutch editions. References will be to the 1555 Leuven edition.

34 J. Monballyu (ed.), *Verzameld werk Philips Wielant, vol. 1. Corte instructie in materie criminele*, Brussel, Paleis der Academiën, 1995, p. 7–48. The two editions of the treatise will be quoted as Wielant, *Corte instructie*, 1st edition and 2nd edition.

35 Monballyu, op. cit., p. 41.

36 Ibid., p. 41–42.

37 *Ibid.*, p. 42–43.

the Court of Flanders, but also to lawyers on local levels. The *Practycke* universalized local and regional knowledge even further, addressing audiences in Dutch, French and Latin editions[38].

The *Corte Instructie* and *Practycke* provide legal advice on, or even legal training in, the practice of criminal law. Although they do not recognize the theatre or the theatrical as a legal category, some sections, particularly those on libel and defamation and injuries by speech, action and writing, turn out to be highly relevant for the study of the theatrical in the sixteenth century. The sections on injury by speech and action in the first version were significantly expanded in the second version of the *Corte Instructie* with a brief section on injuries in writing added. De Damhoudere expanded these sections and added one on injuries by making faces[39].

According to the *Pracktycke*, an act is legally defined as an injury in the case of an intentional and purposeful will to offend or hurt a person, either out of disdain, or to harm, shame, or inflict injustice, to the effect that the targeted person feels hurt. The injured person who decides to press charges should then be able to state under oath that he feels seriously offended. If an injury by speech is legally proven, the perpetrator would be obliged to rectify and compensate the injured party[40].

Typical injuries by speech include blaming a person for his or her physical handicaps, falsely accusing someone of being a liar or a dreamer, threatening people, or speaking blasphemous words against a person, such as in wishing another person evil. The *Practycke* pressed judges to take injuries by speech rather lightly by referring to the Canonists who recommend forgiving injuries for the love of God. Judges, the author insists, need to be cautious and try to mediate and convince the offended party to withdraw the charges if the injuries were only verbal[41].

De Damhoudere and Wielant seem to have been highly interested in the topic of injury by speech, action, and writing. The sections on insults by speech (*by woorde*) and action (*by faite*) include extensive reflections on exceptions or cases in which insulting language or actions should not

38 The Antwerp edition of 1561 for example was addressed a Brabantine instead of a Flemish audience.

39 Wielant, *Corte instructie*, 1st edition, cap. 97–99, 2nd edition, cap. 140–142; De Damhoudere, *Practycke*, p. 251–260.

40 De Damhoudere, op. cit., p. 251.

41 Ibid., p. 251–255.

be considered injuries. Wielant's second version and De Damhoudere extensively expand on these exceptions[42].

The first rule of exception states that insults given in a playful spirit should not be considered legally offensive. The second rule states that, since injuries are defined by the *intention* to hurt, and since speaking the truth lacks that intention, it should not count as an offense in a legal sense, unless it was done in such a biting and sharp way that a person would be utterly humiliated or dishonored. The third rule states that insults should be allowed among legal practitioners in courts of law. Particularly young lawyers, according to the *Practycke*, were fond of using biting, mocking, taunting, and scoffing language in their writings against the representatives of the other party, an issue, the author adds, that is treated in more detail in the Latin edition. The fourth rule states that offensive words spoken by someone who was equally offended or clearly provoked are also an exception to the law[43].

The *Practycke* outlines at length that insulting words spoken in a joking, mocking spirit and out of wit, not to jeer and taunt, but for example to teach and admonish a person instead (if not too often and harshly), should always be excused. The same counts for friends and relatives who for good reasons can speak a bit bolder and with more liberty towards each other; or for an alderman, bailiff, or any other officer of justice, who treats a suspect rather harshly, if it is done for the sake of justice. A person hurting someone for the love of his prince or in honor of his city or borough should also be excused, even though "it is not very Christian-like"[44].

Although the sections on injuries are relevant to the problem of the theatrical in early modern Dutch-speaking culture, De Damhoudere's explicit focus concerning the theatrical is on injuries in writing. This may seem odd, since we might be inclined to link the theatrical to the spoken word, or even action, or to injuries by making faces. While Wielant in his second version focused on the act of writing refrains, songs, booklets or histories, De Damhoudere, expanding this section, explicitly links the writing of texts to spreading them through the spoken word[45].

42 Ibid., p. 251–255; Wielant, *Corte instructive*, 2nd edition, cap. 140–141.

43 De Damhoudere, op. cit., p. 252–255.

44 De Damhoudere, op. cit., p. 252–255, 257.

45 Ibid., p. 259; Wielant, *Corte instructive*, 2nd edition, cap. 142.

The *Practycke* states that injuries in writing happen in wicked, infamous poems, songs, booklets, refrains, plays and public invectives. These various sorts of writing are then immediately related to the wicked tongue which, it is claimed, is worse and harsher than iron armor. Such a serious and therefore a public offence committed by the tongue makes those who allow it to happen as guilty as the writer. Anyone who is a witness to the offence of injury in writing can legally press charges. The *Practycke* stresses that the offence is often committed and typically includes the making of poems, songs, booklets, refrains, ballades, comedies, and public plays out of anger and in order to jeer and hurt someone else's honor and reputation, which is against all justice, conscience, and the truth[46].

The *Practycke* does not distinguish between writing infamous songs, histories, or refrains and having them composed, sung, performed, or sold by others, anonymously or not, with an explicit or an implicit attack on the victim. Making and spreading infamous texts is a capital offence and should be punished accordingly. Thus, De Damhoudere's taxonomy links play and comedy with literature composed in writing and spread in print and manuscript, or through performance.

The entire section on injuries (by speech, action, writing and by making faces), it could be argued, deals with aspects of the theatrical. This can also be seen from the offence of injury by making faces which includes mocking and taunting someone by wearing provocative clothes, disfiguring beards or haircuts, making faces, sticking one's tongue out in someone's face, rolling one's tongue or eyes at someone, threatening a person with bad luck or accidents by gesturing, or wearing a monk's dress to cast blame onto a religious order or a religious person[47]. By arguing that infamous texts are (legally) offensive, the author also explicitly refers to an earlier section on defamation and slander by booklets and libels, which he defines as an act of spiritual theft of someone else's honor and reputation, that should be physically punished[48].

In that earlier section, the *Practycke* does not distinguish between the writers of infamous libels or people who have them made by others.

46 De Damhoudere, op. cit., p. 259.

47 Ibid., p. 160.

48 De Damhoudere, op. cit., p. 226–227.

Infamous libels against princes, the common good, and officers of justice should be immediately reported and handed over to the government. Infamous libels or bills typically included letters spread in the streets or stuck on doors or gates to accuse and blame, or they could be infamous songs dictated and composed to offend. Interestingly, in the section on infamous libels, the *Practycke* again stresses that authors publishing the truth do not commit a crime. If they accuse someone of a capital offence, however, these truth-speaking authors should be willing to confirm and prove the accusations in a court of law, since no one should be accused outside a court of law in grave matters[49].

The question raised by the exception to the crime of slander or defamation is to what extent this might also apply to the injuries by writing. Although the *Practycke* does not mention exceptions to this offence, it could be that exceptions formulated in earlier sections on slander and injuries by speech and action also apply to injuries by writing: writing the truth and texts written in a joking spirit, as part of a joyful exchange or of an intimate group of people, thus might be excluded too.

In De Damhoudere's legal taxonomy, plays are no different from other written texts, and performances make no exception either. Instead, speech, action, and writing are closely bound together, since the written word and the spoken word are conceptually linked. The same rules apply, that take communicative acts, either the written and spoken word or all sorts of gestures, very seriously. This already suggests why theatre plays were singled out in censorship policies: they were much more provocative by nature since, more than any other genre, they combined written scripts, spoken words and all sorts of gestures (not only invoking more senses, but also more legal categories).

49 Ibid., 226–227. Wielant, *Corte instructie*, 1st edition, cap. 88, and 2nd edition, cap. 129 treats libels and infamous texts, and explicitly refers to the spread of songs through performance. Wielant does not deal with exceptions.

THE THEATRICAL IN THE ANTWERP COURTROOM

In the context of growing Lutheran activities in the city, on February 25, 1521, the Antwerp government published an ordinance that confirmed two earlier ordinances by the emperor against the spread of Lutheran ideas that focused on the spoken word (disputations and conversations). The local ordinance targeted citizens who violated this law by printing, selling, and buying Luther's books, and "recommending and praising them" and also, "making, spreading, and posting infamous libels, rhymes, roundels, and ballades in mockery of those who do not adhere to this brother Luther and his writings but renounce him and his ideas instead[50]".

The archives of the Antwerp *vroedschap* or city council preserve a file that was probably created in the 1560s, but also contains the imperial ordinance of 1520, a 1500 ordinance against secret meetings by Philip the Fair, a collection of Antwerp privileges, some cases of heresy from the 1550s and 1560s, and a folder, apparently dating from 1515, with cases concerning blasphemy and injury by speech and the way they were punished (with pilgrimages and fines) in Brussels in the 1430s[51].

These folders closely linked cases of blasphemy, heresy, and injury and are evidence of the ways in which the Antwerp government enhanced its knowledge of the laws and punishments concerning communicative acts. Such inquisitive care can also be observed in the complaints of the Antwerp sheriff against a local printer and two rhetoricians in the 1540s. The proceedings allow probing the legal status of the theatrical from the perspective of the courtroom and the local community.

In 1544 and early 1545, on charges put forward by the sheriff, the Antwerp criminal court (*hoge vierschaar*) began legal proceedings against the followers of a small but highly visible and well-connected heretical

50 P. Génard (ed.), "Ordonnantien van het Antwerpsch Magistraat rakende de godsdienstige geschillen der XVIe eeuw", *Antwerpsch Archievenblad*, 2 (s.d.), p. 308–372, esp. 308–309.

51 Stadsarchief Antwerpen, Archief van de Vierschaar, Amman, inv. nr. 314. Nieuwe religie, 16e eeuw. Informatiën over personen, beschuldigd de nieuwe leer aan te kleven, 1520 tot 1560.

cult that had raised concerns from Martin Luther himself. The group was led by Loys Pruystinck, an illiterate but charismatic craftsman of humble origins. According to the late sixteenth-century Antwerp-born historian Emanuel van Meteren, his followers were "among the best, the richest and the most esteemed citizens who lived together joyously and in an Epicurean manner[52]". Among them, Dominique van Uccle (author of the cult propaganda), a Parisian jeweler, and members of the noble Van Lier family[53].

While he was acting against the Pruystinck cult the sheriff's suspicion was also raised against Mr. Peeter Schuddematte, a schoolteacher and prominent rhetorician, who was charged in January 1545. While he was building his case against Schuddematte after the cult members were found guilty of heresy and executed, the sheriff also put forward charges dating back to 1542 against the young apprentice Jacob van Middeldonck and the high-profile printer Jacob van Liesvelt in May 1545[54].

Van Liesvelt had been charged in 1542 with having printed forbidden books. The charges were renewed in 1544 and accepted as proven in 1547 after a lengthy trial lasting three years. Van Liesvelt was executed by the sword in November 1545 for having transgressed the imperial ordinance of 1540. The verdict by the *vierschaar* shows that the sheriff's case had previously been dismissed on the grounds that the suspicious books had been printed with a privilege before the ordinance of 1540[55].

The young Van Middeldonck had also been charged in 1542 with having staged a printed play that was on the Index, and for having appropriated the text which would make him not only the organizer

52 E. van Meteren, *Belgische ofte Nederlantsche historie van onsen tijden*, Delft, Vennecool, 1605, f. 5: "Ten lesten heeft hy eenen grooten aenhanck aldaer ghekreghen van de beste, rijckste ende deghelijckste geachte burghers de welcke vrolic ende Epicureisch met malcanderen leefden achtende de rechte wetenschap ende gherustheyt der conscientien gevonden te hebben alle inwendighe ende gheestelicke swaricheyt uuter herten stellende".

53 J. Frederichs, *De secte der Loïsten of Antwerpsche Libertijnen (1525–1545): Eligius Pruystinck (Loy de Schaliedecker) en zijne aanhangers*, Gent, Vuylsteke, 1891. G. Waite, *Reformers on stage. Popular drama and religious propaganda in the Low Countries of Charles V, 1515–1556*. Toronto, University of Toronto Press, 2000, p. 66–68, points to the influence of David Joris in Antwerp at the same time (1539–1544). P. Génard, "Personen te Antwerpen in de XVIe eeuw voor het feit van religie gerechtelijk vervolgd. Lijst en ambtelijke bijbehoorige stukken", *Antwerpsch Archievenblad*, 7 (s.d.), 469–472; ibid., 8 (s.d.), p. 322–472, esp. 322–336.

54 Génard, op. cit., 7 (s.d.), 463–467; ibid., 8 (s.d.), esp. 346–362.

55 Génard, op. cit., 346–353.

but also the (co-) author of a suspect play. His case was probably dismissed on grounds similar to Van Liesvelt's. He might have claimed that the play had been staged earlier with the consent of the authorities of Middelburg, and was printed with a privilege in Antwerp in 1539, which is what he argued in 1544, when the charges against him were renewed[56].

On May 7, 1546, the *vierschaar* evicted Van Middeldonck, but he was ordered to pay the expenses of both parties in the proceedings "for reasons moving the aldermen aforementioned". The verdict summarized the charges and counter charges put forward by the defendant[57].

Van Middeldonck had been charged with having participated in the company of rhetoric the *Damastbloeme* and staged the *batement* "*den boom der Schriftueren*" (the tree of the Scriptures). This play, or its title, smacked of heresy against "our Holy Christian Religion and the institutions of the Holy Roman Church". He was accused of having written, or at least read the prologue, and of having been the leader or *facteur* of the play. Some of the names of characters had been altered, the sheriff argued, yet the play staged in Antwerp had the same content and argument as the Middelburg play that had been censored because it was suspect. Van Middeldonck had been threatened to name the actors, but refused to do so[58].

The defendant agreed that a couple of years before a group of boys calling themselves the *Damastbloeme* had staged the play. He denied having known or understood the content of the play, arguing he was only 15 or 16 at the time. He claimed that his age and the fact that he was only an ordinary craftsman were proof that he had no great knowledge of the Scriptures. He also pointed out that he regularly attended Church, confession, and mass, behaved like a good Christian, was a man of good reputation, and had never been suspected of any kind of heresy[59].

He then refuted the charge that he had written the prologue to the play, adding that he had never even composed any refrains. Although

56 Génard, op. cit., p. 346–362.

57 Ibid., p. 359–362.

58 See for the content of the printed play Waite, op. cit., p. 167–169. The play had probably also caused problems in Zealand in 1539; see C. Rooze-Stouthamer, *Hervorming in Zeeland (ca. 1520–1572)*, Goes, De Koperen Tuin, 1996, p. 116.

59 Génard, op. cit., p. 359–362.

he admitted having read the prologue, he claimed not even to have understood its content. He also denied having been the leader of the group, arguing that he was an unlearned person deficient in the skills and knowledge needed to alter or stage such a play. He also pointed out that the play had been printed and sold publicly in Antwerp with the title-page claiming that it had been performed in Middelburg by consent of the government. While denying his role as *facteur*, he pointed to the habit of boys and children, who often read old printed and manuscript prologues, as he had done[60].

The *vierschaar* accepted most of his argument. Its verdict shows a rather precise knowledge of the world of rhetoric and of the knowledge and skills required to write, stage, direct and understand a play, as well as of the role of young men and children in rhetorical culture. Whether or not Van Middeldonck's argument was the truth (we will never know), it was convincing enough to the *vierschaar* because it must have matched the theatrical knowledge shared by sheriff and aldermen.

Although it could of course be argued that the defendant was acquitted on other grounds, such as the alleged (but unproven) dislike of the Antwerp *vierschaar* for the anti-heresy policy of the central government, the cases against the Pruystinck cult, Van Liesvelt, and schoolteacher and rhetorician Schuddematte do not support this view. The time and procedural care that were devoted to the prosecution of Van Middeldonck show that a strong sense of the seriousness of the matter was driving the Antwerp government, rather than a lack of interest in heresy.

The case of Van Middeldonck shows how local knowledge of theatrical practices helped dismiss the case against the young man. The same sort of knowledge led to the execution of the rhetorician Peter Schuddematte. These cases suggest that the fact that the charges were put forward during a final crackdown on a cult believed to be dangerous, might have helped the sheriff. Peter Schuddematte was charged on January 15, 1545 for unknown reasons. The charges were taken seriously and the *vierschaar* granted the sheriff the time (a couple of years) needed to acquire information and build a case that would convince the court[61].

60 Ibid., p. 359–362.

61 Génard, op. cit., p. 330–334.

On February 20, 1545, the sheriff was permitted to add the script of a play to the charges "in as far as it would be possible to acquire the script". The play was kept by the deans of the chamber of rhetoric of the *Olijftack* (Olive Branch)'[62]. On February 27 the *vierschaar* allowed Schuddematte to read the charges and have the list of witnesses and some additional information he needed to prepare his defense. The case was continued until May 1545, and was resumed in August 1546 after the execution of Van Liesvelt (1545) and the acquittal of Van Middeldonck (May 1546)[63].

On August 13, 1546, a book called "den Babel van Vilvoorden" was added to the charges and discussed several times in the next few months[64]. This book might have been the play that had been recovered from the Olive Branch. Schuddematte's lawyer was allowed to review the imperial ordinances and the book, which suggests that the content of the book was considered heretical. Schuddematte was a teacher and prominent rhetorician, and therefore not an ignorant person. He had also been banished from Oudenaarde in 1532 for unknown reasons[65]. The fact that he had once more transgressed the heresy laws might have sealed his fate.

After more than two years, the sheriff succeeded in convincing the *vierschaar* of his guilt. The verdict has not been preserved, but a loyal

62 Ibid., p. 359–364.

63 Schuddematte was a member of the Gillyflowers at the time, but he had been active in other chambers, including, apparently, the Olive Branch. He became a citizen of Antwerp 24 October 1533. H. L. de Groote, "De zestiende-eeuwse Antwerpse schoolmeesters", *Bijdragen tot de Geschiedenis inzonderheid van het oud Hertogdom Brabant*, 50 (1967), 179–318, esp. 302, claims he was executed for heresy by the sword, 25 May 1547. Cf. Van Bruaene, *Om beters wille*, 110, 137–138, 140, who claims that Schuddematte had been involved in a Bible translation project. Cf. also J. Decavele, *De dageraad van de reformatie in Vlaanderen, 1520–1565*, Brussel, Paleis der Academiën, 1975, vol. 1, p. 206–207, 268, 374. Most accounts of the Van Middeldonck and Schuddematte-cases are built on assumptions rather than the details of the sources provided by Génard. Decavele also refers to a request sent by Schuddematte to the Secret Council to revoke his banishment. Archives Générales du Royaume, Brussels, Varia D, 3028, f. 150vo-151 (an old reference that I have not yet been able to check). Decavele claims it does not provide any information on the reasons for this punishment.

64 Génard, op. cit., p. 364–365, 368.

65 The banishment from Oudenaarde became relevant to the case on November 5, 1546. Génard, op. cit., p. 367, 369, 370. On 18 March 1546 (O.S.) the Antwerp court had received answers from Oudenaarde. See also J. Decavele, *De dageraad van de reformatie in Vlaanderen, 1520–1565*, Brussel, Paleis der Academiën, 1975, vol. 1, p. 206–207, 268, 374.

Catholic chronicler noted that on May 10, 1547 "Mr. Peeter Schuddematte, a schoolteacher, who was a gifted Rhetorician" was executed for heresy in front of the city hall[66].

The former town secretary Jacob van Wesembeke claims in his *La description de* l'estat *succes* et *occurrences, advenues au Pais Bas au faict de la Religion* of 1569, that Schuddematte had been executed "*pour avoir composé quelque balade, touchant quelques cas commis par aucuns cordeliers*[67]". Although Wesembeke, appointed secretary in 1546, must have known of the verdict against Schuddematte, he clearly downplays the seriousness of the case, ignoring the book or the play *Babel van Vilvoorden*, in an attempt to paint the merciless character of the religious persecutions of the sixteenth century.

The time it took the *vierschaar* to convict Schuddematte apparently raised some eyebrows elsewhere concerning Antwerp's willingness to execute the law. A letter of November 7, 1545 from the *vierschaar* to the attorney-general of Brabant, explains why the case against the teacher had been delayed by a few months. One reason stands out that concerns conditions set by the Broad Council, representative of the citizenry, for the outlawing of Schuddematte as citizen. Outlawing a citizen was needed when a convict went into the hands of the sovereign, represented by the sheriff, for examination under torture and for execution[68].

The Broad Council had delayed permission until the *vierschaar* agreed not to accept charges against Schuddematte's pupils and their parents if they were based on names Schuddematte might come to mention under torture or pressure. The Council expressed the fear that writing exercises given by Schuddematte would include "cladden of refreynen" (draught copies or refrains) taken home and read by parents. Since teachers used to visit their pupil's families, the Broad Council also feared

66 *Chronycke van Antwerpen sedert het jaer 1500 tot 1575, gevolgd van: Eene beschryving van de historie en het Landt van Brabant, sedert het jaer 51 vóór J.-C., tot 1565 na J.-C., volgens een onuitgegeven handschrift van de 16e eeuw met Fac-simile van het HS*, Antwerpen, Van Dieren, 1843, p. 45.

67 The Cordeliers or Franciscans were often attacked or mocked in rhetorician as well as anti-clerical and Protestant literature, but mockery was not heresy. The court files show no reference to Franciscans. Wesembeke also, falsely, claimed that Van Liesvelt had only been executed for having printed a Bible with the marginal annotation "que la salvation de l''homme procédoit seullement par Jesu-Christ". C. Rahlenbeck (ed.), *Mémoires. Jacques de Wesembeke*, Brussels, Heussner, 1859, p. 68.

68 The decision to have him tortured was taken May 29, 1545. Génard, op. cit., p. 347–348.

that Schuddematte might have engaged them in discussions that might raise suspicion against innocent people[69].

Similar fears were expressed concerning the members of the Gillyflowers and other chambers that Schuddematte had been a member of, where similar problems might occur should he mention names under torture. The Council argued that rhetoricians daily engaged themselves in composing all sorts of *batementen*, *balladen*, *refereynen*, and *spelen van sinne*, in preparation for performances, just for pleasure or for other reasons. Often the *facteurs*, actors, and others kept minutes, draught copies, and abstracts at home. This meant that texts of suspicious content by Schuddematte might be found among them, without them being aware[70].

The cases of Van Middeldonck and Schuddematte show a detailed knowledge on the part of the local council and court of the theatrical world of rhetoric. Since the aldermen used these arguments to explain the delay of Schuddematte's case, they must have expected the attorney-general to share their knowledge. Interestingly, in both cases, the *vierschaar* was anxious to have written proof, that is, copies of the suspect plays and books, supporting the charges put forward by the sheriff[71].

CONCLUSIONS

Knowledge of the rhetorical-theatrical world was created and used by governments, councils and courts in the Dutch-speaking Low Countries; it was universalized in laws, ordinances and sixteenth-century juridical literature. The epistemological status of the theatrical in these circles underwent some changes in the course of the sixteenth century, but in general the theatre play and other forms of performative literature were not strictly distinguished from a wider set of communicative practices (writing, speech, and action), instead they were conceptually linked.

69 Génard, op. cit., p. 373–375.
70 Ibid., p. 373–375.
71 Ibid., p. 347–348.

Although this might seem to lead to the conclusion that sixteenth-century law did not accept a *status apart* for the theatre or for the performative event among other communicative practices, a critical probing of the evidence however does suggest a separate status of some sorts of the theatrical interaction.

First, Wielant's instructions and De Damhoudere's expansions suggest that the link between writing, action, and speech might have given the theatrical an exceptional position in relation to pure writing. They seem to point out that the court room, the family, and meetings of friends, as well as festive gatherings, or speech and actions done in a witty spirit, to speak the truth, promote the common good or defend the reputation of the prince, all formed "spheres of freedom". Its limits were loosely defined by the purposeful and successful attempt to hurt a person (laws on injury and slander) and more strictly by the institutionalized truth in matters of state and religion (the laws on blasphemy, heresy, and lèse-majesté).

Secondly, while this first conclusion builds on a hypothetical reading of various sections of Wielant's and De Damhoudere's arguments, evidence from the Van Middeldonck and Schuddematte-cases also suggests that the performative event, with its live and festive nature and the involvement of quite a number of people with varying responsibilities, was somewhat privileged over the written text and its maker. In other words, the hierarchy in responsibilities that can be assumed from these two cases is: firstly the script and its maker; secondly, the organizer(s) of the performance; thirdly, the performers; to which fourthly might be added the audiences (who were witnesses to the event and among whom we might expect the informants that caused investigations).

The personal responsibilities for a problematic performance increased with the involvement, understanding, and purposefulness invested in the event. A young, unlearned, decent actor went unpunished. A teacher, esteemed rhetorician, and maker of blasphemous or heretical texts was found guilty, yet those who might have read or even performed his texts were thought to be innocent. The focus on the script, with relative neglect of the performance, is evident from these two cases and from investigations into scandalous plays in Holland and Zeeland. Censorship measures also focused on having scripts checked by experts prior to performance. This might be related to the priority given to evidence in writing in courts of law, but it also seems related to the notion that the written text and its maker were the root of the problem, and that if the root were attacked, the problem would be solved[72].

The performative event seems to have been a problematic target for the law and courts of justice while the theatrical text was not distinguished in any way from other forms of performative literature or even other sorts of writing. However, in circles of anti-heresy Catholic reformists of sixteenth-century Holland, another attitude towards the theatre play seems to have been developing. They seem to have targeted the theatre play in particular, issuing special measures against plays, favoring a pre-emptive censorship of texts by experts in theology that would lead to the establishment of the (failed) censorship committee of 1551 in Holland. Their negative attitude towards the play also seems to have influenced the 1560 ordinance and was perpetuated by the Calvinists ministers of the Dutch Republic after 1572.

The (long-term) effect of the new paradigm created by the coalition of groups of Calvinists and humanists, and an increasing number of local governments, was the rise of a new theatrical culture. In Holland, the new theatrical paradigm would be epitomized after the fusion of the two chambers of rhetoric of Amsterdam in 1632 and the construction of Jacob van Campen's Amsterdam city theatre in 1637.

Arjan VAN DIXHOORN
Utrecht University
University College Roosevelt
Middelburg

72 The idea to attack the authority problem of performative literary culture at the root by eradicating the chambers of rhetoric was expressed in the letter of 1550 that led to the establishment of a censorship committee in Holland. Van Boheemen and Van der Heijden, op. cit., p. 677–678.

LE THÉÂTRE DES RHÉTORICIENS ET LES AMBIGUÏTÉS DE LA CENSURE DANS LES PAYS-BAS PRÉ-MODERNES (XVe-XVIIe SIÈCLE)[1]

L'histoire de la censure est un sujet difficile à aborder. Même si la censure officielle est loin d'être absente de notre société contemporaine, nous avons tendance à considérer nos lois sur la diffamation comme rationnelles, en même temps que nous jetons un regard négatif, ou du moins condescendant, sur les stratégies de la censure sous l'Ancien Régime. En outre, les études sur la censure historique présentent de grandes différences en ce qui concerne à la fois leur approche et leurs présupposés. Sans surprise, la plus grande part des recherches sur la censure pré-moderne est consacrée à la régulation de l'imprimerie. Au début de la période pré-moderne, le nouveau medium qu'elle représentait ouvrit des possibilités sans précédent pour la dissémination d'une grande variété d'opinions et d'idées hétérodoxes et non-conventionnelles. Dans le même temps, il devint possible pour les autorités d'adopter de nouvelles techniques plus sophistiquées pour réguler l'expression publique, parce que les textes imprimés étaient des objets matériels dont la production résultait de processus technologiques complexes. C'est pour cette raison que, pendant une longue période, les historiens de la censure se sont concentrés sur des institutions telles que l'Inquisition romaine, l'Index et les corps d'État de la censure, dont l'efficacité n'a jamais sérieusement été mise en doute[2].

1 Je tiens à remercier vivement Katell Lavéant et Marie Bouhaïk-Gironès pour la traduction.

2 E. Tortarolo, « Censorship in Early Modern Europe », *Journal of Modern European History*, 3, 2005, p. 18-22. Sur la question de la censure dans les Pays-Bas du seizième siècle, voir entre autres H. van Nierop, « Censorship, illicit printing and the revolt of the Netherlands », *Too mighty to be free. Censorship and the press in Britain and the Netherlands*, A. C. Duke et C. A. Tamse (dir.), Zutphen, De Walburg Pers, 1987, p. 29-44 ; A. G. Johnston, « L'imprimerie et la Réforme aux Pays-Bas, 1520-c. 1555', *La Réforme et le livre. L'Europe de l'imprimé (1517-v. 1570)*, J. F. Gilmont (dir.), Paris, Éditions du Cerf, 1990, p. 155-186 ;

Plus récemment, de nombreux chercheurs ont soutenu que même si les autorités civiles et religieuses ont inventé tout au long de la période pré-moderne toutes sortes de mécanismes ingénieux pour contrôler la publication et la prolifération des textes, le succès de ces mesures n'était jamais garanti et a toujours dépendu des personnes, des circonstances et de négociations[3]. Dans cette approche plus nuancée, la censure reste une pratique culturelle facilement reconnaissable. Des penseurs postmodernes du fait historique tels que Michel Foucault et Stephen Greenblatt ont en revanche mis en avant le fait que la censure était omniprésente dans la société pré-moderne et qu'elle s'exerçait via un large éventail des discours, et non par un nombre limité de pratiques institutionnelles[4]. Bien qu'il ne soit pas facile pour les historiens de rendre opérationnel un concept de la censure défini de manière si large, il peut nous aider à nous souvenir que la régulation de l'expression a toujours représenté plus qu'une répression directe ou qu'une relation simple entre le censeur et le censuré. Cette approche est prouvée en particulier en ce qui concerne la censure du théâtre, sur laquelle porte cet article. Le théâtre de la période pré-moderne était un medium mixte éphémère et complexe qui combinait la performance orale, physique et visuelle. Le théâtre pouvait être joué partout, des sphères les plus hautes de la cour jusqu'aux plus modestes prés autour des villages. La représentation pouvait être précédée par des dispositifs élaborés ou être plus ou moins spontanée. De par leur nature même, les performances théâtrales se prêtaient à des interprétations multiples et leur relation – pour peu qu'il y en eût – avec des textes écrits, sous forme manuscrite comme imprimée, restait toujours ambiguë[5]. Par conséquent, pour les autorités, il n'était pas seulement extrêmement difficile sur le plan

---

J. Machiels, *Privilegie, censuur en indexen in de Zuidelijke Nederlanden tot aan het begin van de 18de eeuw*, Bruxelles, Algemeen Rijksarchief, 1997 et, plus généralement, A. Goossens, *Les inquisitions modernes dans les Pays-Bas méridionaux, 1520-1633*, 2 volumes, Bruxelles, Éditions de l'Université de Bruxelles, 1997-1998.

3 D. McKitterick, *Print, Manuscript and the Search for Order, 1450-1830*, Cambridge, Cambridge University Press, 2003, p. 152-153.

4 J. Clare, « Historicism and the Question of Censorship in the Renaissance », *English Literary Renaissance*, 27, 1997, p. 155-176 ; E. Tortarolo, art. cité, p. 20.

5 Sur l'histoire du théâtre aux Pays-Bas à cette période, voir R. L. Erenstein (dir.), *Een theatergeschiedenis der Nederlanden. Tien eeuwen drama en theater in Nederland en Vlaanderen*, Amsterdam, Amsterdam University Press, 1996. Plus généralement, H. Pleij, *Het gevleugelde woord. Geschiedenis van de Nederlandse literatuur, 1400-1560*, Amsterdam, Bert Bakker / Prometheus, 2007.

technique de développer des mécanismes pour contrôler l'expression dramatique. D'un point de vue culturel plus général, ce n'était pas non plus une tâche facile de décider où se trouvaient les limites politiques, religieuses et morales d'un théâtre qui puisse être acceptable.

Cet article analyse la question de la censure du théâtre des rhétoriciens et, plus largement, la régulation des pratiques culturelles des Chambres de Rhétorique dans les Pays-Bas de la période pré-moderne. L'argument central en sera que, même si les rhétoriciens eux-mêmes, tout comme les autorités qui les sanctionnaient, étaient convaincus du besoin de poser des limites au discours et à la performance publics, ces limites sont toujours restées fluides et ont même créé de nouvelles opportunités pour une pratique littéraire riche. Pour soutenir cette affirmation, nous approchons la régulation des pratiques des rhétoriciens de deux façons. Nous discuterons d'abord brièvement le point de vue des rhétoriciens eux-mêmes sur la liberté de parole et d'expression. Ensuite, nous nous concentrerons sur la censure politique et religieuse telle qu'elle était exercée par les autorités centrales. Il faut enfin noter que nous choisissons intentionnellement une approche institutionnelle globale, en laissant de côté le réseau souvent complexe des relations qui se trouvent à la base des politiques culturelles et en insistant plutôt sur des idées, des stratégies et des actions générales, ainsi que sur leurs effets.

RÉGULATION DE LA PAROLE ET DE L'EXPRESSION PAR LES RHÉTORICIENS

Son caractère hautement institutionnel était l'un des traits principaux de la culture des rhétoriciens pré-modernes. Le théâtre des rhétoriciens était en général produit dans un contexte bien défini, à savoir celui des Chambres de Rhétorique. Ces Chambres étaient des guildes ou des confréries surtout composées de laïcs qui formaient leurs membres à la pratique de l'écriture et de la récitation de textes en vers, ainsi qu'à la performance de pièces de théâtre. À partir des années 1450, ces Chambres de Rhétorique s'intégrèrent fortement à la culture urbaine des Pays-Bas. Leurs genres dramatiques de prédilection étaient les pièces allégoriques ou morales *(spelen van zinne)*, les farces *(esbattementen)* et les pièces jouées pendant les banquets *(tafelspelen)*. Les Chambres participaient aux festivités civiques telles que les processions religieuses, les entrées princières et les fêtes pour la célébration de la paix, tout en organisant leurs propres festivals de théâtre et de poésie, dans l'espace public comme dans l'espace semi-privé de leurs lieux de réunion. Les autorités locales encourageaient l'engagement des Chambres de Rhétorique dans la culture publique en ratifiant leurs statuts et en leur accordant des privilèges locaux et des subventions occasionnelles ou permanentes[6].

Il faut souligner que, dans le contexte institutionnel particulier des Chambres de Rhétorique, l'expression était, dans le même temps, à la fois libre et régulée. L'une des notions fondamentales de la culture rhétoricienne était la compétition, entre rhétoriciens individuels comme entre Chambres de Rhétorique[7]. Cela impliquait que l'expression littéraire était formalisée et devait souvent suivre des règles strictes. Par exemple, les rhétoriciens étaient formés à composer des ballades ou *refreinen* comportant un *envoi* prédéterminé. Les invitations pour les festivals de théâtre proposaient une question centrale pour les moralités comme celui de la compétition de Gand en 1539 : « Quelle est la plus grande consolation de l'homme mourant ? ». L'argument central devait être soutenu par une triple démonstration : d'une façon "naturelle" en référant à la Création, d'une façon "scripturale" en référant aux autorités comme la Sainte Écriture et les Pères de l'Église, et d'une façon "figurative" en utilisant des métaphores, des allégories et des images[8]. Paradoxalement, grâce à cette régulation des procédures pour la

6 D. Coigneau, « Rederijkersliteratuur », *Historische letterkunde. Facetten van vakbeoefening*, M. Spies (dir.), Groningen, Wolters-Noordhoff, 1984, p. 35-57 ; A.-L. van Bruaene, « "A wonderfull tryumfe, for the wynning of a pryse" : Guilds, Ritual, Theater, and the Urban Network in the Southern Low Countries, ca. 1450-1650 », *Renaissance Quarterly*, 59, 2006, p. 374-405 ; *Id.*, *Om beters wille. Rederijkerskamers en de stedelijke cultuur in de Zuidelijke Nederlanden (1400-1650)*, Amsterdam, Amsterdam University Press, 2008 ; A. van Dixhoorn, *Lustige geesten. Rederijkers in de Noordelijke Nederlanden (1480-1650)*, Amsterdam, Amsterdam University Press, 2009.

7 A.-L. Van Bruaene, « Harmonie et honneur en jeu : les compétitions dramatiques et symboliques entre les villes flamandes et brabançonnes aux quinzième et seizième siècles », *Le verbe, l'image et les représentations de la société urbaine au Moyen Âge. Actes du colloque international tenu à Marche-en-Famenne du 24 au 27 octobre 2001*, M. Boone, E. Lecuppre-Desjardin et J.-P. Sosson (dir.), Garant, Anvers/Apeldoorn, 2002, p. 227-238.

8 N. Moser, *De strijd voor rhetorica. Poëtica en positie van rederijkers in Vlaanderen, Brabant, Zeeland en Holland tussen 1450 en 1620*, Amsterdam, Amsterdam University Press, 2001, p. 132-146.

compétition littéraire, les rhétoriciens recevaient une liberté considérable dans le développement de leurs arguments. Dans le cas de la poésie et du théâtre religieux, par exemple, ce n'était pas le plus grand attachement aux points doctrinaux qui comptait, mais la réflexion rationnelle et critique sur la façon d'atteindre les vérités religieuses. En d'autres termes, les rhétoriciens étaient formés à penser de manière créative[9]. Il semble que ces pratiques reçurent l'approbation générale du clergé au moins jusqu'aux premières décennies du XVIe siècle. On a peu d'indications que l'Église était opposée à la performance profane de drames religieux par les Chambres de Rhétorique[10]. Au contraire, des clercs présentant différentes formations ecclésiastiques écrivirent des pièces rhétoriciennes et jouèrent le rôle de membres du jury pendant les compétitions littéraires. Les vers composés par les rhétoriciens étaient parfois accrochés dans les églises pour que les paroissiens puissent les lire[11].

L'une des assertions principales des travaux récents sur les Chambres de Rhétorique est que les pratiques littéraires des rhétoriciens et le cadre institutionnel dans lequel elles fonctionnaient contribuèrent de manière cruciale au développement d'une libre culture du débat et de la discussion dans les Pays-Bas de l'époque pré-moderne[12]. Dans leurs lieux de réunion, les rhétoriciens discutaient ouvertement de questions religieuses et politiques et de problèmes sociaux. Pendant les compétitions publiques, ces débats étaient partagés avec un public urbain large et divers[13]. La plupart des rhétoriciens, originaires de la classe moyenne, n'étaient certainement

---

9 D. Coigneau, « Bedongen creativiteit. Over retoricale productieregeling », *Medioneerlandistiek. Een inleiding tot de Middelnederlandse letterkunde*, R. Jansen-Sieben e.a. (dir.), Hilversum, Verloren, 2000, p. 129-137 ; A.-L. van Bruaene, « *In Principio Erat Verbum.* Drama, Devotion, Reformation and Urban Association in the Low Countries », *Early Modern Confraternities in Europe and the Americas*, Ch. Black et P. Gravestock (dir.), Aldershot, Ashgate, 2006, p. 64-80.

10 *Cf.* J. Horowitz, « Le théâtre sacré aux XIVe-XVe siècles : une réflexion socio-religieuse », *Revue d'histoire du théâtre*, 221-222, 2004, p. 58-68.

11 Voir, par exemple, M. E. Kronenberg, « Gemengde berichten uit de kringen van theologen en rederijkers te Antwerpen, Brussel en Gent (begin 16e eeuw) », *Prosper Verheyden gehuldigd ter gelegenheid van zijn zeventigsten verjaardag 23 Oct. 1943*, Anvers, Nederlandsche Boekhandel, 1943, p. 237-238.

12 Le concept d'une « discussiecultuur » néerlandaise a été développé particulièrement dans W. Frijhoff et M. Spies, *1650. Bevochten eendracht. Nederlandse cultuur in Europese context*, La Haye, SDU, 1999.

13 J. Dumolyn et J. Haemers, « "Let each man carry on with his trade and remain silent". Middle-class ideology in the urban literature of the late medieval Low Countries », *Cultural and Social History*, 10, 2 (2013), p. 169-189.

pas des partisans d'une ligne dure en matière politique ou religieuse, mais c'est précisément pour cette raison que leur attitude intellectuelle joua un rôle considérable dans l'élaboration d'un modèle culturel propre aux Pays-Bas, qui finit par faire de la République des Provinces-Unies une exception dans une Europe pré-moderne de plus en plus intolérante[14].

L'attitude créative et réflexive typique de la culture rhétoricienne n'implique pas que les rhétoriciens se posaient en avocats d'une liberté de parole et d'expression illimitée[15]. Le statut des auteurs individuels était presque toujours comme secondaire par rapport aux intérêts du corps collectif[16]. La notion d'harmonie ou d'"amour" était centrale dans les pratiques des rhétoriciens. Elle signifiait que de bonnes relations devaient être maintenues entre les rhétoriciens individuels, entre les Chambres de Rhétorique et entre les Chambres et les autres guildes et institutions urbaines[17]. Selon leurs statuts et autres documents institutionnels, les rhétoriciens étaient en particulier préoccupés par l'usage d'un langage diffamatoire, souvent décrit comme *vilonie*. Les rhétoriciens n'avaient pas le droit de s'insulter ni de se moquer les uns des autres, ni dans les conversations ordinaires ni dans les compositions littéraires. Cette règle s'appliquait en premier lieu à l'intimité des lieux de réunion des Chambres de Rhétorique, mais était souvent étendue à l'espace public. Ainsi, les invitations pour les compétitions publiques incluaient toujours un avertissement visant à interdire l'insulte à l'encontre de personnes publiques ou privées dans les pièces de théâtre et les autres compositions littéraires – avertissement souvent répété par les autorités locales[18]. Il ne s'agissait pas d'une phrase creuse. On a conservé assez de preuves que les rhétoriciens utilisaient

14 G. Waite, *Reformers on Stage. Popular Drama and Religious Propaganda in the Low Countries of Charles V, 1515-1556*, Toronto, University of Toronto Press, 2000 ; A.-L. van Bruaene, *Om beters wille*, *op. cit.*, p. 253-257 ; A. van Dixhoorn, *Lustige geesten*, *op. cit.*, p. 26-34 ; J. van Bloemendal et A. van Dixhoorn, « "De scharpheit van een gladde tong". Literaire teksten en publieke opinievorming in de vroegmoderne Nederlanden », *Bijdragen en Mededelingen betreffende de Geschiedenis der Nederlanden*, 125, 1 (2010), p. 3-28.

15 Pour une discussion plus générale des notions de liberté de parole et de presse, voir J. van Eijnatten, « Van godsdienstvrijheid naar mensenrecht. Meningsvorming over censuur en persvrijheid in de Republiek, 1579-1795 », *Bijdragen en Mededelingen betreffende de Geschiedenis der Nederlanden*, 118, 2003, p. 1-21.

16 Sur le rhétoricien en tant qu'auteur individuel, voir D. Coigneau et S. Mareel (dir.), *Met eigen ogen. De rederijker als dichtend individu (1450-1600)*, Gand, Jaarboek de Fonteine, 2009.

17 A.-L. van Bruaene, « Harmonie et honneur », art. cité.

18 *Id.*, *Om beters wille*, *op. cit.*, p. 241-243.

fréquemment l'expression littéraire pour provoquer leurs compétiteurs et leurs rivaux publics. Les *Baladen van Doornijcke*, écrites en 1521/1522 par le célèbre rhétoricien Mathijs de Castelein, en est un exemple notoire. Dans ce texte, il inclut une véritable diatribe contre les habitants de la ville de Tournai, qu'il accuse entre autres, dans un ironique retournement de perspective, d'avoir mis en scène des pièces injurieuses[19].

Ainsi, la préoccupation des rhétoriciens concernant les propos diffamatoires resta toujours ambivalente. Il en va de même concernant leur position sur le blasphème. Le blasphème peut être vu comme le péché par excellence de l'époque pré-moderne[20]. Cette position est reflétée dans les nombreux statuts de Chambres de Rhétorique qui avertissaient les membres de ne pas jurer ni blasphémer, par habitude et encore moins avec de mauvaises intentions. Ces régulations se conformaient à la sensibilité culturelle générale ainsi qu'au souci propre aux rhétoriciens d'utiliser un langage orné[21]. Pour autant, les rhétoriciens étaient également conscients qu'un langage grossier pouvait être nécessaire pour composer une bonne pièce. Ainsi, les *sinnekens*, qui personnifiaient toutes sortes de vices dans les moralités, devaient leur popularité à leurs propos orduriers et irrévérencieux[22]. Ce paradoxe est illustré dans plusieurs statuts des Chambres de Rhétorique qui stipulaient que les rhétoriciens n'avaient pas le droit de nommer le diable, sauf dans une pièce ou autre composition littéraire, quand une telle transgression était jugée nécessaire[23]. Pour conclure au moins temporairement sur cette question, on peut affirmer que le schéma culturel général qui prit forme au sein de la culture rhétoricienne comprenait un ensemble complexe de valeurs en concernant les limites morales posées à l'expression et à la performance.

19 *Id.*, « De stad als scheldwoord. De *Baladen van Doornijcke* (1521/1522) van Matthijs de Castelein en de stedelijke literaire praktijk van de rederijkers », *Spiegel der Letteren*, 48, 2006, p. 135-147.

20 E. Belmas, « La montée des blasphèmes à l'âge moderne du Moyen Âge au XVIIe siècle », *Injures et blasphèmes*, Paris, Imago, 1989, p. 13-33 ; A. Cabantous, *Histoire du blasphème en Occident, XVIe-XIXe siècle*, J. Delumeau (dir.), Paris, Albin Michel, 1998.

21 A. van Dixhoorn, « Als retorica regeert. Rederijkersregels rond taalgebruik en gedrag in de zestiende en zeventiende eeuw », *De zeventiende eeuw*, 18, 2002, p. 17-30 ; A.-L. van Bruaene, *Om beters wille*, *op. cit.*, p. 243.

22 W. M. H. Hummelen, *De sinnekens in het rederijkersdrama*, Groningen, Wolters, 1958, *passim* ; F. L. Kramer, *Mooi vies, knap lelijk. Grotesk realisme in rederijkersklucbten*, Hilversum, Verloren, 2009, p. 206-259.

23 A.-L. van Bruaene, *Om beters wille*, *op. cit.*, p. 244.

RÉGULATIONS DES PRATIQUES DES CHAMBRES DE RHÉTORIQUE PAR LES AUTORITÉS CENTRALES

Vers la fin du quinzième siècle, les Chambres de Rhétorique étaient devenues une part intégrante de la culture urbaine de Flandres et de Brabant. En Zélande et en Hollande, les premières Chambres étaient en cours d'institution[24]. Il y a peu d'indications que les Chambres de Rhétorique aient été l'objet de mesures répressives sérieuses de la part des autorités avant cette période. Le premier souci des autorités locales était l'ordre public. Les Chambres de Rhétorique pouvaient recevoir un avertissement quand elles diffamaient des personnalités publiques ou des corporations dans leurs pièces ou quand elles provoquaient des troubles, mais d'ordinaire, les municipalités étaient plus inquiétées par le théâtre non organisé et les groupes de carnaval[25]. Comme nous l'avons souligné ci-dessus, le clergé aussi appuyait en général les pratiques des rhétoriciens. Les premières vraies réserves sur les institutions et les pratiques littéraires des rhétoriciens furent exprimées par les autorités centrales. Pourtant, comme je vais le soutenir, la répression directe ne fut jamais un objectif réel de ces mesures. À cette fin, j'analyserai la politique centrale pendant la période qui correspond à peu près au seizième siècle en me concentrant sur deux documents qui ont joué un rôle crucial dans la négociation des limites posées aux pratiques théâtrales des Chambres de Rhétorique : une lettre du duc Philippe le Beau de 1493 et l'édit émis par le roi Philippe II et la gouvernante Marguerite de Parme en 1560.

Le premier document indiquant clairement des intentions de la cour de Bourgogne-Habsbourg de réguler la culture rhétoricienne n'est ni une ordonnance officielle, ni un édit, mais une lettre envoyée par le duc Philippe le Beau à l'un de ses aumôniers le 20 mars 1493. Dans cette lettre, le duc annonçait son intention d'organiser un rassemblement pour toutes les Chambres de Rhétorique néerlandophones dans sa ville de

24 A. van Dixhoorn, *Lustige geesten*, *op. cit.*, p. 35-40.

25 H. Pleij, « Van keikoppen en droge jonkers. Spotgezelschappen, wijkverenigingen en het jongerengericht in de literatuur en het culturele leven van de late middeleeuwen », *Volkskundig bulletin*, 15, 1989, p. 297-315.

résidence, Malines. Ce rassemblement eut lieu le 1er mai 1493[26]. Cette date est remarquable en soi, puisque que la réunion – qui prit place dans une période d'activité politique intense – suivit directement une réunion des États-Généraux (13 avril / 1 mai), le plus haut organisme représentatif des Pays-Bas[27]. La décision de convoquer un groupe de rhétoriciens à cette date et ce lieu exacts peut être décodée comme une indication claire du sentiment d'urgence que la cour ressentait sur cette question. La réunion a rassemblé dix-huit Chambres de Rhétorique de Brabant, de Flandres et de la Hollande[28]. Nous n'avons pas conservé de minutes du rassemblement, mais selon la lettre de Philippe le Beau, les représentants des Chambres de Rhétorique devaient être sommés d'apporter des pièces, des *refreinen* et d'autres textes de jeux rhétoriques pour que l'on puisse parvenir à un consensus après une discussion sur le sujet avec des représentants de la cour[29]. En outre, pendant ou juste après le rassemblement, la cour décida qu'une Chambre de Rhétorique souveraine – nommée *De Balsemblomme* – devrait être établie. Il était initialement prévu que cette Chambre souveraine accompagnerait la cour itinérante (une idée qui fut vite abandonnée à cause des frais élevés que ces déplacements occasionneraient). *De Balsemblomme* reçut autorité pour instituer de nouvelles Chambres et examiner attentivement les statuts des Chambres déjà existantes. L'objectif déclaré de la cour était d'imposer à toutes les Chambres de Rhétorique « des règles et des pratiques poétiques conformes » (« een ghelijcke Reghele ende usance van dichtene »)[30].

Même si la conception de ce que devait être cette conformité selon la cour reste obscure, il est évident que son but était d'établir un certain degré de censure sur les pratiques des Chambres de Rhétorique. Selon toute probabilité, il s'agissait en premier lieu d'une censure politique.

26 R. Haeserijn (éd.), *Oorspronck der cameren van Rhetorycke, statuten ende ordonnancien der selve onder den titel Jesus metter Balsem Bloume*, Gand, Provinciebestuur Oost-Vlaanderen, 1960, p. 21.

27 R. Wellens, *Les États généraux des Pays-Bas des origines à la fin du règne du Philippe le Beau (1464-1506)*, Kortrijk/Heule, Standen en Landen, 1974, p. 228-230 et p. 472-475 ; J.-M. Cauchies, *Philippe le Beau, le dernier duc de Bourgogne*, Turnhout, Brepols, 2003, p. 21.

28 E. Van Autenboer, *Volksfeesten en rederijkers te Mechelen, 1400-1600*, Gand, Koninklijke Vlaamse Academie voor Taal- en Letterkunde, 1962, p. 96-97.

29 R. Haeserijn, *op. cit.*, p. 21.

30 R. Haeserijn, *op. cit.*, p. 26 et p. 79.

L'initiative de Philippe le Beau intervenait peu après la fin d'une décennie de révoltes et de guerre civile, déclenchées par le conflit entre le père de Philippe, Maximilian d'Autriche, et les villes flamandes sur la question de la régence pendant la minorité du jeune Duc[31]. Il existe assez d'indications que, pendant ces années, les spectacles des rhétoriciens dans des villes puissantes telles que Gand et Bruges avaient été de nature profondément politique et avaient promu la cause des villes révoltées. Enfant, le Duc lui-même avait probablement assisté plusieurs fois à la mise en scène des pièces rhétoriciennes politiquement chargées à Gand, où il a fut retenu captif par les rebelles[32].

L'initiative de Philippe le Beau en 1493 peut ainsi être analysée comme une première tentative des autorités centrales de censurer les pratiques des rhétoriciens et, ce faisant, de contrôler l'opinion publique. Il faut souligner que cette campagne pour prendre le contrôle des pratiques littéraires des rhétoriciens ne remporta pas de réel succès. La Chambre souveraine instituée en 1493 se révéla rapidement inefficace[33]. Pourtant, plus généralement, les rapports de la cour avec les Chambres de Rhétorique dans cette période eurent des conséquences importantes pour le développement de la culture rhétoricienne et, plus largement, de la culture urbaine. Avec le soutien direct et indirect de la cour, un nombre important de compétitions rhétoriciennes de grande envergure et souvent interrégionales fut organisé après le rassemblement de Malines[34]. Le plus spectaculaire fut probablement le *landjuweel* d'Anvers en 1496, qui fut directement autorisé par Philippe le Beau et qui rassembla vingt-huit Chambres du Brabant, des Flandres, de la Zélande et de la Hollande[35]. Comme je l'ai montré ailleurs, les grandes compétitions de ce type contribuèrent à l'unification culturelle des

31 W. P. Blockmans, « Autocratie ou polyarchie ? La lutte pour le pouvoir politique en Flandre, d'après des documents inédits, 1482-1492 », *Bulletin de la Commission Royale d'Histoire*, 140, 1974, p. 257-368 ; J. Haemers, *For the common good ? State power and urban revolts in the reign of Mary of Burgundy, 1477-1482*, Turnhout, Brepols, 2009.

32 A.-L. van Bruaene, *Om beters wille*, *op. cit.*, p. 61-63.

33 *Ibid.*, p. 73-76.

34 *Ibid.*, p. 191-192.

35 E. Van Autenboer, « Een landjuweel te Antwerpen in 1496 ? », *Jaarboek de Fonteine*, 29, 1978-1979, p. 125-150 ; W. Waterschoot, « Het Landjuweel te Antwerpen in 1496. Enkele teksten en hun interpretatie », *Jaarboek de Fonteine*, 32, 1980-1981, p. 49-68 ; M. Vandecasteele, « Het Antwerpse rederijkersfeest van 1496 : een onderzoek van de bronnen », *Jaarboek de Fonteine*, 36-37, 1985-1986, p. 149-176.

territoires centraux des Pays-Bas[36]. Pendant ces mêmes années, par la médiation directe et indirecte des délégués de la cour, une part importante du théâtre des rhétoriciens développa un ton résolument dynastique. Ainsi, dans une ville de résidence princière comme Bruxelles, les rhétoriciens organisèrent de plus en plus des pièces adaptées à l'occasion de célébrations publiques dynastiques telles que les entrées joyeuses et les cérémonies de mariage ou de baptême[37]. Dans les grandes comme dans les petites villes, ils mirent aussi en scène des pièces qui promouvaient les dévotions "bourguignonnes" telles que celle de Notre-Dame des sept Douleurs[38]. Ainsi, même si à la fin du quinzième siècle la cour ne réussit pas à contrôler directement les pratiques théâtrales des Chambres de Rhétorique, elle parvint à créer les conditions d'un climat culturel dans lequel ces pratiques théâtrales contribuèrent en partie, mais d'une manière significative, à son propre programme politique.

Après les années 1490, la cour semble avoir graduellement perdu son intérêt pour la culture rhétoricienne. Son engagement positif prit fin à peu près au moment où la pensée réformée était introduite aux Pays-Bas, mais rien ne semble indiquer qu'il ait existé une relation directe entre ces deux faits[39]. Les premières tentatives d'encadrer le théâtre religieux des rhétoriciens ne furent en fait pas entreprises par les autorités centrales, mais au contraire, par les autorités régionales, plus particulièrement dans le nord des Pays-Bas. Là, le mouvement des rhétoriciens était un

36 A.-L. van Bruaene, « Sociabiliteit en competitie. De sociaal-institutionele ontwikkeling van de rederijkerskamers in de zuidelijke Nederlanden (1400-1650) », *Conformisten en rebellen. Rederijkerscultuur in de Nederlanden (1400-1650)*, B. Ramakers (dir.), Amsterdam, Amsterdam University Press, 2003, p. 45-63.

37 S. Speakman Sutch, « Dichters van de stad. De Brusselse rederijkers en hun verhouding tot de Franstalige hofliteratuur en het geleerde humanisme (1475-1522) », *De macht van het schone woord. Literatuur in Brussel van de 14e tot de 18e eeuw*, J. Janssens et R. Sleiderink (dir.), Louvain, Davidsfonds, 2003, p. 141-160 ; *Id.*, « Jan Pertcheval and the Brussels Leliebroeders (1490-1500). The model of a conformist rhetoricians chamber ? », B. Ramakers, *Conformisten en rebellen, op. cit.*, p. 95-106 ; S. Mareel, *Voor vorst en stad. Rederijkersliteratuur en vorstenfeest in Vlaanderen en Brabant (1432-1561)*, Amsterdam, Amsterdam University Press, 2010, p. 143-181.

38 S. Speakman Sutch et A.-L. van Bruaene, « The Seven Sorrows of the Virgin Mary. Devotional Communication and Politics in the Burgundian-Habsburg Low Countries (c. 1490-1520) », *The Journal of Ecclesiastical History*, 61, 2010, p. 252-278 ; S. Speakman Sutch et A.-L. van Bruaene, « La dévotion des sept douleurs de la vierge Marie aux Pays-Bas : propagande princière et sensibilité urbaine », *Jean Molinet et son temps*, J. Devaux, E. Doudet et E. Lecuppre-Desjardin (dir.), Turnhout, Brepols, 2013, p. 45-57.

39 *Ibid.*

phénomène relativement neuf et, pour cette raison, les élites nobles et cléricales régionales – à l'exception d'un réseau d'officiels bourguignons qui voulaient affirmer leur statut grandissant dans la société publique hollandaise[40] – ne le prirent pas tout à fait pour acquis. Contrairement à leurs équivalents dans les Pays-Bas du sud, ces élites traditionnelles étaient moins familiarisées, et par conséquent, moins convaincues par les avantages des pratiques littéraires des rhétoriciens, en particulier du drame religieux mis en scène en public[41]. D'autre part, nous avons des indications que dans les milieux rhétoriciens de Hollande – plus récents et qui cherchaient encore leur propre identité – régnait une plus grande réceptivité pour les idées luthériennes et, surtout, anabaptistes, que dans les Chambres plus établies de Flandres et de Brabant[42]. En tout état de cause, c'est la Cour provinciale de Hollande qui lança une offensive précoce et longue contre les pratiques théâtrales des Chambres de Rhétorique. La Cour de Hollande prescrivit la censure préalable des pièces par les autorités locales dès 1528 et proclama une interdiction provisoire de représentation publique de toutes les pièces des rhétoriciens en 1539[43]. Chose intéressante, ni les autorités locales de la Hollande, ni la cour à Bruxelles ne témoignèrent d'un grand enthousiasme pour soutenir ces initiatives[44].

Le vent tourna quand, au lendemain d'un important festival de rhétorique organisé à Gand en 1539, un grand scandale éclata aux Pays-Bas. Selon le chancelier de Brabant, les pièces jouées pendant ce festival étaient « plain de malvaises et abusives doctrines et séductions, de tout tendant à l'opinion lutheriaine[45] ». Cette fois-ci, les autorités centrales réagirent,

40 S. Ter Braake et A. van Dixhoorn, « Engagement en ambitie. De Haagse rederijkerskamer "Met Ghenuchten" en de ontwikkeling van een burgelijke samenleving in Holland rond 1500 », *Jaarboek voor Middeleeuwse Geschiedenis*, 9, 2006, p. 150-190 ; A. van Dixhoorn, *Lustige geesten*, *op. cit.*, p. 99-105.

41 Sur la culture littéraire de la Hollande dans cette période, voir K. Goudriaan, « Holland in de tijd van Leeu », *Een drukker zoekt publiek. Gheraert Leeu te Gouda 1477-1484*, Delft, Eburon, 1993, p. 31-53 ; H. Brinkman, *Dichten uit liefde. Literatuur in Leiden aan het einde van de Middeleeuwen*, Hilversum, Verloren, 1997.

42 A. van Dixhoorn, *Lustige geesten*, *op. cit.*, p. 270-274.

43 F. C. van Boheemen et Th. C. J. van der Heijden (éd.), *Retoricaal Memoriaal. Bronnen voor de geschiedenis van de Hollandse rederijkerskamers van de middeleeuwen tot het begin van de achttiende eeuw*, Delft, Eburon, 1999, p. 10-11.

44 F. C. van Boheemen et Th. C. J. van der Heijden, *Met minnen versaemt. De Hollandse rederijkers vanaf de middeleeuwen tot het begin van de achttiende eeuw. Bronnen en bronnenstudies*, Delft, Eburon, 1999, p. 51-57 ; A. van Dixhoorn, *Lustige geesten*, *op. cit.*, p. 210-212.

45 L. P. Gachard (éd.), *Relation des troubles de Gand sous Charles-Quint, par un anonyme : suivie de trois cent trente documents inédits sur cet événement*, Bruxelles, Hayez, 1846, p. 256.

et de façon violente. Cependant, elles ne dirigèrent pas leurs mesures répressives contre la Chambre responsable de l'organisation ni contre les autres Chambres qui avaient participé au festival, mais contre l'édition des allégories par l'imprimeur humaniste Joos Lambrecht à Gand[46]. L'édition des pièces fut mentionnée dans une ordonnance impériale et dans un édit impérial contre l'hérésie, tous deux parus en 1540, et fut mise à l'Index de Louvain. Ces actions confirment que, pendant les premières étapes de la répression de la pensée réformée, les autorités centrales concentrèrent leurs efforts sur la régulation de la presse à imprimer[47]. Il faut en revanche reconnaître que l'ordonnance impériale de 1540 exprimait également une intention de contrôler plus largement les mises en scène de pièces de théâtre et d'autres formes d'expression littéraire. L'ordonnance interdit la mise en scène de pièces suspectes, la mention des Saintes Écritures ou d'auteurs religieux dans les pièces et, finalement, le chant, la vente ou la distribution de ballades et de chansons ayant une telle portée[48]. Significativement, ces mesures étaient pourtant été moins répressives que l'interdiction générale des pièces des rhétoriciens qui avait été proposée en Hollande une année plus tôt[49]. Qui plus est, dans les années suivantes, les mesures impériales furent mitigées par des ordonnances locales, promulgués en Flandres avec le soutien de la cour de Bruxelles, en imposant seulement la censure préalable aux représentations[50].

Néanmoins, pendant les années qui suivirent 1540, le contrôle des pratiques des Chambres de Rhétorique s'accéléra, mais l'intensité et le

46 *Spelen van zinne by den xix. gheconfirmeirden Cameren van Rhethorycken binnen der Stede van Ghendt comparerende vertooght : Volghende den Octroye vander K. Maiesteyt, Grave van Vlaendren, onzen geduchten Heere, Schepenen der zelver stede ende Camere van Rhetorijcke vand' helighe Drivuldigheyt ghezeyt de Fonteynisten, verleent ende der quarte wtghezonden op de questye 'welc den mensche stervende meesten troost es ?'*…, Gand, Joos Lambrecht, 1539. Pour une édition contemporaine, voir B. H. Erné et L. M. van Dis (éd.), *De Gentse Spelen van 1539*, 2 volumes, La Haye, Nijhoff, 1982. Voir également W. M. H. Hummelen, "31 augustus 1539. De eerste bundel met rederijkersspelen die bij een wedstrijd opgevoerd zijn, komt uit bij Joos Lambrecht Lettersteker te Gent. Spelen van sinne en hun opvoeringspraktijken", R.L. Erenstein, *Een theatergeschiedenis*, *op. cit.*, p. 98-105.

47 A.-L. van Bruaene, « Printing Plays. The Publication of the Ghent Plays of 1539 and the Reaction of the Authorities », *Dutch Crossing*, 24, 2000, p. 265-284.

48 Pour une édition et une discussion de l'ordonnance de 1540, voir B. De Groote, « De overheid en het Gentse rederijkersfeest van 1539 », *Jaarboek de Fonteine*, 25, 1975, p. 105-118.

49 A. Van Dixhoorn, *Lustige geesten*, *op. cit.*, p. 212.

50 J. Decavele, *De Dageraad van de Reformatie in Vlaanderen*, Bruxelles, Verhandelingen van de Koninklijke Academie voor Wetenschappen, Letteren en Schone Kunsten van België (Klasse der Letteren 76), 1975, vol. 1, p. 20.

caractère des mesures répressives dépendit largement du lieu, du moment, des personnes et des circonstances. En Flandres, Pieter Titelmans, le nouveau et zélé inquisiteur pour les Flandres, Lille et Tournai commença à mener l'enquête sur les pièces des rhétoriciens jouées dans les petites localités et les villages, souvent à l'occasion de compétitions locales ou régionales. Pourtant, si quelques rhétoriciens individuels furent sévèrement punis, des sanctions sérieuses furent rarement prises contre les Chambres de Rhétorique[51]. À Anvers, deux rhétoriciens proéminents, Peter Schuddematte et Frans Fraet, furent exécutés. Mais, dans leurs cas, leurs activités subversives en tant que, respectivement, instituteur et imprimeur, pesèrent lourdement dans le verdict[52]. La suspicion générale pesant sur les institutions et les pratiques des Chambres de Rhétorique resta la plus forte en Hollande. Là, un certain nombre de compétitions prévues furent annulées, tandis que l'inquisiteur Franciscus Sonnius plaidait pour une interdiction générale des pratiques des rhétoriciens ou, au moins, pour une censure de la part des ecclésiastiques bien organisée[53].

La question de savoir si les spectacles dramatiques et les autres formes d'expression des rhétoriciens pendant cette période peuvent vraiment être considérés comme subversifs du point de vue des autorités, a été traitée ailleurs, et ne peut être abordée ici qu'en des termes généraux. Pris individuellement, les rhétoriciens avaient des opinions très variées en matière religieuse, même si la plupart d'entre eux, avec leur arrière-plan social bourgeois, n'était certainement pas extrémiste[54]. Il est important de souligner que les dynamiques de la culture rhétoricienne, avec ses notions de compétition et de liberté de débat, permettaient la circulation rapide des idées dans des cercles étendus (en particulier,

51 J. Decavele, *op. cit.*, vol. 1, p. 206-220.

52 P. Génard, « Personen te Antwerpen in de XVIe eeuw, voor het "feit van religie" gerechtelijk vervolgd. Lijst en ambtelijke bijhoorige stukken », *Antwerpsch Archievenblad*, 8, s. d., p. 374-375 ; J. Decavele, *op. cit.*, vol. 1, p. 206-207 ; P. Valkema Blouw, « The Van Oldenborch and Vanden Merberghe pseudonyms or Why Frans Fraet had to die », *Quaerendo*, 22, 1992, p. 165-190 et p. 245-272.

53 F. C. van Boheemen and Th. C. J. van der Heijden, *Met minnen versaemt*, *op. cit.*, p. 56-57 et p. 234-237 ; A. van Dixhoorn, *Lustige geesten*, *op. cit.*, p. 212-214 et p. 273.

54 W. Waterschoot, « De rederijkerskamers en de doorbraak van de reformatie in de Zuidelijke Nederlanden », *Jaarboek de Fonteine*, 45-46, 1995-1996, p. 141-153 ; G. Waite, *op. cit.* ; G. Marnef, « Chambers of Rhetoric and the transmission of religious ideas in the Low Countries », *Cultural Exchange in Early Modern Europe. Volume 1. Religion and Cultural Exchange in Europe, 1400-1700*, H. Schilling et I. G. Tóth (dir.), Cambridge, Cambridge University Press, 2007, p. 284-293.

pour cette période, dans le contexte des festivals de poésie) et que, par conséquent, elles favorisaient un climat général d'ouverture d'esprit à la pensée religieuse non conformiste. Ce fait, plutôt que les opinions ou les actions de rhétoriciens individuels ou les spectacles de Chambres de Rhétorique spécifiques, fit du mouvement rhétoricien un facteur clé dans la réception plus large de la Réforme dans la région et dans le soutien populaire à la Révolte des Pays-Bas[55].

Bien que des inquisiteurs comme Pieter Titelmans et Franciscus Sonnius eussent déjà lancé beaucoup plus tôt des campagnes contre les pratiques des rhétoriciens, il fallut attendre 1560 avant que les autorités centrales se lancent dans une nouvelle initiative législative. Le 26 janvier de cette année, un édit fut promulgué au nom du roi Philippe II par la cour bruxelloise de la régente Marguerite de Parme. Il avait pour but d'encadrer les pratiques du théâtre, de la poésie et des chansons religieux dans les Pays-Bas. L'édit interdit la distribution et la mise en scène en intérieur de toute pièce, ballade, chanson, comédie, farce et *refrein* qui touche à des questions religieuses ou aux ecclésiastiques. Il imposait la censure préalable par le curé principal, le bailli ou le conseil municipal d'un lieu sur toutes pièces allégoriques, tous tableaux vivants et toutes autres pièces de théâtre en public, jouées à l'honneur de Dieu ou de ses saints et pour la récréation du peuple[56]. Même si le texte ne l'exprime pas directement ainsi – il réfère aussi aux compagnies de théâtre venues de l'étranger – il est clair que l'édit vise particulièrement les Chambres de Rhétorique. Dans les comptes de la petite ville flamande de Tielt, par exemple, il est noté qu'en février 1560, un courrier avait apporté une copie d'un placard qui impliquait que « personne ne jouerait aucune rhétorique de caractère suspect[57] ». Cela est également mis en évidence dans une lettre de Marguerite de Parme à Philippe II dans laquelle elle référait à la mise en scène de plusieurs pièces par les Chambres de

55 A.-L. van Bruaene, « "Of the King's Edict I do You no Command". Vernacular Literary Networks and the Reformation in the Low Countries », *Archiv für Reformationsgeschichte*, 99, 2008, p. 229-255.

56 *Ordonnancien / Statuten, Edicten ende Placcaten, / ghepubliceert in de landen van hervvaerts-ouer, / van weghen der Keyserlicker ende Conijnghlicker / Magesteyten, ende haerlieder Edele Voorzaten…* Gand, Jan van den Steene, 1562, p. 815-816 (publication de l'édit de Flandres). Pour une édition moderne de l'édit publié en Hollande, voir F. C. van Boheemen et Th. C. J. van der Heijden, *Retoricaal Memoriaal*, *op. cit.*, p. 13-15.

57 F. Hollevoet (éd.), *Stadsrekeningen Tielt : 1500-1610*, Tielt, Heemkundige Kring De Roede van Tielt, 2000, p. 444.

Rhétorique bruxelloises en 1559, qui avait suscité une controverse sérieuse dans les milieux gouvernementaux[58]. Pourtant, comme cela avait été le cas depuis les années 1490, la position de la cour en ce qui concernait les Chambres de Rhétorique restait ambiguë et n'était certainement pas exclusivement répressive.

Il faut insister sur le fait que l'édit de 1560 notait explicitement la valeur religieuse et sociale des pièces allégoriques et des tableaux vivants, en contraste avec celle de genres plus informels, moins sérieux ou moins publics tels que les chansons, les farces et les ballades. Par conséquent, l'édit ne mena certainement pas à une interdiction des pratiques théâtrales des Chambres de Rhétorique. Au contraire, au début des années 1560, les Pays-Bas du sud virent une augmentation sans précédent du nombre de compétitions de rhétorique régionales et interrégionales, théâtrales comme lyriques[59]. En Flandres, seules deux compétitions prévues furent supprimées, l'une à Gand en 1561 et l'autre dans la petite ville de Ronse en 1564. Dans les deux cas, cependant, la politique gouvernementale était enchevêtrée avec des intérêts locaux. Ironie de la situation, la compétition qui devait être tenue à Gand en 1561, était organisée par *De Balsemblomme*, une société littéraire qui pouvait encore se targuer de son statut de Chambre souveraine, même si elle avait depuis longtemps rompu ses liens avec la cour. Il est intéressant de constater que l'initiative d'interdire la compétition ne vint pas du gouvernement central, mais du magistrat de Gand. Le conseil municipal se servit de l'édit de 1560 pour revendiquer son autorité sur les activités de la Chambre, et, ce faisant, pour résoudre un conflit en cours entre *De Balsemblomme* et les Chambres locales[60]. En 1564, une compétition rhétoricienne devait prendre place dans la petite ville de Ronse, mais la cour promulgua une interdiction officielle, « craindrant les dangiers et inconveniens qui poroient advenir contre nostre foy cahtolicque ». Ce

58 L. P. Gachard (éd.), *Correspondance de Marguerite d'Autriche, duchesse de Parme avec Philippe II. Tome Premier 14 Août 1559-16 Novembre 1561*, Bruxelles, C. Muquardt, 1867, p. 138. Sur les incidents bruxellois, voir A.-L. van Bruaene, « "Of the King's Edict" », art. cité, p. 233-237.

59 A.-L. van Bruaene, « Sociabiliteit en competitie », art. cité, p. 51, 54 and 56. Dans les Pays-Bas du Nord, cette tendance était moins évidente : A. van Dixhoorn, « Burgers, branies en bollebozen. De sociaal-institutionele ontwikkeling van de rederijkerskamers in de Noordelijke Nederlanden (1470-1650) », *Conformisten en rebellen*, B. Ramakers (dir.), *op. cit.*, p. 79.

60 A.-L. van Bruaene, *Om beters wille*, *op. cit.*, p. 163-164.

cas était également remarquable, car les metteurs en scène avaient non seulement obtenu le soutien du magistrat local mais aussi celui du doyen de Ronse, qui n'était autre que l'inquisiteur flamand, Pieter Titelmans. Par conséquent, il est difficile de comprendre la raison pour laquelle la gouvernante persévéra et continua d'affirmer sa crainte de l'hérésie dans ce cas particulier, contre de l'avis de son inquisiteur, dont l'orthodoxie inébranlable ne pouvait être mise en doute[61]. En Hollande, une première interdiction sur la tenue d'un festival de rhétorique à Gouda en 1564 fut finalement retirée par la Cour de Hollande et la régente Marguerite de Parme, même si l'événement et le contenu des pièces continuèrent à susciter la controverse[62].

Incontestablement, les négociations qui accompagnèrent l'organisation du fameux festival de rhétorique ou *landjuweel* d'Anvers en 1561, l'un des festivals urbains les plus emblématiques du seizième siècle, montrent bien l'attitude de la cour[63]. Dans ce cas, l'édit de 1560 joua un rôle fondamental, non pas pour supprimer la culture rhétoricienne, mais en tant qu'outil pour mettre en place le politiquement et religieusement correct. Rien ne fut laissé au hasard : les négociations entre la ville et la gouvernante durèrent plusieurs mois. Toutes les pièces de la compétition dûrent être soumises aux censeurs officiels. Les Chambres qui présentaient des pièces religieusement ou politiquement suspectes risquaient non seulement des peines sévères, mais aussi la perte définitive de leurs privilèges. Pourtant, il est intéressant de constater que l'interférence de la cour eut également un effet plus positif sur les pratiques littéraires des rhétoriciens. Face au mécontentement causé par la question initiale, considérée comme trop chargée politiquement, il fut demandé à la Chambre organisatrice *De Violieren* de présenter une liste de thèmes au conseil de la gouvernante. Une première sélection fut faite en se basant sur cette liste. Parmi les trois thèmes approuvés par la cour, *De Violieren* sélectionna finalement la question humaniste : « Quelle est la

61 E. Van der Straeten, « De Ronssesche rederykkamers in 1564 », *Aldernardiana en Flandriana*, Audenarde, Vuylsteke, 1867, vol. 1, p. 150-161 ; J. Decavele, *op. cit.*, vol. 1, p. 213-214 ; A.-L. van Bruaene, *Om beters wille*, *op. cit.*, p. 140.

62 F. C. van Boheemen et Th. C. J. van der Heijden, *Met minnen versaemt*, *op. cit.*, p. 59 et p. 251-255.

63 E. Cockx-Indestege et W. Waterschoot (éd.), *Uyt Ionsten Versaemt. Het Landjuweel van 1561 te Antwerpen*, Bruxelles, Bibliothèque Royale, 1994 ; J. Vandommele, *Als in een spiegel. Vrede, kennis en gemeenschap op het Antwerpse Landjuweel van 1561*, Hilversum, Verloren, 2011.

plus grande cause de ce que l'homme désire les arts ? » (« dwelck den mensche aldermeest tot consten verwect »)[64].

On a beaucoup écrit sur l'orientation humaniste et renaissanciste croissante de la littérature vernaculaire néerlandaise en général et de la littérature rhétoricienne en particulier, dans la deuxième moitié du seizième siècle. Le *landjuweel* de 1561 a souvent été considéré en tant qu'événement phare dans ce développement[65]. Bien sûr, le changement dans l'attitude intellectuelle des rhétoriciens eux-mêmes fut déterminant dans ce processus, mais l'impact des politiques gouvernementales ne peut pas non plus être nié. Le fait que la régente choisit plus ou moins elle-même le thème du *landjuweel* n'est peut-être pas plus qu'un fait divers. Il est plus notable que la cour approuva également l'édition des pièces du festival dans deux volumes prestigieux agrémentés des gravures sur bois raffinées[66]. Pour la première fois depuis l'édition malheureuse des pièces de la compétition de Gand de 1539, la renommée d'un festival de rhétorique fut augmentée par la presse à imprimer. L'éditeur des livres du festival d'Anvers n'était autre que Willem Silvius, qui avait récemment été nommé typographe royal par l'approbation personnelle de Philippe II[67]. Pendant le festival, Silvius avait obtenu les droits d'édition par la médiation du Chancelier de Brabant. Avant leur édition, les textes du festival furent examinés attentivement : Silvius dut attendre le privilège jusque respectivement mai et août 1562[68]. Silvius

---

64 E. van Autenboer, *Het Brabants landjuweel der rederijkers, 1515-1561*, Middelburg, Merlijn, 1981, p. 48-56.

65 Voir, entre autres, J. Koopmans e.a. (dir.), *Rhetoric – Rhétoriqueurs – Rederijkers. Proceedings of the colloquium, Amsterdam, 10-13 November 1993*, Amsterdam, North-Holland, 1995 ; B. Ramakers, « De mythe van de grote vertraging », *Queeste*, 5, 1998, p. 58-63 ; J. Koppenol, *Leids heelal. Het Loterijspel (1596) van Jan van Hout*, Hilversum, Verloren, 1998 ; M. Spies, *Rhetoric, Rethoricians and Poets. Studies in Renaissance Poetry and Poetics*, Amsterdam, Amsterdam University Press, 1999 ; W. Waterschoot, *Schouwende Fantasye. Opstellen van Werner Waterschoot*, Gand, Academia Press, 2002 ; A. van Dixhoorn, *Lustige geesten*, *op. cit.*, p. 274-276.

66 *Spelen van sinne vol scoone moralisacien, uutleggingen en bediedenissen op alle loeflijcke consten waer inne men claerlijck ghelijck in eenen spieghel, Figuerlijck, Poetelijck ende Retorijckelijck mach aenschouwen hoe nootsakelijck ende dienstelijck die selve consten allen menschen zijn*, Anvers, Willem Silvius, 1562. Pour une édition contemporaine, voir R. Ryckaert (éd.), *De Antwerpse spelen van 1561 naar de editie Silvius (Antwerpen 1562) uitgegeven met inleiding, annotaties en registers*, 2 volumes, Gand, Koninklijke Academie voor Nederlandse Taal- en Letterkunde, 2011.

67 P. Valkema Blouw, « Willem Silvius's remarkable start, 1559-1562 », *Quaerendo*, 20, 1990, p. 170-172.

68 E. van Autenboer, *Het Brabants landjuweel*, *op. cit.*, p. 20-21.

obtint également la permission de commercialiser deux autres livres de festival en 1564, qui contenaient les productions littéraires d'une compétition à Rotterdam en 1561[69]. Dans ce cas, il semble que la cour ait été moins prudente, dans la mesure où le thème général du réconfort spirituel invitait au moins quelques réponses modérément inspirées par les idées de la Réforme[70]. Il est probable que c'est au moins en partie pour cette raison que l'expérience ne fut pas répétée. Willem Silvius avait aussi prévu d'éditer les pièces de Gouda de 1564, mais, à cause de la controverse entourant cette compétition, une lettre de la gouvernante Marguerite de Parme le lui déconseilla indirectement[71].

Le fait que la cour permit les éditions d'Anvers et de Rotterdam peut être compris comme un contrepoids à l'édit de 1560. Ces livres de festival eurent un impact important sur les développements poétiques au sein de la littérature des rhétoriciens[72]. C'est pourquoi l'on peut dire que, comme ce fut le cas dans les années 1490, les rapports plus positifs de la cour avec cette littérature des rhétoriciens eut plus de résultats que les tentatives de répression directe. Bien sûr, ce ne fut qu'un succès mitigé. Les rhétoriciens continuèrent à écrire des vers subversifs et à utiliser le théâtre pour exprimer leurs opinions religieuses, souvent très variées[73]. Dans un pays à l'aube de la Révolte des Pays-Bas, la situation restait explosive. Mais pour une cour sans l'avantage du recul, on peut considérer que la stratégie de réguler si nécessaire, mais de stimuler si possible, peut être considérée comme très adroite.

L'attitude générale de la cour explique également pourquoi, après le début de la Révolte des Pays-Bas, les appels répétés pour l'interdiction complète de la culture rhétoricienne dans les Pays-Bas du sud espagnols

---

69 *Drijderley Refereynen ghepronuncieert opte Rhetorijck-feest der blauvve Acoleyen van Rotterdam. 1561* [...]. Antwerp, Willem Silvius, 1564 ; *Spelen van Sinne vol schoone allegatien, loflijcke leeringhen ende schriftuerlijcke onderwijsinghen [...]. Ghespeelt ende verthoont met octroy der Coninckclijcker Mat. binnen die stede van Rotterdam by de neghen Cameren van Rhetorijcken die hem daer ghepresenteert hebben den xx. dach in Julio Anno 1561*, Anvers, Willem Silvius, 1564. Voir aussi D. Coigneau, « Drie Rijnsburgse refereinen te Rotterdam 1561 en hun Franse bron », *Verslagen en Mededelingen van de Koninklijke Vlaamse Academie voor Taal- en Letterkunde*, 1977, p. 239-244.

70 F. C. van Boheemen et Th. C. J. Van der Heijden, *Met minnen versaemt*, *op. cit.*, p. 245-248 ; A. van Dixhoorn, *Lustige geesten*, *op. cit.*, p. 247.

71 F. C. van Boheemen et Th. C. J. Van der Heijden, *Met minnen versaemt*, *op. cit.*, p. 254-255.

72 *Cf.* B. Ramakers, « Tonen en betogen. De dramaturgie van de Rotterdamse Spelen van 1561 », *Spiegel der Letteren*, 43, 2001, p. 176-204.

73 G. Marnef, art. cité ; A.-L. Van Bruaene, « "Of the King's Edict" », art. cité.

ne furent jamais suivis[74]. Au lieu de cela, les archiducs Albert et Isabella republièrent l'édit de 1560. Il s'agissait en fait d'une version révisée qui reflétait les sensibilités culturelles de l'ère de la Contre-Réforme. L'édit de 1601 donnait un plus grand rôle au clergé, en particulier au *censor librorum*, dans la censure préalable des compositions littéraires. L'édit stipulait aussi que les spectacles de théâtre ne pouvaient plus être organisés au même temps que les messes et les sermons, auxquels le peuple était censé assister. Le plus important est peut-être qu'en sus de son orthodoxie, c'est aussi la moralité du drame laïque qui devenait un véritable sujet de préoccupation. Les pièces de théâtre devaient désormais ne plus offenser les bonnes mœurs[75]. En somme, une nouvelle ère commençait, dans laquelle le rôle du théâtre des rhétoriciens en particulier et les pratiques dramatiques en général devaient être renégociés[76]. Mais comme cela avait été le cas dès la fin du quinzième siècle, le souhait était présent que les autorités centrales maintiennent l'équilibre en présence.

CONCLUSION

Cet essai a exploré la question de la censure du théâtre des rhétoriciens dans les Pays-Bas à l'aube de l'époque moderne. La censure n'a pas été traitée ici comme une action répressive à sens unique, mais comme un processus complexe dans lequel les ensembles de valeurs et de pratiques des différentes parties impliquées interagissaient de différentes façons. C'était une vérité universellement reconnue dans les Pays-Bas

74 A.-L. van Bruaene, *Om beters wille*, *op. cit.*, p. 174-177.

75 *Tweeden Placaet-Bouck inhoudende diversche Ordonnancien, Edicten ende Placaeten van de Coninclicke Ma.[tem] ende haere deurluchtighe Hoocheden, Graven van Vlaendren, metsgaders van heurliederen Provincialen Raede aldaer, ghepubliceert in den voorghenoemden Lande van Vlaendren t'zedert den Iaere Vyfthien-hondert t'zestich, tot ende metten Iaere zesthien-hondert Negenen-twintich*, Gand, Anna vanden Steene, 1629, p. 28-30. *Cf.* A. K. L. Thijs, *Van geuzenstad tot katholiek bolwerk. Antwerpen en de Contrareformatie*, Turnhout, Brepols, 1990, p. 161-162.

76 A.-L. van Bruaene, « De contouren van een nieuw cultuurmodel. Rederijkers in Vlaanderen en Brabant in de zeventiende eeuw », *Handelingen der Koninklijke Zuid-Nederlandse Maatschappij voor Taal- en Letterkunde en Geschiedenis*, 58 (2005), p. 221-237.

de l'époque pré-moderne qu'il était nécessaire de fixer les limites de l'expression dramatique. La véritable question était de trouver où se situaient ces limites. Les rhétoriciens eux-mêmes étaient très conscients du pouvoir de l'expression verbale (et non-verbale) et ils montraient, par conséquent, une véritable préoccupation concernant les propos diffamatoires et blasphématoires. Dans le même temps, la transgression de leurs propres règles relatives à ces questions faisait partie intégrante de leur jeu rhétorique.

Les autorités locales se préoccupaient surtout de l'ordre public. Les Chambres de Rhétorique furent rarement considérées comme une menace réelle. En général, le clergé appréciait également les pratiques des rhétoriciens. Bien entendu, les choses changèrent drastiquement avec l'introduction de la pensée réformée vers 1520. Mais même après cette date, l'attitude du clergé varia considérablement. C'est pourquoi il est nécessaire de mener davantage de recherches pour mieux cerner les sensibilités culturelles de ce groupe hétérogène. Il existait également des différences nettes dans les actes des hautes autorités laïques. La position des autorités régionales semble avoir dépendu partiellement de traditions culturelles. Cela peut expliquer pourquoi les plus forts appels à la répression de la culture des rhétoriciens furent émis dans les Pays-Bas du nord, où le mouvement était probablement considéré par quelques responsables haut placés comme une indésirable importation du sud.

Finalement, les actions et les stratégies des autorités centrales sont les plus révélatrices des ambiguïtés de la censure dans les Pays-Bas à l'aube de l'époque moderne. Dès la fin du quinzième siècle, la cour montra qu'elle était consciente des dangers potentiels du mouvement rhétoricien. Cela se traduisit par des tentatives de poser des limites à l'expression littéraire en langue vernaculaire. Chronologiquement, la principale aire de préoccupation évolua du domaine de la politique à la fin du quinzième siècle, au domaine de la religion vers le milieu du seizième siècle, jusqu'au domaine de la moralité au commencement du dix-septième siècle. Mais en général – même si quelques officiels à la cour pensaient sans doute autrement – les autorités centrales n'eurent jamais le désir de supprimer complètement les pratiques des rhétoriciens. Il ne faut pas oublier que les Chambres de Rhétorique avaient l'avantage d'être des institutions respectables et clairement identifiables, beaucoup plus faciles à gérer que des groupes de théâtre non organisés. De plus, les quelques tentatives de contrôle direct, comme celle de l'institution d'une Chambre de Rhétorique souveraine ou les interdictions sur l'organisation de compétitions rhétoriques, n'aboutirent guère à de grands résultats. La stratégie de la cour de stimuler l'expression littéraire politiquement correcte et religieusement neutre en encourageant les spectacles et les textes qui se conformaient aux politiques officielles, s'avéra beaucoup plus efficace. Ce faisant, la censure d'État devint un facteur non pas de suppression mais de modelage et, aux moments critiques, de réinvention d'une riche pratique littéraire.

Anne-Laure VAN BRUAENE
Université de Gand

DISCIPLINE IN PLAY-RELATED ACTIVITIES IN COMMUNAL ITALY

Between the middle ages and the Modern Age, local authorities in north-central Italy developed converging disciplinary actions in the contemporary system of play[1], which took into consideration various prospects and requests (public and private, economic and moral, social and religious…). For this reason, games of chance and play-related activities were regulated little by little[2].

In the last centuries of the middle ages (13th-16th centuries)–an age generally characterized by a "codification" of behaviour and social practices–there were several decisive moments for the field of play. Starting from the twelfth century, play took on a different "value" and "position" among man's activities. During the following century, public authorities came to a full awareness of its potential (economic, social, political…). The process of moralization that influenced the customs of fifteenth century society also involved play, along with the growing appreciation for the scenic and propagandistic side of performances

1 For this period, we speak of a true "overall, play-related system" (in which we acknowledge different activities, all in the *ludus* category according to contemporary perceptions), with internal and external interconnections and specificities. See G. Ortalli, "Tempo libero e medio evo: tra pulsioni ludiche e schemi culturali", *Il tempo libero. Economia e società (Loisirs, Leisure, Tiempo Libre, Freizeit)*, S. Cavaciocchi (dir.), Florence, 1995, p. 31–54.

2 I only indicate here a few studies that directly regard the topic. In particular regarding the principles of (romanistic and canonistic-theological) gambling regulations refer to: R. Ferroglio, "Ricerche sul gioco e sulla scommessa fino al secolo XIII", *Rivista di storia del diritto italiano*, 71, 1998, p. 273–387; and G. Ceccarelli, *Il gioco e il peccato. Economia e rischio nel Tardo medioevo*, Bologna, 2003; on play-sports oriented practices, see U. Gualazzini, *Premesse storiche al diritto sportivo*, Milan, 1965. For the application and adaptation of such principles to communal Italy, see the collection of norms in *Statuta de ludo. Le leggi sul gioco nell'Italia di comune (secoli XIII-XVI)*, A. Rizzi (dir.), texts collected by C. Cardinali, A. Degrandi, A. Di Salvo, G. Ortalli and A. Rizzi introduction by G. Ortalli, Rome-Treviso, 2012. In reference to communal Italy, see contributions published in *Gioco e giustizia nell'Italia di Comune*, G. Ortalli (dir.), Treviso-Rome 1993 and A. Rizzi, *Ludus/ludere. Giocare in Italia alla fine del medio evo*, Treviso-Rome, 1995.

and civic rituals. During the age of the Counter-Reformation, the "codification" of behaviour and social practices, with the spreading of rules and regulations of diverse origin, also weighed upon games and similar activities.

The phenomenon of play becomes therefore clearer when considered in the long term, although I will focus here primarily on the fourteenth and fifteenth centuries. During this period, Italian city-states were consolidated and evolved into lordships and principalities or oligarchical republics (Venice, for example) in which associations and "unions" of diverse origins developed (such as trade guilds and religious brotherhoods). One has to take into account a complex political and social reality, as well as a network of different powers and jurisdictions. These entities may in their own time and manner have played an active role in the disciplining of the contemporary system of play, first of all by establishing regulations (and sanctions) on the matter.

Let us begin with an underlying question: could play have been a source of dispute (or agreement) amongst different powers having official jurisdiction in the same territory? What follows are some general considerations regarding fourteenth and fifteenth century Italy, leaving investigations on individual situations for later.

GAMES AND PERFORMANCES IN ITALIAN CITY-STATES: FUNCTION

Play in Italian city-states in the late middle ages (not unlike what happened in other contexts and periods of time) gave rise to certain expectations and took on different values (political, social and economic)[3]. Horse races, tournaments and "sports" competitions

3 On the political value of play and festivities in the middle ages with reference also to the Italian context, refer to the contributions collected in *Festa e politica e politica della festa nel medioevo. Atti del convegno di studio svoltosi in occasione della XVIII edizione del Premio internazionale Ascoli Piceno*, A. Rigon (dir.), Rome, 2008. On the economic (as well as social) effects of gambling, with many references to communal Italy, and also for the bibliography, it is useful to refer to G. Ortalli, *Barattieri. Il gioco d'azzardo fra economia ed etica. Secoli XIII-XV*, Bologna, 2012.

were, first of all, a form of distraction and amusement but were also propagandistic programs useful to the public, also directed outside the community[4]. Any change or significant moment in the life of the community could lead to collective, heart-felt and festive participation. Such festivities were not usually undertaken spontaneously on individual initiative; they often led to theatrical demonstrations and performances (devised for the occasion and often inserted into traditional, festive programs) for the public to celebrate or legitimize an undertaking, a lord or a faction[5]. Good example of this is what happened during the lordship of the Duke of Athens in Florence between 1342 and 1343. The play and performance oriented activities during those two years bear witness to the political ascent of the Florentine lord. Few years later something similar occurred in Rome under the regime of Cola di Rienzo[6]. On the contrary, it was not rare to experience a sort of "short circuit" in the system of play and celebrations, where festivities and performances were interrupted or suspended during times of crisis or disagreement (this happened with horse races, jousts, tournaments...)[7]. In fourteenth and fifteenth century Italy, conflict between factions was still highly present and not completely "tamed". It was not until the century of the Counter-Reformation that the "process of civilization" that occurred from the middle ages to the Modern Age produced results. Political aggressiveness finally gave way to civic rituals with refined allegories and complex political

4 A confirmation of this is given by a decision taken in Florence in the spring of 1392: as an anonymous chronicler notes, the tournament that was to take place on the 21th of April "was postponed" to the 12th of May in order to avoid overlapping with a similar event, organized in Lombardia, which would have prevented "many Lombard lords" to "take part to the tournament in Florence". Cf. *Alle bocche della piazza. Diario di anonimo fiorentino (1382–1401)*, A. Molho and F. Sznura (ed.), Florence, 1986, p. 138.

5 We find many play-related occasions in contemporary sources, organized for various reasons to give visibility and support to a lord or a reigning dynasty, a regime of the few or one of the people. It was mentioned also in Rizzi, *Ludus/ludere*, op. cit., and in A. Rizzi, "Ordinare e guidare: poteri laici e predicazione nella gestione della festa nell'Italia di tradizione comunale", in *Festa e politica*, op. cit., p. 114.

6 On the Duke of Athens, see: Giovanni Villani, *Nuova cronica*, G. Porta (ed.), III, Parma 1991, p. 315; on Cola di Rienzo, see: Anonimo Romano, *Cronica*, G. Porta (ed.), Milan 1981, p. 165–167 and 184–189. Cf. also Rizzi, *Ludus/ludere*, op. cit., p. 191–193, and Rizzi, "Ordinare e guidare", op. cit., p. 115–116.

7 Rizzi, *Ludus/ludere*, op. cit., p. 191; and Rizzi, "Ordinare e guidare", op. cit., p. 113–114 and 121.

messages regulated by a higher authority[8]. On the contrary, in the last centuries of the middle ages, conflicts amongst political factions were made highly visible through play-related competitions. Play then deteriorated not by chance but because of complex, articulate situations, undermining the "authoritative" disciplinary actions. Play, by nature, could be a ritual contest for control over a certain area, for the most part liminal, among opposing groups. Disputes were therefore a show of force to diminish the adversary, they expressed the ability to control a territory and a group of "armed" people or *clientes* as in the *battagliole* (armed encounters or stone throwing amongst rival groups within the city, each with a leader–sometimes a member of the local elite) fought amongst young people belonging to eminent families in fourteenth century Florence[9].

Civic traditions and religious rituals competed to confer an "identity" to public festivities in communal Italy, leading to a characteristic mix of sacred and profane[10]. The importance that was given to play-related events organized at the same time as traditional public festivities explains (and justifies) the attention they received from the authorities

---

8 On the effects of the process of civilization on public rituals as outlined by Norbert Elias, cf. "Ludica. Annali di storia e civiltà del gioco", 1, 1995, p. 53–200 (monograph section of the journal, dedicated to *Gioco, civilizzazione, transizioni / Spiel, Zivilisation, Gesellschaftlicher Umbruch*, with contributions of B. Roeck, G. Ortalli, E. Dunning, P. Spierenburg, A. Nitschke, G. Schwerhoff, R.A. Müller, H. Holländer, I. Gareis, A. Rizzi, G. Andrieu and H. Eichberg).

9 On Florentine battles cf. above all A. Zorzi, "Battagliole e giochi d'azzardo a Firenze nel tardo Medioevo: due pratiche sociali tra disciplinamento e repressione", in *Gioco e giustizia*, op. cit., particularly p. 73–75. Regarding the *battagliola*, more generally, for the contexts in which it is stated and the reference to different interpretations given as well as for the main studies on the topic, cf. A. Rizzi, "Il gioco della 'battagliola'", in *Pace e guerra nel basso medioevo*, Spoleto, 2004, p. 219–254; and A. Rizzi, "Continuità ed evoluzione nelle pugne cittadine fra medioevo ed età moderna: il 'caso' italiano", in *Agon und Distinktion – Soziale Räume des Zweikampfs zwischen Mittelalter und Neuzeit*, U. Israel and C. Jaser, Berlin, LIT-Verlag, 2016, p. 199–219. Fifteenth-century cases of *battagliola* (in the mountain community of Bormio, in Valtellina) were studied by F. Antonacci and M. Della Misericordia, *La guerra dei bambini. Gioco, violenza e rito da una testimonianza rinascimentale*, Milan, 2013.

10 On this aspect of medieval festivities especially in Italian context, see P. Ventrone, "Feste e rituali civici: città italiane a confronto", in *Aspetti e componenti dell'identità urbana in Italia e in Germania (secoli XIV-XVI) / Aspekte und Komponenten der städtischen Identität in Italien und Deutschland (14.-16. Jahrhundert)*, G. Chittolini and P. Johanek (dir.), Bologna-Berlin, 2003, p. 155–191. For an overview, see also J. Chiffoleau, L. Martines and A. Paravicini Bagliani (dir.), *Riti e rituali nelle società medievali*, Spoleto 1994.

(governors and clergymen) and from political leaders (leaders of political factions or representatives of emerging local families)[11]. Multitude of actors, addressees but also game promoters (of different gender, social status, profession, public role and even religion) participated during the celebrations to games and sports competitions. Men and women, town-dwellers and foreigners, nobles and common people, soldiers and students, brigades and people's associations, Guelphs and Ghibellines (supporters of the Pope and of the Emperor), Jews and Christians, town authorities (*podestà*–chief magistrates who acted mostly as judging magistrates–, captains, guilds and priors) and lords (dukes or princes), high prelates or simple clerics: all took part. At times, there was no general consensus on the organized activities[12]; sometimes these activities became a tool between rival groups (supporters and disparagers), further exacerbating the political atmosphere[13].

---

11 One can recall here the importance held by the *palio* in Italian municipalities in the late middle ages, to which we will return below.

12 Many people did not like the feast of the Holy Spirit organized by the Florentine organizers in the church of Carmine instead of the church of Santo Spirito, in 1489: cf. Tribaldo de Rossi, *Ricordanze*, in *Delizie degli eruditi toscani*, t. XXII, Firenze 1786, p. 276. Even the jousts wanted by that the Duke of Athens in Florence at Easter in 1343 were deserted by many ("few citizens played"): important people as well as commoners "started to dislike the methods": Giovanni Villani, *Nuova cronica,* op. cit., III, p. 315.

13 In Florence in September 1342 the "Great" (the old aristocracy of the Florentine commune out of the government) organized "a big feast handling weapons" (*armeggeria*) to celebrate the fact that the Duke of Athens (Gualtieri di Brienne) had been elected lord for life against the will of the Priors, who governed Florence (for this reason, soon after the Duke imprisoned them). Along with the "Great" common people supported the Duke of Athens. The performance of the Great, the "great feast" that followed, desired by the duke himself the following week, but also the sermons and the praise of the Florentine bishop to "glorify the duke, lord of the people", in the chronicler's account, underline the seriousness of the situation: "in this way the duke of Athens usurped the freedom of Florence, betraying it" (cf. Agnolo di Tura del Grasso, *Cronaca senese [...] detta la cronaca maggiore*, in *Cronache senesi*, A. Lisini and F. Iacometti (ed.), Bologna 1931–1939 (RIS², 15/6), p. 533–534). On the contrary, the "feast of fire and lights" organized by the lord of Ravenna, Bernardine of Polenta, in May 1357 for the fall of Cesena in the hands of the papal ambassador (of which da Polenta was a partisan) was the occasion to set off the dissatisfaction of the people of Ravenna against their lord "because of his oppression", cf. Matteo Villani, *Cronica, con la continuazione di Filippo Villani*, G. Porta (ed.), II, Milan, 1995.

GAMES AND PERFORMANCES IN ITALIAN CITY-STATES: REGULATION

In addition to paying particular attention to games and performances, as mentioned earlier, the authorities of the time claimed public control of them, which led to a general policy of containment and regulation of contemporary play-related activities.

The *ius commune* had dictated the fundamental legal principles to regulate play involving money and physical activities. In order to authorize the latter, publicity had to be guaranteed (that is to say it had to occur in a public place and in front of spectators); it had to be carried out *virtutis causa*, *i.e.* to exercise vigour, and not *questus causa*, that is to say not to gain money (civil law); it was not to result in anything dangerous for the body or the soul (canon law), thereby promoting *ludus exercitiorum* (which, for theologians from the thirteenth century on, meant tournaments or chess)[14]. Subsequently, laws were mainly created by the city-states and therefore by lords and princes (as the city-states expanded and evolved into regional states) appointed to control public play through different councils. The Church also became involved in the regulation of the play-related activities of its contemporaries: first of all, through synodical regulations–which became harsher over time–aiming above all at preserving the moral integrity of the clergy by imposing a series of obligations and prohibitions. For example, clergymen had to abstain from any play-related activities (above all gambling but also performances, dances[15], games using balls[16]...). They also had to refrain from excessive and useless expenses

14 See for further analysis: Gualazzini, *Premesse storiche*, op. cit.; Ferroglio, *Ricerche sul gioco e sulla scommessa*, op. cit.; Ceccarelli, *Il gioco e il peccato*, op. cit.

15 G. Bosisio, *Concilia Papiensia, Constitutiones synodales et Decreta dioecesana [...] nunc in unum corpus collecta [...] D. Angelo Ramazzotti sanctae ecclesiae papiensis episcopo*, Pavia 1852, p. 298–300: the clergy is therefore to abstain from "lascivis cantionibus, choreis [...] comoediis, tumultuosis saecularium conviviis aliisque profanis spectaculis" (it is part of: *Constitutiones in synodo papiensi sub [...] Hippolyto Rubeo episcopo papiensi editae et publicatae anno MDLXVI. Cum additionibus et novis Constitutionibus factis in Synodo Dioecesana anno MDCXII [...]*).

16 P. Dinelli, "Dei sinodi della diocesi di Lucca", *Memorie e documenti per servire all'istoria del ducato di Lucca*, VII, 1934, p. 128 (this is part of the second synod of Nicolò Guinigi, 1414).

in favour of jesters and "actors" (*histriones*)[17], from hunting[18] but also from using instrumental music during religious celebrations (because such music was used during profane and obscene performances)[19]... After the Council of Trent, the religious world proved to be more open with regards to physical activity in general–particularly regarding the education of young nobles destined to become part of the government. However, it established precise conditions: the "publicity" of the event had to be guaranteed, it had to be carried out honestly and with moderation, and it had to have a meaningful goal (that is to say, *valetudinis causa*, educational effectiveness and moral utility). Even the statutes of the brotherhoods contained regulations of play (above all, they stated that gambling was forbidden and urged the members to observe ritual practices like chants and processions)[20]. In the fifteenth century, the statutes of the Monti di pietà (credit institutions, without profit aim, founded in Italy during the second half of the 15th century by the Observant Minorites for the poor citizens) also contained regulations. They contained general bans on play, dancing, singing and any other *desonestà*, that is to say deceit, fraud or indecency–this was the opinion of the most of the religious world about these activities in that period–, probably to avoid that officials of the Monte di Pietà used its capital or the same pledges received by creditors (generally valuables) for activities that were forbidden or considered immoral[21].

As mentioned above, local statutory regulations offer a vast view of play regulations in communal Italy. Besides gambling (in many forms), the *ius proprium* regulated several common, traditional play-related

17 R. C. Trexler, *Synodal law in Florence and Fiesole 1306–1518*, the Vatican, 1971, p. 255–256 (the prohibition is found in: *The constitutions of Florence* 1310).

18 Among others cf. Trexler, *Synodal law*, op. cit., p. 189 (the prohibition is found in: *The constitutions of Fiesole* 1306).

19 Bosisio, *Concilia Papiensia*, op. cit., p. 439: "nolumus ut tibiae, buxus, vivolae, aleuthi, cytherae [...] in divinorum officiorum celebratione permittantur" (the prohibition is taken from: *Secundae Constitutiones [...] Hyppolyti De Rubeis Episcopi Papiensis et comitis, conditae in synodo anni MDLXXI. Addendae prioribus Constutionibus cum additionibus factis in synodo dioecesana anno MDCXII*).

20 V. Botteon and A. Barbieri, "Congregazioni di Carità e Istituti pii riuniti in Conegliano. Studio storico amministrativo", *Rivista della beneficenza pubblica delle istituzioni di previdenza e di igiene sociale*, 32/12, 1904, p. 302 and 304–305 (the regulations are taken from: *Statuto della veneranda Scuola di S. Maria dei Battuti di Serravalle*).

21 For the statutes of Monte di pietà di Faenza, for example, cf. V. Meneghin, *Bernardino da Feltre e i Monti di pietà*, Vicenza, 1974, p. 650.

events: horse races, target shooting and *battagliole.* As for target shooting and *battagliole,* in addition to being activities with a play-related and ritualistic aim, the *ratio* of the town authorities was to guarantee that the races and armed challenges were carried out properly and safely and that the local militias (crossbowmen and ground soldiers) received training. When the goal no longer was to train men, statutory laws contained and then abolished these activities altogether. Horse race was one of the symbolic events of communal Italy. In the last centuries of the middle ages, the festivity in honour of a patron saint (with all its religious, civic, ritual, and play-related values) was consolidated in order to "get over the particularisms of the areas of the town (districts, gonfalons, social stratifications) and create a moment of civic religiosity centred on a common tradition, on the sense of the territory and on the military aspect expressed by the horse races"[22]. In many cases this process of unification of the city under the aegis of the government through patron rites such as horse race could be considered as completed only in the fifteenth century. The legal sanction of the statutory regulation made it possible for the horse race–carried out at the same time as the celebrations in honour of the saint–to become a sort of "state" game, the heart of the entire event. In this way the municipality took on the honours and the onus of the management of the race, taking control of public, play-related "areas" over any other opponent. The city-state event *par excellence,* had to be, without a shadow of a doubt, the prerogative of the town.

22 Cf. M. Casini, *I gesti del principe. La festa politica a Firenze e Venezia in età rinascimentale,* Venezia, 1996, p. 121 (from which comes the quotation), with particular reference to the Florentine feast of the patron saint in honour of Saint John and the race organized on the same occasion. For an overview of the function of horse race in the municipalities of Mediaeval Italy cf. Rizzi, *Ludus/ludere,* op. cit. p. 171–204; A. Rizzi, "Le jeu dans les villes de l'Italie médiévale", *Histoire Urbaine,* 1, 2000 (« Les loisirs et la ville: espaces, institutions, pratiques »), p. 54–58; but also *Statuta de ludo,* op. cit., *s.v. palium.* For a more general overview of horse race and its evolution over time, see W. Heywood, *Palio and Ponte. An account of the sports of central Italy from the age of Dante to the 20th century,* London, 1904; and now C. Jaser, "Beyond Siena: the Palio Culture in Renaissance Italy", *Ludica. Annali di storia e civiltà del gioco,* 23 (in press).

PUBLIC PLAY: MANAGEMENT AND CONFLICTS OF INTEREST?

It is therefore suggested that play produced a true "widespread set of rules and regulations" which could not always avoid leading to conflicts amongst authorities and various disciplinary aims. To tell the truth, there are not many indications on the matter (at the moment) but the few we have are sufficient to hypothesize tendencies.

Well-known tale by the fourteenth century chronicler and short story writer Giovanni Sercambi[23], for example, talks about a certain Bioccolo di Boccadivacca from Lucca who had received the podesta's seat of office in Castello Marciano (in the nearby territory) from Mastino II della Scala, prince of Verona. There the Scaliger official repeatedly prohibited a series of games on which the local people used to bet: dice, chess, games with hazel-nuts as well as with small flat stones, balls, tops… The ending of the story is worth noting. Every form of play and amusement being forbidden, the inhabitants resorted to their lord (Mastino) who judged the bans of the podesta to be caused by "damned envy" ("not being able to tolerate that others could enjoy themselves") that is, from a "corrupt" and not "righteous" knowledge of things. The prince took the office away from the official, authorizing (in contrast with the functionary's will) the inhabitants of Castello Marciano "enjoy themselves", but urging them "to use discretion in their play". The conflict between the two authorities was due to a different evaluation of town recreation. The first one deemed the activities dangerous and to be prohibited because he thought they promoted gambling and bets amongst the townspeople with, as a result, a significant, uncontrolled redistribution of money and wealth. The second one, on the other hand, deemed play to be a moderate and inoffensive activity, a form of socialization and a way of reducing daily tension and therefore (one could add) a useful tool for keeping the subjects under control as well as a pleasant reward and compensation for simple and marginal lives.

---

23 Giovanni Sercambi, *Il novelliere*, L. Rossi (ed.), Rome, 1974, vol. II, p. 241–246. But see also A. Rizzi, "La regolamentazione del gioco nelle comunità italiane minori alla fine del medioevo", *Ludica. Annali di storia e civiltà del gioco*, 11, 2005, p. 126–127.

In the literary aspect of the tale, the conflict in the small Veneto town regarding the regulation of local play-related habits could symbolize one vaster than what is known. There are also indications of conflict in other milieus (amongst members of the religious world). Another well-known example occurred in Rome in 1334. Dominican from Bergamo, fra Venturino, had preached, in addition to other things, against "llo ioco de Nagoni" (or of Agone) – that is, the ring race that took place on Carnival Thursday in Piazza Navona –, suggesting that the money spent for the festivity be distributed to the poor. Instead of seeing the requested abolition take place, the monk was mocked by the onlookers and the Romans. And as if it weren't enough, in the end the Pope (from Avignon) took away his right to preach. The request made by the monk appeared to be "anachronistic" and out of place not only to the magistrates but also to the highest religious authority. Few decades later the statute of the city of Rome (1360–1370), confirmed the carrying out of the game and also confirmed the obligation to participate for some people. Paul II made the race part of the traditional, Roman carnival races (along with the ones that the Pope himself added in order to be in the good graces of the people of the eternal city)[24].

In communal Italy, therefore, regulations concerning time and location for play may have led to conflicts amongst different officials or public authorities. Even statutory documentation contains traces of this. Derogations were very important. General prohibitions for play (not only gambling) were almost always counterbalanced by concessions carefully calibrated to the circumstances (time and location) and the people involved in the play-related activities. Each time, the statute drafters had to set the boundaries between the play-related activities that were allowed by local law and those that were not, highlighting and sanctioning any "disciplinary" interference (although coming from public officials and magistrates) that could have gone against the regulations established by those delegated to do so. For example, in Omegna (near Lake Orta) in 1384, after having exceptionally authorized playing with dice (and therefore betting) on market days on the market square ("in quibuscumque nundinis sive feriis [...] in mercato"), the vicar was not to say anything against it ("dominus vicarius de alibi ludendo ut supra

24 Anonimo Romano, *Cronica*, G. Porta (ed.), Milan, 1981, p. 24–27. With reference to Rizzi, *Ludus/ludere*, op. cit., p. 47 and 139–140.

dictum est licentiam dare non possit") and, as if it were not enough, the following was added: "et data non valeat" ("every different authorization was declared null and void"). Few decades before, in Florence (1322–1325), after having set strict regulations for dice and for board games (and the like), the podesta or anyone else was urged not to permit "licentiam ut fiat contra predicta"("to contravene these regulations")[25].

Conflicts deriving from the management of play and festivities could occur along with political-institutional alternations, for example when a communal regime became a lordship, or when a territory was surrendered or became subject to new rulers (as it happened with the expansion of a city). Traditional games and performances could suffer from changes in general circumstances and the political situation of a city or state. Sometimes the horse race (whose importance in communal Italy was mentioned above) was "placed in a higher category" at the time of these transitions and changes. Races continued to be organized in respect of the tradition (even if with some changes) but the reasons for the race were changed. For example, if a race was run to celebrate a saint and a victory (that he had favoured) by a part of the town, it was continued even in a new political situation but it then took on some significance regarding another victory, perhaps the one brought on by the new lord in the town[26]. With the conquest of Treviso, which occurred twice (in 1339 and 1389), we have an example of how Venice prevented possible conflicts that could have occurred in the organization of public play and ceremonies during periods of transition from one regime to another. During the first domination (1339–1380), in its "forward position" on the mainland, Venice decided to keep traditional play-related activities, particularly in Treviso, which was the point of reference for the entire territory. This way, play-related activities could be a tool to mediate

25 Cf. *Statuta de ludo*, op. cit., nn. 667 and 2831. For similar examples regarding not only dice but also other practices (for example the *ludus bilie* or *burianarum*, la *druzzola*...), cf. the regulations at nn. 197 (Casale Monferrato end of XIV century), 237 (Gaeta 1552–1554), 479 (Biella XIV century), 734 (Vigevano 1392), 775 (Moncalieri prior to 1272), 1024 (Revello 1477), 1094 (Chiarentana 1314–1316), 1100 (Empoli 1428), 1508 (Guarcino XV century), 2386 (Bellano 1370), 2389 (Valsassina 1388), 2866 (Ivrea 1329), 2973 (Poggibonsi 1332), 2999 (Rivarolo 1358), 3055 (Torino 1360), 3079 (Valcamonica 1433), 3094 (Venasca probably prior to 1534).

26 On "redefined" horse races, particularly, cf. Rizzi, *Ludus/ludere*, op. cit., p. 182–184; Ead., *Le jeu dans les villes*, p. 57; Ead., *Ordinare e guidare*, op. cit., p. 121, as reference for examples.

between the ruler and the new subjects in such a delicate phase–that of the recent conquest–during which it was certainly more useful and advantageous for the new Venetian lordship to keep an open dialogue with the recent dominions, also by respecting ancient local traditions. This was a pragmatic way, suitable for the circumstances, which confirmed the idea of "good Venetian government": in this case we refer to the ability to take advantage of the best time for intervention. Subsequently, when Treviso became for good part of the Venetian state–the Venetian ruling class having overcome its distrust on forming a territorial state in the nearby mainland[27]–, the central Venetian government began to reinforce its presence in the Treviso area also through propaganda and to get involved in its play-related and festive activities. The central government placed the ancient races "in a higher category" (for example, shifting the traditional Saint Nicholas horse race to the feast of Saint Lucy, the day on which Venice reconquered Treviso) and it established new ones (for example the horse race in the ancient castle of Noale that replaced the running race wanted by the Tempesta family, the ancient lords of the territory)[28]. Venice continued to be interested in the play-related activities of the "subjects" over and beyond the idea of settling its conquests and territorial expansion in the fifteenth century. In the commissions given to its rulers (a series of regulations and government instructions given to its "representatives" before they took on their role in the various "land" or "sea" dominions), it provided regulations on play (gambling in particular but also the crossbow competitions, festivities–for example those organized for the beginning or end of the term of the ruler–, marriages, theatre…)[29], always respectful of local regulations, as explicitly indicated ("statuta et consuetudines terrae tibi commissae serventur", "local statutes and consuetudes have to be always observed")[30],

27 A long debated question; for a summary refer to F. Pigozzo, *Treviso e Venezia nel Trecento: la prima dominazione veneziana sulle podesterie minori (1339–1381)*, Venice, 2007.

28 The case is developed in Rizzi, "Le jeu dans les villes", op. cit., p. 58–61.

29 For examples see A. Rizzi, "'Volentes pro meliori … providere … super ludo'. *Provvedimenti sul gioco per i territori veneziani (secoli XIII-XVI). Ricognizioni preliminari*", in *Historiae. Scritti per Gherardo Ortalli*, C. Azzara, E. Orlando, M. Pozza and A. Rizzi (dir.), Venice 2013 (Studi di storia), p. 218–236.

30 Cf. *Lo 'statuto del podestà di Bergamo': commissione dogale per Lorenzo Bragadin, 1559*, G. Cappelluzzo (ed.), prefaces by S. Di Noto and Emilio R. Papa, Bergamo, 1992, p. 97–98, with reference to local regulations on gambling which the Venetian ruler of Bergamo, Lorenzo Bragadin, should have applied during his mandate.

sometimes making additions to fill in any gaps ("ubi statuta non essent, pars ipsa loco statutorum [debeat] observari", "lacking local statutes, Venetian provisions and regulations have to be applied")[31].

One phenomenon was quite widespread in Italian city-states, starting in the fourteenth century and continuing in the following century: mendicant preaching during Advent or Lent, against what was considered immoral behaviour of the times (including play). The preachers' battle–which put into effect the plan of the late medieval Church to spiritually regenerate contemporary society and itself–led in many cases (probably more than what has been found) to an (often transitory and short-termed) "rewriting" of the norms that penalized gambling but also competitions and traditional civic rituals more than the regulations they aimed to replace. Perhaps the most well-known (and not isolated) example of this is the attempt in the *Statuta* of Bernardine of Siena in 1425 to put an end to the Perugian "stone fight", a battle of stones that took place in the Umbrian city from the thirteenth century on and was still greatly in vogue in the fifteenth century[32]. To recall another example of effective preaching, a few decades later, in 1494, in Florence, during the presence of Savonarola in the city, on the occasion of the feast of Saint John, the chroniclers of the time claimed that "there would be no (profane) feast at all", as was traditional, but only "the procession and the offering". This went on until the death of the Dominican[33]. On many occasions the

31 Cf. *Statuti di Rovereto del 1425 con le aggiunte dal 1434 al 1538*, F. Parcianello (ed.), introductions by M. Bellabarba, G. Ortalli, D. Quaglioni, Venice, 1991, p. 202, with reference to gambling.

32 On the actions of the mendicant preachers regarding play in communal Italy, particularly the norms that derived from them, cf. A. Rizzi, "Dal divieto alla moralizzazione: il gioco e la predicazione al tramonto del medio evo", *Ludica. Annali di storia e civiltà del gioco*, 1, 1995, p. 157–170; Rizzi, *Ludus/ludere*, op. cit., p. 25–39 and 103–147; Rizzi, *Ordinare e guidare*, op. cit., p. 111–133; A. Rizzi, "Regulated play at the end of the middle Ages: the work of mendicant preachers in communal Italy", *Sport and Culture in Early Modern Europe. Le Sport dans la Civilisation de l'Europe Pré-Moderne*, J. McClelland and B. Merrilees (dir.), Toronto, 2009 (Centre for Reformation and Renaissance. Studies Essays and Studies, 20), p. 41–69; A. Rizzi, "Predicatori, confessori mendicanti e gioco alla fine del medioevo", in *Religiosus ludens. Das Spiel als kulturelles Phaenomen in mittelalterlichen Kloestern und Orden*, J. Sonntag (dir.), Berlin-Boston, 2013 (*Arbeiten zur Kirchengeschichte*, vol. 122), p. 97–113. For the perugian statutes by Bernardine of Siena, refer to C. Cardinali, "Il santo e la norma. Bernardino da Siena e gli statuti perugini del 1425", in *Gioco e giustizia*, op. cit., p. 183–191.

33 The chronicler Luca Landucci, reported by P. Gori, *Le feste fiorentine attraverso i secoli: le feste per San Giovanni*, Firenze, 1987 (anastatic reprinting, Florence, 1926 edition), p. 97.

monk pushed the Florentines to make laws against "the sin [...] of play", uttering such threats: "See to it, Florence, and give serious punishments to those who are involved in this. Heaven help you if you do not do it"[34]. Tolerance of play was completely lost in Perugia and Florence and any other place where a clergyman reprimanded it or suggested new regulations. But the *ratio* would not seem so new: this lack of open-mindedness with regard to play was also found in other places during that period, without there being knowledge of any exceptional, external interventions from "on high", as the preaching of Bernardine of Siena was seen by his contemporaries. In some cases, once the flood of emotions instigated by clergymen subsided, the authorities (whether they were compelled to or not) "gave in" again, as anticipated, to a more permissive legislature. It was not therefore the power of regulation (although from on high) but the changing times that definitively put aside certain practices, as in the case of the Perugian stone fight. However, this happened only much later than the end of the middle ages. The regulations upheld by the preachers in the fourteenth and fifteenth centuries regarding play supported–rather than opposed–the city-states, where it was more difficult than in other places to put an end to certain traditional practices, for example, those whose violence in their very nature had gone over the threshold of tolerance for a community or whose organization seemed to require too many expenses[35]. Clergymen made no secret that, in order to have "compelling virtue" (effectiveness), the law had to be "made by the prince [...], for everyone's good"[36].

In communal Italy (as mentioned above) there were various promotors of play and public performances. This situation reflected the particularisms (districts, gonfalons, arms societies, brotherhoods, youth brigades, social parties...) that developed in the city and in local society. In many cases (like Florence) until at least the mid-fifteenth century, there were different types of "tension" characterizing the "commemorative style" of the town. There were those, such as the government, who tried to enhance the civic and processional types of festivities (the feast of the

34 G. Savonarola, *Prediche sopra Aggeo con il trattato circa il reggimento e governo della città di Firenze*, L. Firpo (ed.), Rome, 1965, p. 45.

35 Considerations, in part, in Rizzi, "Dal divieto alla moralizzazione", op. cit.; and in Rizzi, *Ludus/ludere*, op. cit., p. 119–120.

36 G. Savonarola, *Prediche italiane ai Fiorentini*, R. Palmarocchi (ed.), III, 1, Florence, 1933, p. 463.

patron saint, which in time contributed to overcome particularisms) and those, such as the large private family clans, who tried to monopolize late feudal-age events, the carnival or May Day. On the other hand, in Florence, the town, through the Guelph part, could for example try to control jousts and handling of arms (a prerogative of important families), in order to acquire that chivalrous honour middle-class regime needed in order to be legitimized[37]. In several cases, local tensions regarding the management of public festivities could be overcome by having "specialized" locations where these festivities were held: in Alessandria for example, squares were left to the nobles for their recreational activities[38]. While not resulting in a visible dispute, there could however be "diplomatic embarrassment" coming from the outside when, for example, a famous guest refused to respect the established ceremonial procedures for a festivity he was invited to attend[39].

There could be useful indications on "conflicts" concerning play regulations, in documentation concerning judicial practice, as seen in the *consilia* of experts in late-mediaeval law whose opinions about controversial, juridical questions were asked. New views emerged regarding the impunity of the *puer*, guilty of homicide due to play. With regards to different types of play-related activities (like *battagliole*) practiced by minors and perceived as increasingly dangerous, destabilizing and lacking any benefit (in this case, training), the consulted jurists went against the roman-canonistic principle that was generally accepted regarding the impunity of the *puer*, representing the transition from showing tolerance to convicting the minor who committed murder under such circumstances. They indeed characterized the crime as an unintentional offence (a manslaughter) or as a wilful and malicious crime, excluding the idea of fortuitousness or inability on the part of the minor to carry out *dolus*. Therefore, as for violent street play (stone-fights and mock battles) the period of time for

37 Casini, *I gesti del principe*, op. cit., p. 122. Here the author is following R. C. Trexler, "Il rituale della celebrazione: le forme cavalleresche e la festa di San Giovanni", in *Teatro e culture della rappresentazione. Lo spettacolo in Italia nel Quattrocento*, R. Guarino (dir.), Bologna, 1988, p. 71–119.

38 Girolamo Ghilini, *Annali di Alessandria [...] dall'anno dell'origine sua sino al 1659*, Milano, nella stamperia di Gioseffo Marelli, 1666, p. 4.

39 Alfonso Duke of Calabria, for example, refused the procedure established by the Florentine government in 1467 (or 1468) for his participation to the feast of Saint John (the same one which his opponent to the throne of Naples Giovanni d'Angiò had to observe in 1454 on a similar occasion): Casini, *I gesti del principe*, op. cit., p. 127.

innocentia (childhood) and judicial protection was reduced, if not removed. When play-related crimes moved from the fortuitous category to the malicious and *dolus* category, society acquired a disciplinary tool to exert essential control and tame practices deemed increasingly brutal and destabilizing by society[40]. Judicial practice, acquiring new guidelines from law experts, was transformed into an additional tool for regulating contemporary, play-related activities and overcoming or overturning roman-canonistic principles in force.

From the beginning of the fifteenth century on, in the transition from the middle ages to the Modern Age, Italy's political-institutional geography became complicated, with the arrival of vaster regional powers that overlapped or replaced the local ones, without the appearance of a "leader" among them (a national or supra-national power). Rome, Florence, Venice… with their courts or curia, their oligarchies represented several state models with as many ceremonial systems of festivities and public play which left ample traces, although they have been only partially investigated. For this period, it is therefore more difficult to go on proceeding in a general manner, as I have done up to now, in search of any occasions of conflict amongst the various powers in the organization, management and control of the contemporary system of play. It is necessary to analyse the various localized situations separately[41]. We must look at the regulations provided by the competent local magistrates rather than at general regulations regarding the regional state–for instance, in the case of the duchy of Milan, as of now, we have seen only regulations regarding hunting[42]. In Venice, for example, it

40 See E. Orlando, "Gioco, violenza, e punibilità del puer nel basso medioevo. Dalla tolleranza alla repressione, tra caso, colpa e dolo", in *Filii, filiae…: position and role of children in the Adriatic area*, Poreč, 2011 (*The 4th Istrian history biennale*), p. 46–68.

41 For the Renaissance and Modern Age in particular, there are numerous studies on individual Italian situations where civic rituals and religious feasts have been investigated, paying attention to the play-related components of such events. Obviously, as it is not possible to indicate them systematically here, only a few works for Venice will be mentioned (refer to them for a vast bibliography on the matter, useful not only to Venice): E. Muir, *Il rituale civico a Venezia nel Rinascimento*, Rome, 1984 (ed. or. Princeton, 1981); Casini, *I gesti del principe*, op. cit. (this work is interesting because of the original comparison between Venice and Florence, as can be derived from studies on the matter such as R. C. Trexler, *Public life in Renaissance Florence*, New York, 1980); S. Tichy, *Et vene la mumaria: studien zur venezianischen festkultur der Renaissance*, München, 1997.

42 Cf. *Antiqua ducum Mediolani decreta*, Mediolani, 1654, *passim*. The same for Sardegna: F. C. Casula, *La "Carta de Logu" del regno di Arborea*, Cagliari, 1994, *passim* (chapters 24

seems, after a rapid look at the documentation, that the Council of Ten progressively "monopolized" the regulation and management of state, play-related activities starting in the fifteenth century[43], well beyond the middle ages.

CONCLUSION

A general look at late medieval Italy suggests that on many occasions the lay and the religious authorities of the time collaborated and agreed on the actions to take and on the objectives to reach rather than engaged in conflicts related to competence and jurisdiction (even though there are some examples of this). Beginning in the fifteenth century, play-related events, feasts and ceremonies are gradually "differentiated" and "specialized" (while the political-institutional situation undergoes changes). Religious feasts stand apart from "state" organized rituals and ceremonies and public play is separate from private play. In late fifteenth century Florence, the words used by Savonarola during his preaching on the 29th of May 1496 show this clearly. One knows the importance for Florence, during the middle ages, of the feast of Saint John, a civic ritual and religious event, as well as the significance of the horse race in the celebrations. However, the Dominican who was promoting a general moral renewal of Florentine customs, attacked the horse race in such terms: "Do you think it is the time to have a horse race? I tell you that it is a time for crying and not laughing". While a few decades earlier clergymen considered the horse race as Pauline prefiguration of the race towards the greatest good and therefore were not opposed to racing in order to honour the Baptist in the traditional Florentine feast,

and 81–105 deal with the regulation for the *giudicato*–Sardinian district–of Arborea in 1390 that was extended to the entire island in 1421, under Aragonese domination).

43 In the sixteenth century, the Council of Ten also dealt with the regulations for stagings and plays. Cf., for example, Venice state archives (=ASVE), *Consiglio dei Dieci, Misti*, reg. 32, c. 55v: a decree dated of the 29th of December 1580 forbade performances in town, either publicly or privately, also on the occasion of weddings and banquets. The decree was abolished and reinstated on the 25th of September 1581: ASVE, *Consiglio dei Dieci, Comune*, reg. 36, c. 9. Cf., also, Casini, *I gesti del principe*, op. cit.

Savonarola now thought the saint would much rather have the money for the race be given to the poor[44]. There is another indication of the divergence between "sacred" and "profane" management of play-related events. The moralization of customs promoted by mendicant preachers who were successful in late mediaeval Italian cities, supporting even social disciplining (as has been said on the matter of play-related events), encountered some difficulty at the end of the fifteenth century. As was acknowledged later by his biographer with reference to the preaching in Ferrara in April 1486, Bernardine of Feltre "did not work much in that city". In fact, only a few people went to listen to him and preferred to participate in the "jousts and dances" organized at the same time by the city government[45]. Under these circumstances it would be difficult to think of shared social disciplinary actions between civil authorities and members of the religious world as far as play-related events are concerned (like when the regulations in force for play were "rewritten"). From then on, each side was ready to promote and manage play and performances in different locations, under different circumstances and with different objectives. The state would take care of public rituals, including games and performances (in addition to managing the increasingly remunerative field of betting) while the religious orders (above all those created by the Counter-Reformation) would take care of private play, particularly that of the youth destined to govern someday[46]. One cannot exclude however the possibility of having direct conflicts, under particular circumstances, when it came to disciplining play-related activities.

Alessandra Rizzi
Università Ca' Foscari, Venice

44 G. Savonarola, *Prediche sopra Ruth e Michea*, V. Romano (ed.), Rome, 1962, I, p. 270.

45 B. Guslino, "Vita del B. Bernardino da Feltre. Prima edizione integrale con note illustrative di Alberto Ghinato", *Le Venezie francescane*, 27, 1959, p. 30.

46 Cf. also Rizzi, *Ludus/ludere*, op. cit., p. 210; Rizzi, *Regulated play*, op. cit., p. 56–60.

DEUXIÈME PARTIE

CONTRÔLER LES SPECTACLES DANS LA VILLE

« ET DE NE JOUER N'EN PEUT VENIR QUE BIEN. »

L'interdiction et le contrôle du théâtre universitaire à Paris (1450-1550)

Depuis le XIIIe siècle, l'université parisienne accueille au sein des nations et des facultés[1] une population étudiante nombreuse, qui trouve dans le théâtre le moyen de se divertir et bien plus encore[2]. De fait, si les textes conservés sont rares, des témoignages indirects attestent la vitalité des activités dramatiques dans ce milieu, et en particulier les textes réglementaires de l'Université elle-même, de ses collèges ou des autorités politiques. Dans la mesure où il s'agit alors d'interdire et de contrôler les abus, de tels documents donnent du théâtre des étudiants une image évidemment partielle et partiale ; c'est ainsi que l'historiographie moderne a souvent insisté sur sa dimension satirique et frondeuse[3]. Il n'en demeure pas moins que ces textes sont riches d'enseignements et méritent d'être étudiés pour ce qu'ils sont, dans leur contexte singulier de production[4].

Pour la période qui nous intéresse et qui correspond au plein épanouissement du théâtre des farces, moralités et sotties et à la renaissance

---

1 Les quatre nations de la faculté des arts, à Paris, rassemblent les suppôts de l'Université selon leur origine géographique ; les quatre facultés relèvent quant à elles d'une organisation disciplinaire : arts, médecine, droit, théologie. Sur l'histoire de l'université parisienne, voir par ex. J. Verger, *Les universités au Moyen Âge*, Paris, P.U.F., 1973 et A. Tuilier, *Histoire de l'Université de Paris et de la Sorbonne*, t. I : *Des origines à Richelieu*, Paris, Nouvelle Librairie de France, 1994.

2 Sur le théâtre des étudiants à Paris, nous nous permettons de renvoyer à notre thèse de doctorat, *Le théâtre des collèges parisiens au début du XVIe siècle. Textes et pratiques dramatiques*, sous la dir. de P. Galand et M. Huchon, Paris, EPHE, 2013.

3 Voir, par exemple, l'étude classique de L. Petit de Julleville, *Les comédiens en France au Moyen Âge*, Paris, Léopold Cerf, 1885.

4 *Cf.* J. Koopmans, « Polémiques universitaires sur la scène », *Le Théâtre polémique français (1450-1550)*, M. Bouhaïk-Gironès, J. Koopmans et K. Lavéant (dir.), Rennes, Presses Universitaires de Rennes, 2008, p. 77-87.

du théâtre latin, nous avons pu rassembler, en parcourant les travaux des historiens de Paris et de ses institutions ainsi que les recueils et les éditions de documents médiévaux et modernes, une vingtaine de règlements ; ils sont d'origine universitaire au XVe siècle et d'origine universitaire et parlementaire au XVIe siècle[5]. Certes, les lacunes constatées dans les archives de l'Université et du Parlement ainsi que l'absence de dépouillement systématique de ces mêmes archives nous invitent à la prudence dans l'approche chronologique et synthétique des données. Ni la Table de Le Nain, qui répertorie et reproduit un grand nombre d'arrêts du Parlement[6], ni les cartulaires des nations et des facultés publiés aux XIXe et XXe siècles[7] ne peuvent prétendre à l'exhaustivité, pas plus que l'*Historia Universitatis parisiensis* de César Egasse Du Boulay[8]. Cependant, l'inscription de notre corpus dans la longue durée permet

5 Ces textes ont été rassemblés et traduits dans l'annexe I de notre thèse de doctorat, *op. cit.*, p. 548-564. Nous donnons dans l'annexe du présent article les deux textes les plus riches de ce corpus, de 1488 et 1525 (*cf. infra*).

6 Archives nationales, U 493 à U 590, et notamment U 574, « Table des matières concernant les Universités ». *Cf.*, sur la table de Le Nain, L. Le Grand, « La table de Le Nain et les Registres du Parlement de Paris », *La Bibliographie moderne*, 1907, n° 2-3, p. 92-112.

7 *Auctarium Chartularii Universitatis Parisiensis* (*A.C.U.P.*), H. Denifle, E. Châtelain *et alii* (éd.), Paris, Delalain-Didier, 1894-1964, 6 vol. ; *Chartularium Universitatis Parisiensis* (*C.U.P.*), H. Denifle et E. Châtelain (éd.), Delalain, 1889-1897, 4 vol. ; *Commentaires de la Faculté de Médecine de l'Université de Paris (1516-1560)*, M.-L. Concasty (éd.), Paris, Imprimerie Nationale, 1964 ; *Index chronologicus chartarum pertinentium ad historiam Universitatis Parisiensis ab eius originibus ad finem decimi sexti saeculi*, C. Jourdain (éd.), Paris, Hachette, 1862. À ces recueils s'ajoutent les travaux plus récents et systématiques de J. K. Farge, et en particulier l'édition critique des registres 89 et 90 des Archives de l'Université (1490-1515) (*Students and teachers at the University of Paris*, Boston-Leyde, Brill, 2006). Sur les différentes instances de délibération et de décision dans l'université parisienne, *Cf.* M.-M. Compère, *Les Collèges français aux XVIe-XVIIIe siècles. Répertoire, t. 3, Paris*, Paris, INRP, 2002, « Introduction », spéc. p. 24-27, et C. Thurot, *De l'organisation de l'enseignement dans l'Université de Paris au Moyen Âge*, Paris-Besançon, 1850, p. 22-25.

8 C. E. Du Boulay, *Historia Universitatis Parisiensis*, Paris, F. Noël, 1665-1673, 6 vol. Du Boulay, comme recteur puis greffier de l'Université (1662-1678), avait un accès privilégié aux archives de son « *alma mater* » et a reproduit un nombre considérable de documents. Il a ainsi utilisé des sources qui ont aujourd'hui disparu. Cependant, Du Boulay intègre les transcriptions à son propre récit sans présentation ni approche critique, ce qui rend leur examen délicat et le recours aux originaux nécessaires, quand c'est encore possible. *Cf.*, sur le travail de Du Boulay, les introductions de H. Denifle, *Chartularium Universitatis Parisiensis*, *op. cit.* et J. Verger, « Charlemagne fondateur de l'Université de Paris. Les ultimes avatars du mythe de la *translatio studii* dans l'*Historia Universitatis Parisiensis* de C.-E. Du Boulay », *Famille, violence et christianisation au Moyen Âge. Mélanges offerts à Michel Rouche*, éd. M. Aurell et T. Deswarte, Paris, Presses de l'Université Paris-Sorbonne, 2005. Quant à l'œuvre de J.-B.-L. Crevier, *Précis sur l'histoire de l'Université de Paris, depuis son*

d'éclairer, me semble-t-il, certaines données positives. Trois phénomènes méritent ainsi d'être rappelés :

- Depuis le début du XVe siècle, le roi et le Parlement exercent sur le théâtre parisien un contrôle toujours plus pressant[9]. Le théâtre de la basoche est ainsi soumis à la censure[10].
- Au lendemain de la Guerre de Cent Ans, le pouvoir royal tente de mettre au pas l'Université, si fière, depuis sa création, de ses privilèges et de son indépendance. Le Parlement est le principal agent de cette politique[11].
- Enfin, les collèges prennent une place de plus en plus importante au sein de l'institution universitaire et offrent le cadre réel de la vie estudiantine, et donc, des activités dramatiques[12]. Ils sont aussi un moyen efficace de contrôle des enseignements et de la discipline.

À la lumière de ces évolutions et à travers une approche essentiellement chronologique, nous essaierons de voir comment les documents collectés témoignent de ces relations, complexes et dynamiques, qui lient l'Université, les collèges et le pouvoir politique, au tournant des XVe et XVIe siècles ; mais nous nous intéresserons surtout à la façon dont le théâtre lui-même s'inscrit dans ce réseau de relations et dans les différentes sphères de la vie de l'étudiant. Par ailleurs, les documents présentés nous renseignent sur les conditions concrètes du jeu ; en cherchant à le contrôler, les textes réglementaires tentent

---

origine jusqu'en l'année 1600, Paris, Desaint et Saillant, 1761, 7 vol., elle se contente, le plus souvent, de paraphraser l'œuvre de Du Boulay à laquelle elle renvoie à chaque page.

9 Voir G. Cariani « Autorité et théâtre à la fin du Moyen Âge », *Revue d'Histoire du Théâtre*, 45, 1993, p. 35-44 et M. Rousse, « Le Pouvoir royal et le théâtre des farces », *Le Pouvoir monarchique et ses supports idéologiques aux XIVe-XVIIe siècles*, Paris, Publications de la Sorbonne Nouvelle, 1990, p. 185-197.

10 Sur cette question, *cf.* M. Bouhaïk-Gironès, *Les clercs de la Basoche et le théâtre comique (Paris, 1420-1550)*, Paris, Champion, 2007, p. 135-143.

11 Voir S. Lusignan, *« Vérité garde le Roy » : la construction d'une identité universitaire en France (XIIIe-XVe siècle)*, Paris, Publications de la Sorbonne, 1999, notamment le chapitre intitulé « L'emprise croissante du Parlement sur le monde universitaire », p. 43 *sq.*

12 De simples internats pour élèves boursiers, les collèges sont devenus des lieux d'enseignement à part entière, au sein de l'Université. *Cf.*, sur les collèges parisiens à l'époque moderne, M.-M. Compère, *op. cit.*, et G. Codina-Mir, *Aux sources de la pédagogie des jésuites. Le « modus parisiensis »*, Rome, Institutum Historicum S. I., 1968. Voir aussi le premier chapitre de notre thèse, « Les collèges parisiens et l'humanisme », p. 21-106.

en effet de le saisir dans sa réalité matérielle. Ils n'y parviennent pas toujours cependant car le théâtre est un objet labile ; c'est d'ailleurs par commodité et abus de langage que nous parlerons ici de théâtre, pour désigner un ensemble de pratiques dramatiques parfois très différentes les unes des autres.

LA RÉFORME D'ESTOUTEVILLE (1452)

Les années 1450-1550 sont marquées, nous l'avons dit, par un contrôle accru du pouvoir royal et de ses agents sur l'Université. Lors de la Guerre de Cent Ans, celle-ci choisit le parti bourguignon ; le roi tient dès lors cette institution pour suspecte. Ainsi l'ordonnance du 26 mars 1446 revient sur les privilèges que lui avait accordés Philippe Auguste : désormais, les suppôts de l'Université sont placés sous la juridiction directe du Parlement de Paris pour les causes civiles et criminelles.

Une réforme de l'institution est alors à l'ordre du jour, dans les milieux universitaires comme à la tête du royaume ; elle est promulguée en 1452 par le légat pontifical, le cardinal d'Estouteville, avec l'agrément de Charles VII ; elle marque ainsi le rapprochement de la royauté française et de la papauté qui, depuis l'origine de l'Université, exercent conjointement leur patronage sur cette institution. Le texte ne modifie pas en profondeur son organisation, et se contente le plus souvent de restaurer les bonnes mœurs en condamnant les abus de tous ordres. Il s'agit d'imposer une discipline sévère, pour le plus grand bien de la morale et de l'ordre public. Aussi le cardinal consacre-t-il quelques lignes aux fêtes que célèbrent les étudiants, et aux excès qui les accompagnent :

> [...] *ne permittant ipsi magistri scolaribus suis in festis nationum, aut alias, choreas dissolutas et inhonestas ducere, ludos etiam inhonestos et prohibitos agere, habitus indecentes et laicales deferre, maxime qui ad luxum provocent adolescentes : quin potius permittant eos virtuose et eutrapelice ludere, ad laboris levamen et solacium honestum ; nec eis pemittatur in predictis festis libere per vilam, aut de domo in domum circuire, prout ipsam facultatem nuper, honestati eorumdem consulentem, intelleximus statuisse ; quod laudamus et approbamus.*

> « [...] que les maîtres eux-mêmes interdisent aux élèves, lors des fêtes des nations et en d'autres occasions, de se livrer aux danses obscènes et malhonnêtes, d'accomplir des jeux malhonnêtes et proscrits et de porter les habits indécents de laïcs, surtout ceux qui peuvent conduire les jeunes gens à la débauche. Mais qu'ils ne leur interdisent pas de jouer dans le respect de la vertu et avec bonne humeur, pour se récréer et se reposer honnêtement après l'effort. Qu'il ne leur soit pas permis, lors des fêtes susdites, d'aller librement par la ville ou de maison en maison, comme, nous le savons, la faculté elle-même, veillant aux bonnes mœurs de ces étudiants, l'a récemment décidé; ce que nous louons et approuvons[13]. »

Le légat pontifical a bien soin de souligner ce que son texte doit aux mesures prises par l'Université elle-même, lors de délibérations qui ont préparé la réforme[14]. Il s'agit de rappeler que celle-ci émane d'abord des autorités universitaires, si jalouses de leurs prérogatives; le temps n'est donc pas encore venu de convoquer les maîtres pour formuler *ex cathedra* les décisions du Parlement; mais le texte de 1452 n'en répond pas moins aux vœux du souverain et *in fine*, « la remise en ordre » apparaît bien comme « une mise au pas[15] ».

Notre attention est évidemment retenue par l'interdit portant sur les *ludos inhonestos*; il s'agit-là de termes génériques qui ne sauraient désigner à coup sûr des activités dramatiques. Remarquons cependant que l'auteur utilise alors le verbe « *agere* », dont l'un des sens techniques renvoie aux jeux de théâtre[16]; en outre, l'association avec les danses, « *choreas* », semble indiquer qu'il s'agit là d'une activité spectaculaire. Il n'en demeure pas moins que ce texte réglementaire garde une portée très générale et ne distingue pas nettement le théâtre des autres activités festives.

13 *C.U.P.*, IV, n° 2690, p. 730 et C. E. Du Boulay, *op. cit.*, V, p. 575.

14 Voir notamment *C.U.P.*, IV, n° 2588, p. 643; IV, n° 2681, p. 709; C. E. Du Boulay, *op. cit.*, V, p. 560.

15 S. Roux, *La rive gauche des Escholiers (XVe siècle)*, Paris, Éditions Christian, Paris, 1992, p. 142-144.

16 *Cf.* J. Bade, *P. Terentii Aphri comicorum elegantissimi comedie...*, Lyon, J. Huguetan, 1511, chapitre II de ses *Praenotamenta* : on appelle « *comedus qui comedias agit seu ut dicunt vulgatiores ludit.* »

LES DÉCISIONS DE L'UNIVERSITÉ AVANT 1515

Or, c'est peut-être le caractère très général de cette réforme qui explique, du moins en partie, la multiplication dans les décennies suivantes de textes « répétés de la réforme d'Estouteville[17] » ; c'est alors l'Université elle-même qui légifère, sous le regard de l'autorité royale. Ces textes n'ont de cesse, en effet, de reprendre les différents articles de la réforme pour les préciser et les adapter aux réalités pratiques. Et bientôt, toute ambiguïté est levée à propos des « *ludi inhonesti* » : il s'agit bien de théâtre. Si l'assemblée de l'Université qui se tient le 24 novembre 1462 condamne encore les « *inhonestos ludos*[18] », l'historien Du Boulay, lorsqu'il cite l'arrêt du 25 décembre 1483, précise pour sa part qu'il s'agit de « *ludos, seu Comoedias* » dont « les principaux de collèges permettaient la représentation dans leurs collèges », « *Primarii Collegiorum sinebant [...] in suis Collegiis repraesentari*[19] ». Déjà, l'assemblée de la faculté des arts, le 5 janvier 1470, faisait allusion aux représentations de farces et de moralités, « *farsam vel moralitatem*[20] ». Quant aux textes du 5 janvier 1484 et du 27 novembre 1487, ils interdisent clairement de « jouer farces et comédies », « *ludere farsas aut comedias*[21] » et autres « jeux de comédies », « *ludos comoediarum*[22] ». Le vocabulaire devient plus riche et précis. Même s'il existe, du moins pour le lecteur moderne, de vrais flottements terminologiques et si l'heure n'est pas encore aux classifications normatives, le texte de loi tente de mieux cerner son objet[23]. Le théâtre se distingue alors des autres « abus » commis lors des fêtes d'étudiants, comme le port d'armes et les coups de mains.

---

17 J.-B.-L. Crevier, *op. cit.*, IV, p. 250.

18 C. E. Du Boulay, *op. cit.*, V, 656 ; *cf.* J.-B.-L. Crevier, *op. cit.*, IV, p. 283-284.

19 C. E. Du Boulay, *op. cit.*, V, p. 761 ; *A.C.U.P.*, III, col. 538-539. Texte cité par M. Rousse, *Le théâtre des farces en France au Moyen Âge*, thèse d'État dactyl., Rennes II, 1983, IV, p. 91.

20 *A.C.U.P.*, III, col. 130 ; C. E. Du Boulay, *op. cit.*, V, 690-691. Texte cité notamment par M. Rousse, *op. cit.*, IV, p. 75.

21 *A.C.U.P.*, IV, col. 453. Cité par M. Rousse, *op. cit.*, t. IV, p. 93.

22 *A.C.U.P.*, III, col. 654-655 ; C. E. Du Boulay, *op. cit.* V, p. 777. Texte cité notamment par M. Rousse, *op. cit.*, IV, p. 97.

23 Le corpus se prêterait à une analyse approfondie du vocabulaire dramatique, qui excède, cependant, les limites de cet article et ne pourrait prendre sens que dans une étude lexicographique de plus grande ampleur.

S'il n'est pas explicitement question, dans les textes cités, de ces fêtes que condamnait la réforme d'Estouteville, les assemblées se réunissent souvent la veille de quelques-unes des dates les plus importantes du calendrier universitaire : la Sainte-Catherine (25 novembre), la Saint-Nicolas (5 décembre), la fête des Rois (6 janvier). De fait, l'assemblée du 4 novembre 1488, qui précède de peu la Saint-Martin, cite ces fêtes-là[24]. Il s'agit du texte le plus long et le plus riche concernant le théâtre et sa répression au XVe siècle. On peut y lire notamment :

> *Nulla festa sanctorum Martini, Katherinae, Nicholai, sive nationum, provinciarum aut diocesum sive collegiorum fient sive cum mimis, sive facetiis et tapetis, sive cum simplicibus cantilenis pro chorea, sed solum vacetur divinis obsequiis et studiis sicut diebus dominicis quibus fieri est solitum. Possunt tamen virtuose et eutrapelice ludere ad laboris levamen et solatium*[25].
>
> « Interdiction est faite de célébrer les fêtes de saint Martin, de sainte Catherine, de saint Nicolas, comme les fêtes des nations, des provinces, des diocèses ou des collèges[26], que ce soit avec mimes, farces et tentures ou avec de simples chansons pour remplacer la danse ; que l'on se livre seulement au culte divin et à l'étude comme on a l'habitude de le faire les dimanches. On peut cependant jouer dans le respect de la vertu et avec bonne humeur pour se récréer et se reposer après l'effort. »

On reconnaît, dans cette dernière phrase, une citation littérale de la réforme d'Estouteville, qui, de toute évidence, restait le texte de référence en matière de discipline universitaire[27] ; le texte de la réforme est ici glosé. Notons qu'à cette date, les autorités avaient peut-être eu raison de la fête des Fous qui n'est pas mentionnée et ne le sera pas dans les

24 Sur le calendrier des festivités, voir notre thèse citée, p. 118-127.

25 C. E. Du Boulay, *op. cit.*, V, p. 782-783. Cité par M. Rousse, *op. cit.*, IV, p. 98-101. L'ensemble du texte est paraphrasé par J.-B.-L. Crevier, *op. cit.*, IV, p. 433-437. Voir, en annexe, l'édition de ce texte d'après le manuscrit de la Bibliothèque nationale de France.

26 Précisons que provinces et diocèses sont des subdivisions des nations dans l'université parisienne. Nations, provinces, diocèses et collèges célébraient ainsi leurs saints patrons.

27 Le lien direct entre la réforme de 1452 et le règlement de 1488 est clairement établi par Robert Goulet (*Compendium recenter editum de multiplici Parisiensis Universitatis magnificentia...*, Paris, Denis Toussaint, 1517, f° 7r-7v ; traduit par R. Belle Burke, *Compendium on the magnificence, dignity, and excellence of the University of Paris in the year of grace 1517*, Philadelphie, University of Pennsylvania Press, 1928). Notons cependant que la citation de la réforme d'Estouteville que donne C. E. Du Boulay et que nous reproduisons ici ne se trouve pas dans le manuscrit que nous avons consulté à la Bibliothèque nationale de France et que nous nous proposons d'éditer en annexe.

textes que nous avons collectés[28]. En revanche, il est abondamment question, dans la suite du règlement, de la fête des Rois. En effet, cette même assemblée permet les jeux de théâtre seulement à cette occasion. Le texte s'empresse cependant d'en définir précisément les modalités. Jeux et danses ne sont permis que la veille et le jour même après vêpres, et ce pour ne pas perturber l'office divin. Le lendemain, chacun doit se remettre à l'étude. Il s'agit là, semble-t-il, d'une concession accordée aux jeunes gens ; les pratiques dramatiques avaient la vie dure, la multiplication des textes réglementaires depuis la réforme d'Estouteville en témoigne, ainsi que la rigueur des sanctions prévues en 1488 : renvoi des professeurs impliqués, châtiments corporels pour les étudiants.

Du reste, au XVe siècle, il n'a guère été question d'interdire toute activité dramatique, soit parce qu'on ne l'a pas jugé nécessaire, soit parce qu'on ne l'a pas jugé possible. Il semble ainsi qu'il y ait eu place pour un « bon théâtre » : rappelons que les textes réglementaires formulent toujours des interdits, mais disent peu de choses des pratiques sinon permises, du moins tolérées. Celles-ci, cependant, peuvent apparaître au détour d'une phrase. Ainsi, le 5 janvier 1470, la faculté des art condamne non pas le théâtre, mais l'élection du prince des fous et le port de son costume traditionnel, « sauf, ajoute-t-elle, s'il s'agit de jouer une farce ou une moralité[29] ». Ainsi, ce n'est pas tout le théâtre qui se voit condamné, mais certaines pratiques dramatiques, en certaines occasions.

D'ailleurs, la plupart des textes, quand ils justifient leur décision, indique ce qui fait problème. Le plus souvent, il ne s'agit pas seulement de condamner les activités dramatiques au nom de principes moraux et religieux[30] ; il ne s'agit pas seulement de réprimer les dépenses excessives qu'engendrent de telles activités (de fait, on découvre que les étudiants n'hésitaient pas à la dépense et portaient des costumes en tissus précieux, ce que la rigueur cléricale des collèges ne pouvait tolérer[31]) ; il s'agit surtout de limiter la veine satirique et politique du théâtre des étudiants. Ainsi en 1462, interdiction est faite « de jouer des jeux indignes, surtout ceux

28 La fête des Fous fut interdite par Charles VII en 1438 et 1445. Voir A. Tuilier, *op. cit.*, p. 273 et note 29. Voir aussi M. Bouhaïk-Gironès, *op. cit.*, p. 128. Cependant, on continua d'élire un *rex fatuorum* à l'occasion de la fête des Rois, *cf. infra*.

29 « [...] *nisi forsan dumtaxat ludendo farsam vel moralitatem* ».

30 C'est toutefois sur ce point qu'insiste Robert Goulet lorsqu'il évoque les abus des étudiants (*op. cit.*, f° 7v.).

31 *Cf.* le texte en annexe.

qui touchent à l'état des princes et seigneurs[32] ». En décembre 1483 et janvier 1484, ce sont les parlementaires eux-mêmes qui sont victimes d'attaques[33] et ce sont eux qui portent plainte auprès de l'Université. Est-ce un signe qu'alors, le Parlement n'avait pas encore légiféré directement sur ces jeux de théâtre et s'en remettait encore à l'autorité du recteur ?

De fait, l'Université semble garder la main sur ces pratiques dramatiques, qu'elle essaie avec réalisme de contrôler, sans toutefois les interdire absolument. Pour ce faire, elle compte surtout sur les principaux de collèges et les maîtres de pédagogies[34]. En 1462, 1483, 1487 et 1488, l'Université répète inlassablement que tout jeu de théâtre est interdit « s'il n'a été vu et examiné par les principaux ou leurs régents[35] ». Le texte de 1488 ajoute :

> *Et ludantur in propriis collegiis hujusmodi facetiae, ne discurrant inde juvenes per collegia ut evitentur scandala quae ob id evenire solebant.*
>
> « Et que l'on joue les farces de ce genre dans les collèges eux-mêmes afin que les jeunes gens n'aillent pas courir d'un collège à l'autre. De cette façon l'on évitera les scandales que ces déplacements avaient l'habitude de provoquer. »

Cette volonté d'enfermer les jeux de le fête des Rois dans les collèges montre clairement le rôle qu'on souhaite voir tenir à ces institutions dans le maintien de la discipline.

En 1490, on tente de revenir sur les restrictions de 1488, mais en vain[36]. Cependant, dans les années qui suivent, celles-ci semblent tomber en désuétude car Robert Goulet, en 1517, estime que les décisions prises trente ans plus tôt méritent d'être répétées ; il attribue l'échec de ces mesures à l'incurie des principaux et des régents qui sont chargés de les faire respecter[37]. De fait, les professeurs et leurs étudiants n'ont pas cessé de donner, sous le règne de Louis XII notamment, des pièces

---

32 « [...] *ludant inhonestos ludos, maxime statum Principum et Dominorum tangentes* ».

33 Il est question en effet, dans l'assemblée du 5 janvier 1484, de « *quibusdam comediis et farsis curie Parlamenti advocatosque procuratores tangentibus* ». Selon toute vraisemblance, les textes datés de décembre 1483 et janvier 1484 renvoient en fait à la même décision, voire à la même assemblée.

34 Une pédagogie est une école ouverte par un professeur qui loge ses étudiants et enseigne contre rétribution. Elle se distingue donc du collège fondé, qui accueille des boursiers.

35 « [...] *nisi visitatus et examinatus per Principales aut eorum Regentes* ».

36 C. E. Du Boulay, *op. cit.*, V, p. 794.

37 R. Goulet, *op. cit.*, f° 7v.

satiriques qui déplurent au roi[38] ou à l'Université ; le 30 octobre 1514, lors de l'assemblé de la faculté des arts, il est ainsi question de

> *quamdam comediam detractatoriam lusam die mercurii ultima in collegio dive Barbare contra reformationem facultatis artium*[39].
>
> « quelque comédie médisante jouée le mercredi précédent au collège de Sainte-Barbe contre la réforme de la faculté des arts. »

La réforme dont il est fait mention ici est sans doute encore la réforme voulue par d'Estouteville, dont les modalités d'application font encore problème, en ce début de XVIe siècle. L'auteur de notre « *farcia seu comedia* », un professeur dont le nom n'est pas donné (l'éditeur du manuscrit constate qu'un blanc a été laissé), reconnaît les faits mais se défend d'avoir voulu faire du scandale :

> [...] *obtulit illam ostendere facultati. Magister Nicolaus Bouchart, electus in reformatorem facultatis artium pro nacione francie, recitavit etiam qualiter per dictam comediam ipse et alii fuerunt iniuriati, et suplicuit quod facultas provideat, alias non intendit exercere officium.*
>
> « [...] il proposa de montrer [la pièce] à la faculté. Maître Nicolas Bouchart, qui avait été élu Réformateur de la faculté des arts pour la nation de France, dit publiquement combien lui-même et ses collègues avaient été injuriés par ladite comédie et demanda que la faculté prenne des mesures. Sans quoi, il entendait ne pas exercer sa charge. »

Le texte de la « comédie » doit être remis au recteur et examiné par des représentants des nations. Plusieurs points attirent ici notre attention.

---

38 En 1499, dans la *Sottie de l'Astrologue*, des étudiants (?) semblent dire leur opposition au divorce et au remariage du souverain avec Anne de Bretagne (*Cf.* J. Koopmans, art. cité et M. Bouhaïk-Gironès, « La Sottie de l'Astrologue (Paris, 1499 ?) : contextes et polémiques autour de la figure de l'astrologue à Paris à la fin du Moyen Âge », *Le Théâtre polémique français (1450-1550)*, M. Bouhaïk-Gironès, J. Koopmans et K. Lavéant (dir.), Rennes, Presses Universitaire de Rennes, 2008, p. 65-75). Or, Brantôme, écrit M. Rousse, « apporte des restrictions significatives à la liberté qui est laissée [par Louis XII] aux auteurs de jeux théâtraux », en évoquant les menaces qu'à cette occasion (?) le souverain fait peser sur les basochiens et les écoliers (*Œuvres complètes de Pierre Bourdeille, seigneur de Brantôme*, éd. L. Lalanne, Paris, 1873, VII, p. 316 ; *cf.* M. Rousse, art. cité). Il y a fort à parier que le roi, dont la politique menée contre le pape Jules II fut soutenue par l'œuvre dramatique d'un Gringore, n'eut de cesse de contrôler cette parole publique dont il connaissait mieux que d'autres l'efficacité polémique. La légende du bon « Père du peuple » qui laissait toute liberté aux tréteaux parisiens mériterait ainsi d'être réévaluée.

39 Texte édité par J. K. Farge, *op. cit.*, p. 487-488.

Lors de cette assemblée d'octobre 1514, il ne s'agit pas d'interdire à titre préventif les excès des étudiants lors de fêtes à venir, mais de répondre à une plainte précise contre un spectacle donné la semaine précédente, le mercredi 25 octobre, dans un collège bien identifié. Par ailleurs, ce sont les victimes de la satire qui demandent des sanctions, comme l'avaient fait les membres du Parlement en 1483. Et là encore, ce sont des victimes bien singulières. De fait, celles-ci ne sont autres que ces *reformatores* dont la fonction a été créée par la réforme de 1452 et qui ont pour tâche de contrôler les activités des collèges[40]. D'une certaine façon, les *reformatores* sont, dans cette affaire, à la fois juges et parties. On voit que le théâtre permettait aux régents de prendre position dans les débats qui agitaient l'Université parisienne, et d'exprimer, avec une certaine audace, une défiance à l'égard de ceux-là même qui tentaient de les surveiller. Le professeur est déjà au cœur du système de contrôle et de répression en tant qu'*auctor*, c'est-à-dire auteur et surtout garant de la « légalité » et de la « moralité » du spectacle proposé ; mais, souvent à peine plus âgé que ses élèves, il est aussi indiscipliné qu'eux et résiste par le théâtre aux autorités qu'il juge abusives. La responsabilité remonte alors sur les épaules des principaux.

LES ARRÊTS DU PARLEMENT SOUS LE RÈGNE DE FRANÇOIS Ier

Ainsi, au lendemain de l'avènement de François Ier, le Parlement, qui en 1483 s'était plaint auprès de l'Université, s'adresse cette fois directement aux principaux de collèges et les convoque nommément pour les enjoindre de faire respecter sa loi. Le 5 janvier 1516,

> la court a mandé de venir en icelle maistres Jehan Bolu principal des grammairiens du college de Navarre, Bernard Roillet principal du college de Bourgongne, Jacques du Molin principal du college des Bons-enfans, Richard de Wasbourg principal du college de la Marche, Jehan Pelletier sous-principal,

40 *Cf.* R. Goulet, *op. cit.*, f° 7r. Goulet insiste sur le fait que ce sont ces « *reformatores* » qui ont été à l'origine du règlement de 1488 (*cf. supra*). Pour les auteurs et amateurs de réjouissances estudiantines, ce sont donc des cibles naturelles mais dangereuses.

> Jerosme Clitonne et Robert Sueur regens du college du cardinal le Moyne, Pierre Michault et Claude de Montfaucon regens du collège de Boncourt, Jehan Morin principal du college de Harcourt, Estienne le Roux principal du college des Tresoriers et Yves Godestar principal du college de Justice ; ausquels ladite court a faict deffences de ne jouer, faire ne permettre de jouer en leurs colleges aucunes farces, sottises, et autres jeux contre l'honneur du roy, de la royne, de madame la duchesse d'Angoulesme mere dudit seigneur, des seigneurs du sang ne autres personnages estans autour de la personne dudict seigneur, sur peine de punition contre ceux qui feront le contraire, telle que la court verra estre à faire[41].

En vertu des réserves méthodologiques énoncées dans notre introduction, rien ne permet de dire que cet arrêt de 1516 fut le premier arrêt du Parlement jamais prononcé contre le théâtre des étudiants. Il n'en demeure pas moins que, par son origine et son contenu, il se distingue nettement des textes qui, dans notre corpus, l'ont précédé et marque peut-être une nouvelle étape dans les relations que le pouvoir politique entretient avec le monde universitaire et, plus précisément, avec le théâtre des étudiants. En outre, c'est la première fois que, dans nos textes, il est fait une allusion si directe au crime de lèse-majesté. Il est donc tentant de mettre ce texte en relation avec la lettre si souvent citée de Ravisius Textor qui constate les effets bien réels de la répression à la même époque[42] : cette année-là (mais la lettre n'est pas datée), « pour la fête des Rois, trois ou quatre collèges seulement ont joué des mimes et des comédies, et encore, sans aucun trait satirique » ; Maître Durand est maintenu en prison, accusé, comme d'autres, d'avoir attenté « à la majesté royale et féminine[43] ».

De 1516 à 1529, les cinq arrêts collectés reprennent une rhétorique comparable ; ce ne sont pas toujours les mêmes principaux que l'on convoque, mais ces derniers sont censés rapporter l'arrêt à tous leurs

41 M. Felibien et G.-A. Lobineau, *Histoire de la ville de Paris*, Paris, G. Desprez et J. Desessartz, 1725, 5 vol., t. IV, *Preuves*, p. 634. Voir aussi Archives nationales U 2026, f° 9v.

42 *Cf.*, par ex., J.-C. Aubailly, *Le monologue, le dialogue et la sottie. Essai sur quelques genres dramatiques de la fin du Moyen Âge et du début du* XVI*e* *siècle*, Paris, Champion, 1976, p. 441.

43 « *In regum festo tria aut quatuor tantum collegia mimos et comoedias recitauere, et eas quidem satyricis immunes aculeis : timuit enim capiti suo unusquisque, quorumdam periculo factus cautior, qui (quod regiae maiestati et muliebri perduelles stigma inussissent) catenati ad regem non tam ducti, quam tracti sunt. Magister Durandus, cui doleo, adhuc in uinculis est : dolorem tamen, sperato reginae aduentu, ubi se liberum fore confidit, solatur* », *Ioannis Ravisii Textoris Nivernensis non vulgaris eruditionis epistolae*, Paris, Prigent Calvarin et Thomas de Villiers, 1529, lettre 50, f° 37r-37v.

collègues. Il est rarement question d'autre chose que du théâtre, qui se distingue alors des autres abus aux contours mal définis[44] ; cependant, les flottements terminologiques demeurent. On trouve, aux côtés des farces et sotties, des momeries[45] voire des moresques[46], qui correspondent peut-être au latin *mimi* et *choreae*. En 1516 et 1523[47], le greffier qui rédige l'arrêt ne fait pas explicitement allusion aux fêtes lors desquelles ces spectacles pouvaient être donnés, mais c'est à l'approche de la fête des Rois que les arrêts sont rendus (l'un date du 5 janvier, l'autre du 27 décembre). Celle-ci est d'ailleurs très clairement mentionnée en 1525[48], 1528[49] et 1529[50]. Les autres fêtes ont alors disparu des sources collectées.

Pour l'année 1525, nous disposons d'un document précieux, qui mérite notre attention : le greffier rapporte non seulement l'arrêt lui-même, mais surtout le discours du Président devant les principaux réunis, ainsi que la réponse, au nom de ses collègues, du principal du collège de Coqueret, Robert Dugast[51]. Les circonstances sont tragiques : le roi est en captivité et le Président en appelle au respect de la concorde civile. Il évoque assez clairement ce que l'on craint dans ces jeux :

> on a acoustumé, a la feste des Roys, de jouer par les collieges ; et soubz ombre de jeux, s'ilz estoient permis, y auroit quelques gens qui *latenter* pourroient dire des parolles qui pourroient mouvoir le peuple a sedition [...] ; et fault qu'ilz considèrent l'affliction de la chose publicque ; que les jeux, farces, morisques, ce sont choses volontaires et picquantes ; et s'il estoit permis de jouer, il en adviendroit de la follye et ne pourroient les principaulx de collieges estre

44 En 1529 cependant, défense est faite « de ne jouer, ne permettre jouer, ne *aller parmy les rues en armes et tabourins*, la vigille, jour des Roys, et autres en suyvans par les Escholiers, Martinets et autres personnes » (c'est moi qui souligne).

45 Il s'agit, vraisemblablement, de parades avec déguisements. Sur la momerie, *cf.* A. Lionetto-Hesters, « La Momerie, de Marot aux poètes de la Pléiade : histoire d'un genre », *Réforme, Humanisme, Renaissance*, 69, 2009, p. 85-104.

46 Sur l'esthétique de ce spectacle dansé, voir les articles de J. Koopmans, « "genres théâtraux" et "choses vues" : le cas du théâtre profane à la fin du Moyen Âge », *Fifteenth-Century Studies*, 16, 1990, p. 143-156 et « Les Sots du théâtre et les sauts de la Morisque à la fin du Moyen Âge », *Les lettres romanes*, 43, 1989, p. 43-59.

47 L'arrêt de 1523 est donné par M. Félibien, *op. cit.*, IV, *Preuves*, p. 645.

48 Archives nationales, *Registres du Parlement*, X1a 1529, f° 67r-68r ; Archives nationales U 2029, f° 62r-63r ; C. Jourdain, *op. cit.*, n° 1631, p. 331. *Cf. infra*, mon édition.

49 C. E. Du Boulay, *op. cit.*, VI, p. 204. Texte mentionné par J.-B.-L. Crevier, *op. cit.*, V, p. 229.

50 Archives nationales U 2031, f° 116v et 117r. Texte rapidement mentionné par Du Boulay, *op. cit.*, VI, p. 214, qui ne le reproduit pas.

51 Voir, en annexe, l'édition de ce texte.

> maistres ; et s'il advenoit tempeste et sedition en ceste ville, ce seroit pour la mettre en tout le royaume ; ce qu'il fault éviter necessairement et se contenir *in luctu publico* ; et de ne jouer n'en peult venir que bien.

Il semble donc que, dans ces circonstances exceptionnelles, les autorités ne soient plus disposées à faire le tri[52]. La relative tolérance dont jouissait jusque là les jeux de la fête des Rois est alors oubliée. Ici, on interdit toutes les pratiques dramatiques dans la mesure où elles peuvent être liées à d'autres activités subversives, « tempêtes et séditions ». Il s'agit d'une mesure radicale, qui manifeste le désarroi en même temps que le progrès de l'appareil répressif en ces années troublées[53].

L'ATTITUDE DE L'UNIVERSITÉ ET DE SES MAÎTRES

La réponse de Robert Dugast, au nom de ses collègues, rappelle quant à elle que, pendant toutes ces années, l'Université n'a pas renoncé à légiférer. Le principal affirme que l'Université a déjà pris des mesures, quelques jours avant :

> a ja long temps qu'ilz ont adverty les escoliers qu'ilz ne facent en leurs compositions aucunes choses contre l'honneur du royaume ; et le XXVIe jour du moys passé, le recteur feit assemblée où il leur feit promettre *per jus jurandum* qu'ils obvieroient aux disputations et invectives injurieuses et scandaleuses et feit expres commandement qu'on y mettroit *per compita* defenses de non jouer, sur peine de privation des droitz et privileiges de l'université.

Mais l'Université est confrontée à ses propres marges qu'elle ne maîtrise pas ; si les principaux sont au cœur de l'institution, les martinets, étudiants qui fréquentent en externe les collèges, échappent à tout contrôle. Robert Dugast ne manque pas de le rappeler :

52 De même en janvier 1515, quelques jours après la mort de Louis XII, un arrêt (mais il s'agissait alors d'une décision de l'Université) interdisait la fête des Rois et ses jeux. Le deuil devait être respecté. *Cf.* J.-K Farge, *op. cit.*, p. 494.

53 Par la suite, cette politique semble s'inscrire dans la durée, jusqu'à l'interdiction totale des *Regalia*. En 1538 ou 1545 par exemple, c'est, semble-t-il, la fête des Rois tout entière qui est interdite par l'assemblée de l'Université, et non seulement ses jeux satiriques.

> Et pour ce que, soubz ombre des escolliers, aucuns mauvais garsons, comme les imprimeurs et autres, et mesmement les escolliers qui demeurent hors des collieges, ont acoustumé de jouer, et sont ceulx qui pourroient faire la division et sur lesquelz ilz n'ont aucune puissance, supplient la court faire faire defenses de ne jouer et la faire publier.

L'allusion aux imprimeurs ne laisse pas de surprendre. La réponse de Dugast témoigne d'une proximité de l'imprimerie avec le monde du théâtre, au moment où Trepperel publie des recueils de farces dont plusieurs sont incontestablement d'origine universitaire. Par ailleurs, l'insistance sur ces « mauvais garçons [...] sur lesquels [les principaux] n'ont aucune puissance » montre les limites de la juridiction universitaire, et explique peut-être en partie le nécessaire appel à une juridiction plus étendue, celle du Parlement[54]. C'est ce que semble faire l'Université en 1529, puisque le greffier écrit que la décision suit « la requeste baillée a la Cour par les Recteur et Université de Paris ». On est alors frappé par l'inversion de la procédure qui, en 1483, conduisait le Parlement à porter plainte auprès de l'Université. Ainsi se manifeste sans doute l'emprise croissante du Parlement sur la vie universitaire.

L'Université, cependant, ne constitue pas toujours un tout cohérent et homogène. La plupart des collégiens relevaient de la faculté des arts, dont le public est plus jeune et plus turbulent ; ce sont donc ses principaux que le Parlement convoque lorsqu'il est question de théâtre. En 1523, on trouve cependant à leur côté un représentant de la faculté de médecine. Mais le principal du collège de Sorbonne, qui se consacre tout entier à la théologie, n'est jamais du nombre[55]. Les « Sorbonagres », en revanche, sont parfois victimes des tréteaux[56]. Ainsi, en 1521, Noël Béda, le fameux syndic de la faculté de théologie, se plaint devant l'assemblée de l'Université d'avoir été joué sur la scène du collège du Plessis. Les trois facultés supérieures veulent alors interdire ces jeux, tout bonnement ; mais la faculté des arts veut s'en remettre aux principaux de collèges ; l'on décide finalement de permettre les jeux de la fête des Rois, en interdisant seulement

54 On sait que l'Université mena, tout au long du XVIe siècle, une politique visant à faire disparaître ces élèves externes, qui ne portera réellement ses fruits qu'à la fin du siècle.

55 Si le Parlement, en 1523, convoque le maître des théologiens de Navarre, c'est en tant que principal du collège tout entier, qui supervise l'ensemble des enseignements.

56 Nous pensons en particulier à la *Farce des Théologastres*, attribuée à Louis de Berquin (c. 1528) (*cf.* l'édition de C. Longeon, Genève, Droz, 1989).

ceux qui porteraient atteinte au « sang royal[57] ». Cet épisode est riche d'enseignements : on y découvre que la faculté des arts, concernée au premier chef par le théâtre, est la plus bienveillante à son égard, tandis qu'il est sévèrement condamné par les trois facultés supérieures. L'épisode nous renseigne aussi sur la procédure qui aboutit parfois au texte réglementaire : comme en octobre 1514, il y a, à l'origine, une plainte de l'un des membres, ici éminent, de l'Université, qui espère régler le problème sans avoir recours à l'autorité de tutelle, le Parlement. Enfin, une décision concernant la protection de la majesté royale est le produit d'une plainte qui, *a priori*, ne la concernait pas ; il s'agit, pour la faculté des arts, d'une décision *a minima*, qui se contente de rappeler l'évidence.

Il ne faudrait pas conclure de ce qui précède que le théâtre est toujours le fait des novateurs qui s'opposent, grâce à lui, au conservatisme pédagogique et religieux qu'incarnent Noël Béda et les facultés supérieures[58]. C'est ainsi qu'au collège de Navarre, en 1533, des étudiants ont violemment blasonné Marguerite de Navarre[59]. Le théâtre est une arme que les tenants de l'orthodoxie savaient aussi utiliser[60]. Quant aux professeurs humanistes, ils prennent volontiers leur distance avec cette tradition du théâtre satirique, et poussent parfois la législation universitaire à prendre des mesures contre lui. Ce qui se passe alors au collège de Sainte-Barbe en est peut-être l'illustration. L'âge d'or de ce collège coïncide avec le principalat de la famille de Gouvéa, qui assoit la réputation de l'institution comme bastion de

57 C. E. Du Boulay, *op. cit.*, VI, p. 132. L'affaire est résumée par J.-B.-L. Crevier, *op. cit.*, V, p. 147-149. En 1531, à nouveau attaqué, Béda obtiendra, devant cette même assemblée, qu'enquête soit menée à propos de l'auteur de la comédie dont il a été victime ; *cf.* C. E. Du Boulay, *op. cit.*, VI, p. 234 ; J.-B.-L. Crevier, *op. cit.*, V, p. 258-259. Sur Béda et le théâtre, voir notre thèse citée, p. 460-463.

58 Du reste, le clivage entre le parti des novateurs et celui des conservateurs n'est jamais aussi schématique.

59 Le roi ordonne de retrouver l'auteur de cette « comédie ». Ses agents ne peuvent y parvenir; on met alors à l'arrêt le Grand Maître du collège, Étienne Loret ; le principal des grammairiens, Jean Morin, est placé sous surveillance. Sur cette affaire bien connue, voir notre thèse citée, p. 474-476.

60 Rappelons ici que Pierre de la Ramée fut lui-même victime de pièces satiriques, « sous les applaudissements des Aristotéliciens », *cf.* O. Talon, *Academia*, Paris, Matthieu David, 1550, p. 18. Texte cité par M.-D. Couzinet, *Pierre Ramus et la critique du pédantisme. Philosophie, humanisme et culture scolaire au XVIe siècle*, Paris, Champion, 2015, chapitre VI « Le théâtre de l'éloquence », p. 305-379 (ici p. 306).

l'Humanisme[61]. Jacques de Gouvéa le jeune, qui est principal de 1534 à 1541, devient recteur de l'Université en 1538, et obtient très vite un arrêt interdisant les jeux de la fête des Rois[62]. Gouvéa doit aussi se battre dans les murs de son collège : ainsi, en 1539, il interdit la représentation de pièces de théâtre qui ont échappé à son contrôle. Les auteurs de ces pièces, meurtris, sont bientôt à l'origine d'un violent tumulte ; le principal, soutenu par son oncle, Jacques de Gouvéa l'ancien, décide de leur renvoi[63].

Certains humanistes préfèrent se tourner vers de nouvelles formes dramatiques, qui trouvent leurs modèles dans la littérature antique, et notamment dans les éditions récentes de Plaute et Térence. Depuis les premiers essais de Ravisius Textor, le théâtre universitaire se réinvente en effet peu à peu et affiche nettement ses ambitions pédagogiques et littéraires[64] ; il rejette, pour cela, le modèle satirique. Jean Calmus, notamment, fait jouer au collège du Plessis, en 1544, une comédie latine en cinq actes, dont l'édition, publiée en 1552, propose un petit traité sur la comédie antique. Le prologue s'inspire des préceptes de Quintilien et d'Érasme et insiste en particulier sur les vertus morales et pédagogiques du théâtre[65]. En voici les premiers vers :

Non vos latet, scio, Spectatores benevoli,
Quam sit periculosum, ut isto tempore,
Et quam molestum artem exercere Comicam.

« Vous n'ignorez pas, je le sais, spectateurs bienveillants,
Combien il est dangereux, ces temps-ci,
Et combien il est pénible de pratiquer l'art de la comédie. »

---

61 Sur le collège de Sainte-Barbe, voir J. Quicherat, *Histoire de Sainte-Barbe*, Paris, Hachette, 1860-1864 et M.-M. Compère, *op. cit.*, p. 339-344.

62 C. E. Du Boulay, *op. cit.*, VI, p. 330 ; J.-B.-L. Crevier, *op. cit.*, V, p. 340-341 ; *Commentaires de la Faculté de Médecine…*, *op. cit.*, p. 302. *Cf.* A. Tuilier, *op. cit.*, p. 353.

63 Voir le récit de cette affaire par J. Quicherat, *op. cit.*, p. 255-265.

64 *Dialogi aliquot Joannis Ra. Textoris Nivernensis hactenus non editi, studiosae juventuti utiles et jucundi, adjecta sunt animi gratia ejusdem epigrammata aliquot non inutilia*, Paris, Regnault Chaudière, 1530. Voir, sur ces questions et sur cet auteur, notre thèse citée, et notamment notre deuxième partie, « Théâtre et pédagogie. Autour de Joannes Ravisius Textor », p. 179-371.

65 *Comedia recenter edita, autore Ioanne Calmo, cui nonnulla per eundem adiecta sunt, quae non parum ad cognoscendam et scribendam comoediam conferunt*, Paris, Jean Gueulart, 1552. Sur ce texte, nous nous permettons de renvoyer à notre article « Le théâtre des collèges, la formation des étudiants et la transmission des savoirs aux XVe et XVIe siècles », *Camenulae*, 3, 2009 (en ligne).

Notre auteur sait de quoi il parle ; de fait, Calmus, nous dit l'historien Quicherat, était au nombre des auteurs de pièces de théâtre censurés et renvoyés de Sainte-Barbe, en 1539. L'invention de la comédie humaniste constitue peut-être, pour ce professeur assagi, une réponse à la censure et aux excès du théâtre satirique dont il a pu lui-même faire l'expérience[66]. Mieux encore, sous son propre rectorat, en 1545, les jeux de la fête des Rois sont à nouveau interdits[67]. Dans l'esprit de Calmus, il existait vraisemblablement une différence entre, d'une part, le théâtre qu'il interdit comme recteur, et, d'autre part, le théâtre latin qu'il publie. Ainsi, les interdits qui ont pesé sur les activités théâtrales des milieux universitaires, en donnant une place centrale, dès le XVe siècle, aux professeurs de collège – ils s'ouvraient alors à la littérature classique et aux préoccupations de l'humanisme – ont pu être des aiguillons du renouveau[68].

Certes, le théâtre polémique des étudiants ne disparaît pas dans la seconde moitié du siècle, et il est encore fait mention de scandales liés à la satire dramatique[69] ; mais le modèle de la comédie et de la tragédie à l'antique qui échappent à la censure s'impose sur les planches

---

66 Notons que, dès les années 1530, la plupart des prologues de comédies latines font allusion aux risques que courent les auteurs de pièces satiriques et justifient ainsi le choix de formes dramatiques plus innocentes. Tout cela fait écho à la lettre de Ravisius Textor déjà citée.

67 Du Boulay, *op. cit.*, VI, p. 398 et *Commentaires de la Faculté de Médecine…*, *op. cit.*, p. 393.

68 C'est en tout cas ce que semble dire Vauquelin de la Fresnaye dans son *Art poétique* (1605), livre III, v. 87-102 : il oppose nettement le théâtre ancien des étudiants, satirique, et le théâtre nouveau qui trouve son inspiration chez Ménandre et Térence. Il explique le passage d'une esthétique à l'autre par le rôle que tinrent les nouveaux « Apollons » des lettres françaises, dans les années 1550-1560 mais aussi, par les effets de la censure. Sur ce dernier point, il faut cependant faire la part du *topos* historiographique et littéraire : d'une certaine façon, Vauquelin « récrit » le passage de la comédie ancienne d'Aristophane à la comédie nouvelle de Ménandre tel que le présentait Josse Bade (*op. cit.*) à la suite d'Horace. Un tel *topos* participe du discours sur la *translatio studii*. Calmus lui-même, lorsqu'il compose son prologue, a sans doute tout cela en tête, de même que les auteurs de théâtre latin depuis Ravisius Textor.

69 En 1559, l'assemblée de l'Université répète ses interdits (*cf.* C. E. Du Boulay, *op. cit.*, VI, p. 526). En 1579, on joue encore, au collège du Plessis, certaines « farces où l'on avait pris la licence de déchirer la réputation de bien des gens ». Enfin, l'article 80 de l'ordonnance des États de Blois, en cette même année 1579, défend « à tous supérieurs, seigneurs, principaux et régents de faire ou permettre aux écoliers ou autres quelconques jouer farces, comédies, tragédies, fables, satyres, scènes ou autres jeux en latin ou français, contenant lascivités, injures, invectives, convices, ni aucun scandale contre aucun état public, ou personne privée, sur peine de prison et punition corporelle ». Textes cités d'après E. Faguet, *La tragédie religieuse au XVIe siècle*, Paris, Hachette, 1883, p. 61.

des collèges parisiens[70]. Quant au théâtre à visée pédagogique, ce sont les jésuites qui lui donnent, dans les décennies suivantes, son âge d'or.

De toute évidence, les textes réglementaires dont il vient d'être question ne suffisent pas à faire l'histoire du théâtre universitaire au début de l'époque moderne. Un certain nombre de questions restent ainsi sans réponse :

- Les règlements portent d'abord sur le théâtre satirique. Mais quelle était réellement la part de ce théâtre dans les activités dramatiques des collèges ? Faisait-il l'essentiel de la production scolaire ?
- Les textes font parfois allusion aux relations qu'entretient le théâtre universitaire avec le reste de la production dramatique à Paris, et avec les autres formes d'expression publique. Mais quelle est exactement la nature de ces relations ?
- Un point particulier attire notre attention, et montre de façon exemplaire les limites de nos sources : au XVIe siècle, les textes règlementaires cités parlent essentiellement de la fête des Rois. Mais nous avons vu que l'on jouait aussi en d'autres occasions des jeux parfois licencieux. Ces activités, parce qu'elles ne concernaient pas à dates fixes l'ensemble de la communauté universitaire, ont pu échapper aux condamnations les plus générales et les plus officielles. Elles n'en ont pas moins été, semble-il, extrêmement vivantes.

Dans le même temps, notre corpus offre un certain nombre de renseignements précieux. Il confirme d'abord que le théâtre occupait une place très importante dans la vie des étudiants et des maîtres. Il donne par ailleurs des informations essentielles sur les conditions de la représentation : on jouait en public, dans les collèges et au dehors ; les collégiens se mélangeaient parfois à d'autres jeunes gens ; ils faisaient quelques excès vestimentaires et pécuniaires et accompagnaient ces jeux de danses, de musiques et de chahuts divers. Enfin, nos textes, par leur nature même, témoignent parfaitement de l'inscription de ce théâtre dans les différentes sphères de la vie de l'étudiant (le collège, la cité, le royaume), tout en soulignant son caractère souvent insaisissable.

70 C'est aux collèges de Boncourt et de Beauvais que sont représentées les premières comédies françaises de Jodelle et Grévin, dans les années 1550 et 1560.

Et c'est ce caractère insaisissable qui explique, en dernière analyse, le nombre mais surtout la nature et le contenu des interdits. Le mode de production et de réception du spectacle dramatique, collectif et immédiat, ne cesse d'inquiéter les autorités universitaires et politiques. Celles-ci n'hésitent plus, au XVIe siècle, à conjuguer leurs efforts : elles tentent d'enfermer le théâtre dans les collèges et de définir ainsi un lieu et un public, sous la conduite d'un professeur qui devient l'*auctoritas*, l'*auctor* véritable et responsable devant la loi[71]. Au côté d'un théâtre d'étudiants qui, malgré tous ces efforts, continue d'échapper à l'institution ou au contrôle des autorités, les XVe et XVIe siècles voient donc émerger un théâtre *de collège*, à la fois *signé* et *situé*. Dans les années 1530 et 1540, certains contrats demandent même aux professeurs de rédiger des pièces de théâtre pour les « Actes » des collèges[72] : la mise par écrit et sous contrat de telles pratiques, parfois anciennes, me semble témoigner d'une institutionnalisation croissante du théâtre scolaire, au seuil de l'époque moderne.

Mathieu FERRAND
Université de Grenoble Alpes

---

71 Le professeur n'est pas nécessairement l'auteur de ces pièces, au sens moderne du terme, mais, dans le cadre de son magistère, il est bien le garant de sa « légalité ».

72 Voir le contrat d'engagement de François Descobars en tant que régent, au collège parisien de La Marche (4 septembre 1543), dans E. Coyecque, *Recueil d'actes notariés relatifs à l'histoire de Paris et de ses environs au XVIe siècle*, Paris 1905, vol. 1, p 499-500, n° 2708. Voir aussi les contrats d'engagement des professeurs pour le tout nouveau collège de Guyenne, à Bordeaux (contrat du 17 novembre 1533, cité par H. Lagrave, C. Mazouer, M. Régaldo, *La vie théâtrale à Bordeaux des origines à nos jours*, Paris, C.N.R.S., 1985, p. 51 et reproduit dans E. Gaullieur, *Histoire du Collège de Guyenne*, Sandoz et Fischbacher, Paris, 1874, p. 548-549). Signalons enfin l'apparition, dans les archives conservées, d'autorisations spéciales pour des festivités bien particulières : en 1549, les « maistres, principal et boursiers » du collège du Cardinal Lemoine demandent et obtiennent la permission d'« exécuter cette présente année leurs jeux en leur collège » (M. Félibien, *op. cit.*, IV, *Preuves*, p. 744).

ANNEXE

Les textes présentés ci-dessous sont de loin les plus longs et les plus riches de notre corpus[73]. Ils sont en outre représentatifs de la diversité des questions abordées dans les règlements d'origine universitaire (texte 1, XVe siècle) et parlementaire (texte 2, XVIe siècle).

1488, 4 novembre

La faculté des arts, réunie à Saint-Julien-le-Pauvre, édicte des statuts pour réglementer les fêtes des écoliers. Le texte interdit tout abus et insolence. Seule la fête des Rois peut être célébrée par des jeux, mais selon des modalités précisément définies.

On peut lire une paraphrase de ce document, d'après C. E. Du Boulay, dans l'ouvrage de J.-B.-L. Crevier, *Précis sur l'histoire de l'Université de Paris, depuis son origine jusqu'en l'année 1600*, Paris, Desaint et Saillant, 1761, vol. IV, p. 433-437.

Nous avons proposé une traduction de ce texte (avec son édition) dans notre thèse de doctorat, *Le théâtre des collèges parisiens au début du XVIe siècle. Textes et pratiques dramatiques*, sous la dir. de P. Galand et M. Huchon, Paris, EPHE, 2013, p. 555.

(A) Original perdu (?)
(B) Copie du XVIe siècle dans le *Chartularium Nationis Gallicanae*, Paris, BNF, nouv. acq. lat. 2060, f° 178v-179v.

(a) C. E. Du Boulay, *Historia Universitatis Parisiensis*, Paris, F. Noël, 1665-1673, t. V, p. 782-783, d'après un *Liber Picardicae Nationis*.
(b) M. Rousse, *Le théâtre des farces en France au Moyen Âge*, thèse d'État dactyl., Rennes II, 1983, t. IV, p. 98-101, d'après (a).

73 Je tiens à remercier Marie Bouhaïk-Gironès ainsi que Thierry Kouamé et Luigi Sanchi dont les conseils et remarques pour l'édition de ces textes ont été d'un précieux secours. Je rappelle que le lecteur trouvera dans l'annexe I de ma thèse l'ensemble des textes cités dans le présent article.

INDIQUÉ : C. Jourdain, *Index chronologicus chartarum pertinentium ad historiamUniversitatis Parisiensis…*, Paris, Hachette, 1862, p. 305, nº 1473, d'après (a).

Édition d'après (B) (on ne trouve pas, dans ce manuscrit, la citation littérale de la réforme d'Estouteville reprise par C. E. Du Boulay et M. Rousse ; elle figure ici entre crochets) :

Sequuntur statuta praeclare artium facultatis juxta conclusionem concorditer habitam a quattuor nationibus apud Sanctum Julianum Pauperem anno domini 1488, die vero quarta novembris, ad corripiendum abusus et insolentias quae fiebant circa festa sanctorum Martini, Katerinae et aliorum sequentium tam in turpibus facetiis et in excessivis habitibus quam aliis in rebus etiam indecentibus.

Nulla festa sanctorum Martini, Katherinae, Nicholai, sive nationum, provinciarum aut diocesum sive collegiorum fient sive cum mimis, sive facetiis et tapetis, sive cum simplicibus cantilenis pro chorea, sed solum vacetur divinis obsequiis et studiis sicut diebus dominicis quibus fieri est solitum. [*Possunt tamen virtuose et eutrapelice ludere ad laboris levamen et solatium*].

Permittatur tantummodo festum et solemnitas regum sub hac moderatione tamen ut fiat laetitia chorearum solum in vigilia sero et per diem festi post vesperas, ac nihil ante, ut divino servitio plenius ac devotius intendatur.

In crastino autem nihil ludi facetiarum aut simplicium etiam chorearum omnino fiet, sed vel lectiones reddent juvenes scholastici vel scribent, saltem hora postmeridiana vel cum simplici licentia a magistro paedagogo impetrata, ludant in curia collegii, ac se praeparent ad diei proxime sequentis lectionem.

Nulla tapeta, sive locagio, sive mutuo permittantur in praedicto festo regum praeter banccaria, quae sedilibus pro reverentia regis ac dominorum conceduntur apponi.

Permittitur unus mimus, et ad summum duo in praedicto festo regum modo prius dicto, scilicet sero in vigilia et in die post vesperas.

Prohibetur omnino ne occasione mimorum sive facetiarum aut aliarum expensarum pro festo aliqua pecuniae summa quantumcumque parva exigatur, aut recipiatur a juvenibus scholasticis etiam gratis oblata, praeter spontaneam regis oblationem moderatam, ac pecuniam noviter venientium qui vulgo bejauni nominantur, quae pecunia bejaunorum recipi conceditur, juxta antiquam et laudabilem facultatis permissionem.

Prohibentur omnino vestes et indumenta quaecumque de livreta sive de serico, sive de panno quacumque occasione composita, sive ad honorem et comitivam regis, sive ad ludum facetiarum et fatuorum, aut etiam quaecumque indumenta, sive locagio, sive mutuo accepta, nisi sint necessaria ad qualitatem personarum comediae.

Solae illae facetiae conceduntur in memorato festo, quae per magistrum paedagogum, aut alium de suis regentibus fuerint visitatae ad unguem, priusquam in ludum prodeant, ne aliquid mordax, aut alias inhonestum quod viri probi animum offenderet, ullo modo sub risus specie contineant.

Et ludantur in propriis collegiis hujusmodi facetiae, nec discurrant inde juvenes per collegia ut evitentur scandala quae ob id evenire solebant.

Et hanc constitutionem in omnibus suis articulis suo successori faciet jurare dominus rector praesens et posse observari, et omnes singuli sequentes similiter facient.

[Suivent les dispositions prises pour faire respecter le règlement, et notamment les sanctions prévues pour les contrevenants. Les professeurs se verront privés de leurs charges. Quant aux élèves, ils seront soumis aux châtiments corporels.]

1525, 29 décembre.

Le Parlement de Paris convoque les principaux de collèges et interdit tout jeu de théâtre pour la fête des Rois. Les registres du Parlement présentent le discours du président et la réponse, au nom de ses collègues, de Robert Dugast, principal du collège de Coqueret.

(A) Archives nationales, *Registres du Parlement*, X1a 1529, f° 67r-68r.
(B) Bibliothèque Mazarine, ms. 2925 (copie du XVIIe siècle).
(C) Archives nationales, U 2029 (copie du XVIIe siècle).

(a) C. Jourdain, *Index chronologicus chartarum pertinentium ad historiam Universitatis Parisiensis…*, Paris, Hachette, 1862, n° 1631, p. 331.

Édition d'après A :

Ce jour, Maistres Robert Dugast, Estienne Le Roux, Richard Turmante, Jehan de Tartas, Olivier de Lesgier, principaulx des collieges de Coquerel, de Justice, de Harcourt, de Lisieux et du Plessis, et maistre Anthoine Silvestre, maistre des arciens du college de Navarre, Maistre Simon Le Roux, scribe, et Waldequin Thyvet, receveur de l'université de Paris, sont venuz en la court de ceans, ausquelz Maistre Charles Guillart, president en ladite court, a dit que la court les a mandez pour pourveoir aux inconveniens qui peuent arriver en ceste ville de Paris par le moyen des escolliers qui sont de present en l'université ; et scavent la desolation du royaume par la prinse du roy, qui de present est en Espaigne detenu es mains de l'empereur ; ont veu la grant ruyne arrivée devant Pavye et la perdition de tant de gens nobles et des principaulx du royaume qui est telle que le royaume est demeuré sans defense et est *sine capite et viribus* ; et ne consiste la force d'icelluy qu'en l'union et en l'obeissance qui a esté telle qu'elle a conservé jusques a present le royaume en son entier ; est celle qui le defend ; et quant la chose publicque de Rome estoit en sa fleur, elle n'a jamais esté gardée et conservée sinon par l'union des nobles et du peuple ; que cette ville de Paris est composée de toutes nations et diversitez de gens en tous estatz *et in tanta urbe multa sunt et varia ingenia* ; qu'on a acoustumé, a la feste des Roys, de jouer par les collieges ; et soubz ombre de jeux, s'ilz estoient permis, y auroit quelques gens qui *latenter* pourroient dire des parolles qui pourroient mouvoir le peuple a sedition, ce qui n'est requis mais est de nécessité le tenir en paix ; et a Rome, *re publica afflicta, interdicebantur ludi publici*, mesmement *circenses, et utebantur Romani vestibus luctuosis* ; que la chose publicque de France n'eust sceu avoir plus grant mal ne occasion de se doulloir que de la prinse de son prince, joinct la perte des nobles qui y sont morts et la ruyne de la force de France ; et fault qu'ilz considèrent l'affliction de la chose publicque ; que les jeux, farces, morisques, ce sont choses volontaires et picquantes ; et s'il estoit permis de jouer, il en adviendroit de la follye et ne pourroient les principaulx de collieges estre maistres ; et s'il advenoit tempeste et sedition en ceste ville, ce seroit pour la mettre en tout le royaume ; ce qu'il fault éviter necessairement et se contenir *in luctu publico* ; et de ne jouer n'en peult venir que bien. Parquoy la court leur a ordonné et leur enjoinct de ne permettre en leurs collieges de ne jouer aucuns jeux, ne y faire farces ne morisques ; et le tout faire cesser, sur peine de s'en prendre à leurs personnes ; et oultre, de faire savoir au recteur de l'université et aux principaulx des autres collieges ceste presente ordonnance, afin que de leur part ilz la gardent et observent et qu'il n'en arrive inconvenient. Et sur ce a ledit Maistre Robert Dugast, principal dudit college de Coquerel, dit que l'université, voyant la desolation du royaume et le temps tel qu'il est, prevoyant aux inconveniens qui pourroient advenir à cause des jeux, a ja pourveu a ce que la court leur a ordonné et commandé, *agunt enim dies lugubres in cubilibus suis, et non solum diem, sed annum* ; et a ja long temps qu'ilz ont adverty les escoliers qu'ilz ne facent en leurs compositions aucunes choses contre l'honneur du royaume ; et le XXVIe jour du moys passé, le recteur feit assemblée où il leur feit promettre *per jus jurandum* qu'ils obvieroient aux disputations et invectives injurieuses et scandaleuses et feit expres commandement qu'on y mettroit *per compita* defenses de non jouer, sur peine de privation des droitz et privileiges de l'université. Que ledit recteur a esté nouvellement esleu, et n'a encores prins sa chappe, et pour ce qu'il n'a acoustumé aller sans chappe, il n'est venu au mandement qui luy a esté fait ; et supplient la court de le tenir pour excusé ; aussi sont venuz en petit nombre, mais ilz se chargent d'en advertir et faire [et faire] savoir l'ordonnance de ladite court, tant audit recteur que autres, tellement qu'il n'en arrivera inconvenient. Et pour ce que, soubz ombre des escolliers, aucuns mauvais garsons, comme les imprimeurs et autres, et mesmement les escolliers qui demeurent hors des collieges, ont acoustumé de jouer, et sont ceulx qui pourroient faire la division et sur lesquelz ilz n'ont aucune puissance, supplient la court faire faire defenses de ne jouer et la faire publier ; car quant est de ceulx qui demeurent es collieges, ilz en respondront et s'en chargent. Et sur ce leur a ledit Guillart president dit qu'ilz facent faire les defenses particulierement par chacun colliege a leurs escoliers et aux autres, sur peine de privation des droitz et privileges de l'université ; et en cela, s'ilz ont affaire de l'auctorité de la court, elle les supportera et fera ce qu'elle devera. Et quant aux defenses qu'ilz requièrent, la court en advisera pour y pourvoir. Ce fait, se sont les dessus dits retirez.

CURBING CARNIVAL ACTIVITIES BY STAGING CARNIVAL PLAYS?

Renward Cysat's ambigous resolution of jurisdictional conflicts

In the Middle Ages and Renaissance, when the liturgical church calendar still dominated the course of the year, carnival was customarily the period of different kinds of revelries, popular folk traditions and profane spectacles. Exuberant carnival activities often ended up in violations of limits, endangering law and order[1]. Authorities therefore tried to channel and control the festivity. Their difficult struggle against the negative effects of overindulgence of worldly pleasures can be observed very closely in the case of Lucerne, a stronghold of carnival and theatre since the late Middle Ages. A considerable amount of minutes of the city council, legislation and criminal justice is about measures to prevent or punish misconduct during the critical period before Lent.

Complaints about transgressions during carnival already appear in the earliest written records of the city council at the end of the 14th century and are often repeated in almost the same manner during the following centuries[2]. They bear witness of the ongoing conflict between the legislative authority that tried to implement regulations and people that were not willing to refrain from old familiar practices. In contrast to efforts of banning and ruling carnival activities we also

1 Carnival and its impact on social order is one of the main topics of the collaborative research (CRC) 923 "Threatened Orders" based at the university of Tübingen, Germany. Cf. K. Ridder, B. von Lüpke, R. Nöcker, "Carnival From Festival to Revolt. Carnival Theatre during the Late Middle Ages and Early Reformation as a Threat to Urban Order", *Power and Violence in Medieval and Early Modern Theater*, C. Dietl, Ch. Schanze, Gl. Ehrstine (dir.), Göttingen 2014, p. 153–157.

2 Cf. H. Greco-Kaufmann, *Zuo der Eere Gottes, vfferbuwung dess mentschen vnd der statt Lucern lob. Theater und szenische Vorgänge in der Stadt Luzern im Spätmittelalter und in der Frühen Neuzeit*, Historischer Abriss (Band I) und Quellenedition (Band II), Zürich 2009 (=Theatrum Helveticum Bd. 11), p. 193 ff.

find recordings of enthusiastic accounts of excessive celebrations and public performances in the spirit of carnival and a remarkable amount of dramatic texts provide evidence of elaborate stage activities during the Lucerne carnival season. The analysis of different source material shows that the acceptance or interdiction of carnival events varies in the course of time and depends on the prevailing political, moral and cultural climate of the era in question. The social affiliation of the performers and the use of masquerade and disguise seem to be decisive factors. Generally, the attitude of the power holders towards carnival can be described as ambivalent. On the one hand they did not want to abandon traditions that historically were related to religious, mercantile and political interests, on the other hand they lean towards curbing ungovernable customs and tolerating only certain forms of entertainment. The tendency of reducing and modifying pleasures increased continuously in the course of the 16th century, not least driven by the pressure of reformatory movement, and culminated after the arrival of the Jesuits in 1574.

In my paper I'd like to depict the situation in Lucerne at the end of the 16th century when Renward Cysat, director of the famous wine market plays and driving force of the catholic reform, staged his two-day spectacle *Spiegel dess vberflusses vnd missbruchs in ergetzlicheit dess lybs und weltlichen fröwden* (Mirror of the opulence and abuse for delectation and worldly pleasures), also called *Convivii Process*, at the carnival of 1593[3]. Cysat's tragicomedy is based on the widespread French morality *La Condamnation de Banquet* (printed 1507)[4]. The nucleus of the plot is simple: excessive eating and drinking brings about visitations of the personified diseases, Gout, Colic, Jaundice, Quinsy, afflicting the revelers. Both plays, the 3644 verses long French original and the huge

3 H. Greco-Kaufmann, *Spiegel dess vberflusses vnd missbruchs. Renward Cysats „Convivii Process". Kommentierte Erstausgabe der Tragicocomedi von 1593*, Zürich 2001 (= Theatrum Helveticum 8).

4 Nicolas de La Chesnaye, *La Condamnation de Banquet*, J. Koopmans et P. Verhuyck (ed.), Genève, Droz, 1991. After the discovery of an additional textual witness of the French morality, which was enclosed in Cysat's "Convivii Process" manuscript, Koopmans revised his former statements about attribution, dating and localization of *La Condamnation de Banquet.* He now suggests that Guillaume Flamang created the text at the beginning of the 16th century in the region of Chaumont. Cf. J. Koopmans, "La fin du Banquet", *Mainte belle oeuvre faicte. Études sur le théâtre médiéval offertes à Graham A. Runnalls*, D. Hüe, M. Longtin, L. Muir (dir.), Medievalia No 54, Orléans 2005, p. 252–264.

Swiss adaption of 9528 verses, end up in a trial and condemnation of gluttony. Banquet/Convivium is executed, Soupper/Coena is ordered to keep a respectable distance from Disner/Prandium. The French author, addressing an upper class (or courtly) audience, considers revelry merely as a health issue whereas Cysat, pharmacist and clerk of the municipality, situates the vice *Gula* in the context of the local carnival and festivity culture and interprets the consequences against the background of catholic faith.

Regarding the symposium on "Conflicts of jurisdiction and Theatre" there are two ways to deal with Renward Cysat's "Convivii Process": either we consider the staging of the tragicomedy in the context of municipal legislation and jurisdiction, or we take a close look at the conflict expressed in the drama. The fact that Cysat's drama is far more than a translation of the French play–according to his own statement in the preface he adopted only the "substance" and the "argument" of the French author and created a new and extended version incorporating local customs[5]–suggests that both approaches, the one with the focus on the context and the one discussing the drama, are likely to produce similar results.

Rich meals at carnival were already a subject of the earliest written records of Lucerne. Regulations of the monastery "im Hof", at that time proprietor and ruler of the town, reveal that already in the 14th century people gathered on the occasion of the delivery of the tithe within the premises of the monastery and celebrated carnival by sharing opulent meals. After the independence of the town in 1479 the monastery lost its predominance and the social activities of the community shifted to the center of the settlement where the upcoming patricians constructed their representative buildings and places[6]. Festivities in the spirit of carnival, usually held in the pre-lent period, were the most important society events of the year[7]. Apart from their entertaining and community

5 H. Greco-Kaufmann, *Spiegel*, p. 132, V. 42ff.

6 The monastery "im Hof" was located a little distance outside and linked with a wooden bridge to the settlement. Before 1500 the bourgeois center of the town was situated around the oldest church "Kapellkirche", bordered by the Lake of Lucerne and the river Reuss. After 1500 it was dislocated westwards to the wine market (formerly called fishmarket).

7 In the late middle ages the meaning of the German term *fastnacht* was not limited to specific carnival days preceeding lent but denotes just a cheerful festivity, usually consisting of food, drinks and entertainment. After the reformation carnival activities were restricted also in catholic regions and limited to three days per year.

generating function they also provided the perfect settings of legal, economical and political actions (court hearings, interest payments, conclusions of agreements between allies). During the 15th and at the beginning of the 16th century we can observe a well-established culture of mutual carnival visitations between authorities of confederated towns in Switzerland. The merry atmosphere of carnival offered an ideal venue for informal discussions about politically sensitive topics and furthered good relationships and consensus between allies and negotiating partners. As the main festivities were linked with major markets, a lot of people from the urban hinterland came to town and celebrated carnival and successful dealings with excessive consumption of meat and wine, music, dance and manifestations of folk culture. Thus carnival also provided an ideal framework for staging weddings[8] or initiating contacts with a future spouse. In general carnival was regarded as a period of joyful get-together, fleshly pleasures and entertainment, a most welcome interruption of the hardship of everyday life.

But the other side of the coin is that carnival potentially harbored the risk of unwanted activities, transgressions and violence. Under the cover of masquerade it was easy to stage charivaris against disliked persons, invade homes in order to get food and drinks and settle disputes in a rude way. Hilarious carousing and merrymaking in taverns and on the streets could end up in rough brawls and disturbance. Protagonists of impertinent and aggressive behavior were mostly bachelors whereas victims were very often unmarried women and old maids. Rude customs like *Block- oder Eggenziehen* (maids were forced to drag a tree-trunk or a harrow as punishment for not choosing or accepting a husband) and *Kuechlin reichen* (begging for carnival cakes, often combined with assaults and sexual abuse) caused terror and pain among women and sometimes resulted in unwanted pregnancy. The rough goings-on of in many cases alcohol fueled young men were a constant source of annoyance for the authorities. They tried to control and ban carnival practices that offended against common decency and endangered the public order. But interdictions turned out to be in vain. The minutes of the city council, put down on Johannes Baptistae (24th June) 1592, speak volumes. Here are some excerpts:

8 In the Late Middle Ages carnival was customarily the period of weddings.

> [...] regarding strolling around in carnival costumes, disguise and masquerade (in ancient times, as mentioned in an order of 1417, also called in the kind of devils): My aldermen did prohibit this repeatedly and rigorously. But the law was not observed. Regardless the everlasting interdiction, it happened again and again, yet recently, past carnival. [...] In order that it will never be forgotten it is engraved in the chair of the mayor that it must be announced from the pulpit at the beginning of the New Year, for time and eternity. Namely: that nobody, regardless what stand or rank he might be, may adhere to this godless custom and neither disguise nor cover his face or wear costumes other than dressed for churchgoing. [...] or make alarums and excursions rumbling and hammering in streets and alleys and behave impetuous. Everyone is warned: personal injuries occurred while taking an active part in carnival activities will not be persecuted, disadvantages suffered will not be compensated. But legal action will be taken if uninvolved persons are insulted or suffered damages. Offenders will be judged severely[9].

There is no doubt that the staging of Renward Cysat's tragicomedy *Convivii Process*, which took place exactly during the subsequent carnival after the above cited council order, is closely related to the authorities' ineffective attempts to suppress the objectionable customs. In his preliminary remarks the author explains that he rewrote the French play on request of religious and secular superiors and submitted the text to the pastors (the Jesuits) for approval[10]. The preserved list of the cast[11], containing names of distinguished families of the ruling patricians, confirms that the staging of *Convivii Process* is considered an affair of state, joining the rank of the prestigious Lucerne passion play tradition. In fact, the dramatic presentation at carnival in 1593 followed the pattern of the passion plays in many respects (processional entry to the wine market, symbolic order of the stage arrangement, framing by speeches of the *precursor* etc.). The affinity with the tradition of religious plays can also be noted with regard to the contents.

The play starts with an assembly in hell. Lucifer and his servants are discussing the possibilities of getting new souls for their community. The devils *Beelphegor* (gluttony), *Mammon* (avarice), *Asmodeus* (voluptuousness) *Petulcus* (mischief) und *Schlangtüfel* (serpent) boast their specific abilities.

9 Cited in H. Greco-Kaufmann, *Spiegel*, p. 110 (Ratsprotokoll 1592, Staatsarchiv Luzern, RP 43,2, p. 111).

10 H. Greco-Kaufmann, *Spiegel*, p. 132, V. 57ff.

11 H. Greco-Kaufmann, *Spiegel*, p. 485 ff.

Lucifer gives them order to corrupt the humans and sends them to earth. A several hours lasting banquet and spree, dance and frivolous behavior with the *Wynmaitlinen* (wine serving waitresses) demonstrate their success. Although the personified vice of *gula* proves the most successful seducer, her peers don't develop less destructive activities. In the course of the two-day spectacle the infernal staff gets assistance from other vices: *Convivium* (banquet), *Coena* (supper), *Gügerlin* (booze), *Schlafftrunk* (nightcup), *Nachtsupp* (nightsoup), symbolizing gormandizing and crapulence, and *Unzucht* (fornication), *Verwegenheit* (foolhardiness), *Fulentzerin* (laziness), *Bona Societas* (good company), *Hoffart* (pride) and other allegories of immorality. In the tavern and the house of pleasure they suborn the carnival followers to idleness, gambling, lies and deception, arrogance, procuration and prostitution. The debauchery activates the personified diseases. They, in the disguise of terrifying monsters, launch their attack and strike hard, but for he moment they preclude the interference of death. They argue that the carnival addicts should get an opportunity to come to their senses and focus on moderation. But soon after their recovery the convivial companions go for carnival cakes to the hostel of the bawd and continue their life of sin and depravity. On their way home devils turn up und chase them around the place. They catch the bawd and haul her into hell. *Sobrietas*, allegory of soberness, warns the booze buddies. Nevertheless they pursue their drinking and merrymaking. The diseases repeat their assault but this time death claims his right and grabs four of the offenders. They also end up in the jaws of hell[12]. *Excessus* (debauchery), severely hurt, is able to escape. Showing penitence, confessing and getting absolution of his sins by the priest he is finally saved and conducted to the court of *Conscientia* (conscience). The vices, however, are sentenced after long judicial proceedings. Father confessor addresses the audience and preaches insistently about the necessity of *metanoia* (reversion), confession and penitence. The play ends with an adamant refusal of carnival and fleshly pleasures and a vigorous appeal for virtues and temperance.

The staging of "Convivii Process", a giant spectacle of baroque magnificence, marks the culmination point of the ongoing conflict

12 As shown on Cysats sketch for the staging of the easterplay in 1583, the hell was constructed like an enormus mouth with sharp teeth. It could be opened and closed.

between the defenders of a pleasure-seeking lifestyle and the promoters of moderation and morals. Due to the fact that requirements, bans and rules did not bring about the requested change of habits, authorities had to find other ways and means to achieve their objectives. All the more as the pressure of the reformation movement increased and the Jesuits in charge with the cure of souls urged for more support of their fight against carnival and other popular folk traditions. The staging of tragicomedy "Convivii Process" deemed to be appropriate for several reasons. With the two-day spectacle on the main market place during the peak days of carnival the organizers were able to reach a large audience. In particular they could directly address the target group, people from near and far, gathering in town to make merry. Cysat's version of the French background story, enhanced with re-enacted scenes of familiar traditions, reproduced the prevalent local atmosphere during the carnival days very precisely and offered a great potential for identification. Hence it provided an excellent vehicle for conveying the message of the secular and religious leaders of the catholic reform: Those who are unwilling to renounce carnival customs will bear terrible consequences in the afterlife and end up in the flaming pit of damnation. The statement is unequivocal: In case that the conflict cannot be resolved on earth it will be transferred to the domain of eschatology. Jurisdiction will be postponed to the last judgement.

Focussing on the content of Cysat's drama there is no doubt that the threat with eternal pain was intended to act as a deterrent. In fact the topic was also very common in Jesuit sermons. Citing the imminence of apocalypse and doomsday was an important element of the strategy of preachers to convince believers to confess their sins, do penitence and change their lives. But did the rhetoric, that quite often proved successful in church, also have the same effect on stage?

If we imagine well known Lucerne patricians acting in scenes like "devils dancing in front of the tavern while carnival aficionados abandon themselves to vice", "monsters beating the revellers" or "dragging the bawd to hell" it seems likely that the reaction of the local public was laughter rather than contrition. It seems obvious that the entertaining aspect of the theatre event in question was at least as important as preaching morals with a wagging finger. Not to mention that the extensive celebration of sumptuous meals and sensual pleasures onstage bears the risk of provoking a contrary effect and animate the public to behave in the same way.

Although we do not possess any written records about the reception of the dramatic performance at carnival 1593 we might be able to find out if the staging of the morality play really helped the authorities to achieve their aims. Examining the city councils minutes and other source materials of the following years we learn that violations of restrictions regarding carnival and related customs continued to be a widely discussed issue among of the rulers of the town[13]. For this reason we might consider the theatrical campaign against gluttony and carnival activities a complete failure. The fact that Cysat's "Convivii Process" was the very last carnival play that Lucerne patricians staged on the wine market seems to corroborate this interpretation. The dramatic activities of the citizens of the following years were focused on religious topics, the passion of Jesus Christ, miracles, lives of saints and martyrs. Yet the resident Jesuits, initiators of Cysat's unique effort in the field of carnival spectacles[14], continued to pursue their mission by staging didactic plays, however in Latin, very often embedded in a foreign cultural setting and confined to the school-premises[15]. Based on the fact that only the educated elite was able to understand Jesuit dramatic productions the range of influence of their theatrical events can be considered as quite restricted.

After the ambiguous "Convivii Process" experience Lucerne authorities were bound to realize that the staging of the carnival play did not really produce the social disciplining effect they had hoped for. Additional measures had to be taken to tackle the problems. Once more the minutes of the city counsel shed light on their approach to change

13 Records of these activities are collected in chronological order under the keywords "Fastnacht, Fritschi, Kurzweil, Maskenlaufen, Tanz etc." (Carnival, Fritschi, entertainment, masks, dance etc.), H. Greco-Kaufmann, *Zuo der Eere Gottes*, vol. II.

14 Cysats major contributions to the Lucerne theatre traditions were in the field of religious plays. He revised and staged the Lucerne passion play of 1583 and 1597 and prepared the staging of 1614 (due to his sudden death the staging took place in 1616 under the direction of the parish priest) and was the author of the mircale play of the holy cross (written 1575, a staging did not take place due to pestilence).

15 A request for permission to stage vernacular plays in 1581 was turned down by the Provincial superiors of the Jesuit order. Cf. H. Greco-Kaufmann, *Zuo der Eere Gottes*, vol. I, p. 576.

popular festivity culture and implement their moral concept. On the one hand they tried to modify objectionable customs by eliminating the disturbing elements, on the other hand they tried to replace them with new forms of social activities. The former can be illustrated by the taming of the mythic "Brother Fritschi", the most important local masquerade, described in different sources as wild young fellow, mercenary, saint of the battle, old farmer, mediator in political matters and exponent of the rampant medieval carnival culture[16]. Practices around this complex carnival symbol often endangered the public order. But "Brother Fritschi" protagonist of celebrations combined with overindulgence, carousing, music, dance and fights for fun could not be banished, neither with mandates nor interdictions. Records, transmitted by Renward Cysat, tell us the story of an amazing change at the end of the 16th century: "Brother Fritschi", dressed in the colours of the town, riding on horse in the fore of a military parade. The authorities transformed the former carnival customs around "Fritschi" into a strictly organized military event, integrating not only the wild masquerade but also the young hotspurs, preventing them from destructive carnival activities.

In addition to the abovementioned method of modifying, taming and channelling popular traditions we also encounter the creation of new rites with intent to replace unwanted customs. A good example is the institution of the big public prayer. The devotional ceremony, lasting 12, 20 or 40 hours, was arranged by order of the government at different times of the year in town and countryside for various reasons (penitence for sins, natural disasters, wars, pestilence etc.). A record of 1594 indicates that it also served to keep people from "playing, dancing and unnecessary roistering and drinking"[17].

Comparing the three approaches to enforce the renouncement from pleasure-seeking lifestyle and promote virtues and moral conduct we can observe that it is the kind of involvement of the target group that makes the main difference: with regard to the staging of Cysat's morality play the participation of the audience can be described as (more or less passive) watching and listening whereas in modified or replaced customs

16 H. Greco-Kaufmann, *Zuo der Eere Gottes*, vol. I, p. 221 ff.
17 H. Greco-Kaufmann, *Zuo der Eere Gottes*, vol. II, p. 295.

the parties affected played an active role. But in any case: during the event people were absorbed and had no time for deleterious carnival activities. Viewing it in this light we may conclude that the two-day spectacle at carnival 1593 was a success–though not really sustainable.

Heidy GRECO-KAUFMANN
Universität Bern

SUIVRE LA LOI OU CONCOURIR AU BIEN COMMUN ?

Les fabriques de paroisse et les lieux de spectacles dans Londres à la fin du XVIe siècle

À la fin du XIXe siècle, E. K. Chambers a produit une lecture politique très étatiste de la naissance et du développement du théâtre public élisabéthain à Londres[1]. Chambers postulait l'existence d'une pyramide descendante de pouvoirs gouvernant les spectacles, dont témoignerait une pyramide de textes législatifs ou règlementaires. La monarchie d'Élisabeth Ire, par l'entremise du Conseil privé, imposerait à la cité de Londres ses choix politiques, juridiques et même esthétiques en matière de spectacles. La seule marge de manœuvre laissée aux élites civiques, Municipalité en tête, gagnées à un protestantisme radical (puritanisme), aurait été de freiner ou d'essayer de raisonner le pouvoir royal afin de faire disparaître ou, tout au moins, de limiter, les spectacles publics dans la ville. Le théâtre public devrait donc sa naissance à la volonté royale dont la loi serait l'instrument privilégié. Le droit, compris comme expression et outil de cette volonté, modèlerait largement le monde social. Ce positionnement historiographique impose de considérer, d'une part, les textes législatifs produits par la monarchie comme absolument performatifs et, d'autre part, les officiers royaux comme les personnages clefs du contrôle des spectacles publics.

L'interprétation proposée par Chambers est restée, jusqu'à aujourd'hui, dominante dans l'historiographie. Elle a, même, trouvé un nouveau souffle dans les années 1980 en entrant en résonance avec les recherches consacrées à la genèse de l'État moderne. La naissance du théâtre public londonien au XVIe siècle devient un marqueur de la construction de l'État

1 E. K. Chambers, *The Elizabethan stage*, Oxford, Clarendon Press, 1923. Sur les présupposés de la lecture produite par Chambers, voir W. R. Streitberger, « Chambers on the Revels Office and Elizabethan Theater History », *Shakespeare Quarterly*, vol. 59/2, 2008, p. 187-209.

monarchique Tudor. Les spectacles publics seraient une occasion pour la royauté d'accroître le champ de son intervention. Cette dernière prendrait les formes concomitantes de l'établissement juridique d'un cadre législatif de plus en plus extensif et de créations empiriques d'offices spécialement dédiés à la gestion des spectacles[2].

La présente étude entend, à rebours de cette interprétation, montrer qu'il n'existe pas de politique claire, systématique et planifiée de la monarchie vis-à-vis des spectacles, qui se traduirait par l'énonciation de lois, règlements, décrets et autres textes. Au contraire, le théâtre public n'a pas été formalisé juridiquement par le système légal élisabéthain, défini comme un outil constitué par et pour la monarchie. L'interprétation traditionnelle repose, en effet, sur un présupposé erroné de ce que sont réellement l'État Tudor et son mode de gouvernement de Londres. Les relations qu'entretiennent le pouvoir monarchique et les institutions urbaines (la Municipalité de Londres, mais aussi les corps de métier et les fabriques de paroisses qui sont de véritables autorités publiques) sont beaucoup plus complexes et moins univalentes que l'on ne l'a cru. Loin d'agencer leur action au service du souverain, les institutions inférieures possèdent une large capacité d'adaptation du droit positif édicté par la monarchie. Cela découle, d'une part, du fait que le corpus légal élisabéthain n'est absolument pas pensé et constitué en un système unifié et, d'autre part, du fait que tout texte édicté par l'autorité centrale est susceptible d'interprétation par des autorités inférieures à l'autonomie grandissante. Or, ces interprétations, parfois divergentes, des lois, sont loin d'être condamnées par la monarchie ; elles font partie du processus normal, mais souvent discret, d'élaboration des pratiques de gouvernement.

L'étude du développement du théâtre public londonien à la fin du XVIe siècle doit donc prendre en compte ce processus de négociation permanent entre les différents pouvoirs élisabéthains. Pour mettre en lumière ce jeu, nous nous proposons d'analyser la place des fabriques de paroisses londoniennes dans le champ politique qu'est le gouvernement des spectacles publics. Dans un premier temps, nous verrons que, malgré le rôle de contrôle des spectacles confié par la législation royale aux

2 Pour des travaux symptomatiques de cette approche, voir J. Clare, *"Art made tongue-tied by authority". Elizabethan and Jacobean dramatic censorship*, Manchester, Manchester University Press, 1999 et R. Dutton, *Mastering the Revels. The regulation and censorship of English Renaissance Drama*, Londres, MacMillan, 1991.

paroisses londoniennes, ces dernières se montrent pour le moins laxistes. On s'interrogera donc sur les raisons qui peuvent expliquer pourquoi les fabriques de paroisse ont, non seulement, toléré le déroulement des spectacles et l'implantation de lieux pour les accueillir, mais les ont également encouragés. Ce questionnement permettra de mettre, en partie, à nu les structures politiques de l'État Tudor.

LA FRÉQUENTATION DES SPECTACLES : UN LAISSER-FAIRE DES OFFICIERS PAROISSIAUX

LES PAROISSES LONDONIENNES, ROUAGE DU CONTRÔLE DES SPECTACLES ?

Londres possède l'un des maillages paroissiaux les plus denses d'Europe. La Cité compte, à elle seule, cent-onze paroisses (soit un ratio de près d'une paroisse pour 1 500 habitants). Durant le règne d'Élisabeth Ire, elles n'ont cessé de prendre de l'importance dans le gouvernement de Londres, la monarchie et la municipalité leur confiant des attributions religieuses et séculières toujours plus nombreuses[3].

Depuis la Réformation henricienne, tous les souverains Tudor ont accordé une grande importance à la sanctification, par leurs sujets, du sabbat mais aussi des fêtes religieuses et du carême. Au cours du XVIe siècle, s'est donc élaboré un cadre législatif destiné à détourner les Londoniens de la fréquentation des spectacles dominicaux. Dans une injonction de 1548, Édouard VI, en tant que « Chef suprême de l'Église d'Angleterre », rappelle en quoi consiste la sanctification du sabbat qu'il attend des fidèles :

> À partir de maintenant, tous les sujets fidèles et aimants du roi célèbreront et fêteront les saints jours selon les saints plaisir et volonté de Dieu, c'est-à-dire qu'ils iront écouter la lecture et l'enseignement de la Parole de Dieu, ils prieront en public et en privé, ils méditeront sur les offenses qu'ils ont faites à Dieu et sur

3 G. Gibbs, « New duties for the parish community in Tudor London », *The parish in English life*, K. French, G. Gibbs et B. Kümin (dir.), Manchester, Manchester University Press, 1997, p. 163-177 et K. Wrightson, « The politics of the Parish in Early Modern England », *The Experience of Authority in Early Modern England*, P. Griffiths, A. Fox et S. Hindle (dir.), Londres, MacMillan, 1996, p. 10-46.

> la façon de les amender, ils se réconcilieront charitablement avec leurs voisins s'ils sont en désaccord, ils recevront régulièrement la communion du corps et du sang du Christ, ils visiteront les pauvres et les malades, ils se comporteront avec la plus grande sobriété et entretiendront des conversations pieuses[4].

Dans ce contexte, les représentations théâtrales dominicales, fort nombreuses, sont doublement illégales : les acteurs devraient s'abstenir de jouer ces jours-là puisqu'il s'agit d'une activité commerciale rémunérée, identique à n'importe quel autre métier. Quant aux spectateurs, assister à une représentation peut difficilement être assimilé à une œuvre pie, d'autant plus que les horaires des représentations empiètent souvent sur ceux des services religieux.

La monarchie confie l'application des lois régulant les spectacles à ses officiers dans les comtés, les *Justices of the Peace*, aux magistrats urbains et, plus spécialement, aux officiers des paroisses, notamment les marguilliers. En effet, du fait de leur proximité avec les gouvernés, les fabriques semblent être le relais institutionnel adéquat pour contrôler l'implantation des lieux de représentations et leur fréquentation par les Londoniens. En 1559, l'acte d'Uniformité adopté par le Parlement pour rétablir le culte protestant en Angleterre, prévoit que toute personne n'assistant pas à l'office dominical devra verser un shilling à la caisse paroissiale d'aide aux pauvres[5]. Les fabriques sont tenues de nommer des officiers pour relever les noms des paroissiens absents. Dans les années 1570, le Parlement durcit ce contrôle et adopte des lois qui chargent les marguilliers d'organiser des rondes dans leur paroisse pendant les offices afin d'identifier les fidèles qui ne se rendent pas au service[6]. Le 13 mars 1579, le Conseil privé réaffirme, pour sa part, l'interdiction de donner des représentations théâtrales durant le carême et signale, une nouvelle fois, le rôle que doivent jouer les autorités locales, dont les paroisses, dans l'application de cette interdiction[7].

---

4 Injonction d'Édouard VI datant de 1548 ou 1549, éditée dans J. E. Cox (éd.), *Miscellaneous writings and letters of Thomas Cranmer*, Cambridge, Parker Society, 1844-1846, vol. 2, p. 502. Marie Ière et Élisabeth Ière reprendront à leur compte, presque mot pour mot, cette définition du sabbat.

5 Act. 1 Eliz. Chap. 2, édité dans *Statutes of the Realm*, Londres, HMSO, 1819, vol. 4/1, p. 355.

6 E. Carlson, « The Origins, Function and Status of the Office of Churchwarden, with Particular Reference to the Diocese of Ely », *The world of rural dissenters, 1520-1725*, M. Spufford (dir.), Cambridge, Cambridge University Press, 1995, p. 164-207, ici p. 172.

7 J. R. Dasent (éd.), *Acts of the Privy Council of England, 1542-1604*, Londres, HMSO, 1890-1907, vol. XI, p. 73-74.

L'ensemble des institutions londoniennes, religieuses comme laïques, relayent des exigences royales et demandent régulièrement aux marguilliers de faire appliquer les lois royales encadrant les spectacles. Ainsi, une entrée datée du 17 janvier 1593 dans les registres de la fabrique de la paroisse Saint-Margaret Lothbury signale que lors d'une visite pastorale, l'évêque de Londres a fait un sévère rappel à la loi : tous les paroissiens doivent assister aux offices dominicaux et nul ne doit travailler en violation du sabbat[8]. Le Lord maire n'est pas en reste. Les préceptes qu'il promulgue sont publiés en chaire par les vicaires, chaque dimanche. En février 1583, la fabrique de la paroisse de Saint-Botolph Aldgate reçoit ainsi une lettre du Lord maire afin que soit donnée la lecture d'un précepte pris le mois précédent sur les mesures à adopter pour faire face à l'épidémie de peste. Parmi celles-ci, figurent la suspension de l'ensemble des spectacles et l'interdiction faite aux Londoniens de les fréquenter[9]. En 1592 encore, le Lord maire suspend toute représentation théâtrale pour cause de peste. La fabrique d'All Hallows Staining reçoit alors un livre résumant les ordres municipaux en matière de peste, pour que ceux-ci soient appliqués[10].

Les paroisses se voient donc confier un rôle clef d'application des lois édictées, rôle d'autant plus important dans une ville où la municipalité et, plus encore le pouvoir royal, n'ont qu'un personnel très réduit pour faire respecter leurs décisions.

UNE ABSENCE DE MISE EN PRATIQUE DE LA PART DES FABRIQUES

Malgré les rappels incessants des autorités municipales, royales et épiscopales, les fabriques ne luttent pas activement, voire tolèrent, l'organisation et la fréquentation des spectacles, y compris le dimanche.

Si les archives attestant directement du laisser-aller des autorités paroissiales sont très rares, les officiers des fabriques sont régulièrement

8 E. Freshfield (éd.), *The vestry minutebook of the Parish of St Margaret Lothbury in the City of London, 1571-1677*, Londres, Rixon and Arnold, 1887, p. 28. Voir également l'article 18 de la visite paroissiale de l'évêque Edwin Sandys faite en 1571, édité dans W. Frere (éd.), *Visitations articles and injunctions of the period of the Reformation*, Londres, Alcuin Club, Longman, 1910, vol. 3, p. 308.

9 T. R. Forbes, *Chronicle from Aldgate. Life and Death in Shakespeare's London*, New Haven, Yale University Press, 1971, p. 122.

10 A. Povah, *The annals of the parishes of St Olave, Hart Street and Allhalows Staining*, Londres, Blades, 1894, p. 307.

accusés par des pamphlétaires puritains d'être les premiers responsables de la violation du sabbat par les Londoniens. Ces officiers tolèreraient les manquements de ceux dont ils ont la charge pour des raisons strictement mondaines, telles que la préservation de la paix sociale au sein de la communauté de voisinage. Le prédicateur Christopher Fetherston, par exemple, accuse les marguilliers d'être des officiers deux fois parjures : ils dérogent à leur « devoir de magistrats chrétiens » en ne faisant pas respecter les commandements divins, dont la sanctification du sabbat, mais ils méprisent également leur « devoir d'officiers royaux » en bafouant les lois civiles[11].

Ces accusations se vérifient en partie. Durant les années 1580-1600, les troupes d'acteurs donnent très régulièrement des représentations dominicales. Pourtant, aucun acteur ne semble avoir été arrêté par les marguilliers. Quant au nombre de paroissiens londoniens traduits devant les cours ecclésiastiques pour avoir été à un spectacle plutôt qu'à l'office, il est infinitésimal, alors même que les divertissements drainent plusieurs milliers de spectateurs tous les jours. Les marguilliers refusent, la plupart du temps, de punir directement ou de déférer ceux qui ne viennent pas aux offices pour des raisons qui ne sont pas religieuses[12]. Lorsqu'un laïc qui n'a pas honoré le sabbat est convoqué devant une juridiction ecclésiastique, celle-ci ne peut le contraindre à comparaître. Elle doit avoir recours au bras séculier, ici les fabriques de paroisse, qui se montrent peu enclines à obéir à ce type de demandes[13]. Certains évêques constatent même que les officiers paroissiaux ne lèvent pas les amendes sur ceux qui ne se rendent pas au service[14].

11 C. Fetherston, *A dialogue agaynst light, lewde, and lascivious dauncing*, Londres, Thomas Dawson, 1582, p. C4v.

12 Pour l'archidiaconé de Norwich entre 1576 et 1580, seuls 15 % des cas traités par la cour ecclésiastique relèvent d'une violation du sabbat. La quasi-totalité des accusés ont été déférés pour avoir travaillé le dimanche, et non pour s'être livrés à des divertissements. K. Parker, *The English Sabbath : a study of doctrine and discipline from the Reformation to the Civil War*, Cambridge, Cambridge University Press, 1988, p. 64.

13 R. Houlbrooke, *Church courts and the people during the English Reformation, 1520-1570*, Oxford, Oxford University Press, 1979, p. 252.

14 *Ibid.*, p. 154.

REPENSER LE MODE DE FONCTIONNEMENT DE L'ÉTAT TUDOR

Pour comprendre l'absence du respect des lois par des autorités publiques censées les appliquer, il faut avoir à l'esprit que les procédés de gouvernement des institutions londoniennes sous les Tudors répondent moins aux impératifs du respect d'un droit positif qu'à la consonance des décisions à une idéologie politique, le bien commun.

AU CŒUR DE L'IDÉOLOGIE POLITIQUE TUDOR : LE *COMMON WEAL*

Depuis une dizaine d'années, les historiens ont mis en exergue l'importance de la notion de bien commun (*common weal*) dans la pensée et les discours politiques de l'époque Tudor. Le terme de *common weal*, très présent dans les archives des institutions londoniennes, recouvre deux notions politiques qui doivent être distinguées[15]. Dès le XVe siècle, ce terme est utilisé par certains auteurs pour traduire l'expression latine *res publica*, issue de la pensée politique aristotélicienne revue par Cicéron[16]. Le *common weal* se définit alors au XVIe siècle comme « les moyens d'atteindre une bonne vie, grâce à laquelle chaque citoyen et sa maisonnée peuvent remplir leur potentiel moral et économique tout en servant et tirant profit simultanément de ce bien commun ou public[17] ». Le bien commun revêt une dimension chrétienne puisque le bien par excellence est la sanctification collective et individuelle[18].

Le *common weal* doit donc se réaliser dans une structure institutionnelle. Celle-ci est toujours pensée à l'époque moderne sous la forme

15 G. Baldwin, « The "public" as a rhetorical community in early modern England », *Communities in early modern England*, A. Shepard et Ph. Withington (dir.), Manchester, Manchester University Press, 2000, p. 199-215, p. 201.

16 Sur l'importance du *De officis* de Cicéron dans l'Angleterre Tudor, voir S. Hindle, « Law, law enforcement and state formation in early modern England », *Staatsbildung als kultureller Prozess*, R. Asch et D. Freist (dir.), Cologne, Auflage, 2005, p. 209-233, p. 213.

17 Ph. Withington, « Agency, Custom and the English Corporate System », *Identity and Agency in early modern England*, J. Barry et H. French (dir.), Basingstoke, Palgrave MacMillan, 2004, p. 200-222, p. 209.

18 A. Guéry, « L'État. L'outil du bien commun », *Les lieux de mémoire. Volume III. Les Frances*, P. Nora (dir.), Paris, Gallimard, 1992, p. 819-867, p. 827.

de la métaphore du corps naturel, création divine. Au sein du corps, chaque organe doit accéder à un certain bien vivre pour que l'ensemble du corps prospère et réciproquement[19]. Pour définir ce cadre socio-politique institutionnalisé dont le but idéal est de réaliser le *common weal*, on utilise le terme de *common wealth*.

Le royaume d'Angleterre, en tant que régime institutionnel, est qualifié de *common wealth*, de même que les corps politiques inférieurs, comme les cités. Ainsi dans le *De Republica Anglorum* (1583), Thomas Smith, serviteur expérimenté de la monarchie Tudor, définit le *common wealth* anglais idéal comme un grand corps politique composé de corps politiques inférieurs, eux-mêmes composés d'une multitude d'individus[20]. Ces corps autonomes entretiennent entre eux des rapports harmonieux et vertueux, au service d'un ordre social et politique apaisé visant, *in fine*, à la sanctification de tous[21]. Pour cela, les élites socio-politiques qui gouvernent chaque *common wealth* doivent toujours avoir pour mission d'assurer le *common weal* de leur corps pour assurer celui du corps plus vaste. Chaque corps et chaque Anglais, en respectant sa place, participe politiquement à chaque *common wealth* et concourt au *common weal*[22]. *Le common weal*, sorte de norme supra-juridique, définit donc les principes du gouvernement de la Cité, alors que celle de *common wealth* donne des instruments pour la gouverner. Les historiens ne se sont, pendant longtemps, intéressés qu'au *common wealth*, considérant *common weal* comme une simple variante orthographique de ce dernier.

LES FABRIQUES PAROISSIALES COMME *COMMON WEALTH*

C'est dans ce cadre idéologique qu'il faut comprendre le refus des fabriques de se plier aux exigences quant aux spectacles des autorités municipales et royales. Durant la seconde moitié du XVIe siècle, les

---

19 Pour la conception en partie différente du « bien commun » dans l'humanisme civique italien du XVe siècle, voir Q. Skinner, *Les fondements de la pensée politique moderne*, Paris, Albin Michel, 2001, p. 80-86.

20 T. Smith, *De republica Anglorum. The maner of governement or policie of the realme of Englande*, Londres, 1583.

21 Londres s'inscrit dans une évolution européenne. Voir, pour les villes de la France du Nord, G. Saupin, « Les corps de ville dans la France moderne. Tendances historiographiques récentes », *Le bulletin de la S.H.M.C.*, nº 3-4, 2000, p. 123-135.

22 A. McLaren, *Political culture in the reign of Elizabeth I*, Cambridge, Cambridge University Press, 1999.

fabriques évoluent pour répondre aux missions qui leur sont confiées : elles se considèrent désormais comme des *common wealthes* autonomes à l'intérieur du *common wealth* civique. Les membres de la fabrique se posent en représentants naturels de la communauté paroissiale et affirment leur légitimité à gouverner l'ensemble des affaires locales[23]. Loin d'obéir servilement à la législation produite par les pouvoirs centraux, les fabriques estiment être plus à même que ces derniers à déterminer ce qu'est l'intérêt de la communauté dont elles sont les premiers gouvernants mais aussi les premiers représentants. Leurs actions politiques visent alors à un perpétuel accommodement entre les ordres qui leur sont donnés et leur propre conception du *common weal* paroissial. Celui-ci repose avant tout sur l'idée de « fraternité » entre voisins, fraternité dont la communauté paroissiale serait la dépositaire et la gardienne. Ainsi, en 1574, la fabrique de la paroisse d'All Hallows Staining affirme solennellement qu'elle prendra à l'avenir toutes ses décisions en ayant à l'esprit le « maintien de l'amitié entre voisins et de l'amour fraternel », car la première nécessité d'une fabrique est de « faire croître l'amour fraternel et la charité entre nous, comme de bons chrétiens doivent le faire[24] ». Les élites paroissiales londoniennes (et plus généralement les élites civiques) sont donc partagées entre la loyauté monarchique, les nécessités d'obéissance aux gouvernants urbains et leur rôle de protecteurs de leurs gouvernés[25]. Les fabriques ont une position d'interface entre le pouvoir royal et la communauté locale. Elles assurent les tâches parfois contradictoires d'assurer le *common weal* paroissial tout en exécutant les demandes de la politique royale, tant en matière de religion que de police urbaine[26].

La notion de *common weal* invite à donner un sens nouveau au mille-feuille politique qu'est Londres à la fin du XVIe siècle. Chacune des institutions civiques (municipalité, corps de métier, paroisses) se définit

23 J. F. Merritt, « Contested legitimacy and the ambiguous rise of vestries in early modern London », *The Historical Journal*, vol. 54/1, 2011, p. 25-45.

24 *Ibid.*, p. 27.

25 Les relations entre les corporations de métiers et la municipalité sont empruntes des mêmes logiques politiques, voir O. Spina, « La mise en jeu de l'honneur : les cérémonies et leurs acteurs à Londres à la fin du XVIe siècle », *Penser et vivre l'honneur à l'époque moderne*, H. Drévillon et D. Venturino (dir.), Rennes, Presses Universitaires de Rennes, 2010, p. 319-333.

26 J. S. Craig, « Cooperation and initiatives : Elizabethan churchwardens and the parish accounts of Mildenhall », *Social history*, vol. 18/3, 1993, p. 357-380, ici p. 359.

comme un *common wealth* devant veiller au *common weal* de ses membres. Les officiers doivent certes servir leur souverain, mais ils doivent avant tout veiller au *bien commun* de la communauté dont ils ont la charge. La sphère politique du Londres du XVIe siècle ne peut donc être réduite à une simple pyramide institutionnelle dont la monarchie serait le sommet. Or, face à des situations particulières, chacune de ces institutions ne conçoit pas de la même façon ce qu'est le *bien commun*, ce qui crée un espace de « jeu » entre les différentes institutions. Du « jeu » non seulement pour que chaque institution élabore ses propres pratiques et discours de pouvoir, mais du « jeu » également pour interpréter et manipuler à son profit les pratiques et discours de pouvoir d'autres institutions.

OBÉIR À LA MONARCHIE OU RÉALISER LE BIEN COMMUN ? L'exemple de la construction des amphithéâtres

L'attitude des différentes autorités face aux spectacles publics londoniens doit donc être réinscrite dans ce réseau dynamique de pouvoirs dont les équilibres sont en perpétuelle négociation. Moins qu'une politique élisabéthaine des spectacles centralisée et formalisée dans un cadre juridique rigide, il existe un champ de forces dynamique et complexe qui crée de multiples possibilités d'accommodement pour les producteurs et les spectateurs du théâtre public. L'étude de la construction des amphithéâtres londoniens à la fin du XVIe siècle et de la façon dont les fabriques de paroisse ont accueilli ces nouveaux arrivants révèle les processus gouvernementaux de l'État Tudor.

Dans le Londres des années 1590, période de crise économique et sociale aiguë, la monarchie comme la municipalité considèrent de plus en plus que les spectacles menacent l'ordre public de la ville[27]. Elles

27 La monarchie durcit son action après l'affaire de l'*Île des chiens* qui éclate durant l'été 1597. Le Conseil privé fait arrêter plusieurs acteurs à la suite de représentations au *Swan* de cette pièce, alors que tout spectacle avait été interdit quelques semaines auparavant. Voir O. Spina, « L'acteur tient-il la plume du dramaturge ? Étude historique de la place des acteurs au sein du système dramatique élisabéthain », *Histoire, économie & société*, vol. 3, 2008, p. 17-29.

craignent les attroupements de centaines de spectateurs que l'on présente comme des pauvres et des brigands désocialisés[28]. Malgré cela, les fabriques de paroisses tolèrent ouvertement la présence de ces spectacles sur leur territoire, et ne font pas toujours appliquer les différentes lois encadrant les représentations théâtrales.

SAINT SAVIOUR'S HIGH STREET : LES SPECTACLES AU SERVICE DES PAUVRES

Les registres des réunions de la fabrique de la paroisse de Saint Saviour's High Street à Southwark, qui abrite, dans le dernier quart du XVIe siècle, deux amphithéâtres (et même trois durant une brève période) et une arène de combat d'animaux, sont, malgré leur caractère lapidaire et lacunaire, précieux pour éclairer les rapports entre les lieux de spectacles et les autorités paroissiales. Saint-Saviour's a la particularité d'être, depuis 1550, située, pour partie, dans la juridiction de la Cité de Londres (*ward* de Bridge Ward Without) et, pour l'autre, dans le Surrey (manoirs de Paris Garden et de The Clink)[29]. Depuis 1557, elle est dirigée par une *selected vestry*, c'est-à-dire que les membres de la fabrique ne sont pas élus par l'ensemble des paroissiens, mais cooptés par les habitants les plus prééminents[30]. De plus, de création récente (1550), le *ward* Bridge Ward Without compte, hormis l'alderman et son député, très peu d'officiers municipaux. La fabrique y est donc la seule autorité publique. En outre, les élites de Saint-Saviour's sont traditionnellement considérées comme acquises aux idées réformées les plus avancées, puisque, entre 1570 et 1620, les prédicateurs qui sont engagés par la fabrique sont des *godlies*[31].

Le 20 avril 1598, la fabrique dépêche les marguilliers auprès de Francis Langley et Philip Henslowe, respectivement propriétaires des amphithéâtres le *Swan* et le *Rose*, et de Jacob Meade, gardien des ours royaux, qui donne

28 Voir, par exemple, la décision du Conseil privé du 29 juillet 1593, *ACP*, vol. 24, p. 427-429 ou, pour la municipalité, la lettre du Lord Maire à Lord Burghley datée du 3 novembre 1594, London Metropole Archives (désormais LMA), Remembrancia II, n° 73, fol. 33-33v.

29 Vers 1600, moins de la moitié des paroissiens vivent dans la juridiction civique. J. Boulton, « The limits of formal religion : the administration of holy communion in late Elizabethan and early Stuart London », *London Journal*, vol. 10, 1984, p. 135-154, p. 137.

30 J. Boulton, *Neighbourghood and society. A London suburb in the seventeenth century*, Cambridge, Cambridge University Press, 1987, p. 265-266.

31 P. Seaver, *The Puritan Lectureships. The Politics of Religious Dissent 1560-1662*, Stanford, Stanford University Press, 1970, p. 217.

des combats publics d'animaux à Paris Garden. Les marguilliers doivent discuter avec ces personnes, qu'ils qualifient avec déférence de « maîtres », « de l'argent pour les pauvres, eu égard à leurs pièces[32] ». Jusqu'à cette date, aucune occurrence de la présence de ces théâtres n'était apparue dans les archives paroissiales, alors que le *Rose*, par exemple, fonctionne depuis dix ans. Cette irruption tient sans doute à l'adoption par le Parlement, au début de l'année 1598, de l'acte sur les pauvres. Il vise à apporter une solution à une situation économique et sociale très tendue, surtout à Londres, où dans le dernier quart du XVIe siècle, le nombre de pauvres a largement cru. Les fabriques se voient confier l'entretien des nécessiteux de leur paroisse et doivent créer des offices de surveillants des pauvres[33]. Une telle politique d'assistance est d'autant plus nécessaire à Saint-Saviour's que la paroisse est en pleine explosion démographique (la population passe d'environ 3 000 habitants en 1547 à plus de 7 000 en 1603) et qu'elle a connu, en 1597, un pic de mortalité très important à cause d'une épidémie et des hausses importantes du prix des grains[34].

En avril 1598, la fabrique semble donc avoir cherché à faire payer aux propriétaires de lieux de représentations, en sus des dîmes qu'ils versent déjà comme tous les autres paroissiens, une taxe spécifiquement destinée à financer l'aide aux pauvres dont le Parlement lui a confié la charge. Cependant, ces propriétaires semblent peu enclins à satisfaire les demandes de la paroisse puisque, lors de la réunion suivante de la fabrique, le 1er mai 1598, la question est de nouveau débattue. Il est décidé que Langley, Henslowe et Meade doivent être *moved*, c'est-à-dire démarchés, travaillés au corps, pour s'acquitter de cette taxe sur les lieux de spectacles[35]. Brusquement, lors de la réunion suivante, le 19 juillet 1598, après l'élection de nouveaux marguilliers, le ton change radicalement :

> Premièrement, il a été ordonné, lors de cette fabrique, qu'une pétition soit adressée au Conseil [privé] à propos des théâtres de cette paroisse dans laquelle seront exposées les énormités qui menacent notre paroisse, et afin que ces théâtres ne puissent plus accueillir de représentations et soient détruits. Quatre ou deux de nos marguilliers, M. Howse, M. Ironmonger, ou l'un d'entre eux,

32 Réunion de la fabrique du 20 avril 1598, archives de la fabrique, LMA P92/SAV/450, p. 323.

33 Act. 39 Eliz., Cap. 4, édité dans *Statutes of the Realm*, Londres, HMSO, 1819, vol. 4/2, p. 916. P. Slack, *Poverty and Policy in Tudor and Stuart England*, Londres, Longman, 1988, p. 126-129.

34 J. Boulton, *Neighbourhood and Society…*, *op. cit.*, p. 19 et p. 42.

35 Réunion de la fabrique du 1er mai 1598, LMA P92/SAV/450, p. 324.

> présenteront cette pétition avec un des collecteurs pour le Boroughside et un autre pour Bankside[36].

La rhétorique adoptée ici varie considérablement par rapport à celle des précédentes entrées. Elle emprunte, de façon inédite, au registre de la condamnation politique et morale utilisé dans certains préceptes municipaux ou dans des pamphlets *godlies* hostiles au théâtre. Une telle évolution ne s'explique pas par un changement de personnel à la tête de la fabrique : sur les 17 participants à cette réunion, 12 étaient déjà présents le 1er mai et 9 aux deux réunions précédentes traitant de la négociation avec les propriétaires de lieux de représentation. Ils ne montraient alors aucune hostilité aux spectacles. De plus, plusieurs de ces membres sont des voisins et des relations d'Henslowe et de Langley. Comment, dès lors, expliquer le passage du ton déférent des premières entrées aux rudes condamnations contenues dans la prise de position du 19 juillet ?

Le changement d'attitude de la fabrique s'explique sans doute moins par une altération subite du regard porté sur les représentations théâtrales que par le refus réitéré des propriétaires de lieux de spectacle de participer au financement de l'aide aux pauvres. En pétitionnant le Conseil privé, qui, après plusieurs incidents survenus dans des amphithéâtres au cours des années 1590, devait se montrer attentif à ces questions, la fabrique reprend à son compte la rhétorique du danger des pièces de théâtre. Il s'agit donc d'une manœuvre visant à intimider Langley, Henslowe et Meade pour qu'ils acceptent de s'acquitter de ce nouveau prélèvement. Cette stratégie explique que, parmi la délégation que Saint-Saviour's envoie auprès du Conseil privé, figurent les deux collecteurs des pauvres qui ont été nommés dans les premiers mois de l'année 1598[37]. Il est également possible que, parallèlement, la fabrique ait menacé les propriétaires d'être moins tolérante vis-à-vis de leurs infractions à la législation royale. Cette stratégie porte ses fruits : les propriétaires de lieux de représentation s'acquittent rapidement des sommes demandées et on ne trouve, par la suite, plus aucun signe d'hostilité aux spectacles dans les registres de la fabrique. La menace de respecter enfin les lois édictées est donc utilisée par les marguilliers de Saint Saviour's comme une arme dans le rapport de force qui les opposent à Langley, Henslowe et Meade.

---

36 Réunion de la fabrique du 19 juillet 1598, *ibid.*, p. 325.

37 LMA P92/SAV/1396.

Dans les années qui suivent, la fabrique pérennise cette levée d'argent. Lors de la réunion de fabrique du 28 mars 1600, il est décidé que les marguilliers « rencontreront les acteurs », sans doute, la troupe du Lord chambellan, à laquelle appartient Shakespeare, pour établir les dîmes que ces derniers devront payer, ainsi que pour trouver un accord sur les prélèvements pour les pauvres[38]. À la fin de l'année 1599, ces acteurs se sont installés sur Bankside dans un amphithéâtre fraîchement construit, le *Globe*. Ils sont les interlocuteurs des autorités paroissiales parce qu'ils ont financé en grande partie son édification et ils en sont donc propriétaires majoritaires.

CONFLIT DE NORMES : LA CONSTRUCTION DU FORTUNE

Saint-Saviour's est rapidement imitée par les autres paroisses qui accueillent ou comptent accueillir des lieux de représentations, à l'instar de la paroisse de Saint-Giles Cripplegate dans le nord de Londres. En janvier 1600, Edward Alleyn, acteur dans la troupe de l'Amiral d'Angleterre, et son beau-père Philip Henslowe, déjà propriétaire du *Rose*, initient la construction d'un nouveau théâtre, le *Fortune*, sur le territoire de Saint-Giles, dans la partie de la paroisse relevant du comté de Middlesex[39]. Quelques jours après la signature du contrat de construction du théâtre, le Lord amiral Nottingham, sans doute à la requête d'Alleyn, écrit une lettre aux *Justices of the Peace* du Middlesex et à l'ensemble des officiers du comté. Il leur recommande de faire bon accueil à cette construction destinée à accueillir une troupe autorisée à jouer dans Londres par le Conseil privé pour « préparer » les représentations qu'elle donne à la cour lors des festivités. En effet, selon Nottingham, le théâtre que la troupe de l'Amiral occupait jusqu'alors, le *Curtain*, serait dans un état tel qu'il menace de s'effondrer, rendant impossible son utilisation[40]. L'amiral affirme, de plus, que comme la reine « est gracieusement disposée à leur égard », l'ensemble des officiers royaux doivent tolérer et même faciliter l'édification de ce théâtre.

38 Réunion de la fabrique du 28 mars 1600, LMA P92/SAV/450, p. 339.

39 Alleyn acquiert le bail du terrain le 22 décembre 1599, D. Kathman, « Citizens, Innholders and Playhouse Builders… », art. cité. Le contrat de construction du théâtre est signé entre Alleyn, Henslowe et Peter Streete le 8 janvier 1600, R. A. Foakes, *Henslowe's Diary*, Cambridge, Cambridge University Press, 2002, p. 306-310.

40 Lettre éditée dans *ibid.*, p. 288.

Cependant, Saint-Giles Cripplegate compte un grand nombre de paroissiens aux convictions religieuses radicales[41]. Le 9 mars 1600, plusieurs gentlemen et autres habitants de la paroisse, et, parmi eux, Lord Willoughby dont le calvinisme est très marqué, présentent une pétition au Conseil privé[42]. Willoughby et les autres signataires y prennent à leur compte, eux aussi, le discours municipal sur le danger moral et politique des pièces de théâtre. Ils affirment que non seulement la construction d'un théâtre viole la loi royale, mais qu'en sus ce lieu risquerait de créer de « grands désordres » dans la paroisse car il y attirerait des « gens de basse extraction et louches ». Après lecture de la pétition, le Conseil privé souscrit à cette analyse et charge les *Justices of the Peace* du Middlesex de faire détruire la partie de l'édifice déjà construite. Il confie l'application de cet ordre à William Waad, *Justice* du Middlesex, mais surtout clerc du Conseil. L'ordre est contresigné par l'amiral lui-même, mais aussi par le Lord chambellan autre protecteur d'une troupe de théâtre. L'éthos aristocratique du conseiller semble donc plus important que la protection des acteurs, simples serviteurs de second rang.

L'affaire rebondit dans les jours qui suivent, puisqu'une autre pétition est produite au Conseil. Ses rédacteurs, des officiers de la paroisse de Saint-Giles Cripplegate, implorent les conseillers privés d'autoriser la construction du nouveau théâtre dans leur paroisse :

> De par la construction dudit théâtre, une part très importante de l'argent qui y sera gagné hebdomadairement sera versée à notre paroisse au bénéfice de nos pauvres, dont le nombre et les besoins sont si importants ; [cet argent] contribuera largement et régulièrement à l'aide qui leur est apportée. [...] Nous nous satisfaisons tout à fait de ce moyen pour l'entretien de nos pauvres, car notre paroisse n'a pas les moyens de les soutenir[43].

Parmi les vingt-huit signataires de cette pétition figurent les deux surveillants des pauvres de la paroisse et les principaux membres de la fabrique. Saint-Giles a, comme plusieurs autres paroisses, le plus grand mal à venir en aide à ses pauvres résidents. En 1598, à la suite de plusieurs années de

41 Robert Crowley, figure importante du radicalisme protestant, a occupé la charge de vicaire de la paroisse pendant plus de vingt ans. W. Denton, *Records of St Giles Cripplegate*, Londres, Bell, 1883.

42 Lettre du Conseil privé du 9 mars 1600 aux *Justices of the Peace* du Middlesex, *APC*, vol. 30, p. 146.

43 J. P. Collier (éd.), *Memoirs of Edward Alleyn*, Londres, The Shakespeare Society, 1841, p. 58.

crise économique, la municipalité établit une liste répertoriant le nombre de pauvres dans 102 paroisses londoniennes et le compare aux ressources locales (revenus à destination des pauvres, dons charitables, capacité de prélèvement sur les riches) afin de transférer de l'argent des paroisses les mieux loties vers celles qui le sont moins[44]. Parmi les vingt-et-une paroisses incapables de financer de façon autonome leur politique charitable, figure Saint-Giles. Ces transferts financiers entre paroisses organisés par la municipalité ne semblent pas suffire à assurer l'entretien des pauvres de la paroisse. L'implantation rémunératrice d'un théâtre permettrait à la fabrique de regagner une part de son autonomie financière et politique vis-à-vis de la municipalité. En effet, cette taxe sur les lieux de spectacles est perçue au *prorata* des recettes et ces dernières sont particulièrement importantes les jours de fêtes religieuses et les dimanches, jours de représentations légalement interdits... Non seulement les fabriques acceptent la présence des acteurs, mais elles ferment les yeux sur les violations des lois car elles ont tout intérêt à ce que les spectacles soient donnés le plus souvent possible et qu'ils soient très fréquentés.

Cette pétition porte ses fruits. Le 8 avril 1600, le Lord amiral, le Lord chambellan et le secrétaire du Conseil, Robert Cecil, envoient une nouvelle lettre aux officiers royaux du Middlesex pour les informer de l'aval du Conseil à la construction du *Fortune.* La lettre reprend une partie des arguments utilisés par Nottingham, notamment celui de la décrépitude du *Curtain*, le seul nouvel argument invoqué est :

> Que ce lieu est particulièrement adapté à cette activité, comme cela nous l'a été certifié par de nombreux habitants de la liberté de Finsbury dont ce lieu relève, et comme cela nous a été recommandé par certains *Justices of the Peace* eux-mêmes[45].

La pétition des habitants de Saint-Giles est donc présentée comme le motif principal du changement d'avis du Conseil et de la décision d'avaliser l'édification du *Fortune.* Cet argument n'est peut-être qu'un moyen de masquer d'intenses et longues tractations au sein du Conseil privé et à la cour entre le Lord amiral et d'autres conseillers, peu enclins à favoriser la construction sauvage de théâtres aux abords de Londres. Mais une

44 S. Rappaport, *Worlds within worlds. Structures of life in sixteenth century London*, Cambridge, Cambridge University Press, 1989, p. 171-172.

45 Lettre éditée dans R. A. Foakes, *Henslowe's Diary...*, *op. cit.*, p. 290.

autre interprétation ne peut être écartée. Il est possible que le Conseil ait entendu les arguments des nombreux officiers royaux et paroissiaux. L'autorisation du *Fortune* serait une forme de réponse à une demande sociale articulée selon tous les canons du langage politique Tudor (le *common weal*) et portée par les élites locales reconnues (la fabrique et les *Justices of the Peace*). Or, la légitimité du gouvernement royal à diriger le *common wealth* anglais repose sur sa capacité à répondre, au moins en partie, aux demandes des institutions inférieures. Le Conseil privé apparaît, dans cette affaire, moins comme un lieu d'élaboration d'une politique qu'un lieu d'arbitrage entre les différentes logiques de pouvoir verticales et horizontales, au sein duquel est formulé un discours unique capable de satisfaire toutes les aspirations politiques perçues comme légitimes.

CONCLUSION
Existe-t-il une politique Tudor des spectacles ?

En définitive, il n'y a pas, comme on l'a longtemps cru, opposition entre des institutions civiques hostiles aux spectacles et une monarchie défendant ces derniers. La tolérance des marguilliers vis-à-vis des spectacles dans des paroisses traditionnellement qualifiées de radicale et en proie à des difficultés de maintien de l'ordre, s'explique par le fait que les organisateurs de divertissements versent une partie de leurs gains aux fabriques pour l'entretien des pauvres. Les acteurs, comme les propriétaires de lieux de spectacles, loin d'être perçus comme des marginaux, sont des interlocuteurs valables pour les fabriques[46]. Ils ont, par ailleurs, très bien compris l'intérêt qu'ils avaient à légitimer leur activité en mettant en avant leur nouveau rôle social de pourvoyeurs de revenus pour les nécessiteux, eux que l'on accusait de pousser les pauvres londoniens à dépenser leur argent de façon inconsidérée. Ainsi, la fréquentation des représentations, souvent présentée dans les textes antithéâtraux comme

46 Edward Alleyn et Phillip Henslowe sont même cooptés dans la fabrique de Saint-Saviour en 1607. I. W. Archer, « The City of London and the theatre », *The Oxford handbook of early modern Theatre*, R. Dutton (dir.), Oxford, Oxford University Press, 2009, p. 396-412, ici p. 400.

un danger pour la survie du *common weal* londonien, a été utilisée comme un moyen de lever de l'argent pour assurer la cohésion du *common weal* paroissial et, par-delà, du *common weal* londonien lui-même.

L'étude des rapports entre les paroisses et les lieux de spectacles de la fin du XVIe siècle montre, ainsi, que l'architecture juridique censée encadrer le théâtre n'existe pas en soi. Paradoxalement, le renforcement des attributions confiées par l'État Tudor aux fabriques de paroisses conduit celles-ci à faire des choix qui peuvent brouiller la politique monarchique autant que la politique municipale en matière de spectacles. Le soutien par l'institution locale paroissiale et la légitimation par l'esprit de la politique chrétienne l'emportent sur la lettre des lois élisabéthaines. Les paroisses ne sont donc pas qu'un rouage de l'administration civique ou royale : elles en sont un acteur à part entière[47].

Il semble que, aux yeux des gouvernants, prédomine la nécessité de répondre aux attentes d'un *common weal* chrétien, dont le contenu et les modalités ne sont jamais définis précisément, sans pour autant que l'obligation de s'y référer pour définir les actions politiques légitimes soit remise en cause et soit éclipsée par un légalisme strict qui consisterait en un respect du droit positif. Les textes législatifs se révèlent être moins des discours performatifs visant à modeler le réel qu'un objet de dialogue et d'ajustements entre les différents protagonistes du *common wealth* londonien. Ainsi, d'une part, la prise de décision au sein de la monarchie élisabéthaine résulte de processus sociaux, politiques et économiques multiples qui conduisent les autorités à faire évoluer ou même à ignorer les lois et les directives adoptées précédemment ; d'autre part, la législation est un cadre soumis à négociation et redéfinition au sein du champ de forces politiques que dessinent les différentes institutions londoniennes. La portée des textes législatifs est perpétuellement négociée dans la mise en pratique de ces derniers.

Olivier SPINA
Université Lumière Lyon 2

47 M. Berlin, « Reordering rituals : ceremony and the parish, 1520-1640 », *Londinopolis. Essays in the cultural and social history of early modern London*, P. Griffiths et Marc S. R. Jenner (dir.), Manchester, Manchester University Press, 2000, p. 47-66.

TROISIÈME PARTIE

CONFLITS ET PROCÈS

ÉTUDES DE CAS

QUAND UN HONORABLE BOURGEOIS DE MALINES,

« marié avec une bonne et honeste femme », s'encanaille dans une troupe de théâtre en marge de la bonne société (1475)

Une première distinction pour les types de théâtre médiéval est celle entre le théâtre organisé et subventionné par des autorités publiques d'une part, et le spectacle spontané des rues et des places d'autre part. Dans le premier secteur, on distingue la culture courtoise des jongleurs et joueurs de farces qui s'exhibaient dans les cours princières de l'Europe, et, d'autre part, le théâtre urbain, soit ecclésiastique, soit bourgeois. Dans les trois circonstances, les activités se déroulent dans un cadre bien structuré : la cour princière, la paroisse, les organisations urbaines des chambres de rhétorique. À la cour, les artistes sont d'habitude des professionnels, par contre, dans les villes, les rhétoriciens sont souvent des amateurs locaux[1]. Aux anciens Pays-Bas, entre 1400 et 1650, on estime la présence d'environ 220 chambres de rhétorique et associations littéraires qui employaient des poètes et des musiciens locaux[2]. Dans tous ces cas, il existait un financement plus ou moins « officiel » : le troubadour reçoit un salaire ou un forfait, le groupe urbain une subvention ou une rémunération par prestation[3]. Souvent cependant les artistes refusaient de se plier aux attentes idéologiques de la cour et des magistrats urbains, ce qui amenait parfois les mécènes à supprimer leurs subsides[4]. En dehors de ces circuits « officiels » il existait

1 A. E. Knight (dir.), *The Stage as Mirror. Civic Theatre in Late Medieval Europe*, Cambridge, Brewer, 1997, p. 1-5.

2 A.-L. Van Bruaene, *Om beters wille : Rederijkerskamers en de stedelijke cultuur in de Zuidelijke Nederlanden (1400-1650)*, Amsterdam, Amsterdam University Press, 2008, p. 20.

3 K. Lavéant, *Un théâtre des frontières. La culture dramatique dans les provinces du Nord aux XVe et XVIe siècles*, Orléans, Paradigme, 2011, mentionne des subsides à des compagnies joyeuses de Lille à Ypres en 1425 (p. 449 et p. 484).

4 G. Nijsten, « Feasts and Public Spectacle : Late Medieval Drama and Performance in the Low Countries », A. E. Knight (dir.), *The Stage as Mirror. Civic Theatre in Late Medieval*

du théâtre et des spectacles spontanés, incrustés dans la vie populaire du « petit peuple », des hommes et des femmes soi-disant « sans histoire ». Surtout pendant les jours de carnaval, les gens du commun organisaient des cortèges et des représentations satiriques, des fêtes de renversement du genre « Blauwe Schuit » (Bateau Bleu), dans lesquelles ils pouvaient librement exprimer leurs frustrations et leur critique sociale sous forme de satire sur les abus des dirigeants de la ville et des bourgeois aisés.

Une seconde distinction typologique est celle entre acteurs professionnels et amateurs. Les amateurs sont, en général, les membres des chambres de rhétorique et les participants aux fêtes urbaines improvisées. Parmi les professionnels, il faut mentionner d'abord les artistes individuels, ménestrels, musiciens, déclamateurs, auteurs et acteurs, engagés par les princes pour se charger des divertissements à leur cour. Déjà au XIIe siècle il existait cette brillante activité littéraire et artistique à la cour d'Éléonore d'Aquitaine, de Marie de Champagne et de Philippe d'Alsace en Flandre[5]. Au XIIIe siècle, le même type d'artistes est également accueilli pour les fêtes qu'organisent les bourgeois des villes, telle celle d'Arras, qui n'hésite pas à donner un podium à des auteurs du niveau d'Adam de la Halle. À partir de la deuxième moitié du XIVe siècle apparaissent dans les anciens Pays-Bas les « gesellen van den spele » (« compagnons de jeux »). Selon Theo Meder[6], Herman Pleij[7] et Herman Brinkman[8], il s'agit souvent de déclamateurs individuels, mais parfois de vraies troupes de théâtre qui jouent en premier lieu dans leur propre ville, et très sporadiquement dans d'autres endroits[9].

Brinkman hésite cependant à considérer ces « gesellen van den spele » comme de vrais professionnels, et préfère réserver ce terme pour une

Europe, Cambridge, Brewer, 1997, p. 107-143.

5 M. D. Stanger, « Literary Patronage at the Medieval Court of Flanders », *French Studies*, 11 (1957), p. 214-229.

6 Th. Meder, « Omstreeks 1266. In *Der naturen bloeme* worden sprooksprekers en acteurs vergeleken met een Vlaamse gaai. De vroegste bronnen van het wereldlijk theater », R. L. Erenstein (dir.), *Een theatergeschiedenis der Nederlanden : tien eeuwen drama en theater in Nederland en Vlaanderen*, Amsterdam, Amsterdam University Press, 1996, p. 16-23.

7 H. Pleij, « Volksfeest en toneel in de middeleeuwen. II. Entertainers en akteurs », *De Revisor*, 4 (1977), p. 34-41.

8 H. Brinkman, « Spelen om den brode : het vroegste beroepstoneel in de Nederlanden », *Literatuur*, 17 (2000), p. 98-106.

9 Gl. Wickham, *The Medieval Theatre*, 3e éd., Cambridge, Cambridge University Press, 1987, p. 179-196.

catégorie qui n'apparaît que dans la deuxième moitié du XVe siècle, la niche très spécifique des vraies troupes théâtrales itinérantes. Ce sont des indépendants, qui viennent se présenter de ville en ville, pour un ou deux spectacles, qui travaillent à leur propre compte, et qui perçoivent un droit d'entrée auprès des spectateurs[10]. À Paris la première preuve formelle de l'activité d'une troupe professionnelle de ce type date de 1486[11]. En Italie le phénomène a démarré, vers 1545, avec la Commedia dell'Arte[12]. Peter Meredith a mis radicalement en doute leur existence en Angleterre avant 1500[13], mais d'autres chercheurs signalent des acteurs professionnels itinérants dès 1339[14]. Dans les anciens Pays-Bas on a appelé cette catégorie de troupes professionnelles « kamerspelers » (« joueurs de jeux de personages en chambre »). Willem M. H. Hummelen les avait retrouvé surtout après 1550, mais aussi sporadiquement depuis la fin du XVe siècle[15]. Herman Brinkman a eu le mérite d'inventorier les cas les plus anciens du théâtre professionnel, qui se distinguent nettement des chambres de rhétorique. Les cas les plus explicites sont ceux de la troupe de Mathieu Cricke, active en 1475 dans plusieurs villes de la

10 H. Brinkman, « Spelen om den brode », p. 10-104.

11 M. Bouhaïk-Gironès, « Comment faire l'histoire de l'acteur au Moyen Âge ? », *Médiévales*, 59 (automne 2010), p. 107-125 ; M. Bouhaïk-Gironès et K. Lavéant, « S'associer pour jouer. Actes notariés et pratique théâtrale, XVe-XVIe s. », *Le Jeu et l'accessoire. Mélanges Michel Rousse*, M. Bouhaïk-Gironès, D. Hüe & J. Koopmans (dir.), Paris, Classiques Garnier, 2011, p. 301-318. Pour la France, voir aussi S. K. Wright, « Records of Early French Drama in Parisian Notary Registers », *Comparative Drama*, 24, 1990, p. 232-254.

12 M. A. Katritzky, *The Art of Commedia : a Study in the Commedia Dell'Arte 1560-1620*, Amsterdam et New York, Rodopi, Internationale Forschungen zur Allgemeinen und Vergleichenden Literaturwissenschaft, 2006, p. 31-44.

13 P. Meredith, « The Professional Travelling Players of the Fifteenth Century : Myth or Reality ? », *European Medieval Drama*, 2 (1998), p. 21-34.

14 J. M. Wasson, « Professional Actors in the Middle Ages and Early Renaissance », Medieval & Renaissance Drama in England. An annual Gathering of Research, Criticism and Reviews, J. L. Barroll et P. Werstine (dir.), vol. 1, Cranbury (N.J.), Associated Univ. Presses, 1984, vol. 1, p. 1-11 ; J. M. Wasson, « The English Church as Theater Space », A New History of Early English Drama, J. D. Cox et D. S. Kastan (dir.), New York, Columbia University Press, 1997, p. 35 ("earliest professional performance in 1348") ; J. H. McCarthy, « The Sanctuarie is Become a Plaiers Stage : Chapel Stagings and Tudor "secular" drama », Medieval and Renaissance Drama in England, S. P. Cerasano (dir.), Cranbury (N.J.), Associated Univ. Presses, 2008, vol. 21, p. 56-57 ("from 1339 on").

15 W. M. H. Hummelen, « Kamerspelers : professionele tegenspelers van de rederijkers », Oud Holland, 110, n° 3-4 (1996), p. 117-134 ; W. M. H. Hummelen, « Performers and Performance in the Earliest Serious Secular Plays in the Netherlands », Comparative Drama, 26 (1992), p. 19-33.

Flandre et du Brabant, et du groupe de Jacob van der Straten à Gand en 1477. Un cas probable, mais moins certain, malgré sa dénomination, est la mention fort précoce d'une représentation à Malines en 1427 par une troupe gantoise, de « ghezellen van de cameren van Gheynt ». Dans une certaine mesure cette catégorie est proche des artistes de cour, puisqu'il s'agit de professionnels ou de semi-professionnels. Mais ils s'en distinguent nettement par le fait qu'ils ont un lien direct avec un public payant indéfini, qu'ils ne connaissent pas d'avance. Ainsi ils peuvent se passer en général des subsides des grands seigneurs et des autorités publiques, une condition qui les a largement libérés de la censure du contenu de leur production artistique. Ils appartiennent donc au secteur du marché libre, à l'initiative privée, et, peut-être, sporadiquement à un monde en marge de la bonne société, peu ou pas contrôlé, peu ou pas saisissable. Il n'est en effet pas aisé de retrouver ces spectacles peu spectaculaires, ces loisirs banals pour un auditoire qui ne dépassait pas les limites des villages et des quartiers populaires. Pour les acteurs de ces troupes ambulantes, le silence des sources s'explique facilement par le fait que par défaut de subsides ils n'apparaissent donc guère ou pas dans les comptes urbains, mais aussi parce qu'ils avaient parfois intérêt à rester dans l'ombre, en dehors de tout contrôle des autorités publiques, après qu'ils s'étaient risqués à ironiser ou ridiculiser l'*establishment* de leur temps. Leur public est donc un public libre, de circonstance, et pas nécessairement fidèle. À chaque représentation les acteurs doivent conquérir et mériter leurs spectateurs. À cause de ce dernier élément, ils se distinguent assez peu des jongleurs et trouvères des cours d'Europe du XIIIe siècle, dont le portrait psychologique qu'en ont formulé Carla Casagrande et Silvana Vecchio est, *mutatis mutandis*, merveilleusement applicable aux attitudes mentales des acteurs itinérants des anciens Pays-Bas de la fin du moyen âge : « les jongleurs sont de partout, mais n'habitent nulle part ; présents dans les villes et dans les campagnes, ils ne sont ni paysans ni citadins ; ils traversent toutes les classes sociales, mais n'appartiennent à aucune. Ils sont à la cour des puissants, mais ils ne sont pas leurs hommes[16] ».

Un cas excellent pour illustrer les débuts dans les anciens Pays-Bas du professionnalisme au théâtre est l'aventure rocambolesque

16 C. Casagrande et S. Vecchio, « Clercs et jongleurs dans la société médiévale (XIIe et XIIIe siècles) », *Annales, Économies Sociétés Civilisations*, 34 (1979), p. 913-928, en particulier p. 914.

de Mathieu Cricke[17]. En octobre 1475, Charles le Téméraire, duc de Bourgogne, accorde sa grâce à l'acteur Mathieu Cricke et à ses sept complices[18]. Ils avaient été mis en prison à la suite d'une plainte de Jan van Musene, bourgeois de Malines, pour le rapt de sa maîtresse, l'ancienne prostituée Maria van der Hoeven, devenu actrice vers 1471 dans la troupe de Cricke. Cricke et ses coïnculpés introduisent la lettre de rémission, qu'ils avaient obtenu, auprès du Parlement de Malines, pour y être entérinée dans les registres, étape normale prévue dans le système de la grâce princière afin d'éviter des malversations et de laisser la parole à la partie adverse. Et, en effet, Van Musene et les siens y font opposition. Conformément à la procédure, les conseillers de ce tribunal entament une enquête approfondie afin de vérifier la véracité du délit présumé et la légitimité de l'opposition. De multiples témoins oculaires des événements ont été interrogés de manière critique par les conseillers du Parlement de Malines. Le verdict final de la cour ordonne la ratification et l'exécution de la mesure de grâce, et acquitte Cricke et ses co-prévenus de l'accusation de rapt. Ils sont pourtant condamnés, dans un second verdict, pour les plaintes de violence physique et verbale contre Van Musene et les siens. La perception de l'amende imposée dans le verdict a traîné pendant des années. Une procédure de pardon telle que celle décrite ici est tout à fait régulière au XVe siècle[19]. Ce qui est

17 J'ai également étudié le cas en détail dans cet ouvrage, qui livre également l'édition des documents d'archives : P. Arnade et W. Prevenier, *Honor, Vengeance, and Social Trouble. Pardon Letters in the Burgundian Low Countries*, Ithaca et Londres, Cornell University Press, 2015.

18 Archives départementales du Nord, Lille, B 1698, f° 22 v° – 24 r° ; Archives générales du royaume, Bruxelles, Grand Conseil de Malines, Première instance, 2683, a et b ; *ibid.*, Chambres des Comptes, Reg. 21.438 à 21442 ; édition de ces textes : W. Prevenier, « Vorstelijke genade in de praktijk. Remissiebrief voor Matthieu Cricke en diens medeacteurs voor vermeende vrouwenroof in oktober 1476, slechts geïnterineerd na kritische verificatie door de raadsheren van het Parlement van Mechelen », *Bulletin de la Commission royale d'histoire*, 175 (2009), p. 225-258 ; H. Brinkman, « Spelen om den brode », p. 103-104, a déjà fait mention de ce cas, à base de mon exposé à un colloque de 1997, mais à ce moment je ne disposais que de l'une des quatre séries de textes que j'ai édités en 2009.

19 Sur la procédure du système de grâce, voir : M. Boone, « Want remitteren is princelijck. Vorstelijk genaderecht en sociale realiteiten in de Bourgondische periode », *Liber amicorum Achiel de Vos*, L. Van Parys, e.a. (dir.), Evergem, Oost-Vlaams Verbond van de Kringen voor Geschiedenis, 1989, p. 53-59 ; H. De Schepper, « Het gratierecht in het Bourgondisch-Habsburgse Nederland, 1384-1633. Vorstelijk prerogatief en machtsmiddel », H. Coppens et K. Van Honacker, *Symposium over de centrale overheidsinstellingen van de Habsburgse Nederlanden*, Brussel, 1995, p. 43-87 ; M. Vrolijk, *Recht door gratie : gratie bij doodslagen en andere delicten in Vlaanderen, Holland en Zeeland (1531-1567)*, Hilversum, Verloren, 2004, p. 39-48, 62-72, 375-406.

exceptionnel c'est que quatre types divergents de documents ont été conservés dans le cas de Cricke : la lettre de rémission, la requête aux fins d'entérinement, le rapport de l'enquête, les paiements de l'amende. Il est vrai que l'octroi de grâce est le privilège exclusif du prince, qui l'exerce librement et sans limites. L'opportunité juridique et politique de l'exécution effective dépend, cependant, de la vérification des faits par une des hautes cours de justice princières. Les quatre dossiers conservés pour ce cas ouvrent simultanément plusieurs fenêtres qui permettent de saisir les points de vue contradictoires des témoins, des juges et des fonctionnaires, et d'appréhender finement les attitudes d'hommes et de femmes de différentes couches sociales, leurs mentalités, les limites de tolérance et d'intolérance de la société du XVe siècle.

Mathieu Cricke, natif de Bruxelles, dirigeait donc un groupe théâtral composé de trois acteurs masculins, Mathieu inclus, qui passent, sans doute à juste titre pour de « povres compaignons[20] ». Après une de leurs multiples représentations, dans l'une ou l'autre salle à Bruges, en 1471, Cricke sent un besoin irrésistible de se décharger de ses soucis professionnels. En se promenant, la nuit, dans le quartier chaud de la ville de Bruges, il y remarque une prostituée séduisante, Maria van der Hoeven, et réalise qu'elle pourrait être la chance de sa vie. L'introduction d'un personnage féminin dans sa troupe, pense-t-il, devrait inévitablement mener au succès. Il paie la somme classique de rachat au souteneur de la fille, et prend la mère de la femme également à sa charge, mère qui était fort heureuse « qu'il voulsist oster sadite fille dudit lieu publicque et le prendre avec luy[21] ». Ce passage du monde de la prostitution à une profession honnête ne doit pas trop nous étonner à Bruges à la fin du XVe siècle. Malgré le risque réel de stigmatisation la prostitution était pour beaucoup de jeunes femmes une étape en route pour une carrière réelle. Guy Dupont, dans son livre sur la prostitution à Bruges, note trois échappatoires pour les filles de joie brugeoises : un mariage honnête, la maison de reconversion (Bruges a créé un cloître de pénitentes

20 En fait la lettre de rémission mentionne sept "compaignons" dirigés par Cricke (W. Prevenier, « Vorstelijke genade », p. 234, lignes 2-4), mais plus loin (ligne 8) le texte spécifie que Cricke gagnait sa vie en jouant avec Copin van der Streke et Josse de Backere. Les cinq autres compagnons ne sont sans doute pas des acteurs, mais des « hommes de main », engagés par Cricke pour l'aider à récupérer son actrice Maria van der Hoeven dans ses multiples cavales avec son amant Jan van Musene.

21 W. Prevenier, « Vorstelijke genade », p. 240, n° 5.

de Marie-Madeleine en 1459[22]), et, enfin, la voie qu'a choisi Maria, le théâtre[23].

Une fois partie de Bruges, la nouvelle équipe de trois acteurs et une actrice se déplace constamment de ville en ville, et recueille partout un enthousiasme fou. Trop bien même. Car, lors d'une représentation donnée à Malines, Maria rayonne une telle capacité de séduction érotique qu'elle fait tourner la tête à un bourgeois fortuné de la ville, Jan van Musene, « qui est homme marié avec une bonne et honneste femme, et de laquelle il a de beaux enffans[24] ». Il parvient à éblouir la jeune fille par son statut social, et encore plus par le don de précieux bijoux. Il sait la convaincre de devenir sa maîtresse et de quitter son acteur. Mathieu ne désarme pourtant pas, parvient à retrouver sa bonne amie. À son tour il use amplement des ressources de son charme, et finit par culpabiliser l'ancienne actrice en lui faisant comprendre que, faute de rôle féminin, il fut « constraint de cesser à jouer[25] ». Il n'est pas exclu que des arguments moins affectifs ont pu jouer, notamment l'existence probable d'un engagement contractuel, qui créait des obligations professionelles de la part de Maria. Grande est néanmoins l'émotion de ces retrouvailles. Maria remonte avec grand succès sur les planches pour quelques soirées que Cricke organise à Anvers. Malheureusement sa belle est capricieuse, elle prend à nouveau la poudre d'escampette et rejoint son riche séducteur malinois. Mathieu se met, de nouveau, à la recherche de sa vedette-fétiche en cavale avec son amant dans les marches de Brabant, rate quelques traces dans les faubourgs de Malines et à Aarschot, mais découvre le couple à Diest. Mathieu entre la pension où le couple adultère logeait, reconquiert une fois encore le cœur de l'infidèle en ravivant ses sentiments de culpabilité. Elle rejoint encore une fois la troupe, « confessant qu'elle avoit largement meffait et grandement dommagé Mathis, mais elle se amenderoit et lui aideroit arriere a gaigner sa perte[26] ». À chaque réconciliation, Mathieu et Maria s'amusent follement en jeunes amoureux,

---

22 Ce système fut bien répandu en Europe : L. L. Otis, « Prostitution and repentance in late medieval Perpignan », *Women of the Medieval World : Essays in Honor of John H. Mundy*, J. Kirshner et S. F. Wemple (dir.), Oxford, Basil Blackwell, 1985, p. 137-160.

23 G. Dupont, *Maagdenverleidsters, hoeren en speculanten. Prostitutie in Brugge tijdens de Bourgondische periode (1385-1515)*, Brugge, Genootschap voor Geschiedenis te Brugge, 1996, p. 36-37, 40-43, 105-107.

24 W. Prevenier, « Vorstelijke genade », p. 241, n° 8.

25 W. Prevenier, « Vorstelijke genade », p. 241, n° 9.

26 W. Prevenier, « Vorstelijke genade », p. 242, n° 23.

faisant la fête, goûtant la bonne chère, les bons vins et les jeux d'amour jusqu'au petit matin. Dans une taverne de Gempt, village entre Diest et Louvain, Mathieu et Maria « soupperent et firent bonne chiere, et apres lesdis Mathieu et Marie allerent reposer ensemble, jusques au lendemain qu'ilz se leverent ». La fête continue à Louvain où ils soupèrent joyeusement : « Apres le souper retournerent couchier en leur logiz. Et le lendemain eulx levez, allerent tous desiuner en une taverne de vin, la ou ilz furent jusques pres du disner[27] ». La vie de bohême ne semblait jamais finir. Mais tout d'un coup le drame éclate à Louvain. Le destin, en la personne de Jan van Musene, va frapper plus fort qu'auparavant. Cricke et ses sept compagnons sont arrêtés, et mis en prison à Malines, à cause d'une plainte de Van Musene qui les accusait d'avoir enlevé et ravi Maria Van der Hoeven, « contre son gré ». Cricke, évidemment, proteste, introduit une demande de grâce auprès du duc de Bourgogne, Charles le Téméraire. À sa grande joie la troupe bénéficie de la bonne volonté ducale, et est remise en liberté. Le dernier mot est cependant aux officiers de justice du Parlement de Malines, la plus haute cour de l'État bourguignon, qui doit confirmer la grâce ducale. Cricke et ses coïnculpés introduisent leur lettre de rémission aux fins d'entérinement auprès du Parlement de Malines, mais Van Musene et les siens y font opposition[28]. Conformément à la procédure, les conseillers de ce tribunal entament une enquête approfondie. Pas moins de dix-huit témoins oculaires des événements ont été retrouvés par les officiers de justice et interrogés de manière critique à Diest, Gempt et Louvain[29]. Le verdict final de la cour ordonne, en 1476, la ratification et l'exécution de la mesure de grâce. Cricke et ses co-prévenus sont acquittés de l'accusation de rapt. Ils sont par contre condamnés à titre subsidiaire pour les plaintes de violence physique et verbale contre Van Musene et les siens.

La lettre de rémission de Cricke ouvre une fenêtre assez inattendue sur une niche bien spécifique et mal connue du monde du théâtre, celle d'une troupe itinérante, qui n'a point de local fixe, qui déambule de ville en ville, qui semble appartenir à une certaine sous-culture. Ces informations sont involontaires, venues à la surface uniquement par la coïncidence des démêlés de la troupe avec la justice. Les rapports des

27 W. Prevenier, « Vorstelijke genade », p. 237, § 2 et 3.
28 W. Prevenier, « Vorstelijke genade », p. 239-245.
29 W. Prevenier, « Vorstelijke genade », p. 246-254.

officiers de justice se caractérisent avant tout par un discours juridique, la lettre de rémission reflète les arguments que Cricke et les siens croyaient être utiles pour obtenir grâce, mais les dépositions des témoins oculaires possèdent plutôt la parole directe, dans la véracité de leurs pensées.

Ce sont en effet des bribes de phrases du dossier Cricke qui jettent quelque lumière sur la vie de ces artistes bohémiens. D'abord il est clair que la troupe improvise et voyage selon l'inspiration du jour et, sans doute, en fonction du succès relatif des lieux où ils se manifestent, et, depuis l'affaire Van der Hoeven, selon les péripéties sentimentales. En quelques jours ils se déplacent de Bruges à Malines, de Malines à Anvers. L'essentiel de leur train de vie se résume à la fréquentation d'auberges après-spectacle, selon la célèbre formule de François Villon, « Tout aux tavernes et aux filles[30] ». Nos artistes fréquentent sans doute surtout les cabarets à bière, mais ils ne méprisent nullement les tavernes à vin et les bons restaurants. En Angleterre les « taverns » à vin furent plutôt élitaires, les « alehouses » plus populaires, mais dans les anciens Pays-Bas cette distinction fut beaucoup moins stricte, voire parfois inexistante, car le vin y était déjà une boisson populaire au même titre que la bière[31]. Dans le procès de Mathieu Cricke, Gossin de Villers, aubergiste de l'Hostel de l'Homme Sauvaige à Gempt-lez-Louvain, décrit l'arrivée de la troupe chez lui : « vindrent huit compaignons estrangiers en son hostel, environ heure de souper, et amenerent avec eulx une jeune fille, et souperent illec, faisant grand chiere, ryant et buvant l'ung a l'autre, sans ce que ladite fille fist aucun semblant que aucune force luy euyst esté faicte. Et apres qu'ilz eurent soupé ladite fille ala couchier avec Mathijs Crycke, a present impetrant, sans aucune contrainte en une chambre à part, et ses compaignons en une autre[32] ». Une promiscuité naturelle caractérisait donc le comportement de Cricke et ses acteurs. Elle était assez normale dans les auberges, où les bourgeois se mêlent aisément et sans trop de complexes aux gens de métiers, travailleurs, marginaux, agitateurs, prostituées. Le résultat c'est que les auberges

30 François Villon, *Œuvres*, A. Longnon (dir.), 4e éd. revue par L. Foulet, Paris, Champion, 1966, p. 67.

31 P. Clark, *The English Alehouse. A Social History 1200-1830*, Londres-New York, Longman Group United Kingdom, 1983, p. 4-5 ; R. Van Uytven, « Scènes de la vie sociale dans les villes des Pays-Bas du XIVe au XVIe siècle », *Mémoires de la Société d'Agriculture, Sciences et Arts de Douai*, 5e s., 8 (1983), p. 11-31.

32 W. Prevenier, « Vorstelijke genade », p. 253-254, no 16.

sont le théâtre habituel de rixes entre ceux qui ont trop bu, riches et pauvres. La moitié des meurtres graciés dans les lettres de rémission résultent de bagarres d'auberges.

Venons au point de l'interaction entre acteurs et spectateurs, et celui de « la salle immaîtrisable », selon la formule de Christian Biet. La présence d'un personnage féminin dans la troupe est tout à fait exceptionnelle pour le XVe siècle, même dans un groupe aussi peu orthodoxe que celui de Cricke. Mes confrères Bart Ramakers et Herman Brinkman m'ont confirmé qu'ils n'ont pas rencontré d'autres cas dans les anciens Pays-Bas du XVe siècle. Simon Schama ne situait le premier cas en Hollande qu'au milieu du XVIIe siècle : « *In 1655 the first actress appeared in the Amsterdam theater, strengthening the clergy's view that it was the sink of the vilest iniquity*[33] ». Il avait raison de ne pas manquer d'expliquer l'absence des actrices par la vive opposition du clergé. Cette critique cléricale contre les femmes au théâtre existait comme thème idéologique depuis bien longtemps, et tout au long du moyen âge, où l'on mélangeait allègrement les deux catégories de « meretrix » et « joculatrix[34] ». Le phénomène est lié à l'antiféminisme omniprésent chez les théologiens et les moralistes médiévaux[35]. Dans les régions limitrophes des Pays-Bas bourguignons, par contre, on trouvera quelques cas d'une présence d'actrices dans des compagnies de théâtre, un à Amiens en 1502[36], et deux cas à Metz, en 1468 et 1485[37]. Il faut remarquer cependant que les cas de Metz proviennent de sources « littéraires », et relèvent

33 S. Schama, *The Embarrassment of Riches : An Interpretation of Dutch Culture in the Golden Age*, Londres, Fontana Press, 1991, p. 408.

34 W. Hartung, *Die Spielleute, eine Randgruppe in der Gesellschaft des Mittelalters*, Wiesbaden, Steiner, 1982, p. 65-72 ; W. Hartung, *Die Spielleute im Mittelalter : Gaukler, Dichter, Musikanten*, Düsseldorf, Artemis & Winkler, 2003, p. 194, 224, 231, p. 245.

35 J. M. Ferrante, *Woman as Image in Medieval Literature, From the Twelfth Century to Dante*, New York, Columbia University Press, 1975, p. 20-26 ; C. Frugoni, « La femme imaginée », *Histoire des femmes en occident*, G. Duby et M. Perrot (dir.), t. 2, *Le moyen âge*, Paris, 1990, p. 357-437 ; R. H. Bloch, *Medieval Misogyny and the Invention of Western Romantic Love*, Chicago, University of Chicago Press, 1991, spécialement le chapitre 3 ; E. J. Burns, *Bodytalk : When Women Speak in Old French Literature*, Philadelphie, University of Pennsylvania Press, 1993, p. 71-82 ; F. Gray, *Gender, Rhetoric, and Print Culture in French Renaissance Writing*, Cambridge [England], New York, Cambridge University Press, 2000, p. 16.

36 G. Lecocq, *Histoire du théâtre en Picardie*, Paris, Librairie H. Menu, 1880, p. 138 : on a payé 22 sols et six deniers « à six compaignons et une fille pour avoir joué aulcuns esbattements devant Messieurs » (= les échevins).

37 J. Enders, *Death by Drama and Other Medieval Urban Legends*, Chicago, University of Chicago Press, 2002, p. 17-28, 29-30.

plutôt du genre « légendes urbaines ». C'est en Italie, dans les troupes de la Commedia dell'Arte, au milieu du XVIe siècle, notamment dès 1564, qu'il faut situer l'avènement définitif d'actrices, dans le cadre de la professionnalisation du théâtre moderne[38]. Ce phénomène ne se généralise en France qu'au début du XVIIe siècle, quand les grands écrivains, Molière et Corneille, ont insisté pour que les rôles de femmes soient tenus par des actrices[39].

La présence d'une jolie femme sur l'avant-scène a de tout temps eu un potentiel érotique pour les spectateurs. Mais la mise en scène présente des variantes inattendues et déroutantes. Le chroniqueur Philippe de Vigneulles raconte qu'au cours de la représentation du « Jeu de Sainte Catherine » à Metz en 1468 un certain Henry de la Tour faisait preuve d'une telle passion pour le personnage de la sainte qu'il demandait en mariage l'actrice, Marthe Didier, fille d'un vitrier, qui jouait ce rôle d'une façon si touchante et si convaincante que le gentilhomme était visiblement incapable de faire la distinction entre les deux identités[40]. Encore plus ambigu est la seconde anecdote, racontée sur la veuve de Saulnière, bourgeoise nantie de Metz, en 1485, devenant amoureuse d'un jeune acteur masculin aux traits bien féminins, qui interprétait, par moyen d'un *cross-dressing* le caractère féminin dans le « Jeu de martyre de Sainte-Barbara[41] ».

Dans le cas de Van Musene et Cricke il y avait certainement en plus un parfum de fruit défendu. Maria Van der Hoeven était une ancienne

38 F. Tessari, « Sotto il segno di Giano : La Commedia dell'Arte di Isabella e Francesco Andreini », *The Commedia dell'Arte. From the Renaissance to Dario Fo*, Ch. Cairns (dir.), Lampeter, Edwin Mellen Press, 1989, p. 1-33 ; K. McGill, « Women and Performance : The Development of Improvisation by the Sixteenth-Century Commedia dell'Arte », *Theatre Journal*, 43, n°. 1 (Mars 1991), p. 59-69 ; J. Tylus, « Women at the Windows : "Commedia dell'arte" and Theatrical Practice in Early Modern Italy », *Theatre Journal* 49, n° 3 (Oct. 1997), p. 323-342. Sur la question des actrices en France avant le XVIIe siècle, voir L. R. Muir, « Women on the Medieval Stage : The Evidence from France », *Medieval English Theatre* 7 n° 2 (1985), p. 107-119, A. Evain, *L'apparition des actrices professionnelles en Europe*, Paris, L'Harmattan, 2001, et la bibliographie citée dans l'article de C. Sponsler, « Drama », dans *Women and Gender in Medieval Europe : an Encyclopedia*, M. Schaus (dir.), New York, Routledge, 2006, p. 232-234.

39 M. Baschera, *Théâtralité dans l'œuvre de Molière*, Tübingen, G. Narr Verlag ; Paris, Papers on French Seventeenth Century Literature, 1998, p. 120.

40 Enders J., *Death by Drama*, p. 1, 17-28 ; Dubech L. (dir.), *Histoire générale illustrée du théâtre*, t. 2, Paris, Librairie de France, 1931, p. 84 ; Jean-Julien, *Le théâtre à Metz, notes et souvenirs*, Paris, Louis Geisler, 1908, p. 9.

41 J. Enders, *Death by Drama*, p. 1, p. 29-30.

prostituée. Cette expérience a sans doute enrichi sa palette de séductrice. Le bourgeois malinois n'avait besoin que d'une seule performance sur la scène pour tomber éperdument amoureux de l'actrice : « ladite Marie en jouant lesdis jeux de personnaige en notre ville de Malines tint parolles a ung nommé Jehan de Musene[42] ». L'impact du charme de Maria ne faiblissait d'ailleurs pas au cours de l'aventure. Quand, quelques semaines plus tard, Maria quitte une fois de plus Van Musene pour une autre cavale avec son acteur, la veuve Lysebethe Hekelmakers, hôtesse de l'hôtel à Diest où Van Musene et Maria venaient de passer une nuit d'amour, décrit dans sa déposition pour l'enquête des conseillers de la Cour de Malines la peine d'amour du bourgeois : « Et demoura ledit Jehan ce soir en l'ostel d'icelle deposante, fort regretant ladite Marie, disant a ladite qui parle ces propres et mesmez parollez : "Je vouldroye ycy tenir Marie, ma chiere amye, entre mes brachs, et que mon coeur et le sien se deussent fermer et estaindre". Et cedit soir prinst ledit de Musene ung oreillier sur lequel ladite Marie avoit couchié, disant que de icellui oreillier, il se donroit a entendre qu'il auroit ladite Marie entre ses brachs, et que de ce il se lairoit contenter, avec pluseurs autres lamentations et regretz[43] ».

Il est clair que ces artistes bohémiens ne pouvaient guère vivre du soleil et de la pluie. Ils demandaient certainement un droit d'entrée aux spectateurs, comme c'était d'usage pour d'autres groupes de théâtre. Nos textes ne révèlent point le montant. Mais il est vraisemblable que la vie de théâtre était pour Cricke et les siens un métier à part entière, par lequel il pouvait vraiment gagner sa vie[44]. D'après le témoignage de Cricke, la cavale de Maria avec Van Musene provoquait instamment la mise à sec des revenus de la troupe : « qu'il souffroit pour ce qu'il n'avoit avec lui ladite Marie, pour ce que par ce moien tout son stil et la maniere de gaigner la vie de lui, de ladite Marie et de pluseurs autres personnes, cessoit[45] ». Mathieu Cricke, malgré la qualification « povre compaignon » dans la lettre de grâce, ne fut nullement démuni de ressources. D'abord il savait payer, en 1471, au maquereau brugeois la somme classique afin de libérer Maria : « paia oudit lieu de Bruges

42 W. Prevenier, « Vorstelijke genade », p. 234.

43 W. Prevenier, « Vorstelijke genade », p. 251, n° 9.

44 W. Prevenier, « Vorstelijke genade », p. 240, n° 3 : « il a acoustumé de gaigner sa vie a jouer jeux de personnage en chambres ».

45 W. Prevenier, « Vorstelijke genade », p. 241, n° 13.

en l'acquit d'icelle Marie huyt escus ou environ, lui fit faire robes et autres habillemens et se lui aprint a jouer lesdis jeux de personnages et ystores[46] ». Pendant quatre ans il a entretenu la fille (et sa mère) : « ledit Mathis a gouverné et alimenté, vestu et chaussé a ses despens lesdites mere et fille, gardé a son povoir que ladite fille ne habandonnast son corps publicquement, comme elle faisoit au tamps qui la print avec luy[47] ». Enfin, on ne manquera pas de noter qu'un des textes sur Cricke mentionne « que jouaient avec lui lesdis Coppin et Josse et autres ses serviteurs et serviteresses[48] ». Cette phrase pourrait signifier que Cricke et ses deux acteurs gagnaient si bien leur vie, qu'ils pouvaient se permettre d'embaucher des serviteurs, hommes et femmes. Katell Lavéant m'a justement suggéré que le texte pourrait impliquer que ces serviteurs ont participé comme acteurs aux représentations. Coppin et Josse seraient alors des associés, les autres plutôt des apprentis, sans doute au service de Mathieu pour un temps restreint.

Un autre élément intéressant apparaît pendant le procès devant le Parlement de Malines. À un moment donné, Maria van der Hoeven réclame de pouvoir garder les vêtements et les bijoux dont elle disposait comme actrice. Cricke prétend par contre que le matériel d'infrastructure de la troupe est uniquement son affaire. Les conseillers ducaux lui donnent raison : « Item et au regard des robes et joiaux que ladite Marie demande elle n'a cause de ce faire, car tout appartient audit Mathis, servans a jouer lesdis jeux de personnage, et non point a elle ne a son estat[49] ». Dans ce contexte Cricke réfère aussi à l'existence entre lui et Maria van der Hoeven d'une « convention », qui prévoyait que si Maria le quittait sans cause elle n'aurait droit à « ce que ledit Mathis lui vouldroit donner » ? Cet accord avait été consigné dans des « lettres d'instrument », c'est-à-dire dans un acte notarial[50]. Dans un autre passage on note que Maria « se mist en son service pour le aydier a jouer lesdis jeux de personnaige ».

46 W. Prevenier, « Vorstelijke genade », p. 240, n° 6.

47 W. Prevenier, « Vorstelijke genade », p. 240, n° 7.

48 W. Prevenier, « Vorstelijke genade », p. 240, n° 3.

49 W. Prevenier, « Vorstelijke genade », p. 245, n° 44.

50 En fait la première fonction de cet instrument notarial fut la notation d'un accord amiable entre Cricke et Van der Hoeven pour une plainte précédente de Maria pour des violences physiques, infligées quelques années avant 1475, dont elle avait accusé Cricke. Puisque cet acte n'est pas conservé il n'est pas certain qu'il comprend également un contrat d'acteur, mais l'hypothèse reste fort probable, vu l'autre passage disant que Maria « se mist en son service ».

Ces détails suggèrent l'existence d'un contrat de travail entre Maria van der Hoeven et Cricke, une condition juridique qui, selon les recherches récentes de Katell Lavéant et Marie Bouhaïk-Gironès, est loin d'être exceptionnelle au XVe siècle. Les contrats retrouvés pour le nord de la France à la fin du XVe siècle mentionnent en général quatre à cinq acteurs par troupe de théâtre[51]. Cela expliquerait pourquoi, pendant son passage à Bruges en 1471, l'équipe de Cricke alors composée de trois acteurs, et démunie sans doute d'apprentis, fut en quête d'un quatrième acteur.

Le dossier Cricke ne nous informe que très peu sur les sites exacts des représentations de la troupe. L'expression jouer « jeux de personnaige en chambre » suggère qu'ils jouaient à l'intérieur et donc pas dans la rue. Le système de déplacement des troupes itinérantes est très mal connu. De récentes recherches ont mis en lumière que les acteurs professionnels opèrent soit dans une auberge, soit dans une chambre d'une maison particulière, prêtée ou louée par le propriétaire, ce qui permettait plus aisément de demander une contribution financière[52]. À Malines, la troupe de Cricke logeait dans l'hôtel Rupelmonde, sur l'Yzeren Leen, en face de l'Hôtel « De Noord », où ils ont probablement joué. Avant l'époque des compagnies professionnelles on jouait plutôt en plein air. Carol Symes est convaincue qu'à Arras, au XIIIe siècle, les performances ne s'organisaient guère dans des bâtiments spécifiquement construits dans ce but, et peu dans les tavernes, plutôt en plein air, sur les places, dans les rues, dans les cours de cloître[53]. Même à la fin du XVe siècle les troupes de compagnons continuaient à se présenter dans les rues. Une lettre de rémission, concernant un homicide à Lille en juillet 1474[54], nous raconte qu'une troupe de compagnons donne un spectacle sur la place dite du Petit Frêt à Lille de « certains jeux de personnages que faisoient illec sur eschauffaulx et hours pluseurs compaignons », c'est-à-dire une construction de charpente servant d'échafaud[55]. « Et

51 M. Bouhaïk-Gironès et K. Lavéant, « S'associer pour jouer », p. 301-318.

52 K. Lavéant, « Le théâtre à l'auberge : l'hôtellerie, lieu de représentations dramatiques dans les villes du Nord aux XVe et XVIe siècles », *Drama, Performance and Spectacle in the Medieval City – Essays in honour of A. Hindley*, C. Emerson, M. Longtin et A. Tudor (dir.), Leuven, Peeters, 2010, p. 149-162.

53 C. Symes, *A Common Stage : Theater and Public Life in Medieval Arras*, Ithaca (N.Y.), Cornell University Press, 2007, p. 212.

54 Archives départementales du Nord, Lille, B 1695, f° 36 v°.

55 K. Lavéant, *Un théâtre des frontières*, p. 69-70 et p. 451, mentionne une compagnie de la Place du Petit Frêt à Lille ; J. Finot, « Les représentations scéniques données à l'occasion de

après la fin de leur jeu, pour tant que sur leur eschaffault qui estoit fait sur chariotz pour mener aval la ville », ils se déplacent sans doute pour donner un autre spectacle[56]. La lettre note, en outre, que « entre lesquelz compaignons feussent venus jouer ceulx de la place des Gingans », une co-production de deux compagnies donc[57]. Dans ce cas-ci il ne s'agit pas de groupes d'acteurs professionnels, mais de compagnies joyeuses bien établies dans plusieurs quartiers de Lille, obtenant régulièrement des subventions des échevins[58]. La compagnie des Gingans fut, selon Katell Lavéant, au sommet des troupes de quartier de Lille[59]. Dans une autre lettre de rémission, concernant un homicide à Middelburg (Walcheren), en janvier 1489, le ménestrel hennuyer Jehan Claeys s'exécute d'abord devant un public local en plein air, notamment sur le Dam de la ville marchande, pour ensuite donner une apparition à l'intérieur de l'Hostel de la Platte à l'invitation de la colonie des marchands espagnols de la ville Zélandaise, à l'occasion de la grande fête de leur nation[60].

Un aspect que les documents judiciaires permettent beaucoup moins de juger concerne le type de répertoire. Dans la lettre de Cricke ne figure aucun titre de pièce, aucune référence au genre de théâtre, sauf qu'il s'agit de « jouer jeux de personnaige en chambre », un terme qui ne réfère point à un type spécifique de théâtre. Le terme « personnaige » peut être une allusion à « l'acteur », mais aussi bien au « personnage incarné ». Bien que les textes ne soufflent mot sur la tendance idéologique des pièces, il ne me semble pas exclu que la troupe de Cricke s'aventurait à une approche de critique sociale avec un ton plutôt anti-bourgeois.

Mon hypothèse découle de quelques allusions, à la fin de la procédure du procès de Cricke et les siens, dans les comptes du *receveur des exploiz* du Parlement de Malines. Les acteurs furent, au début de 1476, après

la procession de Lille par les compagnons de la place du Petit-Fret au XVe siècle », *Bulletin historique et philologique du comité des travaux historiques et scientifiques* (1897), p. 504-520.

56 Sur ces constructions temporaires, échafauds et chariots transformés en scène, voir : K. Lavéant, *Un théâtre des frontières*, p. 16.

57 K. Lavéant, *Un théâtre des frontières*, p. 449, mentionne l'activité des compagnons des Gingans en 1425 ; A. E. Knight, *Les mystères de la procession de Lille*, Genève, Droz, 2001, p. 45 ; A.-L. Van Bruaene, *Om beters wille*, p. 31.

58 Ces compagnies participent d'ailleurs annuellement ou quasi-annuellement à la procession de Notre-Dame de la Treille et mettent en scène de courtes pièces dans ce contexte : un certain nombre d'entre elles ont été éditées par A. E. Knight, *Les mystères de la procession de Lille*, 5 vol., Genève, Droz, 2001-2011.

59 K. Lavéant, *Un théâtre des frontières*, p. 64-65, 449-451, 484.

60 Archives départementales du Nord, Lille, B 1706, f° 14 v°.

une longue enquête judiciaire, acquittés pour l'abduction supposée de Maria Van der Hoeven, mais néanmoins condamnés pour des délits mineurs, notamment quelques violences physiques et verbales (« pour certaines batures, envahissemens et injures par eulx commises es personnes de Jehan van Musene et Marie van der Hoeve[61] »), à une amende de 200 livres de 40 gros. La moitié de l'amende est payée immédiatement par le patron de la troupe, Mathieu Cricke, lui-même. Les autres membres de la troupe n'étaient point si prompts à payer. La perception de la deuxième moitié de l'amende, imposée dans le verdict, a traîné pendant pas moins de cinq années. En 1477, une année après le verdict de la cour, Cornille Franceis, huissier d'armes de monseigneur le duc, avait la charge d'aller requérir cette somme auprès des acteurs récalcitrants, qui habitaient à Malines. Il a fait preuve de toute la diligence due. Mais, dit le texte, « il les veoit estre en telle disposition et voulenté que pour riens il ne les eust ozé executer ». Le receveur ducal envoyait ensuite l'*amman* de Malines, un policier donc, « qui pareillement a fait difficulté de la mettre a execution pour le temps qui court, disant aussi qu'il a parlé a eulx, et lui ont dit et respondu qu'ilz sont bourgeois de ceste dicte ville, par qouy selon leurs privileges l'on ne les puet executer se premierement ilz ne sont convenus et convaincus par loy[62] ». Les acteurs et leurs hommes de main avaient donc trouvé un bon argument de procédure pour ne pas devoir payer l'amende, l'argument formaliste de l'immunité des bourgeois, à défaut d'une condamnation par la cour de justice urbaine de Malines.

Ce n'est que dans les comptes du receveur des exploits du Parlement de Malines de 1478 que nous apprenons les vraies raisons de la timidité de l'huissier, de la réticence de l'*amman* et du receveur ducal pour aller réclamer la dette auprès des malfaiteurs. Il paraît, dans ce compte, qu'à la demande du receveur les échevins de la ville de Malines ont finalement condamné, pour la deuxième fois, la troupe de Mathieu Cricke. Nous apprenons également qu'un des compagnons, Peter Gommaer, est insolvable, et que son père, Jehan Gommaer, boucher à Malines, a promis de payer pour lui. Malheureusement, le boucher n'est pas n'importe qui. Le receveur note, en soupirant : « Toutesvoies ce non obstant et mesmement pour ce que ledit Gommaer est homme

61 W. Prevenier, « Vorstelijke genade », p. 255, a.

62 W. Prevenier, « Vorstelijke genade », p. 255-256, c.

de grant port entre le populaire, fort dangereux et plain de mauvaix langaiges. Et n'y a huissier qu'il le oze executer. Pourquoy l'on n'y oze bonnement aller a la rigeur[63] ». Ni le père, ni le fils ne paient donc un sou. Aucun huissier n'avait le courage d'aller réclamer les arrérages dans ce quartier mal famé de la ville de Malines. Les autorités publiques hésitent essentiellement à cause de l'impact que le boucher est supposé d'avoir sur les couches populaires de la ville, et donc par peur d'une révolte sociale. Selon le compte de l'année suivante, celui de 1479-1480, le receveur n'a toujours pas avancé dans cette affaire, malgré « toute dilligence a luy possible ». De nouveau il n'arrive qu'à pousser des soupirs : « Car il n'y a nulz des huissiers de mondit seigneur, ne sergens de ladite ville, quy en veullent ne ozent prendre la charge ». Cette fois-ci il cite clairement les causes de la réticence des autorités publiques devant ce danger social : « Et ce pour cause que icelluy Gommart est homme fort redoubté en ladicte ville, tant pour malvais et dissolut gouvernement de deux ou trois de ses filz demourans avec luy, quy sont haussagiers et fort dangereux de la main comme autrement. Et pour ce icy neant[64] ». Comme par miracle, en 1480-1481, les dernières dix livres de l'amende sont payées.

L'utilité de cette dernière partie du dossier judiciaire de Cricke est de révéler le contexte social dans lequel opérait ce directeur de théâtre itinérant. Peter Gommaer, le compagnon récalcitrant pour payer l'amende, n'est pas un des trois acteurs formels de la troupe, mentionnés explicitement au début de la lettre de pardon. Il pourrait être plutôt un homme de main temporaire, jouant le garde du corps de Mathieu Cricke. Mais même si Cricke n'a pas engagé Gommaer et certains autres comme vrais acteurs, lui aussi s'est encanaillé dans un milieu plutôt marginal et subversif. Cricke se comporte tout au long du récit comme un vrai bohémien. Son train de vie fut très proche de ses hommes de main, si l'on juge par les interminables ripailles dans les auberges et tavernes de vin de Gempe et de Louvain. Il est peu probable que Cricke n'aurait pas trouvé de l'inspiration pour ses pièces de théâtre dans les fascinants dialogues pendant ces multiples soirées culinaires et alcooliques, dans les « mauvaix langaiges » de Gommaer, décrits par le receveur du Parlement découragé. Pouvons-nous supposer que les performances théâtrales de

63 W. Prevenier, « Vorstelijke genade », p. 256, d.
64 W. Prevenier, « Vorstelijke genade », p. 256, e.

Cricke ont déployé un discours de critique sociale, voire le ton subversif de messages contre l'ordre établi ? Nous ne disposons d'aucune information explicite du répertoire de la troupe. Ne doit-on pas plutôt supposer que Cricke a appliqué l'auto-censure, pour ne pas provoquer inutilement les autorités publiques des villes où il veut gagner son pain ? Peut-être le flirt de Cricke avec la marginalité s'est limité au fait, exceptionnel en 1475, de présenter une actrice dans ses jeux. Ce parfum érotique était certainement l'atout principal de son succès, comme Cricke le souligne maintes fois, mais une approche qui ne risque pas trop de provoquer la censure des autorités. De fait, le XVe siècle présente une assez large tolérance, aussi bien dans les arts graphiques comme en littérature et au théâtre, comme le prouvent les innombrables farces contenant des allusions sexuelles et des situations obscènes.

Un. Nous connaissons assez bien, surtout depuis quelques années, les compagnies de rhétoriciens et autres acteurs, subsidiés ou embauchés par les magistrats urbains et par les cours princières. Nous connaissons peu les troupes itinérantes et bohémiennes. Cette maigre récolte est d'une logique parfaite. Les mécènes du théâtre subventionné nous ont légué leurs comptes, leurs paiements, leurs édits, leurs mesures de censure, parfois même des manuscrits de pièces dans leur bibliothèques. Une comptabilité écrite était pour Mathieu Cricke certainement le dernier de ses soucis. Mais, d'autre part, le silence des sources ne signifie nullement qu'une réalité ponctuelle n'ait pas existé. C'est comme si le scandale du Watergate n'avait pas eu lieu si on n'avait pas trouvé le « smoking gun » de Richard Nixon. La meilleure, sinon l'unique, chance de retrouver le théâtre bohémien, ce sont les liasses des cours de justice. Le train de vie peu conventionnel, sinon anarchique, l'absence d'un logement fixe, le mépris de la morale traditionnelle, l'interminable fréquentation de tavernes, endroits par excellence de rixes, de prostitution et de crimes mineurs, tout cela devait alerter l'attention des baillis et autres hommes de justice. Ainsi on peut espérer retrouver ce « petit peuple » dans les comptes des baillis et dans les registres des cours de justice. Sources excellentes en ce domaine, mais malheureusement exceptionnelles, les lettres de rémission racontent le crime, mais surtout le contexte social, surtout si une enquête critique du juge d'instruction et des dépositions de témoins sont disponibles, comme dans le cas de

Mathieu Cricke, accusé d'un rapt de femme. Dans les 2 250 lettres de rémission disponibles aux Archives départementales du Nord à Lille[65], entre 1386 et 1500, je n'ai trouvé que trois lettres qui font des allusions à des activités de théâtre et à des acteurs. La première, celle de Cricke, nous parle d'un groupe itinérant, se déplaçant de ville en ville. La deuxième, à l'occasion d'un homicide à Lille en juillet 1474, présente deux groupes sédentaires lillois, des « compagnies joyeuses », ayant respectivement la place dit Petit Fret et la Place des Gingans comme territoire. Le dernier texte, celui de Middelburg de janvier 1489, est un cas mixte : l'acteur, un ménestrel, vient de l'extérieur (le Hainaut), mais semble avoir domicile plus ou moins fixe en ville[66]. Ces trois cas ne présentent sans doute qu'une minime partie de la réalité totale. De nombreux groupes marginaux ont été suffisamment malins pour échapper à toute répression.

Deux. L'élément le plus inattendu que le dossier Cricke (et les autres) nous révèle, c'est bien le caractère mixte, socialement et géographiquement, et cosmopolite des personnages, aussi bien des artistes que des spectateurs du théâtre. Dans la troupe de Cricke, Mathieu lui-même venait de Bruxelles, son actrice Maria fut fille de joie à Bruges, mais était originaire de Diest, certains de ses acteurs ou collaborateurs faisaient partie du petit peuple, et même des « classes soi-disant dangereuses », de Malines. Mais il n'y a pas que des marginaux dans l'histoire : le principal spectateur, Gerard van Musene, appartenait à l'élite bourgeoise de la même ville de Malines. Dans le cas de Lille, de 1474, le spectateur responsable de l'homicide, est Raucquin van den Berghe, natif de la ville hanséatique de Lübeck, à ce moment serviteur d'un maréchal de logis du duc de Bourgogne. Dans le cas de la fête espagnole de Middelburg, en 1489, le ménestrel est « un povre homme », qui habite Middelburg, mais est natif du comté de Hainaut. Il avait amené quelques jongleurs (« momeurs »). La victime est un tambourin natif de Nivelles. La fête est organisée par les marchands espagnols en Zélande, mais ils y avaient invité plusieurs bourgeois et bourgeoises de la ville de Middelburg. La fête espagnole avait donc bien un parfum international. Le choix des

65 Archives départementales du Nord, Lille, B 1681 à 1710.

66 Archives départementales du Nord, Lille, B 1706, f° 14 v° : « menestrier de rebecque, natif de notre pays de Haynaut, povre homme, marié, demourant en notre ville de Middelburg ».

marchands de la pièce demandée au ménestrel hennuyer, un récit qui s'appelle « La Savoynne », souligne le cosmopolitisme de l'événement[67].

Trois. Ces derniers détails me permettent de mettre en vedette une conséquence intéressante du fait que beaucoup de spectacles théâtraux se passaient sur la place publique, ouverte à tous et à toutes. Certes, aussi dans les Pays-Bas du XVe siècle, la vie sociale et culturelle se passait pour une grande partie dans le monde clos des élites, dans le charme discret des maisons des grands patriciens, devant les tapisseries des manoirs des grands ducs d'Occident. Mais la culture de la rue existait également. Elle était l'endroit idéal où des gens de toutes couches sociales avaient l'occasion de se rencontrer, et de consommer les mêmes soirées lyriques. Carol Symes a bien entrevu que « public space » correspond à une réalité évidente au XIIIe siècle : « I argue that the common stage which came into being in Arras testifies to an early manifestation of what Jürgen Habermas delineated as the *public sphere*[68] ». Dans une étude de 1994, j'ai avancé la thèse que, particulièrement pour l'activité littéraire à Arras au XIIIe siècle, bon nombre de spectacles littéraires organisés sur les places publiques ne s'adressaient pas à un seul « intended audience », pas à un seul auditoire homogène. Il y a lieu de penser à un brassage social des spectateurs et non à une condition de ségrégation sociale[69]. Ainsi je m'opposais à la thèse de Herman Pleij qui croit plutôt à des goûts bien distincts des élites nobles et élites bourgeoises[70]. Les patriciens de la ville, les marchands locaux et étrangers, les familles nobles, mais aussi les communs et les gens de métier, tous étaient présents ensemble devant les mêmes échafauds, ou dans les mêmes auberges, pour une consommation commune de pièces de théâtre, mettant en

67 Archives départementales du Nord, Lille, B 1706, f° 14 v° : « ledit suppliant vint avecq aucuns momeurs qu'il avoit mené aval notre dite ville de Middelbourg, jouant devant eulx d'une rebecque sur le Dam en icelle ville, a l'ostellerie a La Platte illec, auquel lieu aucuns marchans espaignars tindrent lors une feste ou royaulme entre eulx, ou il y avoit pluiseurs bourgois et damoiselles de ladite ville – lesdis marchans le firent jouer une divisse qui s'appelle La Savoynne ».

68 C. Symes, *A Common Stage*, p. 3.

69 W. Prevenier, « Court and City Culture in the Low Countries From 1100 to 1530 », *Medieval Dutch Literature in its European Context*, E. Kooper (dir.), Cambridge Studies in Medieval Literature, Cambridge, University Press, 1994, p. 23-24.

70 H. Pleij, *De sneeuwpoppen van 1511 : literatuur en stadscultuur tussen middeleeuwen en moderne tijd*, Amsterdam, Meulenhoff, 1988, p. 151-160 ; H. Pleij, « The Rise of Urban Literature in the Low Countries », *Medieval Dutch Literature in its European Context*, E. Kooper (dir.), Cambridge Studies in Medieval Literature, Cambridge, University Press, 1994, p. 62-77.

scène toutes les classes sociales. Le fait que dans une pièce comme *Robin et Marion*, composée par Adam de la Halle à Arras vers 1276, il y a de l'humour et de l'ironie sur le dos de toutes les couches sociales montre que tout le monde peut donc s'amuser. Le cas Cricke prouve que le brassage social pouvait aller encore plus loin, et que la réalité de la vie était capable de dépasser la fiction de l'échafaud. Le bourgeois malinois Van Musene y voyait l'occasion belle pour faire connaissance de l'actrice Maria Van der Hoeven, et de la persuader de quitter son patron et amant Mathieu Cricke. En séduisant une ancienne prostituée, non seulement Van Musene n'hésitait pas à s'encanailler dans un milieu marginal qui n'était pas le sien, mais, encore plus surprenant, il pouvait se le permettre malgré son statut social et politique en ville. C'est justement à cause de ce statut que le scandale public était évité. Dans ce cas précis l'entrée de Van Musene dans ce monde inhabituel fut sans doute facilitée par le fait que la troupe de Cricke jouait probablement dans l'hôtel malinois du Noort, un local de fête bien réputée, car on y organisait des banquets pour des groupes très variables, comme pour l'archiduc Maximilien en 1486[71]. Van Musene n'était pas du tout le seul membre des élites sociales à Malines qui, à cette époque, s'était risqué dans des aventures adultérines. Philippe Wielant, juge très honorable auprès du Parlement de Malines, se permettait de reconnaître en 1482 l'existence d'une fille illégitime[72]. À Malines, l'excuse ultime pour un Van Musene fut en fait le comportement d'un homme d'Église, l'évêque de Cambrai, Jean de Bourgogne, fils illégitime lui-même du duc Jean sans Peur et d'Agnès de Croy, qui absent la plupart du temps de son siège de Cambrai, préférait résider à Malines, où les frivolités furent encore plus acceptables, car l'évêque se vantait d'avoir produit 22 enfants illégitimes. Il existait en effet une grande tolérance dans les Pays-Bas bourguignons envers les relations extra-conjugales. Cette sexualité illicite était considérée comme un jeu social acceptable et accepté. Le ton était donné par les ducs de Bourgogne, notamment Philippe le Bon, fier de ses 26 bâtards et 33 maîtresses. Le modèle de

71 A. Rydam, « De namen en de korte geschiedenis der huizen van Mechelen », *Handelingen van de Koninklijke Kring voor Oudheidkunde, Letteren en Kunst van Mechelen*, 5, 1894, p. 344 ; dessin dans H. Installé, *Historische Stedenatlas van België. Mechelen*, Brussel, 1997, p. 114-115.

72 J. Monballyu (dir.), *Filips Wielant Verzameld werk. Corte Instructie in materie criminele*, Bruxelles, 1995, p. 11-12.

la cour bourguignonne fut largement imité par les élites bourgeoises, mais aussi dans la société dans son ensemble[73]. Ce comportement a invité les historiens à appeler les Pays-Bas du XVe siècle « a bastard-prone subsociety[74] ». L'adultère faisait partie du « way of life », il fut un jeu social, sans stigmatisation pour ceux qui s'y adonnaient, ni pour les enfants illégitimes, qui furent légitimés sans trop d'obstacles. Ces frivolités ne mettaient guère en danger la respectabilité sociale.

Pour terminer, je me permets de rappeler la thèse de Frits Van Oostrom sur la perméabilité des audiences des romans de chevalerie, qu'il ne considère pas comme de la littérature courtoise ou de la littérature urbaine, mais comme de la « littérature des élites », au pluriel[75]. C'est ainsi que je suis enclin à souscrire à l'expression de Carol Symes, que déjà au XIIIe siècle, « theater was open to all[76] ». Il n'est sans doute pas trop risqué de penser que les élites avaient des goûts communs, et que patriciens et petit peuple également consommaient simultanément le théâtre des compagnies joyeuses et autres rhétoriciens, et même les pièces légères d'un certain Mathieu Cricke. Cela rejoint une des trouvailles de la recherche d'Anne Laure Van Bruaene, c'est-à-dire l'ordonnance par laquelle les échevins d'Ypres interdisaient pour cinq ans les « jeux de personnages sur kar » en juillet 1428, parce que certains acteurs avaient chanté des chansons satiriques contre le magistrat à l'occasion du malaise économique et social dans la ville[77]. Cela porte à croire que les échevins avaient raison de craindre que ces acteurs étaient en mesure d'atteindre avec leurs spectacles publics toutes les couches de la population, et donc d'influencer fortement l'opinion publique globale. Ainsi Van Bruaene est arrivée à nuancer la thèse de Herman Pleij faisant des chambres de rhétorique des instituts de culture urbaine par excellence et des instruments des classes dirigeantes[78]. Elle est convaincue que les rhétoriciens

73 M. Bergé, « Les bâtards de la maison de Bourgogne », *L'intermédiaire des généalogistes*, 60, 1955, p. 316-408 ; M. Carlier, *Kinderen van de minne ? Bastaarden in het vijftiende-eeuwse Vlaanderen*, Bruxelles, Koninklijke Vlaamse Academie van België, 2001, p. 251-254.

74 M. Carlier, *Kinderen van de minne ?*, p. 129-131.

75 F. Van Oostrom, *Stemmen op schrift : geschiedenis van de Nederlandse literatuur vanaf het begin tot 1300*, Amsterdam, Bakker, 2006, p. 232.

76 C. Symes, *A Common Stage*, p. 3.

77 A.-L. Van Bruaene, *Om beters wille*, p. 31.

78 H. Pleij, « Inleiding », H. Pleij (dir.), *Op belofte van profijt : stadsliteratuur en burgermoraal in de Nederlandse letterkunde van de middeleeuwen* Amsterdam, Prometheus, 1991, p. 8-51 ; A.-L. Van Bruaene, *Om beters wille*, p. 232, 251-252.

ne reculaient point, du moins pas avant le XVIIe siècle, « à vilipender la politique locale, et à coucher en joue les groupes sociaux[79] ».

Le cas de la troupe de Mathieu Cricke illustre bien la potentialité des troupes de théâtre itinérantes et indépendantes d'attirer à leurs représentations des audiences socialement variées, des gens du peuple et des membres des élites urbaines. Il n'est pas du tout certain que leurs pièces aient exprimé des critiques politiques ou religieuses, qui auraient pu être considérées comme subversives et donc dangereuses pour l'ordre établi. Mais il est presque certain que l'équipe de Cricke a mis l'érotisme au centre de la thématique de leurs pièces. La tolérance pour tout ce qui touche l'érotisme fut assez large au XVe siècle[80]. Néanmoins, la seule présence d'un personnage féminin, interprété exceptionnellement pour le XVe siècle par une vraie actrice, fut certainement un défi pour les moralistes conservateurs et les puristes de l'époque, mais également une attraction de poids pour les non-conformistes et pour la grande majorité du public qui aimait savourer les ragots, les cancans, les ironies, l'érotisme et autres excitations de la vie[81].

Walter PREVENIER
Université de Gand

79 A.-L. Van Bruaene, *Om beters wille*, p. 254.

80 B. Roy, *L'Érotisme au Moyen Âge : études présentées au troisième colloque de l'Institut d'etudes médiévales à l'Université de Montréal*, [Montréal], Aurore, 1977 ; A. de la Croix, *L'érotisme au Moyen Âge : le corps, le désir et l'amour*, Paris, Tallandier, 1999.

81 Je tiens à remercier tous ceux qui ont posé des questions et suggéré des pistes de recherches lors du colloque organisé à Amsterdam le 26 et 27 novembre 2009. Je remercie particulièrement mes anges-gardiens à Amsterdam, Jelle Koopmans, Katell Lavéant et Marie Bouhaïk-Gironès, qui m'ont fourni un grand nombre de références, et qui, par leurs remarques judicieuses, ont fortement influencé mes conclusions.

"CHEVAUCHEES, MASCARADES ET JEUX ACOUSTUMEZ"

Jurisdiction over carnival in sixteenth-century Rouen

Carnival in sixteenth-century Rouen, then the second-largest city in France, was a remarkable public event. Three days of celebration, from *Dimanche gras* to *Mardi gras*, were orchestrated by a festive society called the *Abbaye des Conards*. First, on the Sunday, a procession of hundreds, at times thousands of people marched through the city, led by the leader of the festive society, the *abbé des Conards*. The procession consisted of groups of men in masks and costumes, some of these chosen randomly, some in carefully coordinated groups. Some of these groups conveyed comic or satirical messages, through poems that they either carried on placards, or pronounced at regular intervals, or distributed to onlookers as pamphlets. Many groups were accompanied by torches, and by fifes, drums and other instruments.

In 1541, for example, the group *Pere en fosse* were dressed in mourning, but with extravagant silk trimmings, gold buttons and a white feather in their hat, their horses draped with black cloth covered in skulls. Each carried a tablet inscribed with a couplet describing how they were wasting their dead father's inheritance.

Even more spectacular were the *tableaux vivants* performed by allegorical characters on elaborately decorated carts. In 1541, seven chariots embellished in "antique" style carried the "*Lessive de l'abbé*", in which allegorical figures representing society and its vices–Nobility, Church, Justice, Poverty, Ambition, Avarice, Favour, etc.–performed all of the tasks of laundering while dressed in spectacular costumes. As well as its satirical messages, this group was advertising the production of one of the plays that would be performed at the Abbot's banquet on the Tuesday, *Eglise, Noblesse et Pauvreté qui font la lessive*[1].

1 J. Beck, *Théâtre et propagande aux débuts de la Réforme*, Genève-Paris, Slatkine, 1986, p. 103–124.

After the parade ended, the masked participants, especially the bachelors, dispersed through the city showing off their costumes, and visited people holding open houses, especially where there were women. At these houses they performed skits and danced, and probably received wine in return. On *Mardi gras*, the Abbey sponsored a public banquet in a large hall, open to all for a reasonable price, where a stage was set up and plays were performed for the large audience.

This tradition evolved autonomously, without input from or regard for the city's authorities, and by 1541 had become an elaborate event involving up to two thousand in the parade itself and likely many more spectators. That year, the Abbey published a detailed description of the yearly carnival titled *Les triomphes de l'Abbaye des Conards*, which provides us with these details[2]. As its carnival celebration evolved and its impact on the public spaces of the city became more pronounced, it increasingly came to the attention of Rouen's judicial authorities. The result was less a clash than a negotiation, a process of getting to know each other that eventually became a mutual accommodation.

There were two formal judicial authorities in Rouen who had an impact on carnival performances. The first was the *Bailliage* of Rouen, the long-standing local court of first instance for the city that was also in charge of the city prison and of keeping public order. Its archives do not survive, but it was likely the point of contact between the Abbey and the judicial authorities in the first part of the century, as it dealt with local public order matters. However, in the 1530s, the Abbey came to the attention of the *Parlement* of Normandy, the royal court of appeal founded in 1499. While the Parlement heard appeals from local courts all over the province, it also had a role in maintaining public order, and soon began pronouncing edicts about public order in Rouen, the city in which it sat and in which many of its magistrates lived[3]. Over the course of the century, the Parlement significantly expanded its role in Rouen's civic affairs, and inevitably this expanding role brought it into contact with the expanding

2 M. de Montifaud (éd.), *Les triomphes de l'Abbaye des Conards*, Paris, Librairie des Bibliophiles, 1874: "Pere en fosse", p. 61–63; "Lessive de l'Abbé", p. 46–53; for the post-parade activities, p. 76–80. A copy of the original book (Rouen, Nicolas Dugord, 1587) can be found in the Bibliothèque Municipale de Rouen (BMR).

3 J. Dewald, *The Formation of a Provincial Nobility: The Magistrates of the Parlement of Rouen, 1499–1610*, Princeton, N.J., Princeton University Press, 1980, p. 34–35.

carnival activities of the Conards. In 1541 and 1542, the Abbey of the Conards appealed decisions of the Bailliage to the Parlement, and had them overturned. From that point onwards, the Parlement and the Conards dealt directly with each other and the Bailliage was no longer a factor.

But there was another claimant for jurisdiction over carnival in Rouen, and that was the Abbot of the Conards himself. In its origins, this claim was facetious, part of the comedy of carnival, although it sprang out of genuine jurisdictional concepts. As the Abbey's public activities, including masking, playing music, and mockery of individuals, triggered increasing interaction with the judicial system, this independent organization that had once felt free to perform without seeking anyone's permission became increasingly entangled with the courts. Yet in the end, although its encounters with the judicial system led to restrictions on its independence, they also led to the transformation of what was once merely a joyful pretended jurisdiction into a genuine jurisdiction over carnival celebrations, backed by the law.

THE JURISDICTION OF THE ABBOT OF THE CONARDS

The Abbot of the Conards' claim of jurisdiction over carnival was part of the comedy of the festive season. The Abbot asserted a self-appointed jurisdiction over everyone and everything that is foolish. By implication, that meant that his jurisdiction was universal. In 1586, he was described as "*monarque universel / De tous Conards residens soubs le ciel*"[4].

In the carnival of 1541, this facetious jurisdiction was played out primarily in the preparations leading up to carnival. The Abbot was portrayed as a ruler who holds court, presides over legal cases, pronounces judgements and fines, issues edicts, and receives taxes. His council included a chancellor, cardinals, and "*officiers domestiques [et] sauvages*". He referred to himself with the royal "we" and his edicts were

4 *Triomphes*, p. 105.

announced and enforced by his judicial officers, "*nos huissiers, nos sergens et bedeaux, baillis, prevosts*"[5].

The Abbot's facetious edicts were part of an imaginary code of law, the "ordonnance Conarde". These edicts were directed to Conards and also to various character types and professions, for example:

> Aux bons pions et taverniers
>
> *Et pour se monstrer bon divin,*
> *De jour l'eglise, au soir taverne*
> *Faut hanter: mais qu'on si gouverne*
> *Sans troubler service du vin*[6].

The Abbot's various edicts and pronouncements were signed (from a tavern, with nonsense verse), and proclaimed throughout the city, in a parody of how a genuine edict was published:

> *Fait au conseil logé au bois Saint-George,*
> *Present l'abbé, lequel trempoit sa gorge,*
> *Ainsi signé: Regnaud tirelardon*
> *La tantirely mirely guodon*[7].

The Abbot also claimed facetious powers of taxation. One of the titles consistently given to the Abbot in various Conard texts is "resveur [receveur] en decimes". The "decime" was a tax on the clergy, specifically on the nominal value of their benefice, instituted by Francis I in 1516 with the consent of the Pope[8]. The Conards used a similar claim in 1550 when King Henry II, after his ceremonial entry into Rouen,

5 *Triomphes*, p. 18, 21. It is worth noting that even non-festive confraternities might sometimes create elaborate festive jurisdictions on their feast-days, such as the tradition of "reinages" in the Limousin. In 1599, the confrérie de Sainte-Anne in Bas-Limousin featured "roi, reine, le migon du roi, le lieutenant du roi, un capitaine, le lieutenant du capitaine, un porte-enseigne, le fou de la confrérie, le lieutenant du fou, un vigneron, un porte-epée, le fait-à-sa-guise, le tâte-salé, le fauconnier, un évêque, un prêtre, le paresseux, le lieutenant du mignon, un sergent-majeur, un lieutenant de port-enseigne, le bouteiller du roy" (S. Capot et P. D'Hollander (dir.), *Confréries et confrères en Limousin du Moyen Âge à nos jours*, Limoges, Presses Universitaires de Limoges, 2009, p. 55).

6 *Triomphes*, 22. "Pion" means drinker (E. Huguet (dir.), *Dictionnaire de la langue française du seizième siècle*, Paris, Champion, 1925–1967, vol. 5, p. 791).

7 *Triomphes*, p. 28.

8 *Triomphes*, p. 1 (title page), 5. There may be a pun here between "resveur" (dreamer) and "receveur" (tax collector). For the *decime* see R. Briggs, *Communities of Belief: Cultural and Social Tensions in Early Modern France*, Oxford, Clarendon Press, 1989, p. 191.

asked to see them perform. They presented a play called *La farce des veaulx*, the farce of the calves. The play's concept was that every element of society owed a tithe (*dime*) to the Abbot, and the play consists of the Abbot's officials processing the calves sent as payment by all members of society–including the Parlement ("Souverain cour"), and the Bailliage. Calves were a byword for foolishness, and each calf has characteristics that reflect on or provide an opportunity for sardonic comment about the giver (those of the Parlement, for example, are thin and malnourished from avarice)[9].

But underneath all of this comedy lay some genuine jurisdictional claims and activities. First, while the *Abbaye des Conards* was not in any way a real abbey, it was in fact a recognized and formal confraternity, the Confraternity of Bonnes-Nouvelles, a priory just across the river from the city. It was made up of respectable laymen, members of Rouen's "middling sort"–artisans, merchants and minor officials who earned stable incomes and owned property. The confraternity owned possessions, and it participated in serious civic processions along with other confraternities and corporations of the city[10].

Confraternities were recognized to have a certain amount of jurisdiction over the moral behaviour of their own members, for example being able to issue fines for misbehaviour such as public drunkenness or failure to attend mass. In Paris, the *Basoche* of the law clerks, which was both a festive and a professional society, was recognized to have jurisdiction over the professional and moral behaviour of the clerks. In a style evocative of the Conards, it had an elaborate system of partially-facetious, partially-serious officers, and could issue edicts regarding the activities of its members[11]. The Abbot's facetious edicts about the behaviour of "Conards" or his "suppots" were thus based on a playful expansion of a real and widely recognized form of jurisdiction.

This playful expansion took place, first, in terms of the scope of these moral judgements. Sometimes moral judgements were turned upside

9 *La farce des veaulx jouée devant le Roy en son entrée à Rouen* [1550], Paris, Techener, 1834. See discussion by S. Beam, *Laughing Matters: Farce and the Making of Absolutism in France*, Ithaca, Cornell University Press, 2007, p. 54.

10 D. Reid, "Carnival in Rouen: A History of the Abbaye des Conards", *Sixteenth Century Journal* 32:4 (2001), p. 1032–1037.

11 M. Bouhaïk-Gironès, *Les clercs de la Basoche et le théâtre comique: Paris, 1420–1550*, Paris, Champion, 2007, p. 57–63.

down, such as the example above that punningly reverses the common injunction to attend mass without disruption by requiring people to drink in taverns without disruption. At other times the scope of these judgements was more ambitious than the petty trespasses a confraternity would normally deal with, chastising broader moral misbehaviour in society as a whole, such as ambition and avarice in the "Abbot's Laundry". While this expanded moral jurisdiction remained facetious, it gained resonance from being based on a genuine and familiar structure.

The second way in which this confraternal jurisdiction was playfully expanded was by widening the of number of people subject to it, beyond the small genuine membership of the confraternity. Anyone who deserved the title "conard" was considered part of the Abbot's realm–a title that could be adopted freely, but could also be assigned involuntarily.

This claim encompassed, first of all, those who voluntarily joined with the Abbey to participate in the carnival celebrations, a much greater number of people than just the association's formal members. This jurisdiction over the participants in carnival was exercised in part through the question of the right to wear masks during carnival. In 1541, one of the Abbot's edicts proclaimed that only those who accompanied the Conards' parade could do so:

Aux porte-masques autres que ceux qui nous accompagnent
au jour de nostre monstre

Aucuns follets et frais ponnus
N'auront liberté de porter
Masque, sur peine d'atempter,
Si avec nous ne sont venus[12].

Since wearing masks was the very basis of celebrating carnival, by extension the Abbot was claiming jurisdiction over carnival itself.

In 1541, this was simply the twenty-first of a list of twenty-five facetious edicts. In 1557, however, it took a step towards reality. In response to an uncertain legal situation regarding masking, the Conards

12 *Triomphes*, p. 25–26. "Follets" is a diminutive of "fou," and "frais ponnu" means "freshly laid," that is, young and inexperienced. The injunction may thus be directed at new participants in carnival. "Atempter" could be a variation on "attemperer," meaning to regulate or temper, or else "attempter," meaning being the object of an attack. See *Dictionnaire de la langue française du seizième siècle*, vol. 1, p. 378.

directly requested permission from the Parlement to perform their carnival celebrations. In its response, the Parlement granted permission but restricted it to "*ceux qui accompagneront l'abbé seulement*"[13]. In 1570, as we shall see in more detail below, this intent was transmuted from a negative restriction into a positive jurisdiction: the Abbot was given the right to govern who could wear masks during carnival. The Parlement proclaimed that no-one could wear masks during the days when the Conards were performing "*sans l'expresse permission congé et licence*" of the Abbot, backed by the full force of the law. From that point on, the Conards proudly proclaimed their Abbot's formal legal jurisdiction over any person who wished to wear a mask during carnival[14].

There was also another aspect to the Abbot's claimed jurisdiction, one that extended beyond those who voluntarily participated in carnival. Anyone who inadvertently qualified themselves as foolish by their ridiculous misbehaviour was also considered to have put themselves under his jurisdiction. As with the claim over carnival participation, this claim was put into practice, but in this case without the need for any kind of judicial support.

At the end of the *Mardi gras* banquet, the Abbot was presented with a series of cases of actual foolish behaviour on the part of local individuals over the past year, each one "*redigez en rethorique de grande joyeuseté.*" In consultation with his council, he decided on a winner and a runner-up who would be awarded the "crosse au Conards", the Abbot's crozier, for the most foolish act of the year. In 1541, the winner was a solicitor who had bet his wife in a dice game. The Abbot, his council, and probably a large crowd processed to the houses of the winner and the runner-up, where, accompanied by torches and drums, the Abbot pronounced the verdict (the narrative uses the legal term *arrest*) in a loud voice to his new subjects, who were "*declarez et approuvez sots et glorieux Conards,*" and presented with the *crosse*[15]. It was a typical example of festive societies

13 M. Rousse, "Le Théâtre des farces en France au Moyen Âge", Thèse de Doctorat ès-lettres, Université de Haute-Bretagne Rennes 2, 1983, vol. 5, p. 81. The code for this document in the Archives départementales de la Seine-Maritime should be 1 Mi 345, but the microfilm could not be found when I tried to consult it in 2009.

14 Archives Départementales de la Seine-Maritime (ADSM), 1 B 619, 3 February 1570. All references to the ADSM are to the records of the Parlement de Normandie, *arrêts sur rapport*, unless otherwise noted. *Triomphes*, p. 93, 101.

15 *Triomphes*, p. 80.

using ritual humiliation to punish members of the community who had transgressed social norms, similar to a charivari.

The idea that an association that organizes festive celebrations had jurisdiction over those who behaved foolishly, at least during carnival, may not have been unique to Rouen. In what is probably a *cause grasse*, a facetious trial, at the Parlement of Paris on *mardi gras* in 1473, the Basoche asked that what appears to have been a genuine if ridiculous lawsuit between quarrelling prostitutes be handed over to their jurisdiction because "*toutes lesdictes parties sont vrayes bazochiennes*". It looks like a similar concept to the one used by the Abbot–that people can fall under a festive society's jurisdiction by virtue of foolish behaviour[16].

The Conards were not, for the most part, trained in law–in Rouen, the law clerks engaged in their own festivities through the Basoche, which was a separate organization (although in at least one instance they appear to have cooperated with the Conards in putting on a carnival *cause grasse*)[17]. The Conards' works do not usually engage with legal terminology, judicial citations and court procedure to the extensive degree that characterizes Basoche works[18]. The Conards play with the legal terminology and procedure that would have been familiar to them as men of business who had recourse to the law in the course of their affairs and their participation in city life. They used it primarily as a way to embellish the parodic status of their Abbot and give verisimilitude to his jurisdiction over foolishness in the lead-up to carnival. In the comic and satirical material of the carnival procession itself, not all that much legal terminology is used, and issues of justice are dealt with in only the most general manner and in conjunction with other forms of authority such as nobility and the church.

While the real–life examples judged for the "crosse au Conards" were described as "cases", it seems that they were presented more as stories than as the more legalistic *causes grasses* of the Basoche. There is

---

16 M. Bouhaïk-Gironès, *Les clercs de la Basoche*, p. 161. Bouhaïk-Gironès proposes other explanations for this turn of phrase. The Basoche's claim for jurisdiction was not granted. It is not clear if the case was in fact a genuine one that the court chose to play for laughs for carnival, but to me this seems the most likely interpretation.

17 M. Bouhaïk-Gironès, *Les clercs de la Basoche*, p. 76–77. For the example of cooperation, in 1551, see M. Rousse, "Le Théâtre des farces", p. 74, and E. Philipot, *Six farces normands du recueil La Vallière*, Rennes, Plihon, 1939, p. 83.

18 See M. Bouhaïk-Gironès, *Les clercs de la Basoche*, p. 126, 178–183.

no indication in 1541 that the legal debate that was the heart of a *cause grasse* was present[19]. Rather than choosing between two plaintiffs, the Abbot was choosing the best of a series of narratives presented to him. A skit called *Les deux soupiers de Monville*, which was probably performed during the banquet on *mardi gras*, gives a sense of this storytelling. In it, a character described as the "Huissier," which refers to the satirical writer Jacques Sireulde, is chastised by the other characters for having insulted the Abbot and leading them to do so as well. At the end, each of the characters asks forgiveness from the Abbot, who grants it with the phrase "*Ton cas t'est ce jour d'uy remys*"[20].

THE CONCERNS OF THE COURTS

The relationship between the self-proclaimed facetious jurisdiction of the Abbey of the Conards and the official judicial authorities of the city was complex and ever-changing. The courts throughout the century focused on trying to mitigate specific concerns about the Conards' activities. Despite the range and recurrence of these concerns, the courts never went the next step to try to prohibit the Conards or their activities completely, even at times when it was prohibiting other theatrical activities. At first, the responses of the courts were reactive and occasional–either responding ahead of time to reports of what the Conards planned, or after the fact to what they had done during carnival. From 1570, however, the Conards arranged a consistent policy with the authorities that gave them secure privileges in exchange for some limitations that addressed the courts' ongoing concerns.

The concerns of Rouen's courts with regards to the Conards' activities can be sorted into two rough and sometimes overlapping categories:

19 M. Bouhaïk-Gironès, *Les clercs de la Basoche*, p. 178. The Conards may have been involved in *causes grasses* later in the century. In addition to apparently working with the Basoche to perform a *cause grasse* in 1551, there is a *cause grasse* attributed to the Abbey of the Conards published in 1566 (p. 181), although by that time the Conards were famous enough that some facetious works may have been attributed to them for marketing purposes.

20 M. Rousse, "Le Théâtre des farces", p. 111–117.

actions and words. The law's interest in the theatre is often discussed primarily in terms of the impact of the words spoken, bringing up questions such as libel, political and religious commentary, and censorship. But a performance is also an event, one that brings together a large audience. The mere act of gathering a crowd was a significant issue for early modern cities, bringing up concerns about public order and the potential for criminal activity. The strength of the focus on the Conards' actions was probably due to the fact that, first, the Abbey's carnival performance included not just a small acting troupe or even a whole confraternity, but hundreds and at times thousands of people, and, second, that they performed their parade in public space, through several of the central locations of the city. Their actions thus had a huge impact on public order in the city. The most significant of these actions was wearing masks; other concerns about their actions included playing musical instruments in public, and intimidation.

MASKING

The core issue in the relationship between the Abbey and the law courts was the wearing of masks during carnival. Masks–anything that covered the face and made it difficult to identify individuals, "*desguisans le visage*"–were feared because they provided an opportunity for anonymous action that could disrupt public order–the settling of private scores, the commission of property crime, even rioting and rebellion. These concerns were emphasized by the manner in which edicts controlling masking were sometimes accompanied by prohibitions on carrying weapons while wearing masks. But masks were also essential for producing a successful carnival. In 1541, when the Parlement briefly ordered the Conards not to wear masks at night in Rouen, the Conards considered holding their event in another city because the right to wear masks was so essential to the success of their celebrations[21].

The first edict of the Parlement related to wearing masks was issued in January 1514, clearly in anticipation of carnival. It did not mention the Conards by name, but prohibited "*a toutes personnes de quelque estat quilz soient de porter ou achapter aucuns faulx visages masques*

21 *Triomphes*, p. 14. The appendix provides a chronological listing of judicial decisions relating to the Abbaye de Conards and carnival in sixteenth-century Rouen.

nez ou barbes fainctz ou aultre choses desguisans le visage". It also prohibited merchants from selling masks, and prohibited people from following the tradition of receiving maskers in their homes. Anyone who owned masks was required to hand them in to the Bailliage, as if they were dangerous weapons. The edict also refers to an earlier pronouncement by Rouen's Parlement, in May 1508, which similarly banned masking. That edict was pronounced ahead of Rogations, the other time of the year in which the Conards organized celebrations in the early part of the century[22].

The Parlement repeated this kind of blanket condemnation of masking several times in the 1550s, at a time of high anxiety when poverty was a serious problem and Calvinism was on the rise. But, remarkably, the Conards received a specific exemption from this general prohibition. When the Parlement issued a pre-carnival edict banning all masking in 1557, the Conards quickly applied to the court for permission to engage in their usual celebrations, and the Parlement granted permission to wear masks to those who were part of their carnival procession[23].

At other times during the century, the Parlement's concern with the wearing of masks was more targeted. It focused on wearing them at night, when they were most effective at obscuring people's identity. In 1541, the first time the Conards approached the Parlement for support in their carnival activities, the Parlement initially restricted the wearing of masks at night, but later relented on appeal. In 1569, as the Conards restarted their carnival activities after they had been interrupted by the first part of the Wars of Religion, the Parlement got wind of their plans and issued a restriction that no-one should wear masks after the night watch set out. The next year, 1570, when the Conards submitted a formal appeal that included a request for a monopoly over masking, the permission was granted with the proviso that no-one should wear

22 ADSM, 1 B 348, 7 January 1513 (old style). I use standard dating in the text, but where relevant I will provide the old style (o.s.) dates in the footnotes in order to exactly match the dating provided in the archival record. The old style applies to January-March, up to the year 1566. In 1567 the Parlement began using the Jan. 1 new year. The Parlement of Paris issued a similar edict against masking because of its "scandal and inconvenience" a few months later (see S. Beam, *Laughing Matters*, p. 63).

23 ADSM 1 B 568, 16 January 1556 (o.s.). This edict refers to a previous edict of 21 January 1551 against masking (but the archives do not include records from that date). Another edict from 1559 also included a prohibition against masking (1 B 578, 27 January 1558 (o.s)). M. Rousse, "Le Théâtre des farces", p. 81.

masks after ten at night–a continuation of their earlier concern, but in February still leaving several hours of darkness during which masks could be worn[24].

It is worth noting that the Parlement's consistent concern with wearing masks at night may have had some justification. Modern research in social psychology has shown that the perceived anonymity created by both darkness and disguise can have the effect of encouraging unethical and aggressive behaviour–even when the anonymity is more perceived than real[25]. Of course, part of the purpose of carnival was to provide a space where people could speak and behave in a manner that was loosened from the usually restrictive norms of early modern France, and masking was an effective way to create this atmosphere. But combining it with darkness increased the perceived and likely the real risk of expanding beyond looser norms of speech and behaviour to genuinely disruptive, dangerous or criminal behaviour. In trying to control masking at night, the Parlement was acting purposefully on its mandate to maintain public order.

While the concern about wearing masks at night was a constant one throughout the century, the concern about masked individuals carrying weapons tended to appear only around times when civil discord was on the Parlement's mind. It first appears in 1557, when Calvinism was starting to gain strength in the city. After the end of the Wars of Religion, in 1594, the Parlement allowed Conards to re-start their activities, but began adding a further proviso to the annual edict that specified that no-one wearing a mask could carry a weapon–a logical concern after a civil war that had divided the city[26].

The centrality of masking in carnival, as respectively a right for the Conards and a cause for concern for the Parlement, comes through in the understanding they reached in 1570. As well as simply requesting a general permission to conduct their festivities (including "mascarades"),

24 *Triomphes*, 14. ADSM 1 B 616, 26 February 1569. ADSM 1 B 619, 3 February 1570.

25 See C. Zhong, V. Bohns and F. Gino, "A Good Lamp is the Best Police: Darkness Increases Dishonesty and Self-Interested Behavior," *Psychological Science*, 21 (2010), p. 311–314; J. Hirsch, A. Galinsky and C. Zhong, "Drunk, Powerful and in the Dark: How General Processes of Disinhibition Produce Both Prosocial and Antisocial Behavior," *Perspectives on Psychological Science*, 6 (2011), p. 415–427.

26 M. Rousse, "Le théâtre des farces", p. 81. ADSM, 1 B 707, 20 December 1594. The Parlement also prohibited carrying arms while masked during carnival season in 1621, after the Conards had ceased to be active (ADSM 1 B 892, 3 February 1621).

the Abbey also applied specifically for a monopoly over masking: "*que defences soient faictes a toutes personnes autres que de leur societe et adveu porter masques aupres la ville durant lesdictes jours gras.*" The Parlement replied by upholding the requested monopoly in the strongest terms: "*a ladicte court faict et faict expresses inhibitions et defenses a toutes personnes de quelque estat qualite et condition quelles soient autres que de la societe desdicts abbe conardz supposts … de porter masques … sans l'expresse permission congé et licence dudict abbé*". Masking was the key to both the celebration and the danger of carnival[27].

The court's attitudes towards masking evolved back and forth over the course of the century. Blanket condemnation was clearly ineffective, and so the court and the Conards evolved ways of managing it that addressed the court's underlying concerns–that masking should be kept under control and not be combined with aggravating factors such as nighttime or weapons.

MUSIC

In addition to masking, Rouen's courts were troubled by the practice of playing instruments, notably fifes and drums, in public. The Conards (and other performers) used instruments, first, as a way to advertise their upcoming events by playing instruments to get people's attention before making announcements around the city. The Conards also used instruments as an essential part of the carnival performance–many of the costumed groups in their procession were accompanied by fifes and drums to create a striking and festive effect.

The fear of the courts was that when instruments were used to "*assembler le peuple*", the resulting crowd of excited populace could lead to disorder. But, like masks, the Conards considered playing instruments essential to the success of their celebration. As they said at one point, "*Tels sont les timbres et cloches du couvent*"[28]. In 1541, the Conards faced a crisis because the Bailliage had issued a pre-carnival prohibition on playing instruments in public[29]. The Conards and their supporters first

27 ADSM, 1 B 619, 3 February 1570.

28 *Triomphes*, p. 6.

29 The Conards refer to the order having been issued by the "police", which is more likely to refer to the Bailliage than to the city council, the only other authority that could have issued such an order; in addition, at the end of the parade the narrative specifically

protested this ban by making a huge racket outside one of the city gates with whistles and bells, making "*plus de bruit que ne fist l'artillerie de Grecs à la prinse de Troye*". More significantly, this ban was the spur that prompted the Abbey to go over the heads of the local jurisdiction to the Parlement itself. The Conards sent a request to the Parlement asking them to allow the Conards to "*triompher en phiffres et tabours*" during carnival. The Parlement at first granted them permission to celebrate "*en la maniere accoustumée*" during the three days of carnival, presumably including music, meaning that they were granted an exemption from the Bailliage's restriction. But as noted above, this permission restricted them from wearing masks at night. When it relented after a further appeal, the Parlement was more specific in allowing them to play "*Phiffres, tabours*" as part of their celebration[30].

In the 1550s, the general prohibitions of masking issued by the Parlement also included prohibitions on playing fifes and drums in public. A theatre troupe was specifically banned from playing the drums to advertise, although the Conards appear to have remained exempt from this constraint as well. In 1569, the court prohibited drumming as well as masking after the beginning of the night watch. When the court granted the Conards' request for a monopoly over masking in 1570, the court specifically added the right to play fifes and drums to the Conards' monopoly, even though they had not requested it[31]. The courts considered playing instruments in public to be a public order concern similar to masking, one that needed to be carefully managed.

INTIMIDATION

Another aspect of the Conards' behaviour became more troubling to the courts later in the century, as social values changed. This was the danger of intimidation–through visiting houses in the expectation of wine, when they might not be welcome, and through the awarding of the *crosse*. The first sign of this came in 1541, when the Parlement's

notes that it passed by the Bailliage tower and prison, where a poem was posted assuring Conards they could pass by it without danger (*Triomphes*, p. 75), suggesting there had been reason for Conards to fear action by the Bailliage.

30 *Triomphes*, p. 5–6, 8, 13–15.

31 ADSM, 1 B 567, 24 October 1556; 1 B 568, 16 January 1556 (o.s); 1 B 573, 27 January 1558 (o.s); 1 B 619, 3 February 1570.

initial decision required them not to commit any "*force ou exaction*", but this was superceded by the far more liberal subsequent decision that year. In 1557, the court again required them not to practice any "*exaction*", but there was no specific reference to this issue in the formal permissions starting in 1570. Late in the century, this concern emerged more prominently. In 1596, they were prohibited from "*exiger aucune chose de quelque personne que ce soit*". Two years later, in 1598, a Rouennais went to court for protection from being harassed in his home by the Conards, probably because he heard that he was going to be awarded the "crosse" and feared that if he put up resistance he would be attacked.

For many different reasons, urban festive traditions were breaking down by the end of the century. Whereas in 1541, many people in Rouen had "open houses" where they welcomed the arrival and performance of groups of Conards and were happy to serve them wine in return, it may be that there were fewer and fewer houses who did so as the century went on. The reason for this could have been the distrust and economic hardship caused by civil war, increasing distaste for traditional rituals influenced by changing religious standards (both Protestant and Catholic), or simply an emerging culture that was no longer as oriented towards a communal civic ethos. Whatever the combination of reasons, the result may have been increasing tensions when Conards tried to enforce traditional hospitality on unwilling households, leading to concerns about them exacting wine and hospitality forcefully. The emergence of concerns about exactions in court decisions were manifestations of the fact that Rouen's citizens were losing interest or toleration for these activities[32].

WORDS

The awarding of the "crosse"–a punishment for foolishness–was the bridge that carried the Conards' actions into the realm of words. They believed that the jurisdiction over foolishness embodied in the tradition of awarding the *crosse* also meant they had the right to use words to mock or satirize foolishness in society, both in individual cases and in general terms. The Conards asserted this right explicitly in their verse appeal to the Parlement in 1541, where they compared themselves to

32 M. Rousse, "Le théâtre des farces", p. 81. ADSM, 1 B 716, 27 January 1596; 1 B 727, 24 January 1598; *Triomphes*, p. 76 (open houses). See D. Reid, "Carnival in Rouen", p. 1050–1052.

the "mirror of Socrates" that reveals the flaws in individuals and in society as a whole[33].

Before the final years of the sixteenth century, the Bailliage and the Parlement did not show much concern for the Conards' satire of general foolishness in society, which included general mockery of the law, the church, the nobility, and many different vices and character types. Nor did the courts show much concern in the early years if individuals who were members of the Conards' own class were targeted for mockery in the Abbey's performances, such as the solicitor who was awarded the *crosse* in 1541, or the *huissier* mocked in the play *Les deux soupiers de Monville*. These seem to have been treated both by the courts and by the individuals involved as essentially internal issues within the social group of the Conards themselves–in a sense, treating them as part of the Abbey's jurisdiction. It was not until the end of the century that people from their own milieu would go to the courts for protection from the Conards[34].

On the other hand, from the beginning the courts showed a great deal of concern if the Abbey targeted prominent individuals, and they moved strongly to prevent this from happening. One of the Parlement's overarching concerns in everything it did was avoiding "scandale", meaning public outrage or disorder, and attacking someone prominent was sure to cause scandal in Rouen society[35]. The very first time the Conards came to the attention of the court, it was because the court heard in 1536 that they planned to "*deshonnorer injurier et scandaliser aucuns bons personnages de la ville*".

The Conards appeared on the Parlement's radar at this time because they were taking on a more prominent role in Rouen in the 1530s. This was the same period of time when, for example, they intervened in the pamphlet quarrel between the poet Clément Marot and the Norman priest and poet François Sagon. They also began to be referred to in other works of the period, and the evidence of 1541 suggests that their carnival activity became more elaborate. Moreover, they took part as a respected confraternity in solemn civic processions in 1535 and 1542. In

33 *Triomphes*, p. 12.

34 ADSM, 1 B 727, 24 January 1598; see also a similar case from the Norman town of Vire, 1 B 763, 23 Dec. 1603.

35 J. Dewald, *The Formation of a Provincial Nobility*, p. 62–63.

part, their new-found prominence was the result of a period of considerable prosperity for Rouen and, thus, for the artisans and merchants who were members of the Abbey[36]. The newfound ambition and aggression of the Conards brought them to the attention of Rouen's highest court and forced it to find ways to deal with them.

In the 1536 case, it appears that the court was not all that familiar with the Abbey, referring to them as "*aucuns ceulx disans et nommans conards et leurs complices et alliez*". Having heard reports that they were boasting that they would attack prominent figures in the city, the court moved pre-emptively to prohibit them from doing so. The court shows some awareness of the range of tactics available to the Conards in their performances, prohibiting not only attacks by "*parolles diffamatoires*" but also by "*effigie ou painctures*" and "*audiences en lieux publiques*", which could refer to mock trials[37].

The tactic that would attract the most judicial attention, however, was the printing press. In their public performances, the Conards reinforced their messages by taking advantage of new ways to use this relatively recent technology. In the 1530s, Rouen's printing industry was developing a new market in short pamphlets of news and comic verse[38], and by using this new printing medium to distribute their verse the Conards could expand the scope and effectiveness of their mockery.

The Conards handed out printed pamphlets extensively in the 1541 carnival, but the targets of their mockery were generic social types, and after carnival the Bailliage had no problem granting them a privilege to print the description of the celebrations, including this satire. It was a different case the next year, in 1542, when the Bailliage threw eleven Conards into prison after the carnival procession because of the printed

36 D. Reid, "Carnival in Rouen", p. 1039–1043.

37 ADSM 1 B 447, 20 May 1536 (this edict was pronounced in advance of Rogations, when the Conards also performed in the early part of the century). This concern over attacks on prominent individuals was common in French authorities' response to theatre (S. Beam, *Laughing Matters*, p. 34). The same year, the Parlement of Paris reminded the Basoche not to single out individuals in their performances (M. Bouhaïk-Gironès, *Les clercs de la Basoche*, p. 140), a concern that it repeated several times during the century.

38 D. Reid, "Carnival in Rouen", p. 1042; M. Walsby, "Printing in Provincial France in the Early Sixteenth Century", *The Book Triumphant: Print in Transition in the Sixteenth and Seventeenth Centuries*, M. Walsby and G. Kemp (dir.), Leiden, Brill, 2011, p. 110–111; A. Pettegree, "A Provincial News Community in Sixteenth-Century France", *The French Book and the European Book World*, A. Pettegree (dir.), Leiden, Brill, 2007, p. 19–42.

material they had distributed. It appears that they had attacked a more identifiable target–the city council or some of its individual members. The Conards appealed to the Parlement to be released from prison, and this appeal was granted for technical reasons. At the same time, the court recalled the prohibitions it has issued in 1536, and added a proviso to deal with printed works, prohibiting the Conards from "*faire escrire ne imprimer pour publyer ne faire aucuns escripteaux, dixains ne autres dittez ou libelles*" without judicial permission[39].

Only three years later, however, in 1545, the Conards conducted a mock trial of an effigy of a canon of the cathedral, and in 1546 they attacked another canon with "*libellos famosos*", probably printed pamphlets. In each case the Cathedral chapter complained to the Parlement[40]. After this point, however, there are no further indications of attacks by the Conards on specific high-ranking individuals.

By the 1550s, there was sufficient concern about printed texts in Rouen that two censors had been appointed to review works before they were published. In October 1556, in fact, after review by the censors, the Parlement prohibited a troupe of actors from performing a particular play. A few months later, in February 1557, when the Parlement gave the Conards permission to perform their plays and their procession after it had otherwise banned masking and other celebrations, it was clearly still concerned about what they might do–yet it nonetheless granted them permission to perform. The conditions it imposed reflected its previous problems with the Conards' attacks on individuals, both spoken and written. It specifically required that they not offend any individual "*en faict, dit, ny par parolle, ny par ecrit*". It also specified that they should not offend "religion" in general–but unlike the situation at the end of the century (see below), there is no indication that calling themselves an Abbey, dressing in ecclesiastical garb, and parodying gestures such as giving a benediction were considered offensive, as these behaviours continued unchanged until 1587. The Parlement also delegated commissioners to observe the festivities and report any contraventions on the Thursday after *mardi gras*[41].

39 ADSM 1 B 2051, 27 March 1541 (Registres d'audience).

40 M. Rousse, "Le théâtre des farces", p. 55–57.

41 ADSM, 1 B 567, 1 B 568, 16 January 1556 (o.s.). M. Rousse, "Le théâtre des farces", p. 81.

In 1570, when the Parlement officially recognized the Conards' monopoly over carnival, it was less specific and simply said that they should perform their usual processions, masquerades and plays "*sans scandale et sans offenser le public directement ou indirectement.*" The Parlement appears to have been less concerned about what the Conards might do than it had been in 1557. It may be that the Parlement felt it didn't need to be more specific because it was confident that the Conards would restrain themselves–in the midst of the Wars of Religion, the Conards' writings from this period included far less social satire and relied more on burlesque humour[42].

It was not until 1587 that the Conards got into trouble for broader social satire, specifically of the Church. Even then it was not for their contemporary material, but for their writings from almost half a century earlier. Ahead of the 1587 carnival, the Conards decided to republish the description of the 1541 carnival, with additional material from the 1580s appended[43]. While the contemporary material was harmless, the anti-clerical satire that was included in the 1541 carnival was a different matter. It consisted of traditional complaints about corruption in the Church that had not raised an eyebrow at the time, and had not stopped the Bailliage from giving them permission to publish the text. In 1587, on the other hand, it appeared in a very different light at a time of religious tensions, when an ultra-Catholic party was forming in the City in response to the Protestant Henri of Navarre becoming heir to the throne. In a different context, the same text had quite a different meaning.

The Conards' reprinting of this text may not have been entirely innocent. For one thing, the permission to publish the book was granted by none other than the Abbot himself, in a parody of the usual wording, adding supervision of the printing press to the wide range of jurisdictions he already claimed[44]. More seriously, it suggests the Conards were aware that the book would not pass muster from the real authorities. As well, there is some reason to suppose that the Conards were not sympathetic to the ultra-Catholic faction in Rouen. The next year, one of their chariots featured four characters "revestues d'habits fort riches" who were struggling to seize a sceptre, symbolizing "*la contrarité, la convoitise et*

42 ADSM 1 B 619, 3 February 1570. *Triomphes*, op. cit., p. 81–110.

43 This edition is the one that has survived to the present, exists in the BMR, and whose 1874 edition is being used here (*Triomphes*).

44 *Triomphes*, p. 2.

l'ambition de plusieurs qui veulent parvenir au sceptre", which looks like a reference to the well-known ambitions of the Guise. If that is the case, the republishing of this text may well have been a deliberate poke at the rising power of the ultra-Catholic party in Rouen[45].

The Catholic Church responded aggressively to the publication of this book. At least one prominent preacher denounced the Conards from the pulpit[46]. The Archbishop's vicar-general submitted an appeal to the Parlement asking for exemplary punishment for the authors and printers of this book because it was "*scandaleux contre l'honneur de dieu et de la religion catholique*", and for the appointment of commissioners to go to bookshops to find and destroy the book. It also added a demand that the Conards be forbidden to wear or publish anything scandalous to the Church[47].

The Parlement summoned the publishers to answer the charges, and allowed the vicar-general to visit bookstores in the company of a member of the court and destroy all copies (although they were not entirely successful, as this is the book that still survives)[48]. While the court did not mention any restrictions on the Conards, the Abbey did not perform as usual that year. While there was a carnival procession, an eyewitness states that it was not as big as usual, and it was not identified with the Conards.

The next year, in 1588, the Conards eliminated all religious references, calling themselves the "Maison de Sobriété" led by the "Père de Sobriété" in their request to the Parlement and in their procession. While the Parlement's permission was worded identically to previous years aside from the name change, the same eyewitness in his description says that the change was a response to a directive from the court, to the point where they no longer made the gesture of benediction[49].

45 BMR MS M 41 (Journal of curé of St. Martin du Pont), f. 28v (reprinted in *Revue de Rouen et de la Normandie* 2, 1540, p. 251–254). The publishers of the 1587 edition of the *Triomphes*, Nicolas Dugord and Loys Petit (see *Triomphes*, op. cit., p. 2), may both have been from families that included Protestant members, which is also suggestive of a milieu that was not sympathetic to the ultra-Catholic party (E. Lesens, "Imprimeurs et libraires rouennais et dieppois, protestants, avant 1789", *Bulletin historique et littéraire de la Société de l'Histoire du Protestantisme Français* 34 (1887), p. 333).

46 BMR MS M 41, f. 15v.

47 ADSM, 1 B 689, 17 January 1587.

48 ADSM, 1 B 689, 17 January 1587.

49 ADSM 1 B 694, 13 February 1588, BMR MS M 41, f. 28v.

Concern about the Conards' writings, in other words, had gone from the personal to the political at the end of the century. Although they wrote little social satire in the later part of the century, reviving the memory of what was once perfectly acceptable satire earlier in the century was enough to land them in trouble. It also meant that the acts of religious parody that had until then been considered harmless, such as calling themselves an Abbey, dressing in clerical garb, and using religious gestures, were now seen as problematic.

On the other hand, as long as they kept their satire indirect and part of their performance, rather than written down, the Conards still had some scope for expressing satirical opinions in way that did not give the authorities reason to respond. Although they could not wear ecclesiastical garments, through the chariot displaying a struggle for the sceptre they were still able to mock the grasping ambitions of those who were trying to take the throne of France, in a way that was clear to spectators but was not specific enough to prompt any formal action against them. What did prove to be effective against them was informal action; after the ultra-Catholic Holy League took over Rouen in 1589, the Conards stopped performing their carnival celebrations for the duration of its regime[50].

Curiously, the Parlement allowed them to return to the designation of "Abbey" when they started up again after the city returned to royalist control in 1594. The Conards may have been taking advantage of a desire to get away from an ultra-Catholic atmosphere. When the Conards briefly tried to revive their celebrations in 1609 after an interruption of several years, however, they renamed themselves the "Maison Conarde", once again removing the religious reference[51].

50 Not only are there no records of them performing or receiving permission to perform, but in 1594 in their request to the Parlement they refer to their "faceties et joieusetes accoustumees faire avant les derniers troubles" (ADSM 1 B 710, 20 December 1594).

51 ADSM 1 B 710, 20 December 1594; 1 B 797, 3 February 1609.

THE PLAY OF JURISDICTIONS OVER CARNIVAL

There were, thus, many different reasons why carnival in Rouen might need to be regulated. There were also multiple bodies that might perform this regulation–the Bailliage, the Parlement, and the Abbey of the Conards itself. The nature of this regulation shifted around constantly over the course of the century.

FROM BAILLIAGE TO PARLEMENT

There is every reason to suppose that, up to 1542, the Bailliage was the primary jurisdiction for regulating carnival celebrations in Rouen to whatever extent they were regulated. The Bailliage, which had existed in Rouen long before the Parlement was established in 1499, was in charge of maintaining local public order, whereas the Parlement's mandate was province-wide. In 1536, the first time the Parlement intervened in the Conards' activities, it instructed the Bailliage to carry out its orders. In 1541, it was almost certainly the Bailliage that issued a local decree banning the playing of music in public, and in 1542 it was the Bailliage that arrested eleven Conards in response to a complaint from the city council.

Over the course of the sixteenth century, however, the Parlement's ever-increasing interest in the local affairs of Rouen meant that power in the city gradually shifted to it from the city council and the Bailliage. In 1541, the Conards took advantage of this process, and played off the two jurisdictions against each other by appealing the Bailliage's ban on playing instruments in public over its head to the Parlement.

The Conards may have had some reason to feel that the Parlement would be sympathetic. It was an interesting time for the Parlement–it had only just been reconstituted after being suspended by the King for bad behaviour–but it is hard to say how that would have affected the Parlement's decision in this case. More to the point, perhaps, in their internal deliberations during carnival season in 1542 magistrates were forbidden from wearing masks and attending theatrical performances (*momeries*)–suggesting that some of the members had been in the habit of doing so and could be sympathetic to carnival celebrations[52].

In their approach to the Parlement, the Conards engaged in a kind of banter with the magistrates, perhaps in an attempt to bring the court into the spirit of the event. They submitted their request in jovial verse–which may seem astonishing, but a similar request in verse from the *basoche*, in 1570, can still be found in the archives[53]. The Parlement's initial response was brief and to the point, giving them permission but prohibiting masks at night. The Conards then turned to one of their members, Jacques Sireulde, who was one of the ushers (*huissiers*) of the Parlement and who would have known the magistrates well. He submitted a further brief poem requesting that the court "*jours et nuicts les veuillez dispenser / Masques porter*". This time, the court replied with a joyful poem of its own, fully in the spirit of carnival, allowing them to "*Aller masqué, triomphant, phaleré, / Les jours et nuicts en triomphes exquis*". It added–overriding the jurisdiction of the Bailliage–"*Ne soyent en riens par aucuns empeschez*" and then integrated its usual caution, "*Sans faire mal qu'aprés n'en soit enquis*"[54].

The joyful spirit of this response is remarkable and unusual, and it suggests that Sireulde took advantage of his connections to lobby the Parlement, and perhaps target magistrates whom he knew would be sympathetic.

When, a year later, the Conards again successfully appealed to the Parlement to overrule the Bailliage in the case of the eleven imprisoned Conards, the Parlement essentially established that the Conards were now under its direct jurisdiction. In 1545 and 1546, the cathedral chapter complained directly to the Parlement about the Conards's behaviour; and in 1557, the Conards successfully applied directly to the Parlement for permission to perform after the Parlement's general prohibition of

52 A. Floquet, *Histoire du Parlement de Normandie*, Rouen, É. Frère, 1840–1842, vol. 2, p. 93. The Rouen Parlement, like that of Paris, was also supportive of the Basoche's festive theatre (M. Rousse, "Le théâtre des farces", p. 75; M. Bouhaïk-Gironès, *Les clercs de la Basoche*, p. 77).

53 Reprinted in A. Floquet, "Requête en vers français adressée, le 25 février 1570, au parlement de Normandie par les suppotz de la basoche de Rouen. Arrêt du parlement sur cette requête", *Bibliothèque de l'école des chartes*, 1:1 (1840), p. 99–102. Also, M. Rousse, "Le théâtre des farces", p. 89–90. The request is primarily for a defence of its professional privileges, but also refers to their tradition of planting a May tree.

54 *Triomphes*, p. 11–15.

masking ahead of carnival season[55]. The Abbey no longer answered to the local court but directly to the highest court in the province.

One complication is that, for some of these cases, there are no records in the archives of the Parlement itself. The reason may be that the Parlement, before 1570, did not want to accord to the Conards the degree of recognition that would be granted by a formal *arrest.* In 1557, the question of the Conards' request was discussed in private, and the Parlement decided that its decision would not be "*dellivré arrest en forme*" but rather that "*la requeste sera souscrite du greffier*", that is, the decision would simply be written at the bottom of the Conards' own submission when it was returned to them. This procedure is the same as that described by the Conards in their account of 1541, when they say that the Parlement's replies were written below their submissions, which would explain why there is no record of the 1541 decision in the Parlement's records[56].

CONTRAST WITH THEATRE

It is remarkable that the Parlement gave the Conards permission at all in 1557, as it was in the midst of a crackdown on the theatre. The anxieties about poverty and Calvinism in this decade led not only to the appointment of censors, but also to increasing disapproval of festive activity. In May 1556, the treasurers of the municipal poor house had petitioned the Bailliage to forbid any theatrical activity whose subject was not pious[57]. The Parlement, meanwhile, was in the midst of implementing a crackdown on public disorder, including public performance.

In particular, it was once again extending its jurisdiction, this time to control theatre in Rouen. In 1556, two ushers of the Parlement interrupted and stopped a theatrical performance organized by a group of well-known performers led by a Pierre Le Carpentier, known as Le Pardonneur. The actors had already received permission to perform from the Bailliage, as was apparently the usual custom. They complained to the Parlement that they had permission to perform and had invested heavily in the production. The Parlement showed it was concerned with

55 ADSM, 1B 2051, 27 March 1541 (o.s.); M. Rousse, "Le théâtre des farces", p. 55–57, 81.

56 M. Rousse, "Le Théâtre des farces", p. 81. *Triomphes*, p. 13–15.

57 C. de Beaurepaire, introduction to J. Sireulde, *Le trésor immortel tiré de l'écriture sainte*, Rouen, Léon Gy, 1899, p. xlvii, l.

both the words and the deeds of the troupe. It decreed that they had to submit the text of their plays to the censors, who rejected one of the farces but allowed the other plays. It also prohibited the players from advertising their performances by parading through the streets beating drums. The Parlement also ordered that, in future, it would review all requests to perform theatre, essentially taking over jurisdiction over theatre in the city[58].

The Parlement's anxiety about public disorder increased in the following months. In the lead-up to the 1557 carnival season, the King's attorney-general complained about people ignoring a prohibition on carrying weapons and wearing masks. In reiterating this prohibition, the Parlement threw in a clause forbidding actors to perform in public: "*a tous badins et auteurs de farces ne autres telz jeux de plus et ingerer de se promener par la ville sonner tabourins ne jouer leur jeux*"[59].

It was likely in response to this edict that, three weeks later, the Conards appealed directly to the Parlement for permission to celebrate carnival. They presumably wanted to ensure that this wide-ranging decree against wearing masks and performing in public did not apply to them. When the court granted this exemption, the unusually detailed restrictions and conditions it included–limiting the time period, forbidding attacks on individuals or the church, specifying supervision and potential punishment–were a symptom of its anxiety. Nonetheless, it is remarkable that they were allowed to produce their parade and theatrical performances at all, given how the court was soon to react to a different request for theatrical performance[60].

Ahead of carnival season in 1558, the actor Le Pardonneur applied to the Bailliage, as was the custom, for permission to produce some more plays with a new troupe, no doubt seeking to take advantage of the crowds and festive atmosphere of carnival to increase his audience. The Bailliage gave him permission, but ordered him to also go to the Parlement as per the 1556 decree. In his request to the high court he tried to play to the court's respect for precedence, noting that "*de tout temps il a esté accoustumee en ceste ville de Rouen jouer moralitez et farces.*" He also sought to directly address their concerns about the content of

58 ADSM 1 B 1556, 24 October 1556.

59 ADSM, 1 B 568, 16 January 1556 (o.s).

60 M. Rousse, "Le théâtre des farces", p. 81.

plays by promising that they contained no scandalous material. His timing was bad, however. The Parlement, clearly still anxious about public order and specifically complaining that vain expenses would be better spent on poor relief, prohibited him absolutely from performing, in what was merely a preface to a sweeping condemnation of all forms of disorder, including carrying weapons, playing dice and cards, and prostitution[61]. It also forbade wearing masks, receiving maskers in one's home, and selling masks, as it had in 1513. Despite this prohibition, we know that the Conards continued performing, because their carnival is attested in 1562.

The cases of the theatre troupe and the Conards make an interesting contrast. While the Conards ended up transferring themselves to the Parlement's jurisdiction through appeals to get around the Bailliage, the theatre troupe was happy with the Bailliage's jurisdiction and was transferred forcefully to the Parlement. One factor for the differing treatment may well have been that the Conards were a well-established and formal confraternity, a legally recognized group with a reputation and resources that could be held accountable. The theatre troupes, by contrast, while largely made up of locals, were ad-hoc affairs without formal status.

A related issue may have been precedent. By the 1550s, the Conards had been performing consistently, at the same time of year, for at least two decades and probably much longer–likely as far back as anyone could remember. Jonathan Dewald, in his study of the Parlement of Rouen, notes that the court did not have a systematic body of written law to refer to in order to interpret many situations, and thus had to rely heavily on precedent and tradition[62]. The Conards had already survived several different complaints from the city council and from the cathedral chapter. The Parlement's response had been to put conditions on their activities, but it did not try to abolish such an established tradition. In their request of 1557, the Conards emphasized this tradition and the fact that the Parlement had recognized their activities in the past, emphasizing that their performances during carnival were "accoutumez," customary,

61 ADSM, 1 B 577, 27 January 1558 (o.s).

62 J. Dewald, *The Formation of a Provincial Nobility*, p. 36–39. In 1528, a lawyer for the Paris Basoche successfully defended their right to their jurisdiction in part using the argument that "they have been established for so long that there is no memory otherwise" (S. Beam, *Laughing Matters*, p. 82).

and the court echoed this language in its decisions. Le Pardonneur, in his request, also emphasized that theatrical performances in general were customary, but for his troupe this argument did not carry weight, perhaps because theatre troupes changed over time he could not claim precedent for his particular troupe.

As well, while the Parlement's desire to avoid scandal was a regular sticking point in its dealings with the Conards, it may also have played in the Conards' favour. The parade of the Conards was one of the highlights of the year in Rouen, popular and widely viewed. In 1551, the country gentleman Gilles de Gouberville spent the winter in Rouen, and going to see the parade of the Conards was one of the few events he made note of in his journal[63]. The Abbey was made up of respectable men, pillars of their community. To try to prohibit such a popular and traditional event completely could have caused even greater scandal and possibly disorder in the city.

The most significant difference, however, may not have been legal but practical. The conclusion to the Parlement's long public order decree in 1558 is significant. Having banned a wide range of common activities, the Parlement has to direct the personnel of the Bailliage to enforce these decrees, and also direct the city's militia companies to apprehend infractors[64]. In other words, after taking over jurisdiction from the Bailliage, the Parlement then has to request that same Bailliage to do the actual enforcing. And, given that the sergeants of the Bailliage were limited in number, it has to also call on the city's militia companies.

The Parlement's problem was that its only direct enforcement personnel were a dozen ushers. That may have been enough to stop a theatrical performance by a small group of actors, so the theatrical ban was likely effective. But it was nowhere near enough to stop a parade of hundreds of able-bodied men. Only another large group could stop them, such as the city's militias–but they were members of the same social group as the Conards, and quite likely some people were members of both. While the Parlement's theoretical jurisdiction was extensive, in practice it needed the cooperation of others in the city to make its

63 G. de Gouberville, *Journal de Gilles de Gouberville* II, A. de Blangy (ed.) (*Mémoires de la société des antiquaires de Normandie*, 32), Caen, Henri Delesques / Rouen, Lestringant/ Paris, Honoré Champion, 1895, p. 134.

64 ADSM, 1 B 577, 27 January 1558 (o.s).

decrees effective. The Parlement had already, in the past, issued decrees banning masking that appear to have had little effect. It simply could not enforce a ban on masking or carnival by itself without the support of significant other forces in the city. Over the course of the century, it had realized that working with the Conards while controlling their excesses was more effective.

FROM FACETIOUS TO LEGAL JURISDICTION

That the Abbey's carnival festivities could be stopped with the support of a large group of fellow-citizens was demonstrated just a few years later. In 1562 the emerging Calvinist movement, which included many men from the same social group as the Conards themselves, stoned the carnival parade[65]. The Calvinists were, in effect, trying to assert their own jurisdiction over carnival activities, and in April of that year they took over the city in practice, forcing the Parlement into exile. Although their temporary jurisdiction was destroyed when the King retook the city in October, their effect on carnival may have lingered, as the Conards appear to have been inactive in the following years.

The Conards began reasserting their festivities in 1569, when the Parlement heard "*certains avertissements*" about planned carnival celebrations. It consulted with a new jurisdiction implemented in the city as a result of that decade's disturbances, the *lieutenant general du Roy*, the Sieur de Carrouges, before making a decision, and then issued the decree that no-one should wear masks or beat a drum after the night watch set forth–a reflection of its previous concerns about masking at night[66].

It was the next year, 1570, that the Conards submitted their request to the Parlement seeking to formalize their role in carnival. Simultaneously, they submitted the same appeal to the King's lieutenant-general. It is possible that these requests were the result of preliminary negotiations with the two jurisdictions, but there is no way of knowing.

They may have taken this action because their legal situation had become less certain. The force of precedence was weakened because they had been interrupted. As well, the presence of a new jurisdiction in the form of the King's lieutenant-general, specifically appointed after the

65 T. de Bèze, *Histoire ecclésiastique des églises réformées au Royaume de France*, G. Baum and E. Cunitz (éd.), Paris, Librairie Fischbacher, 1883, p. 713.

66 ADSM, 1 B 616, 26 February 1569.

city was recaptured from the Calvinists with a mandate to keep order, meant that there was a new source of potential uncertainty in terms of reaction to their activities. By accepting the need to get permission to perform their activities, they were losing an independence they had previously enjoyed, but it was a trade-off that made sense in uncertain times, because gaining formal legal recognition also promised to give them greater security and recognized legal rights.

The court, noting the agreement of the King's lieutenant-general, granted their request to perform their "*chevauchees mascarades es jeux acoustumez*"–the inclusion of "*jeux*" meaning that theatre was also allowed. As noted above, it expressly asserted the Conards' monopoly over wearing masks and playing instruments, applying it to everyone no matter what their "*qualité, estat et condition*" and ordering it published across the city to the sound of a trumpet.

Unlike earlier examples where the court gave its permission in a deliberately casual manner that did not appear in its formal records, this decree was formal and public. The decision was less restrictive than that of 1557 in some ways. Although it established a limited restriction on masking at night, it did not specify specific restrictions on what the Conards said, it did not specify supervision or threaten punishment for misbehaviour, nor did it explicitly limit the permission to the three days of carnival[67].

The court was, in effect, granting the Conards jurisdiction over carnival in Rouen–they could decide who would take part, in exchange for accepting limited restrictions. This decree was an extension of a common procedure in medieval and early modern cities. Authorities lacking the bureaucratic mechanisms to regulate an activity would deputise a self-managing group to do it for them, in return granting them a monopoly over the activity. Maintaining this monopoly gave the group a self-interested incentive to enforce regulations. Many guilds managed their trades under this arrangement, but it could be applied in cultural matters as well. In Paris, the Confraternity of the Passion had a long-standing monopoly over the production of mysteries, which the Parlement of Paris transformed in 1548 into a monopoly over secular theatrical productions in the city when it banned mysteries[68].

67 ADSM, 1 B 619, 3 February 1570.

68 S. Beam, *Laughing Matters*, p. 131. M. Bouhaïk-Gironès, *Les clercs de la Basoche*, p. 129–130, 138–139.

The Parlement had realized that, given its limited enforcement personnel, blanket banning of carnival activity did not work. By granting the Abbot jurisdiction over wearing masks in carnival, a large and well-established group of citizens now had a self-interest in managing the masking that had so troubled the court. The Conards, in turn, gained prestige, participants, and possibly money from the formalization of their claimed jurisdiction over wearing masks. In its pronouncements in the 1580s, the Abbey puts a lot of emphasis on this official jurisdiction over masking granted by the court[69].

The same permission was granted in most subsequent years in the 1570s and 1580s[70]. After the end of the second civic insurrection of the Wars of Religion, the takeover by the Holy League from 1589–1594, the Parlement continued to grant the permissions with much the same wording, although it now added additional conditions. In 1595, the King's Attorney General made a specific complaint after carnival about the Conards causing scandal, and yet they were again granted permission to perform in 1596, although with an added directive that they should behave modestly and without exacting anything[71]. Although the Parlement could probably have refused permission by this time, after the second serious interruption to the Conards' carnival caused by the Holy League, it continued to allow them to perform.

CONCLUSION

Throughout the sixteenth century, the Abbey of the Conards was able to play the legal system to maintain its ability to celebrate carnival. The legal system was, first of all, a source of humour and a way to enhance the facetious status of the Abbot. When it came to the reality of legal issues, the Abbey played Rouen's jurisdictions against each other, using the Parlement to escape the local control of the Bailliage. It used its legal status and its long tradition of performance to enable its supporters to

69 *Triomphes*, p. 93, 94, 100, 101,

70 See D. Reid, "Carnival in Rouen", p. 1048 and S. Beam, *Laughing Matters*, p. 135.

71 ADSM, 1 B 107 (Registres secrets), 20 February 1595; 1 B 716, 27 January 1596.

wear masks, play instruments and perform plays in public when others were forbidden to do so. It adapted to changing times and addressed the concerns of Rouen's authorities while maintaining its ability to celebrate and to mock. Eventually, from 1570 onwards, it established a special status for itself and transformed its joyful claim to jurisdiction over carnival into a real, legally recognized jurisdiction, gaining the right to choose who could participate in the public festivities.

By the end of the century, changing values meant that new legal issues came to the fore. The Wars of Religion meant that the Abbey's use of clerical costume came under scrutiny. And changing social values meant that citizens of their own social class became less tolerant of the Conards' visitations and awarding of a *crosse* of foolishness. The Abbey's claim of jurisdiction over foolishness was being contested, not by the courts, but by its fellow-citizens. It was not legal cases or decisions, but rather these shifting values that meant that the Conards faded away around the turn of the seventeenth century.

After their disappearance, the Parlement continued to issue carnival-time decrees, although these no longer mentioned the Conards. These decrees now implicitly accepted that masks would be worn, but they put familiar conditions on them: that they should not provide cover for the distribution of libellous pamphlets; that they should not include ecclesiastical garments; and that maskers should not carry weapons[72]. The Abbey had taught the Parlement that carnival could only be controlled, not prohibited, and even after the Abbey of the Conards disappeared, the legal issues and concerns they had raised continued to be in play.

Dylan REID
University of Toronto

72 ADSM, 1 B 829, 16 February 1613; 1 B 892, 3 February 1621; 1 B 927, 21 February 1626.

APPENDIX

The following is a chronological list of judicial interventions regarding carnival or the Abbey of the Conards in Rouen during the sixteenth century. Relevant non-judicial events are noted in italics.

Dates are given according to the modern calendar; source references match the calendar used in the archival record (noted as (o.s.) where the old style calendar was used).

ADSM: Archives Départementales de la Seine-Maritime. All references to the ADSM are to the records of the Parlement of Normandy, *arrêts sur rapport*, unless otherwise indicated.

* Asterisks indicate sources that are transcribed in full in ROUSSE, M., "Le Théâtre des farces en France au Moyen Âge", Thèse de Doctorat es-lettres, Université de Haute Bretagne Rennes 2, 1983, vol. 5. Available online at http://scd-fonds.uhb.fr/TR2RousseT5.pdf

Date	Description	Source
7 January, 1514	The Parlement bans masking. No mention of Conards.	ADSM 1 B 348, 7 January 1513 (o.s.)
20 May, 1536	The Parlement intervenes to prevent Conards from attacking prominent individuals (note: ahead of Rogations).	ADSM 1 B 447, 20 May 1536*
30 January – 21 February, 1541	The Bailliage bans playing instruments in public. The Conards appeal to Parlement and receive an exemption.	*Les triomphes de l'Abbaye des Conards*, p. 5–15
27 March, 1542	Eleven Conards are arrested by the bailliage after carnival, at the request of city council, for distributing libellous pamphlets. The Conards appeal to the Parlement, which releases them.	ADSM 1 B 2051, 27 March 1541 (o.s.) (*Registres d'audience*)*

16 February, 1545	The cathedral chapter complains to the Parlement about an attack on a canon.	ADSM, G 2158, f. 117v–118r (Délibérations du chapitre de la cathédrale)*
11 March, 1546	The cathedral chapter complains to the Parlement about an attack on a canon.	ADSM, G 2158, f. 240v–241vr (Délibérations du chapitre de la cathédrale)*
16 January, 1557	The Parlement bans masking and theatrical performance ahead of carnival.	ADSM 1 B 568, 16 January 1556 (o.s.)*
9 February, 1557	The Conards appeal to the Parlement for permission to perform carnival celebrations and theatre. Permission is granted, with various conditions.	ADSM, 1 Mi 345 (*registres secrets* of Parlement) (currently lost)*
27 January, 1558	A theatre troupe requests permission to perform plays during carnival period; granted by Bailliage, but refused by Parlement.	ADSM, 1 B 578, 27 January 1558 (o.s.)*
1562	*Calvinists attack Conards' carnival procession; possibly carnival celebrations cease for a few years.*	BÈZE, T. de, *Histoire ecclésiastique des églises réformées au Royaume de France*, 713.
26 February, 1569	The Parlement hears that carnival celebrations are being organized, and prohibits them from continuing after the night watch begins.	ADSM 1 B 616, 26 February 1569*
3 February, 1570	The Conards appeal to the Parlement and the *lieutenant du roi* to be given	ADSM, 1 B 619, 3 February 1570*

	permission to perform carnival celebrations and for a monopoly over masking during carnival season. Permission and the monopoly are granted, with light conditions; the monopoly is also extended to playing musical instruments.	
1571–1586	In most years in this period, the Conards request permission to perform and a monopoly over masking from the Parlement and the *lieutenant du roi*, and it is granted.	ADSM, various
17 January, 1587	The Vicars General of the Archbishop of Rouen complain to the Parlement about the re-publication of the *Triomphes de l'abbaye des Conards*. The Parlement investigates and orders the book destroyed.	ADSM, 1 B 689, 17 January 1587*
13 February, 1588	The Conards remove all clerical references from their name and activities ("Maison de sobriété"). Request and receive permission to perform from the Parlement and the *lieutenant du roi.*	ADSM 1 B 694, 13 February 1588*
1589	*Holy League takes control of Rouen. Parlement is divided. The Conards in 1594 indicate that their activities were interrupted during this period.*	
20 December, 1594	Rouen having returned to royal control, the Conards apply to Parlement under their old name and receive permission to perform, with the added condition that maskers must not carry weapons.	ADSM, 1 B 707, 20 December 1594*

20 February, 1595	The King's attorney-general complains to Parlement about Conard behaviour during carnival.	ADSM, 1 B 107, 20 February 1595 (*Registres secrets*)
27 January, 1596	Conards apply for and receive permission to perform from the Parlement. Condition added that they must not exact anything from anyone.	ADSM, 1 B 716, 27 January 1596
24 January, 1598	Christoffe Ludot appeals to Parlement to prohibit the Conards from harassing him. The Parlement orders them not to harass him or anyone else.	ADSM, 1 B 727, 24 January 1598*
3 February, 1609	Now as "Maison Conarde," apply for and receive permission to celebrate carnival from the Parlement.	ADSM, 1 B 797, 3 February 1609*
16 February, 1613	Ahead of carnival, Parlement forbids distribution of defamatory pamphlets under the pretext of masking. No reference to Conards.	ADSM, 1 B 829, 16 February 1613
3 February, 1621	Parlement forbids those wearing masks from carrying weapons. No reference to Conards.	ADSM 1 B 892, 3 February 1621
21 February, 1626	Parlement prohibits wearing clerical costume under the pretext of masking. No reference to Conards.	ADSM, 1 B 927, 21 February 1626

CONFLICTS OF JURISDICTION IN GOLDEN AGE SPANISH THEATER

A Panoramic Overview and Enquiry into Antonio de Soria's 1644 Trial vs. the Villa de Madrid Regarding the Ban on the *Comedia*

Among the several art forms that flourished during the Spanish Golden Age of the sixteenth and seventeenth centuries (1500–1680), literature deserves a special mention, both due to its weight in the society of the time and to its current consideration. Novels and poetry, written by the likes of Miguel de Cervantes, Mateo Alemán, Garcilaso de la Vega, Luis de Góngora, or Francisco de Quevedo, certainly enjoy the aforesaid appreciation, but theater, the famous *comedia*, has claimed the lion's share in this respect. Golden Age theater has come to our times in record numbers of texts (in the tens of thousands), autographs (in the hundreds), and even seventeenth-century playhouses or *corrales*, a living testimony to the obsession with their theater that, according to foreign visitors, characterized Golden Age Spaniards. In contemporary Spain, both the general audience and the critics have responded enthusiastically to their ancestors' devotion for the playhouse, generously dedicating their leisure or professional time to the subject.

Among the themes that these scholars of Golden Age theater have privileged, legal matters hold a paradoxical position: conflicts of jurisdiction are both one of the most and least studied areas in the field. On the one hand, critics have dedicated reams of paper to explore conflicts of jurisdiction within the plot, in fact one of the most popular subjects amongst scholars, to the point that the presence of a conflict of jurisdiction in a Golden Age play has been an important factor contributing to its canonization amidst the legions of texts available. On the other hand, scholars have largely ignored the question of conflicts of jurisdiction outside the plot, that is, real and practical legal conflicts involving the staging, management, or distribution of the *comedia*. These clashes were nevertheless quite real and important, because, if Golden Age Spanish theater frequently staged conflicts, it turns out that the staging itself, the daily running of the theatrical system, also produced a number of clashes that the juridical machine tried to prevent. This conflicting jurisdiction regarding the *comedia* is precisely the subject that our present article will explore in a panoramic fashion. Our analysis will begin with a swift overview of criticism about conflicts of jurisdiction within the plot of the *comedia*, and then will move on to a description of legal practices involving the *corrales*, touching upon some examples of legal conflict. Finally, our article will focus on a case study that will shed some light on several of those aspects: the 1644–1645 legal suit involving contractor Antonio de Soria, then rightful exploiter of all the Madrid *corrales*.

As for internal, plot aspects, the popularity of conflicts of jurisdiction can be gauged by considering that critics have even defined a whole subgenre within the *comedia* around it, a subgenre that we can term the *comedia de villano* or *comedia villanesca*[1]. To build this category they have put together plays featuring a conflict between the Crown and the nobility, a clash in which the Crown would eventually rule in favor of the *villanos* (literary, inhabitants of a *villa*, or town) that had risen up against a nobleman because of an abuse of power. It is the case of three famous *comedias* by Lope de Vega (*Fuenteovejuna*, *El mejor alcalde, el rey*, and *Peribáñez y el comendador de Ocaña*) and one by Pedro Calderón de la Barca (*El alcalde de Zalamea*, based on a previous version by Lope). In these texts, local jurisdiction in the hands of a *villano*, usually a mayor, clashes with corrupt authority represented by a degenerate nobleman holding office, usually a *comendador* of one of the military orders. The subject can also appear in similar, more radical forms, as in the case of *La estrella de Sevilla* (attributed to Lope de Vega), in which the Seville judges (the *veinticuatro*) remind the king himself that his authority knows limits, as defined by their jurisdiction. As we could expect given post-Romantic fervor for rebellious heroes and peoples, there has been a lively debate about the extent of this criticism of absolute authority, and about the supposed "democratic" tendencies of playwrights and

1 L. A. Blecua Perdices, "*Peribáñez*: valor y sentido de la comedia villanesca", *Cuadernos de teatro clásico* 17 (2002), p. 163–188.

audiences alike[2]. In any case, and notwithstanding the resolution of these debates, it is a fact that acute conflicts of jurisdiction appear in several *comedias*, that the topic interested Golden Age playwrights (some of these *comedias* were revisited and rewritten decades later), and that contemporary critics recognize its importance as subject matter in the plot. In fact, some scholars have even approached the subject from a legal perspective[3], even departing from the field of Law rather than literature[4].

As we have advanced above, this situation contrasts with the study of actual conflicts of jurisdiction affecting the *comedia*, a field that scholars

2 J. A. Maravall, *La cultura del Barroco: análisis de una estructura histórica*, Barcelona, Ariel, 1975; M. McKendrick, *Playing the King: Lope de Vega and the Limits of Authority*, Woodbridge, Tamesis, 2000; N. Salomon, *Lo villano en el teatro del Siglo de Oro*, transl. Beatriz Chenot, Madrid, Castalia, 1985.

3 B. P. E. Bentley, "*El mejor alcalde el Rey* y la responsabilidad política", *Lope de Vega y los orígenes del teatro español: actas del I Congreso Internacional sobre Lope de Vega*, Manuel Criado de Val (dir.), Madrid, EDI-6, 1981. P. 415–424; W. R. Blue, "The Politics of Lope's *Fuenteovejuna*", *Hispanic Review* 3 (1991), p. 292–315; J. T. Bravo Vega, "Errar lo menos: notas para una interpretación de *El alcalde de Zalamea*", *Calderón entre veras y burlas: Actas de las II y III Jornadas de Teatro Clásico de la Universidad de la Rioja*, J. T. Bravo Vega and F. Domínguez Matito (dir.), La Rioja, Universidad de La Rioja, 2002, p. 15–34; G. M. Burton, "Justice in *Peribáñez*: The Creation of a New Order in Language", *Romanic Review* 84 (1993), p. 475–492; M. L. Castro Rodríguez, "La desacreditación del comendador en *Fuente* Ovejuna y *Peribáñez y el comendador de Ocaña*", *Cuatrocientos años del «Arte nuevo de hacer comedias» de Lope de Vega: actas selectas del XIV Congreso de la Asociación Internacional de Teatro Español y Novohispano de los Siglos de Oro: Olmedo, 20 al 23 de julio de 2009*, G. Vega García-Luengos and H. Urzáiz Tortajada (dir.), Vol. 2., Valladolid, Universidad de Valladolid, 2010, p. 359–367; S. Fischer, "Staging Lope de Vega's *Peribáñez*: The Problem of an Ending", *Bulletin of Hispanic Studies* 82 (2005), p. 157–180; A. M. García Gómez, "Pedro Crespo, padre y juez, en la primera versión de *El alcalde de Zalamea*", *Memoria de la palabra: Actas del VI Congreso de la Asociación Internacional Siglo de Oro, Burgos-La Rioja 15–19 de julio 2002*, F. Domínguez Matito and M. L. Lobato (dir.), Madrid, Iberoamericana, 2004, vol. 1, p. 841–852; C. M. Gasta, "The Politics of Agricultre: Dramatizing Plight in Lope's *Fuenteovejuna*", *Bulletin of the Comediantes* 55 (2003): 9–21; D. R. Larson, "Rape, Redress, and Reintegration: Ritualized Social Drama in *El mejor alcalde, el rey*", *La violencia en el mundo hispánico en el Siglo de Oro*, J. M. Escudero and V. Roncero López (dir.), Madrid, Visor, 2010, p. 125–136; Matas, Julio, "El honor en *Fuenteovejuna* y la tragedia del Comendador", *Lope de Vega y los orígenes del teatro español*, p. 385–390; G. Ribbans, "The Meaning and Structure of Lope's *Fuenteovejuna*", *Bulletin of Hispanic Studies* 31 (1954), p. 150–170.

4 J. F. Acedo Castilla, "La conducta penal del Capitán Atayde en *El Alcalde de Zalamea*", *Boletín de la Real academia Sevillana de Buenas Letras: Minervae baeticae* 28 (2000), p. 125–141; A. Biglieri, "El derecho público en *El alcalde de Zalamea*", *Urbe et ius: revista de opinión jurídica* 5 (2006), p. 24–27; A. Rodríguez Raimúndez, "Aspectos jurídico-procesales de El mejor alcalde, el rey, de Lope de Vega", *La ley: revista jurídica española de doctrina, jurisprudencia y bibliografía* 5 (1996), p. 1403–1411.

have largely neglected. Partly, this dereliction stems from the fact that jurisdiction over the Madrid commercial[5] *corrales*--the best documented case, and the one upon which we will focus--seems extraordinarily clear for Early Modern standards. The steps leading to this legislation in Spain, which we will examine later in some detail, are related to the development of professional theater itself or, to be more precise, to the development of a permanent urban theater that stemmed from the previous itinerant troupes. In this evolution the contribution of Italian companies touring Spain from circa 1575 was essential, as their technical and professional innovations allowed the nascent Spanish theater to consolidate[6]. Thus we find the notices relating to the first theatrical performances associated to hospitals and charitable institutions, a link that is a definite trait of the *comedia*[7]. In 1568, the Cofradía de la Pasión y Sangre de Jesucristo[8] begins organizing regular theater shows, and in its wake we find like institutions staging theater all through the Crown of Castile (Zamora, 1574; Valladolid, 1575; Toledo, 1576; Seville, 1585; Granada, 1588; Murcia, 1592; Lima, 1594; México, 1597; Córdoba, 1602) and Aragón (Valencia, 1566; Barcelona, 1579). As permanent theaters, the hospitals used the *corrales*, the interior courtyards of residential buildings[9], an originally very simple space that quickly developed as the popularity of the spectacle grew.

5 We will exclude the King's playhouse, where private shows were staged. In Madrid itself, and excluding other royal residences, like Aranjuez, these shows first took place in the old palace, the Alcázar, where the *salón grande* or *salón de comedias* would be put to good use. Then, from 1633 on, the King could enjoy *comedias* in his own *ad hoc* space, the *Coliseo* in the new Buen Retiro palace (J. Thacker, *A Companion to Golden Age Theatre*, Woodbridge, Tamesis, 2007, p. 129).

6 O. Arróniz, *La influencia italiana en el nacimiento de la comedia española*, Madrid, Gredos, 1969; N. L. d'Antuono, "Lope de Vega y la *commedia dell'arte*: temas y figuras", *Cuadernos de Filología* 3 (1981), p. 261–278; J. V. Falconieri, "Los antiguos corrales en España", *Estudios escénicos* 11 (1965), p. 91–118; J. V. Falconieri, "Historia de la *commedia dell'arte* en España", *Revista de literatura* 11–12 (1957), p. 3–37 and 69–90; R. W. Listerman, "Some Material Contributions of the *Commedia dell'Arte* to the Spanish Theater", *Romance Notes* 17 (1976), p. 194–198; N. D. Shergold, "Ganassa and the *Commedia dell'Arte* in Sixteenth-Century Spain", *Modern Language Review* 51 (1956), p. 359–368;. D. Shergold, *A History of the Spanish Stage from Medieval Times until the End of the Seventeenth Century*, Oxford, Clarendon, 1967.

7 J. M. Díez Borque, *Sociedad y teatro en la España de Lope de Vega*, Barcelona, Bosch, 1978, p. 3.

8 B. García García, "Los teatros madrileños y la Cofradía de la Soledad", *Pygmalion* 0 (2009), p. 21–49, p. 29–30.

9 Díez Borque, *Sociedad*, p. 5–9.

The *cofradías*' administration of the Madrid *corrales* was from the beginning controversial, as literary sources testify[10]. Nevertheless, Bernardo García García's detailed study of the case of a pioneer charitable-theatrical institution, the Cofradía de la Soledad, shows that legislation advanced quickly thanks to royal support. Thus, circa 1565 the main royal institution in the kingdom, the Consejo de Castilla ("Counsel of Castile"), encouraged the aforementioned Cofradía de la Pasión to found a hospital in Madrid and therefore to extend its charitable scope. Nevertheless, the hospital turned out to be so expensive that the Cofradía de la Pasión obtained from the Consejo de Castilla a monopoly over all plays represented in Madrid in order to pay for the daily running of the charitable institution[11]. That very important privilege, dating from before 1572, meant the beginning of official legislation on the *aprovechamiento de comedias* ("use of *comedias*") by charitable organizations, the *cofradías*. Protected by this privilege, in 1574 the Cofradía de la Pasión began to build one of the historical theaters of Golden Age Madrid, the Corral del Príncipe. Nevertheless, and spurred by the Cofradía de la Pasión's success, on the same year of 1574 another charitable institution, the Cofradía de la Soledad, began to build their own *corral*, thereby infringing on the royal privilege mentioned above. The reason for this audacity was that the Cofradía de la Soledad had in fact a brighter theatrical tradition than the newer Cofradía de la Pasión, as it had already been involved in Madrid's theatrical spectacles during the 1560s. This tradition was probably essential in the development of the legal suit that quickly followed the Cofradía de la Soledad's initiative: the Cofradía de la Pasión complained to the Consejo de Castilla and obtained on May 7, 1574 a renewal of their monopoly and a sanction against the Cofradía de la Soledad. Nevertheless, shortly later, and for unknown reasons, the two institutions agreed to split the management and earnings from the Madrid playhouses: two thirds for the Cofradía de la Pasión, and one for the Soledad[12]. This Consejo de Castilla decision

10 J. Hesse, *Vida teatral en el Siglo de Oro*, Madrid, Taurus, 1965; H. Recoules, "Les allusions au théâtre et à la vie théâtrale dans le roman espagnol dans la première moitié du XVIIe siècle", *Dramaturgie et société. Rapports entre l'œuvre théâtrale, son interprétation et son public aux XVIe et XVIIe siècles*, Ed. J. Jacquot, Paris, CNRS, 1968, 133–148.

11 C. Davis and J. Varey, *Los corrales de comedias y los hospitales de Madrid: 1574–1615. Estudio y documentos*, Madrid, Tamesis, 1997, p. 89–102; García García, "Los teatros madrileños", p. 30.

12 García García, "Los teatros madrileños", p. 32–33.

and the subsequent agreement between the two *cofradías* established the key legislation regulating the management of the Golden Age playhouses. In it we see that the *aprovechamiento de comedias*, the essential link between commercial theater and charitable institutions, was already in effect in 1574. This peculiar link was further strengthened when, in 1579, the *cofradías* bought the Corral de la Cruz, and shortly later when they built the Corral del Príncipe, in 1582[13]. These actions turned the *cofradías* into de facto owners of the playhouses that they had been renting before.

With some minor changes, essential for the understanding of the case we will examine below, the *aprovechamiento de comedias* situation would last until the end of the Habsburg period. By 1630 the theaters provided funding for six Madrid hospitals, although by that date the two *cofradías* (de la Pasión and de la Soledad) did not control the theaters directly. Rather, they chose to retain ownership of their *corrales*, but now outsourcing its exploitation to private contractors, charging a flat fee for that right[14]. As we will see below, contractors often did not meet the demands of the *cofradías*, and that meant that, in those frequent cases, it was the Ayuntamiento de la Villa de Madrid ("Madrid Town Council") who had to pay the difference[15] in order to maintain the essential hospitals running. This constant nuisance led to the elimination, in 1638, of the connecting point provided by the *cofradías*: that year the Ayuntamiento took charge of the administration of the *corrales*[16], deriving directly from it the income, some of which it would give the

13 Díez Borque, *Sociedad*, p. 9–10; C. Pellicer, *Tratado histórico sobre el origen y progreso de la comedia e histrionismo en España*, Madrid, Administración del Real Arbitrio de Beneficencia, 1804, p. 59.

14 In the beginning, the individual *corrales* were rented on a daily basis directly to the troupes themselves, especially during those periods of the year most propitious for theater shows, such as the San Juan festivities (J. Deleito y Piñuela, *También se divierte el pueblo (recuerdos de hace tres siglos)*, Madrid, Espasa Calpe, 1954, p. 270). For example, Casiano Pellicer informs us that the *cofradías* rented a *corral* to the company of Ganassa in 1574 for 10 *reales* a day (p. 54). From 1615 on, the *cofradías* would rent the right of exploitation of both *corrales* yearly (usually in contracts lasting two or four years [H. A. Rennert, *The Spanish Stage in the Time of Lope de Vega*, New York, The Hispanic Society of America, 1909, p. 204–205]) to individuals who would then, in turn, rent them to the troupes (Díez Borque, *Sociedad*, p. 11–12).

15 By 1616, the Ayuntamiento's contribution amounted to 54.000 *ducados* per year (Díez Borque, *Sociedad*, p. 12).

16 Díez Borque, *Los espectáculos*, p. 22; *Sociedad*, p. 12.

cofradías for their hospitals. Rapidly, the Ayuntamiento centralized the administration of the *corrales*: in 1639 it created an *escribanía de protección* ("bureau of protection") to process all economical affairs relating to the playhouses[17]. Therefore, by 1638 a public institution, the Ayuntamiento, was directly managing the commercial theaters of the Spanish capital.

Nevertheless, and mirroring the double aspect of Madrid (Villa y Corte, Town and Court), the Ayuntamiento de la Villa was not the only public organization in charge of the Madrid theaters. The fact that the Crown also participated in their administration is revealed by a document preserved in Madrid's Archivo Municipal[18]. This undated document, probably drafted in the seventeenth century by order or the Ayuntamiento to clarify some juridical point, explains how the main *corrales* in the Villa, the Corral de la Cruz and the Corral del Príncipe, came into existence and, more importantly, how they were governed. The document begins by telling the story of the establishment of the *corrales* in relation to the two main *cofradías* and their hospitals[19], as we explained above. Then it adds that, in 1608, shortly after the return of the court to Madrid in 1606 after its Valladolid sojourn, the Crown produced more legislation and began intervening directly in the supervision of the theaters. Philip III named a person from the Consejo de Castilla (Juan de Tejada) Lord Protector of the hospitals and, consequently, of everything regarding the *corrales*: "*cometiéndole la protección y gobierno de dichos hospitales, y en su consecuencia de todo lo que tocaba para el buen régimen de los corrales de comedias*". To better pursue this management, the Consejo de Castilla issued new legislation for theater impresarios, governors of the *cofradías*, contractors, and all the *corral* personnel, a legislation that was printed and publicly exhibited in the *corrales*[20]. The Consejo de Castilla produced, thus,

17 Díez Borque, *Sociedad*, p. 18.

18 The document, 2-467-10, was included as number 73 in J. E. Varey and N. D. Shergold's essential *Teatros y comedias en Madrid: 1600–1650. Estudio y documentos*, p. 184–187. We will modernize the spelling of this document and of numbers 43 and 44, used below and corresponding to Antonio de Soria's *pleito*.

19 By 1630, the hospitals were already six, the Hospital de la Corte, the Hospital de la Pasión, the Hospital de Niños Expósitos, the Hospital General, the Hospital de Antón Martín, and the Hospital de Desamparados (Díez Borque, *Sociedad*, p. 13). This testifies to city growth during that period, but also to the rising economic importance of the theater, and therefore of its administration.

20 The 1608 legislation can be found in J. M. Díez Borque (*Los espectáculos*, p. 25–32).

> *reglas para lo que debían observar los autores de comedias, los comisarios de las cofradías, los arrendadores, ministros y demás dependientes que asistían a ellos, y dichas ordenanzas se imprimieron y mandaron fijar una en cada corral, para que se supiese la obligación de cada uno y se castigase al que contraviniese a ellas*[21].

However extensive and clear this legislation may seem, there was a clear potential for conflict stemming from the dual ruling by the *Protector de comedias*, as the Protector was commonly known, and the Ayuntamiento. As we explained above, during the financial problems of the 1630s contractors began to show that they could not meet their payments to the hospitals, and the Ayuntamiento had to provide the money so that the hospitals would not go bankrupt. It was precisely the King's Protector, then don José González, who in 1632 and in the King's name asked the Ayuntamiento to contribute 4000 *ducados* and to apparently--the text is in this respect ambiguous--administer the *corrales*, but conjunctly with the Protector. The document explains that the Protector had communicated to the Ayuntamiento: "*que S[u] M[ajestad] le había remitido, y a esta Villa, la administración de los corrales de comedias, mandando le asistiese a ella el Corregidor y dos Comisarios que se nombrasen para todo lo que fuese necesario tocante a dichos corrales*"[22]. That meant that this particular council, although under the presidency of the Protector, had a majority of municipal members. This double public administration, by the Town Council (Ayuntamiento) and Crown (Protector), would continue during the rest of the century, and it meant, in practice, that the Ayuntamiento would run their important decisions by the Protector, to obtain his approval, as, and as our documentation attests, it happened in 1635 regarding a building expansion of the *corrales*. In this case, the Ayuntamiento men in charge of the *corrales* agreed to the request, but only as long as the Protector approved it first: "*estuvieron llanos con que esta Villa lo hiciese, con que primero se diese cuenta al señor José González del Consejo y Cámara de S[u] M[ajestad], superintendente de los dichos corrales*

21 "Rules that *comedia* impresarios, *cofradía* commissaries, subletters, ministers and all other employees assisting them must abbey, and the aforesaid rules were printed and posted one in each *corral*, so that everybody's duties were known and that those who did not meet them were punished". The legislation was expanded in 1615, among other things to specify that all *comedias* had to be approved and licensed by the Protector (Shergold and Varey, *Teatros y comedias*, p. 185). We modernize spelling and punctuation in all quotes from Shergold and Varey.

22 Shergold and Varey, *Teatros y comedias*, p. 186.

de comedias"[23]. The Protector's approval seems to have been essential even for such apparently minor issues, even though, in this occasion, the problem was resolved quite harmonically. In any case, this double supervision meant that there were two different institutions in charge of the *corrales*: the Consejo de Castilla, represented by the Protector, and the Ayuntamiento.

The Protector, as member of the Consejo de Castilla, was beyond municipal jurisdiction and operated as the highest authority in all matters regarding the theater[24]. For example, the Protector had to authorize companies and even individual plays, controlled the accounting of the *corrales*, approved their subcontracting every two or four years, and named special *alguaciles* (policemen) for the playhouses. These two *alguaciles de comedias*[25] depended directly from the King's House, as they took their orders from the Consejo de Castilla. In fact, the *alguaciles de comedias* were also subordinated to the *alcaldes de casa y corte*, the policemen and judges in charge of the King's court.

In turn, the Ayuntamiento, as institution in charge of the *cofradías*, enjoyed economic autonomy from the Protector and the Crown. It managed the daily functioning of the *corrales*, auctioned the subcontracts, and named its own *alguaciles*, under the jurisdiction of the municipal Corregidor, to maintain public order in and around the playhouses[26]. Nevertheless, even here there was a characteristic overlap, or at least connection between the Ayuntamiento and the Crown: the Corregidor was the royal official that presided over the city councils or *ayuntamientos*. The Madrid Corregidor named his two lieutenants (*tenientes de corregidor*), who had to be confirmed by the Consejo de Castilla and who were in charge of overseeing all municipal establishments, and among them the *cofradías*. The Corregidor and *tenientes* were assisted by forty *regidores*, city noblemen and burghers who took part in the council of the Ayuntamiento, and who were further aided by a variety of technical and practical officers, such as scriveners, plumbers, architects, lawyers, and policemen (*alguaciles*). Naturally, these *alguaciles* appointed by the

23 Shergold and Varey, *Teatros y comedias*, p. 187.

24 Díez Borque, *Sociedad*, p. 19.

25 Originally there were indeed two *alguaciles de comedias*, one for the Corral de la Cruz, and one for the Corral del Príncipe, although by 1641 the number was rather two per *corral*.

26 Díez Borque, *Los espectáculos*, p. 23.

Ayuntamiento frequently came in conflict with the *alcaldes de casa y corte* mentioned above, the policemen directly named by the Consejo de Castilla: theoretically, the *alcaldes de casa y corte* had jurisdiction over the King's court (Corte), and the Ayuntamiento over the city (Villa). Nevertheless, given the dual character of Madrid, both city and court (Villa y Corte), the respective areas of domain could be difficult to distinguish, as was the case with the *corrales*. This is not the opinion of the leading expert in the field of *corral* jurisdiction, José María Díez Borque, for whom there existed a perfectly clear division of functions and of hierarchy emanating from the power of the *Protector de comedias*, and therefore from the King himself:

> *El Protector de hospitales o Protector de comedias tenía jurisdicción total, como vemos, sobre las restantes jerarquías de la organización teatral. Por debajo de esta autoridad, única y englobadora, existió una perfecta distribución jerárquica de cargos con atribuciones concretas y perfectamente delimitadas*[27].

Although it is true that both Ayuntamiento (through the Corregidor) and Protector (via the Consejo de Castilla) ultimately derived their power from the King, the fact is that few power structures in Early Modern Europe were ever a clear-cut as Díez Borque claims, even in a place that enjoyed such a thoroughly developed bureaucracy as Spain did. Moreover, as the information provided by Díez Borque himself shows--see, for example, the case of the *alguaciles*, above--, the double-headed administration of the *corrales* had plenty of room for conflicts of jurisdiction. Nevertheless, the case study of a particular 1644–1645 trial will show that, as Díez Borque claims, the system did indeed work, at least as long as the Ayuntamiento was willing to compromise and did not operate contrary to the Protector's wishes.

The case in point produced one of the most interesting and voluminous series of documents among those collected by Varey and Shergold: the 1644–1645 trial of subcontractor Antonio de Soria vs. the Villa de Madrid. It is a case that exemplifies how the system worked despite the aforementioned potential clashes, and how different parties could

27 Díez Borque, *Sociedad*, p. 20. "The Protector de Hospitales or Protector de Comedias had total jurisdiction, as we can see, over the other authorities of the theatrical organization. Below this authority, unique and all-encompassing, existed a perfect hierarchical distribution of positions with concrete and perfectly delimited duties".

subtly exert pressure on the King regarding one of the most controversial topics related to Golden Age Spanish theater: the total prohibition of the *comedias*.

In fact, in order to understand the Antonio de Soria trial, which began on October 12, 1644, we must turn the clock back a few days. On October 6, 1644, Queen Isabel de Borbón died, an event that triggered the accustomed corollary to royal mourning: the closing of the *corrales de comedias*. Playhouses had been unpopular with moralists since the times of Philip II, and there was a long history of controversies regarding their morality, a debate most famously studied by Emilio Cotarelo y Mori. Moralists opposing the *comedia* were not merely content with the public censorship exerted on theater both by the Consejo de Castilla and the Inquisition: they also advocated a full ban of theatrical activity. As Cotarelo y Mori proved, royal mourning was a wonderful occasion for these powerful anti-*comedia* pundits, who, for example, in November 1597 convinced Philip II to close the *corrales* to honor the death of Philip's daughter, Catalina Micaela. This temporary interruption became permanent in May 1598, when Philip decreed the *sine die* closure of the playhouses. In the dark waning of Philip's reign, plagued by economic, military and demographic turmoil, the moralists had finally prevailed. It was only the death of the old King on that same year that allowed the *corrales* to reopen, after the customary mourning period[28]. Similar temporary closings would take place in 1611 (death of Margaret of Austria, Queen of Spain), 1621 (death of Philip III), and in our date of 1644. Every single one of these interruptions threatened to be permanent, as the moralists' attacks against theater revived with them. What prevented the feared decree of prohibition was a combination of political and economic considerations. On the one hand, the government realized the need for public distractions and the people's love for the theater; on the other hand, there were the essential economic arguments: the *corrales* supported the hospitals. This was the decisive factor, one that

28 Augustin Redondo has shown how the ascetic sadness of the last years of Philip II's reign quickly gave place to a festive atmosphere at Philip III's accession to the throne. This new mood is reflected in the appearance of several works of literature–most famously the first part of *Don Quixote*–sometimes related to the direct patronage of Philip III and his *valido*, the Duke of Lerma (J. Domínguez Búrdalo and A. Sánchez Jiménez, "El mundo del libro a través de las relaciones clientelares en la Sevilla de entresiglos (1582–1621)", *RILCE* 25 (2009), p. 256–317, p. 258–263).

the very opponents of the *comedias* recognized, and one that the critics have duly underscored: theater kept the hospitals running, and therefore it could not be forbidden[29]. In short, the *comedia*'s association with charity allowed it to eventually prevail in the long-lasting controversy[30]. This peculiar justification is, according to Díez Borque, characteristic of a transitional moment such as the Spanish seventeenth-century: "*la explotación económica de la comedia, la comercialización no pudo justificarse en sí misma sino que necesitó, como paliativo moral, la justificación por sus fines benéficos*"[31]. Economic gains could not stand by themselves to defend the *comedia*, and only became effective arguments when linked to moral concerns. Such was the case in Philip II's times, and such it was, as we shall see, in 1644.

In that year, Queen Isabel's death meant the automatic ban on theatrical activity: on the very next day, October 7, the Protector notified the *corrales* that they must close[32]. This decree effectively triggered the flurry of legal activity that we are going to analyze, as on October 12 Pedro Trigoso, Town Pursor (Receptor de la Villa) sued Antonio de Soria because he owed the Madrid Ayuntamiento money (3.000 ducados) from the *arrendamiento* (rent) of the *corrales*[33]. Before October 19, this subcontractor, the aforementioned Soria, replied to the judge that it was rather the Ayuntamiento the one who owed him the money that he had already advanced regarding the 1644–1645 *arrendamiento.* In 1641 (beginning at San Juan, in June), Soria had agreed to pay the Ayuntamiento the sum of 64.680 *ducados* in the span of four years to be able to use (and rent out) the *corrales.* By October 1644, Soria had already paid the equivalent of three years of contract (48.510 *ducados*, that is, 533.610 *reales*), and even some of the 1644–1645 rent above that (Soria adds the receipts to prove it). Therefore, Soria argued, the Ayuntamiento must pay him back the whole amount corresponding to 1644–1645, until the theaters reopened, since, he argued, the real theater season only began in October, and he had lost more than he had made during the summer months of

29 C. Sanz Ayanz, and B. J. García García, *Teatros y comediantes en el Madrid de Felipe II*, Madrid, Universidad Complutense, 2000, p. 77.

30 Díez Borque, *Los espectáculos*, p. 22.

31 Díez Borque, *Sociedad*, p. 13.

32 Varey and Shergold, *Teatros y comedias*, p. 111–112.

33 Varey and Shergold, *Teatros y comedias*, p. 100.

1644. In short, the Ayuntamiento owed him, Soria reckoned, a total of 57.862 *reales*[34]. The conflict was, of course, served.

Representing the Ayuntamiento, Trigoso replied on October 31, 1644, arguing that the contract Soria had signed did not specify anything about summer or winter months, and that therefore he owed Madrid a full sum corresponding to the period from June 1644 to June 1645. In addition, Trigoso appends a curious comment on the *comedia* ban:

> *los dichos cuatro meses [of rent corresponding to 1644 and 1645 for which Soria has already paid] no han llegado y hasta que lleguen puede haber accidentes por los cuales se vuelva a dar licencia para que haya comedias, y por la necesidad de los hospitales la real piedad de S[u] M[ajestad] podrá dispensar el justo sentimiento de la dicha muerte*[35].

Trigoso thinks that the ban will not last long, because unknown events ("accidentes") can occur to convince the King to reopen the *corrales*, and because His Majesty's Royal Piety ("la real piedad de S[u] M[ajestad]") will realize that the economic needs of the hospitals are reason enough to shorten the mourning. That is, an Ayuntamiento official functioning as such expresses in legal correspondence that the Protector and the King can (and the implication is that they should) reopen the *corrales* to put an end to these problems and to the hospitals' economic trouble.

What Soria thought about this last remark we do not know, for he only insisted in the point that the *comedia* season really began in October, not in June, and that he had incurred serious losses due to the King's ban. With this reply, the trial proceeded under the authority of the Madrid Corregidor (representative, let us remember, of the King at the Ayuntamiento): on November 28 Soria was called to testify, on December 10 the Ayuntamiento expropriated and auctioned goods worth 3.000 *ducados* belonging to one of Soria's associates, Juan de la Mota. And so it went, with the examination of witnesses, during the rest of December, 1644[36]. Soria's (and now also Mota's) complaints to

---

34 Varey and Shergold, *Teatros y comedias*, p. 100–101.

35 Varey and Shergold, *Teatros y comedias*, p. 104. "The aforesaid four months [of rent corresponding to 1644 and 1645 for which Soria has already paid] have not arrived yet and until they arrive there could be many accidents through which the license for *comedia* representation can be renewed, and taking into account the needs of the hospitals H[is] M[ajesty]'s royal clemency can dispense with the just sentiment caused by the aforesaid death".

36 Varey and Shergold, *Teatros y comedias*, p. 104–110.

the Corregidor were constant during this period, and forced the royal official and his *regidores* at the Ayuntamiento to look for more details, and also for precedents for Soria's case. Therefore, on December 9, 1644, they ordered Soria to relate in detail how much he had made by month during the years of the contract[37], and on November 29, 1644, commissioned a series of legal experts to look up what the corresponding authorities had done in similar cases during previous *comedia* bans. Nevertheless, this enquiry only recalled former conflicts, because, as we know and as the Corregidor found out, before 1638 the style of managing the *corrales* was totally different: during the time of Margaret of Austria's death (1611) the hospitals perceived the rent directly from the managing *cofradías*, and therefore the municipal and royal authorities did not intervene, and in 1621 (death of Philip III) these *cofradías* had in fact subtracted a sum from the part of the contract not fulfilled due to the ban. The Ayuntamiento had found in the past a different jurisdictional distribution and within it an unfavorable precedent, and was now at a loss. Despite the pressure they undoubtedly exerted on the Protector to reopen the *corrales*, a pressure reflected in the October 31 Trigoso letter to Soria, they must have perceived danger at hand if they rejected Soria's claims and if the relentless subcontractor chose to appeal to a different branch of royal authority in charge of the *comedias*, the Protector and Consejo de Castilla, that he could have reached directly or through a suit at the kingdom's Chancillería in Valladolid.

This puzzling information and unwelcoming perspective led the Ayuntamiento to seek a settlement. On December 20, 1644, the Ayuntamiento's lawyers and *comisarios* met and agreed that Soria was indeed right in his claim that the best months for theater were the Fall and Winter ones (in itself a very valuable piece of information for scholars). Therefore they concluded that the Ayuntamiento must pay back to Soria an amount equivalent of the income he had made in the years past corresponding to the *comedia*-less months for which Soria had already paid[38]. They had, thus, agreed to come to a settlement (*ajuste*)

37 The result of this request is a priceless account by Soria of theater proceedings during 1641–1644, specifying how much every section of the *corral* yielded, and even who rented the VIP areas in the *corrales*, the *aposentos* (Varey and Shergold, *Teatros y comedias*, p. 116–123; p. 126–148).

38 Varey and Shergold, *Teatros y comedias*, p. 126.

somewhat favorable to Soria. And favorable it was indeed, because when the actual document was drafted, the Ayuntamiento agreed to return to Soria everything he had paid for the 1644–1645 year till that point in time, including the summer months before the *comedia* ban[39]. In short, the Ayuntamiento solved a potentially very complicated and awkward case, one that could have resulted in serious conflicts of jurisdiction between the Ayuntamiento and the Consejo de Castilla, by meeting all the demands of the *corrales* subcontractor.

To sum up, our overview has allowed us to explore how several civil institutions, mainly the King's Consejo de Castilla and the Madrid Ayuntamiento, regulated and oversaw Madrid's playhouses or *corrales de comedias* during the Spanish Golden Age. We have seen how the system was far from simple, and how it left ample room for conflicts of jurisdiction, even if we leave out the delicate matter of the Inquisition and Church jurisdiction, and focus solely on civil institutions. Nevertheless, a case study of a 1644–1645 legal suit involving the ban on the *comedias* has proven that the system did indeed work and that it strove to prevent such conflicts. The documents of the trial do show tensions and subtle pressures exerted by one of these institutions, the Ayuntamiento, on the King. But they also prove that it was these conflicts that made institutions seek settlements with plaintiffs rather than face each other. At least, the 1644–1645 suit by Antonio de Soria seems to suggest that possibility, after the Ayuntamiento made every concession to this subcontractor, even beyond the legal experts' advice, possibly to avoid Soria's appeal to the King's *Protector de comedias*. In any case, the examination of conflicts of jurisdiction in the daily running of Spanish Golden Age theater seems a necessary and fruitful venture, and a subject that should be further explored in future studies.

Antonio Sánchez Jiménez
Université de Neuchâtel

39 Varey and Shergold, *Teatros y comedias*, p. 148–150.

QUATRIÈME PARTIE

JUSTICE EN SCÈNE

"IN HEMDE ENDE IN BROECK"

The performance of justice in late medieval Utrecht

On 2 June 1423 somewhere in the city of Utrecht, Claes, son of Jan Ridder, broke a glass window in his drunken revelry. Although at the time when the case was written down he had already made amends by having the window repaired, the consequences of his action were extensive. First, he had to spend time in the so called *vleyshuus* (literally "meat-house"), the house of the butchers' guild which, because of its location near the town hall, functioned as a prison[1]. From there he was subsequently ordered to come before the city council at the *banklok*, the clock which was used to call gatherings of citizens and warn the city in case of fire or other imminent danger. On this occasion Claes would wear a simple shirt and pants, emphasizing his position as penitent. Arriving at the *banklok*, he was made to beg forgiveness from the Council for his deeds, and in addition pay the city of Utrecht a fine of 5000 "stones". The procedure to be followed was read aloud before the gathered populace and the whole occasion was recorded in detail in both the so-called *Buurspraakboek* and *Raads Dagelijks Boek*[2].

Entries like this are numerous in the Council's documents of legal practice. They portray transgressors being punished in plain sight for an array of different offenses, from counterfeiting to manslaughter and more. These penal occasions always seem to follow a general predetermined script, even though individual details may vary. After imprisonment the accused has to come before the city council at the *banklok*, beg the authorities for forgiveness, and compensate the city for his transgression. What we essentially see here is the public face of the Council's legal

1 A. J. van den Hoven van Genderen, "Op het toppunt van de macht (1304–1528)", R. E. de Bruin e.a. (ed.), *Een Paradijs vol weelde. Geschiedenis van de stad Utrecht* (Utrecht: Matrijs, 2000) 112–189, at 141 (map).

2 Het Utrechts Archief (HUA) 701-1.16: *Buurspraakboek* 1418–1425, 199r; HUA 701-1.13: *Raads Dagelijks Boek* 1414–1425, 150v.

process; a performance of its claim to justice[3]. The offender's crime and its resulting punishment were open for all to see, as was his shame at his humiliating position. In addition to any further–often monetary–penalties, the public character of the occasion could function as a form of punishment in its own right.

This performative aspect of the judicial process, common to much late medieval and early modern legal practice, takes a central place in many of the broader theories on the changing role of punishment in western society[4]. Michel Foucault in his *Surveiller et punir: naissance de la prison* (1975) saw the disappearance of public executions as one of the defining differences between the premodern and modern practice of punishment. Whereas the premodern emphasis on the physical body as direct object to be punished required a publicly-witnessed spectacle, the modern "penalization of the soul" took place in concealed spaces, like the prison cell, considering the body mainly as an intermediary to reach the true object of punishment[5]. One central reason Foucault provided for this change was the way in which it allowed authorities to better control the practice of punishment, because of the absence of a participating and often uncontrollable public[6]. Pieter Spierenburg has also tried to explain the change from public to private punishment in the context of social control by authorities. According to Spierenburg the importance of public punishment lay in its function as a display of

3 In order to avoid confusion over the use of terminology, it is important to note from the start that the terms "performance" and "performative" are used here in the sense of situations in which an act or series of acts–in this case parts of the legal process–are acted out in public. This definition is especially used to contrast it with the terms" application in the Austinian vein as statements which, instead of describing a state of affairs, perform an action by themselves. The latter use would imply that statements made in this performative context were necessarily effective, which is most certainly not the way in which I would present the legal process in these cases. For a decent introduction into Austinian theories of performativity, see: J. Loxley, *Performativity*, London & New York, Routledge, 2007.

4 Note that legal performances were certainly not limited to the late medieval and early modern periods. For a pre-medieval example see: K. M. Coleman, "Fatal Charades. Roman Executions Staged as Mythological Enactments", *The journal of Roman studies* 80 (1990), p. 44–73.

5 M. Foucault, *Surveiller et punir. Naissance de la prison*, Paris, Gallimard, 1975, p. 9–35, translated as M. Foucault, *Discipline and Punish. The Birth of the Prison*, AlA.len Lane (tr.), London, Penguin Books, 1977, p. 3–31. In what follows I will cite from the English translation.

6 Foucault, *Discipline and Punish*, p. 57–65.

repression, a way to impress the crowd by acts of physical punishment. Only when a generally more humanitarian mentality broke through, this display and therefore the public character of punishment lost its role for authorities and disappeared from legal practice[7].

Both Foucault and Spierenburg agree on the central importance of performative justice for premodern authorities. They also seem to suggest that changes in punishment were effected by authorities consciously searching for the most effective means of penalization. Several late medieval historians have instead emphasized the role of the other parties in the judicial performance, namely the convict and the spectators. Esther Cohen presents executions in late medieval France as ritual occasions directed by the authorities to present contemporaries with a picture of the majesty and full efficacy of the law. Even though these events were staged by the authorities, Cohen stresses the relation they formed between the authorities, the public and the condemned. All parties had to play their role and shaped the ceremony either directly or indirectly[8]. Claude Gauvard also sees the performance of justice in the form of death penalties primarily as a coherent ritual process involving different parties. Although the convict plays a less prominent role in her view, the ritual occasions required the common consent of both the authorities and the public opinion as reflections of the values and order of society. Only when both parties agreed on the content and procedure of penalization could the ceremony succeed[9].

What all these authors seem to agree on, even though they hardly make this explicit, is the function of public punishment as communicative device. Be it as an instrument for social control or as ritualized performance of communal values, in all cases the judicial spectacle is used to exchange certain messages and ideas between a society and its authorities. Elaborating on this view, I will regard

---

7 P. Spierenburg, *The Spectacle of Suffering. Executions and the Evolution of Repression. From a Preindustrial Metropolis to the European Experience*, Cambridge, Cambridge University Press, 1984, p. 72–73, 77, 80.

8 E. Cohen, "'To die a criminal for the public good': The execution ritual in late medieval Paris", *Law, Custom, and the Social Fabric in Medieval Europe. Essays in Honor of Bryce Lyon*, B. S. Bachrach and D. Nicholas (dir.), Kalamazoo, Western Michigan University, 1990, p. 285–304.

9 C. Gauvard, "Pendre et dépendre à la fin du Moyen Âge. Les exigences d"un ritual judiciaire", *Riti e rituali nelle società medievali*, J. Chiffoleau, L. Martines & A. Paravicini Bagliani (dir.), Spoleto, Centro Italiano di studi sull"alto Medioevo, 1994, p. 191–211.

public punishment primarily as an intersection of different means of communication. I agree with authors like Cohen and Gauvard that the performance of justice was essentially a ritual occasion. However, taking into account recent anthropological and historical discussions on rituals and ritual behaviour, I will argue that these rituals of justice were not limited to the judicial performance itself. Instead these events formed the locus of an interlocking system of communicative devices, combining textual, oral, visual, symbolic and performative characteristics. Focusing on the case of the late medieval city and episcopal see of Utrecht, I will show the interaction between the different means of communication constituting such legal performances and the attempts of late medieval authorities to control these communicative events in all their aspects.

LATE MEDIEVAL UTRECHT AND ITS SOURCES

As an episcopal see, the late medieval city of Utrecht had for a long time been subordinated to the bishop and his administrative and judicial apparatus. During the late thirteenth century this dependence on the bishop and his institutions gradually decreased. Several civic institutions began to develop and take over more and more judicial, political and administrative functions and powers. Most important among these was undoubtedly the Council of Utrecht. This body managed to acquire both extensive political and crimino-judicial powers in the city, and formed the primary representative of the civic government in regional politics. While growing independence from the bishop gave the citizens more autonomy in handling their own affairs, it also increased internal discord. Several groups, usually headed by important families, struggled for the newly acquired positions of power in the city. Since these civic factions often sought cooperation with regional powers, the struggles tended to cross the city borders into the broader political arena and stimulated the involvement of local lords in city politics[10]. Because of

10 J. Smithuis, "Politiek en geweld in een laatmiddeleeuwse stad. Utrecht, 1400–1430", *Tijdschrift voor geschiedenis* 123, no. 2 (2010), p. 241–253, at p. 249.

this combination of internal discord and external pressure the political landscape of late medieval Utrecht was very turbulent, even resulting in several violent power changes within the ruling elite. The legitimacy of a central urban government formed by the Council and other civic institutions was far from given in this situation[11].

It is in this context that we encounter cases like that of Claes, son of Jan Ridder, mentioned above. Our main sources for these judicial performances are two series of registers called the *Buurspraakboek* and the *Raads Dagelijks Boek*. The former contains records of the public events called the *buurspraak*, which were essentially occasions during which measures and verdicts were proclaimed by the Council for the inhabitants of the city[12]. As mentioned, these proclamations were made next to the *Buurkerk*, one of Utrecht's major churches, in which the *banklok* was located. In cases like these it is always difficult to reconstruct the exact audience reached by the proclamations. However, judging by internal evidence, like the types of measures proclaimed and the different social groups–citizens as well as non-citizens–addressed, we can assume that it was at least intended to be received by a majority of the city's population, be it directly or by word of mouth. Linked to the *Buurspraakboek* is the *Raads Dagelijks Boek*. This series of registers was mainly used to document different cases of civil and criminal law that came before the Council, and was therefore less concerned with the public pronouncements[13]. However, often the word *cloc* would be written in the margins next to an entry in the *Raads Dagelijks Boek*, indicating that it would be pronounced or dealt with at the *buurspraak* and was hence also written in the *Buurspraakboek*. Both the *Buurspraakboek* and the *Raads Dagelijks Boek*

11 For a general history of the city of Utrecht in the fourteenth and fifteenth centuries, see: Hoven van Genderen (2000).

12 HUA 701-1.16. This inventory number covers 22 registers for the period between 1385 and 1579, with gaps for the years 1391–1396, 1536–1542 and 1555–1560. I have based my findings for this paper on the seven surviving registers for the period between 1385 and 1425. Decent though non-professional transcriptions of this material can be found at HUA 1128-2.8.3029 through 3035.

13 HUA 701-1.13. This inventory number covers 28 registers for the period between 1402 and 1577, with a gap for the years 1555–1569. I have based my findings for this paper on the three surviving registers for the period between 1402 and 1425. Decent though non-professional transcriptions of this material can be found at HUA 1128-2.8.3001 through 3003.

therefore contain many records of the practice of performative justice in late medieval Utrecht[14].

One should note, however, that the available sources for this period usually record only part of the communicative processes taking place. True, the later Middle Ages saw a marked increase in the amount and types of texts produced, allowing historians to engage with the large numbers of non-elites constituting past societies in ways that are unthinkable for earlier periods[15] . We should, however, not overlook the fact that many people's voices were still excluded from the sources. And this is especially true of legal records such as the *Buurspraakboek* and *Raads Dagelijks Boek*. Even though they present us with an apparently close look into the lives of ordinary people, showing us their habits, problems and conflicts, this view is always mediated by a legal and political institution with its own agenda as to the city's affairs. In light of the communicative process I attempt to grasp here, this is an important point to note, as it means that our default view of the process is indeed heavily biased.

It is certainly possible to catch glimpses of the communicative practices of groups and people not directly related to the city's authorities. In 1408, for example, the Council issued a prohibition on the spreading of written or spoken messages intended to start unrest or discord, because

14 For the first quarter of the fifteenth century the *Buurspraakboek* contains 126 entries of this kind and the *Raads Dagelijks Boek* 175, for averages of 5 and 7 entries per year respectively. These numbers concern individual entries. Often one entry covers several individuals, who are sentenced *en masse*. Within the chosen time-span we find references to 187 individuals in the *Buurspraakboek* and 244 in the *Raads Dagelijks Boek*, giving averages of 7 and 10 individuals per year respectively. Note that many entries in the *Buurspraakboek* and *Raads Dagelijks Boek* overlap, as they were judged significant for both registers.

15 As evidenced during the past few decades by a surge of publications on the lives of ordinary people in late medieval society, of which the following can pretend to be no more than a very limited cross-section: E. Le Roy Ladurie, *Montaillou, village occitan de 1294 à 1324*, Paris, Gallimard, 1975; R.E.V. Stuip and C. Vellekoop, *Gewone mensen in de Middeleeuwen: bundel studies aangeboden aan F.W.N. Hugenholtz ter gelegenheid van zijn afscheid*, Utrecht, HES uitgevers, 1987; N. Z. Davis, *Fiction in the archives: pardon tales and their tellers in sixteenth-century France*, Cambridge, Polity Press, 1988; J.-C. Schmitt, "Les 'superstitions'", *Histoire de la France religieuse: Des dieux de la Gaule à la papauté d'Avignon (des origines au XIVe siècle)*, J. Le Goff, R. Rémond and P.-A. Février (dir.), Paris, Seuil, 1988, p. 417–551; Thomas N. Bisson, *Tormented Voices: Power, Crisis, and Humanity in Rural Catalonia 1140–1200*, Cambridge & London, Harvard University Press, 1998; M. Goodich (dir.), *Voices From the Bench: the Narratives of Lesser Folk in Medieval Trials*, New York, Palgrave MacMillan, 2006.

word of such messages had reached the Council[16]. In the politically tense environment of late medieval Utrecht, entries like this can give us a sense of the contending messages that were exchanged in the city. However, the image presented to us of these counter-messages is mediated by the judicial and political authority responsible for drawing up the records. Regardless of the actual content of the messages, they are presented as unwanted breaches of communal peace and stability. For what was supposedly a multifaceted process of public communication, in which different parties and individuals brought to the fore their ideas on the constitution of Utrecht politics and society, for most of these voices we have only circumstantial evidence. This does not make the points made in this contribution less valid. The fact that the sources that have survived from this period show such a biased image of the communicative practices in the city emphasizes the importance for authorities of controlling the form and content of these practices. As I will show in this contribution, the descriptions given of the occasions of public punishment in Utrecht functioned as a means to provide the public with an authoritative interpretation of the events, and thereby limit the effectiveness of alternative interpretations of these potentially heavily contested happenings. This sensitizes us to the nature of the sources, which were not so much objective descriptions of the events they record, but texts created and used within a complex process of the public negotiation of social, political and legal "truth".

16 HUA 701-1.16: *Buurspraakboek* 1405–1409, 105r: "*Voirt laet die raet enen ygeliken weten dat hier voerden kerken ende der gueder lude husen ende up anderen steden smadelike rimen ende ander scrifte gescreven siin, die in sraets handen gecomen siin, die grotelic tot onruste ende twidrachten in onser stat dragen moghen. Daer om gebiet die raet enen ygeliken die dat ghedaen heeft off daer scout aen heeft, dat hij dat belie binnen achtedagen voer den raet. Et yemant die dat niet en dede, endet die raet dan terwaerheit vonde, dat woude die raet rechten aen siin liif.*"; idem. 105r-v: "*Voirt verbiet die raet enen ygeliken up siin liif dat nyemant en scrive vuer enigen kerken, husen ofte anderen steden enige rimen ofte andere scriften, die upten rade ofte yemant anders tot twidrachten draghen moghen ofte daer perlement of comen mocht. Ende dat oick det geliix nyemant den raet ofte yemant anders en spreke daer onrust ofte twiste of comen mocht. Et yemant die dat verbrak endet die raet ter waerheit vonde, dat woude die raet rechten aen siin liif.*"

LEGAL PERFORMANCE AND RITUAL THEORY

Before we take a closer look at the role of the textual sources, it is necessary to deal with the legal performances as real-time activities. As already mentioned, historians like Cohen and Gauvard have increasingly started to regard penal ceremonies as ritualized events. Although I agree with this interpretation, it is instructive to determine more precisely what we actually mean when we speak of ritual occasions, how the legal performances fit this model, and which implications this has for our understanding of these performances as communicative medium. For much of the twentieth century, a "ritual" was regarded as a specific type of action. From Arnold van Gennep (1909) and Émile Durkheim (1912) to Edmund Leach (1954), John Beattie (1966), Victor Turner (1967) and other important theorists of religion and society, the difference between ordinary and ritual action was seen as a difference in kind[17]. Recently, however, scholars have started to question this binary opposition between ordinary and ritual acts. As early as 1980 Jonathan Z. Smith argued for an understanding of ritual as a means to make ordinary things significant. According to Smith, ritual places a focussing lens on certain actions by routinizing and rationalizing them, which provides these actions with a special significance[18]. Rather than seeing ritual as a fundamentally distinctive type of action, this school of thought regards ritualized actions as only qualitatively different from other actions. The work of Smith therefore sensitizes us to the close connection between ordinary and ritual acts, as well as the specific way in which ritualized action functions differently.

---

17 A. van Gennep, *Les rites de passage*, Paris, Émile Nourry, 1909; É. Durkheim, *Les formes élémentaires de la vie religieuse. Le système totémique en Australie*, Paris, Alcan, 1912; E. Leach, *Political Systems of Highland Burma. A Study of Kachin Social Structure*, London, Bell, 1954; J. Beattie, "Ritual and social change", *Man. New series*, 1 (1966) 60-74; V. Turner, *The Forest of Symbols: Aspects of Ndembu Ritual*, Ithaca, Cornell University Press, 1967; for a general overview of the broad range of applications of the concept of ritual, see: D. Parkin, "Ritual", *International Encyclopedia of the Social & Behavioral Sciences*, N. J. Smelser & P. B. Baltes (dir.), Oxford, etc., Elsevier Science, 2001, 13368-13371.

18 J. Z. Smith, "The bare facts of ritual", *History of Religions*, 20 (1980), p. 112–127, at p. 112–117.

Returning to the penal events themselves with these theoretical considerations in mind, we can see how the occasions were used to place a Smithsonian "focussing lens" on specific acts and movements. Firstly, the performances had an inherently repetitive character, or were at least presented as such. As mentioned before, most of these entries in the *Buurspraakboek* and *Raads Dagelijks Boek* seem to follow the same succession of acts. In 1402, Marten, son of Henric, and Marten, son of Bruninc, were condemned for trespassing and intimidation. As a result, after being imprisoned in the gatehouse of saint Catherine's gate for a time, they would have to come before the Council in shirt and pants, beg forgiveness for their deeds and pay a fine of 10.000 "stones"[19]. Likewise, in the case of Aelbrecht, son of Jan, son of Lubbrecht, who was condemned for sexual assault in 1409, the culprit was described as coming from the *vleyshuus* before the Council in shirt and pants, begging forgiveness, and paying a fine in "stones"[20]. And the same can be found even later in the fifteenth century, as when Henric, son of Ponskijn, was punished for participation in an illegal fight not only by the loss of his citizenship, but also by having to go through the whole process of public punishment as described before[21]. There were variations on this pattern. As can be seen in Appendix 1, the entries recording these performances can be subdivided into several elements, such as the culprits' outfit during the occasion, the plea for forgiveness, and the specifics of the fine or monetary compensation[22] . Some elements, such as asking

19 HUA 701-1.16: *Buurspraakboek* 1396–1402, 333v: *"Want Marten Henrix soen ende Marten Bruninx soen bi avont ghecomen ziin in eens ghoets knapen huys daer hi mit sinen gasten over tafel zat ende at ende anxte daer enen goeden knaep. Daer omme hebben zi gheleghen op sinte Katerinen poorte ende ziin hier ghecomen in hemde ende in broeke ter klocken ende zellen den rade bidden verghifnisse. Ende elc van hem beyden zel gheven tebeteringhe X*[M] *steens."*

20 HUA 701-1.16: *Buurspraakboek* 1405–1409, 112v: *"Want Aelbrecht Jan Lubbrechts soens soen een vroukijn onredelike aengeverdicht heeft op sinte Jans kerchof ende daer veel onsedicheit ghedreven heeft. Daer om heeft hij int vleyshuus gheleghen ende is hier gecomen ter clocken in hemde ende in broec, ende sel den rade verghiffenisse bidden ende hi sel den rade te beteringe gheven V*[M] *steens."*

21 HUA 701-1.16: *Buurspraakboek* 1418–1425, 227v: *"Want de raet van der stat out ende nye ter waerheyt uutgegaen ende ondervonden hebben dat Henric Ponskijnszoen in den vechtelic ende oploep dat des dynsdages nae sinte Johansdach lestleden geschiet is buten sinte Katherinenpoorte mede toegelopen ende geweest is met eenre grave ende dair enen mede geslagen heeft. Daerom heeft hij int vleyshuys gelegen ende is hier gecomen in hemde ende in broek ter clocken ende zel den raide verghifnisse bidden ende zel den raide te betering geven X*[M] *steens. Ende raet neemt hem sijn borgerscapp."*

22 The word used in the sources for this fine is *beteringe*. According to the Dictionary of Middle Dutch. (E. Verwijs & J. Verdam, *Middelnederlandsch woordenboek*, The Hague, 1885–1971), the term *beteringe* could be used in the sense of a fine, but also more generally

forgiveness from the Council or appearing either bareheaded or in shirt and pants, appear in most entries, while elements such as the payment of a fine or imprisonment preceding the public occasion are less frequent. This is where the records show most variation on the pattern presented earlier, by omitting one or more of the "standard" elements that are part of these penal occasions[23]. Other variations appear where uncommon elements are added. These usually consist of additional punishment, such as the loss of citizenship or another favourable position in the city. In some cases the culprit has to make a "willekeur". This was an official promise made by the wrongdoer to do or abstain from doing something, usually under threat of a harsher penalty.

In a few rare cases we encounter a remarkable variation on the act of asking for forgiveness itself. For example, in 1422 Lamme Kyes was sentenced for hiding prisoners, who had supposedly escaped from custody. Not only was he ordered to appear before the Council in shirt and pants, but he also had to acknowledge in public that he had forfeited his life[24]. And it could become even more dramatic, such as in 1416, when Jorden Walmer had to appear before the Council with a bare sword in hand, declaring his life forfeit and begging the Council for mercy[25]. Entries such as these are very rare. In the first quarter of the

---

as a compensation or reconciliation. Since a plethora of other words was used in Middle Dutch to indicate a fine, such as *boete*, *bekeuringe*, *core*, *pene*, and many more, which, moreover, did not usually carry this additional sense of a compensation or reconciliation, it is not unlikely that the use of *beteringe* will have been understood by contemporaries as refering to compensatory or reconciliatory activity. In this contribution, I will therefore use both the terms "fine" and "compensation" for this *beteringe*.

23 Proportionally this "standard" pattern of 1) presentation in shirt and pants or bareheaded, 2) asking the Council for forgiveness and 3) paying a monetary sum, appears in 49 % (61 of 124) of the cases in the *Buurspraakboek* and 42 % (79 of 174) of the cases in the *Raads Dagelijks Boek*. The most common omission in the *Buurspraakboek* is the payment of a fine, while the *Raads Dagelijks Boek* omits the payment of a fine and the appearance in pants and shirt or bareheaded almost equally often.

24 HUA 701-1.13: *Raads Dagelijks Boek* 1414–1425, 141v: "*Want Lamme Kyes gevangen versteken heeft ende siin liif daer an verbuert hadde ende daer om twe jaer in onser stat vangnisse gelegen heeft. Is hij hier gecomen in hemde ende in broec ter clocken ende sel bekennen dat hij siin liif verbuert heeft. Ende die raet out ende nye doet hem grote genade, ende hij sel den rade verghifnisse bidden, ende de raet neemt hem siin borgerscap.*"

25 HUA 701-1.13: *Raads Dagelijks Boek* 1414–1425, 50r: "*Want Jorden Walmer op onser stat knaep gevochten heeft ende Jacop Henricsoen sonder woirde of brueken gesteken heeft, ende voel onsedicheit bedreven heeft, daer om heeft hij lange tijt int vleyshuys gelegen, ende sel comen ter naester clocken in hemde ende broeck ter clocken mit enen blancken zweerde ende belien dat hij siin liif verbuert heeft ende bidden om genade. Ende die raet sel hem genade doen van sinen live.*

fifteenth century we encounter only three of them in the *Buurspraakboek* and five in the *Raads Dagelijks Boek*. Furthermore, most of them are related to very serious matters: usually treason, breaking of the peace or other types of grave resistance against the civic authorities or social order. This is not only reflected in the addition of the "life forfeiture" clause, but also in the relatively high level of additional punishments, such as fines in the hundreds instead of tens of thousands of "stones". Rather than fundamentally different penal occasions, these entries seem to record an aggravated variant of the standard procedure of legal performance, in which the central aspect of publicly begging the Council for forgiveness is given additional emphasis. In general, then, the legal performances followed a pattern centred around the public call for forgiveness from the Council, taking place in front of the town's *banklok*. By adding specific elements to the standard chain of actions, certain aspects of the punishment could be further emphasized.

This creation of focus was not just achieved by schematization. As their name already suggests the judicial performances were explicitly public occasions. They will have been clearly visible manifestations of the Council's jurisdiction, taking place in front of the centrally located *Buurkerk* and its bell tower, which contained the clock that was crucial in the community's system of public communication and was therefore at the centre of its attention. Furthermore, in most cases the convict had to travel through the city in order to reach the location of the ceremony. Apart from the *vleyshuus*, several different buildings appear to have functioned as prisons, usually one of the city gates or towers[26]. However, regardless of the exact building in which the prisoner was contained, it was always located at some distance from the *Buurkerk*. In combination with the stipulation to appear bareheaded, in simple garb or even both, this meant that the convict had to move through the city clearly visible and recognizable for spectators. The visualization of punishment therefore played a central role in the involvement of the general public in the legal process, and contributed to focusing attention on the acts performed during these occasions.

Ende die raet verbiet hem die stat X iaer lang naest comende ende hij en sal mit genen nien heere incomen ende een mile vander stat."

26 D. Berents, *Misdaad in de Middeleeuwen. Een onderzoek naar de criminaliteit in het laat-middeleeuwse Utrecht*, Utrecht, Stichting Stichtse historische reeks, 1976, p. 44–45.

Understanding the legal performances as ritual occasions, however, brings with it a number of hotly debated issues regarding the workings of ritualized action. Following from the more general scholarly debate on the roles of structure and agency, scholars of ritual have concerned themselves with the question of the influence of an individual actor's intentions on the ritual occasion as a whole. Is a ritual actor free to use ritual as a communicative medium, or does the medium impose a certain structure and logic that limits the actor's freedom of acting? Both approaches have found an eager following. But that does not mean that the distinction is as absolute as it initially seems. Several authors have been able to transcend the limits imposed by both approaches and arrive at a concept that combines the communicative structures of ritual action with the possibility for strategic acting by its agents. Catherine Bell, for one, has explicitly argued for questioning and reinterpreting the traditional conceptual categories of ritual action. Although her focus on the ritualization of acts as a culturally strategic way of acting at first seems to situate her on the "agency side" of the theoretical spectrum, a closer look at her conceptualisation of ritual action shows the importance of communicative structures for the understanding of these acts. According to Bell, ritualized acts are strategic in the sense that they are used to construct and reconstruct a certain communicative environment by means of particular ritual schemes. The environment that is constructed through the ritual schemes in its turn provides legitimacy and value to these same schemes by appearing to be their place of origin, instead of the individual ritualized acts that actually produce them. In Bell's concept of ritualized action the social agents both produce the communicative environment, and use its schemata to interpret reality[27].

The conceptualisation proposed by Caroline Humphrey and James Laidlaw starts from the opposite side of the theoretical spectrum. According to them, what makes an act into a ritual act is the severance of the link between the "intentional meaning" of the agent performing the action and the identity of the act. In contrast with ordinary acts, which are given shape by the actor's intentions, ritualized acts appear to be pre-existing entities by which the actor conforms to a socially stipulated

27 C. Bell, *Ritual Theory, Ritual Practice*, Oxford, Oxford University Press, 1992, p. 1–9, p. 140–142.

order. This does not mean that the intention of the ritual "author" is non-existent. There can be, and usually are, authorial intentions involved in the performance of ritual. However, the identity of the act–i.e. how it appears to others–is unrelated to these personal intentions[28]. What the theories of Bell and Humphrey and Laidlaw have in common, then, is the way in which they conceptualize ritual action as a process of close interaction between communicative structures and social agents. No action is possible without one or more individuals purposefully initiating it. However, by ritualizing a certain action, the social actor creates an explicit link with a communicative system and its schemata, in order to legitimize the action in question. This system, in turn, shaped as it is by the actions of ritual actors and the expectations of onlookers, limits the options available to the ritual actor.

In understanding the occasions of public punishment, it is worthwhile to take into account these theoretical issues raised in the broader debate on ritual. They sensitize us to the difficulties of understanding ritualized action as a communicative medium, both for the ritual actor using it and the scholar trying to grasp it. It is not easy to apply such theoretical issues, based as they often are on anthropological fieldwork, to the situation of late medieval Utrecht. As will become clearer when we treat the relation between performance and text, the records we have of the penal occasions allow us a limited and highly subjective view of the actual practice. However, by deducing the ritualized character of these occasions from their textual remains, and using this characterization in its turn to plausibly reconstruct the general nature of these actions, I think we are provided with a first insight into the issues involved in the legal performances of late medieval Utrecht. The possibilities of–as well as the limits imposed by–the use of ritualized means of communication, will be shown to have had a profound effect not only on the actual legal practice, but also on the formation of the textual record.

28 C. Humphrey and J. Laidlaw, *The Archetypal Actions of Ritual. A Theory of Ritual Illustrated by the Jain Rite Worship*, Oxford, Clarendon Press, 1994, p. 1–5.

RITUAL MEANING

Any communicative process requires at least a sender and a receiver. Whereas up until now we have concerned ourselves mainly with the message-sending activities of ritual actors, it is crucial not to lose sight of the other side of the process: the reception of ritualized messages. A central–and again highly problematic–notion in this light is the concept of ritual "meaning". By schematizing reality, emphasizing some of its aspects while downplaying others, judicial performances formed a medium to transmit certain messages about this reality. The ritualized acts performed were therefore infused with meaning. Here, however, we enter a complex and dangerous domain, where one has to be careful not to lapse into pure speculation. Not only is it problematic for a historian–as it is for an anthropologist–to assign a certain meaning to acts from a society that one does not belong to, but it is also unlikely that the meaning of ritual acts was in any way fixed or universally acknowledged by every individual taking part in or witnessing the ritual event[29]. The first problem can be tackled–at least partially–by reconstructing the social and discursive context of these ritual practices. The second opens up a whole new field of issues, with which I will deal later on.

In order to grasp the referential framework of the judicial performances in Utrecht it is instructive to have a closer look at some of their constitutive aspects. One of the most obvious referential elements of these occasions was probably the convict's outfit. As seen before and in Appendix 1, there were two main ways in which the culprit could be ordered to come before the Council: either in a simple garb of shirt and pants or bareheaded. The exact difference between both types of penal appearance is not easy to pinpoint, and speculating on it would merely distract from the central point made here about the use of clothing as

29 These problems have been addressed by different scholars, anthropologists as well as historians. See for example: T. Gerholm, "On Ritual. A Postmodernist view", *Ethnos. Journal of Anthropology* 53 (1988), p. 190–203, at 194; G. Koziol, *Begging Pardon and Favor. Ritual and Political Order in Early Medieval France*, Ithaca, Cornell University Press, 1992, p. 289–324; P. Buc, *The Dangers of Ritual. Between Early Medieval Texts and Social Scientific Theory*, Princeton, Princeton University Press, 2001, p. 3–4.

referential medium. Slightly broadening our view instead, we encounter similar examples of the importance attributed to a culprit's appearance in late medieval legal practice all over Europe[30]. Furthermore, the types of clothing worn–or, for that matter, omitted–often closely resemble outfits encountered in the context of practices of spiritual penitence[31]. Although one has to be careful to make broad claims based on a few examples, there does appear to be a more general referential system at work in these cases. It is probably safe to argue that the social function of clothing is common to most–if not all–human societies. For medieval societies, at least, many authors have recognized the importance of outfits both as personal and collective means of identification[32]. More than a simple means of recognition, clothing, and more in general appearance, was primarily a medium for the staking and refuting of claims to a certain position in society. This of course made it an ideal venue for ritualized punishment, both in a "secular" and in a more religious context. So we see in the case of Utrecht. Being ordered to appear either bareheaded or in a simple garb before the Council placed the convict in a specific relation to the rest of society. Stripped of the visible signs of his social position, his claim to a certain status within the city would be

30 See, for example: A. Musson (dir.), *Crime, Law and Society in the Later Middle Ages*, Manchester, Manchester University Press, 2009, p. 220: "*...walking barefoot and with his head uncovered bearing a crucifix in his hand...*"; S. K. Cohn jr. (dir.), *Popular Protest in Late Medieval Europe. Italy, France, and Flanders*, Manchester, Manchester University Press, 2004, p. 192: "... [the captain of the village of Montataire] *had him led barefoot in his shirt to the cross in front of the palace...*"; P. J. P. Goldberg, *Women in England, c. 1275–1525. Documentary Sources*, Manchester, Manchester University Press, 1995, p. 234: "... *they shall stand there with bare feet and the hair of the head hanging loose for the whole time that they may be seen by all travelling on the road...*".

31 See in particular: M. C. Mansfield, *The Humiliation of Sinners. Public Penance in Thirteenth-Century France*, Ithaca & London, Cornell University Press, 1995, p. 113, 127, 264, 268, 274, 279; for comparable practices in a less public setting, see: R. C. Trexler, *Public Life in Renaissance Florence*, New York, Academic Press, 1980, p. 176: "*...his dress: a nightgown with knees bare, nothing on his head, and around his neck a* corregia *or halter, which was traditionally used as a sign of desperation by which people pleaded for commiseration.*"

32 J. Schneider, "Kleiderordnungen", *Lexikon des Mittelalters* vol. 5, Stuttgart, Metzler, 1991, p. 1198–1201, at 1198; E. Vavra, "Kleidung, I. Weltlicher Bereich", ibid. 1197–1198; J. Keupp, "Macht und Mode. Politische Interaktion im Zeichen der Kleidung", *Archiv für Kulturgeschichte* 86, no. 2 (2004), p. 251–281; P. von Moos, "Le vêtement identificateur. L'habit fait-il ou ne fait-il pas le moine?", *Micrologus. Natura, scienze e società medievali. Nature, Sciences and Medieval Societies* 15 (2007), p. 41–60; G. Bartholeyns, "L'enjeu du vêtement au Moyen Âge. De l'anthropologie ordinaire à la raison sociale (XIIIe-XIVe siècles)", ibid., p. 219–257.

symbolically nullified for the duration of the ceremony, as he was cast in the role of penitent. In order to restore his former place, the convict had to reconcile himself with the city he had wronged by his crime, echoing the common penitential scheme of public submission and satisfaction[33].

This reconciliation itself was also filled with references to claims on the ordering of society. As we have seen, late medieval Utrecht was certainly no haven of peace. Internal and external struggles made its political arena a turbulent field of operation. The descriptions of the judicial performances, however, suggest otherwise. In the wording of these events both the unity of civic society and the role of the Council as its main representative are explicitly emphasized. If we recapitulate the case of Claes, son of Jan Ridder, we remember that he had to beg for forgiveness "from the Council" and pay a fine "to the city". To grasp the implications of such wording, it is instructive to touch briefly on the broader developments of late medieval legal practice. In contrast to most current western societies, centralized legal and political institutions were by far not as dominant in late medieval Europe. They developed in a society in which many different forms of social organization, and their resulting legal and political practices, were in order. One's immediate family and relatives or sometimes broader groups of dependents formed for many the primary social frame of reference[34]. In this context, practices like feuding and vendetta took an important place next to centralized and semi-centralized forms of justice like law courts and legal officials[35]. What we see in late medieval Europe–and more specifically in Utrecht–is a competition not only between different legal institutions, but also between a variety of legal practices and forms of social organization.

33 Mansfield (1995), p. 124.

34 P. C. M. Hoppenbrouwers, "Maagschap en vriendschap. Een beschouwing over de structuur en functies van verwantschapsbetrekkingen in het laat-middeleeuwse Holland", *Holland: regionaal-historisch tijdschrift* 17 (1985) 69–108; Gerd Althoff, *Spielregeln Der Politik Im Mittelalter. Kommunikation in Frieden Und Fehde*, Darmstadt, Wissenschaftliche Buchgesellschaft, 1997, p. 1–4.

35 J. Büchert Netterstrøm, "Introduction. The study of feud in medieval and early modern history", *Feud in Medieval and Early Modern Europe*, J. Büchert Netterstrøm & B. Poulsen (dir.), Aarhus, Aarhus University Press, 2007, p. 9–67, at 15, 58–59, 64–65; T. Dean, "Marriage and mutilation. Vendetta in late medieval Italy", *Past and Present* 157 (1997), p. 3–36; C. N. W. M. Glaudemans, *"Om die wrake wille". Eigenrichting, veten en verzoening in laat-middeleeuws Holland en Zeeland (ca. 1350 – ca. 1550)*, The Hague, Facilitaire dienst / Multimedia, 2003, p. 34–69.

In this light, the wording of entries like those regarding Claes receives a new layer of meaning. The fact that Claes is sentenced to compensating the city instead of, for example, the owner of the window he has broken, is a clear indication of the social body that is regarded–or rather claimed–to have been injured by the act. Instead of an individual or a group of relatives, Claes has harmed Utrecht society as a whole by his drunken behaviour. This in its turn implies that the legitimate layer of social organization on which crimes like those of Claes should be regarded is that of the city. Rather than fighting petty feuds about mutual infringements, citizens should think of Utrecht society as a unity whose peace and order could be violated by individual culprits. But the image presented of a "correctly" ordered society does not stop here. Apart from the monetary compensation required of Claes, he also has to compensate his society morally by begging forgiveness for his deeds. And by explicitly naming itself as the recipient of this moral compensation, the Council here stakes a further claim about this ordering of Utrecht society. For not only should individual citizens regard the city of Utrecht as their primary moral frame of reference, but they are moreover to acknowledge the Council as its main representative.

In the description of the compensation required of Claes, we also encounter more explicit references to emphasize its ideally communal character. As noted above, the fine imposed in these cases was stated in numbers of "stones". These "stones", as we may read in the book of Utrecht bylaws entitled *Die Roese*, were meant for the maintenance of the city wall[36]. Apart from its defensive function, this stone wall, completed during the fourteenth century, formed an essential element in the social and political life of Utrecht. The protection and maintenance of the city wall was carried out by the twenty-one guilds, which constituted the most significant form of political organization in the city and derived a major part of their legitimacy from exactly this assignment[37]. The maintenance of the wall, then, was an important communal effort in the city of Utrecht and a contribution to this joint task meant a contribution to society as a whole. This fits in with a

36 S. Muller (ed.), *De middeleeuwsche rechtsbronnen der stad Utrecht* I, The Hague, Nijhoff, 1883–1885, p. 352; also see: S. Muller (ed.), *De middeleeuwsche rechtsbronnen der stad Utrecht*, Inleiding, The Hague: Nijhoff, 1883–1885, p. 76.

37 Hoven van Genderen (2000), p. 131.

broader tendency of the Council's records to emphasize the individual's responsibility of contributing to the collective project that was the city's welfare. We see this for example in the numerous ordinances regarding the cleanliness of public spaces, like streets, canals and squares. The Council's attempts at motivating people to contribute to the public health of the city came in many shapes: from regulations to restrict the presence of pigs on the streets, to the appointment of special individuals, called *slijkburgers*, charged with keeping certain places clean in exchange for the advantages of citizenship[38]. And the same emphasis on individual contributions to the common cause is implicit in the oft-repeated exhortation that citizens should take an active part in the guilds' voting process[39].

Seen within this social-discursive context, the "stones" fine created a semiotic link between the culprit's wrongful behaviour and an individual's responsibility towards society. The harm done to society by his irregular conduct was to be repaid by a specific type of communal service: a contribution to the project of the city wall. That the link created between criminal acts and communal responsibility had primarily a semiotic character, is confirmed by the fact that the compensation itself was in the end little more than a monetary fine. At least from the 1390's on, as *Die Roese* states, the culprit was expected to pay a certain amount of money for each "stone", rather than bring them himself[40]. It is even questionable if the money collected in this way was actually used for the city wall, since the wall had probably been finished in the

38 For regulations on pigs, see for example: HUA 701-1.16: *Buurspraakboek* 1418–1425, 11v; for the granting of citizenship in exchange for a cleaning duty, see for example: HUA 701-1.16: *Buurspraakboek* 1410–1414, 161r; for the loss of citizenship as a result of failure to comply with such a duty, see: HUA 701-1.16: *Buurspraakboek* 1410–1414, 168r; see F. Camphuijsen & J. Coomans, "De middeleeuwse stad en zijn varkens", *Madoc* 28.3 (2014) p. 140–148 for recent work on pig regulations in the medieval Low Countries; also see: J. Coomans, "Varkens van de werf. Stadsreiniging in laatmiddeleeuws Utrecht" *Oud-Utrecht* 85.3 (2012) p. 60–66 for recent work on the practice of city cleaning in late medieval Utrecht.

39 See for example: HUA 701-1.16: *Buurspraakboek* 1418–1425, 118r: *"Ende waer yemant van onsen borgeren die ghildebrueders sijn ende lot aentasten mogen in horen ghilde op Onser Vrouwen avont ende dan niet ter morgensprake en quaem ende mede lotede in horen ghilden daer sij ynne horen, die verboerde de stat een jaer lang ende een myle van der stat te wesen. Also verre hij also starck van lijve is dat hij ter morgenspraec comen mocht."*

40 Muller, *De middeleeuwsche rechtsbronnen*, p. 200: *"...zo wie datter stat van dezer tijt voert broekich wart, ende diemen op steen zet der stat tegheven..., die zel voer elc M steens der stat gheven alzo vele ghelts alse daer zi horen steen om verdinghen weder der stat tychelaers."*

late 1360's[41]. Any "stone" fines acquired after that time could only be used for repairs. Seeing the probable irregularity of both the need for repairs and the collection of "stone" fines, and the resulting divergence between income and expenses of "stone money", it is highly unlikely that every one of these fines will have been directly used for repairs. But, even though the actual practice of communal compensations will have differed from what was suggested in the verdicts, the fact that the fine was still presented as such is relevant, as it explicitly referred to a communal, rather than an individual, compensation.

RITUALIZED PERFORMANCE AND THE TEXTUAL RECORD

As noted before, it is not without risk to try and "explain" ritual occasions like the performances of justice in late medieval Utrecht. Even when one is able roughly to reconstruct the social and discursive frame of reference of the participants and spectators of these events, there is–for historians at least–the problem of sources. The numerous attempts to identify–albeit in a very broad sense–acts which can be titled rituals, have received criticism most notably from Philippe Buc. For Buc the term "ritual" is little more than the designation of "a practice twentieth-century historians have identified as ritual"[42]. Questioning the use of the term "ritual", he sensitizes us to the problematic relationship between the performance and textual reception of these events. His focus on this textual reception leads Buc to argue that it is only possible for historians to identify interpretations of rituals–usually by one of the parties involved–instead of the ceremonies themselves. The texts recording rituals were themselves elements of the practice of power, and therefore inherently polemical and partisan[43]. It is important to keep this in mind when regarding the practice of performative justice in Utrecht. As noted before, these occasions were noted down in the

41 Hoven van Genderen (2000), p. 129.

42 Buc, *The Dangers of Ritual*, p. 2.

43 Ibid., p. 248–261.

Buurspraakboek and the *Raads Dagelijks Boek*, both sources produced by the Council. In light of the precarious position of the Council in the political and legal constellation of late medieval Utrecht, we should most certainly not take these sources at their word. The picture presented of the judicial performances is above all an idealized representation of the actual events by one of the parties deeply involved in its execution and with a strong interest in using its communicative potential.

But does this make the performances themselves unimportant or even unintelligible? The ideas of Buc have in their turn been criticized because of their tendency to disregard the performative aspect of rituals entirely in favour of textual reproduction and interpretation[44]. Christina Pössel has recently argued that, instead of choosing between either the performance or the textual and oral interpretation of rituals, we should actually be looking at the interaction between both. Rituals had two loci, one performative and one in words, which gave these occasions both short–and long-term effects[45]. This is most certainly the case for the judicial performances in late medieval Utrecht. By leaving out the actual performances of justice, we lose sight of the concrete object of textual interpretation and the essential relation between real acts and their reproduction in words. However, where Pössel maintains a clear division between the two loci of rituals, one performative with short-term effects and one textual with long-term effects, the relation between performance and text in the Utrecht sources seems more complex. It appears that the ritualized acts themself were more closely bound up with their textual deposition than Pössel's theory permits.

Recapitulating the performance in which Claes, son of Jan Ridder, was punished for his misbehaviour, it is instructive to regard the relation between the moment at which the actual event took place and the moment at which it was noted down in the *Buurspraakboek* and *Raads Dagelijks Boek*. For this we should take a closer look at the exact wording of the records. In the *Buurspraakboek* the event is recorded as follows:

---

44 G. Koziol, "Review Article. The Dangers of Polemic. Is Ritual Still an Interesting Topic of Historical Study?", *Early Medieval Europe* 11.4 (2002) p. 367–388, at 372–377; C. Pössel, "The Magic of Early Medieval Ritual", *Early medieval Europe* 17.2 (2009), p. 111–125, at p. 118–119.

45 Pössel, "The Magic of Early Medieval Ritual", p. 124.

> For Claes, son of Jan Ridder, has in drunkenness broken a glass [window], which he has had repaired since. Therefore he has lain in the vleyshuus and has come here to the clock in shirt and pants and shall ask the Council for forgiveness and give our city a fine of 5000 stones[46].

In the *Raads Dagelijks Boek*, on the other hand, we read:

> Claes, son of Jan Ridder, shall come before the clock in shirt and pants and give the Council a fine of 5000 stones, because he has in drunkenness broken a glass [window] at night, actum the Wednesday after the Octave of Pentecost, which he has made to be repaired again[47]...

If we consider the tense of the verbs used in the account of Claes, we notice that neither of the records postdates the actual event it describes, and that both are situated at a different moment. In the record from the *Raads Dagelijks Boek* only the crime of Claes is stated in the past tense. The penal occasion before the *banklok* will, according to this account, still have to take place. In the *Buurspraakboek*, on the other hand, we, as readers of the record, find ourselves in the midst of the proceedings. Not only does this account state the perpetration of the crime in the past tense, but according to the record Claes has already come from the *vleyshuus* before the Council. Only the acts of begging forgiveness and paying a fine will still have to happen[48].

Based on this internal evidence we can roughly identify not only the course of events surrounding the judicial performances, but also the place of our texts within this whole process. After a crime was committed, the

46 HUA 701-1.16: *Buurspraakboek* 1418–1425, 199r; "*Want Claes Jans Riddersoen in dronckenscap een glas entwe geworpen heeft, dat hij weder heeft laten maken. Daerom heeft hij in"t vleyshuus geleghen ende is hier gecomen in hemde ende in broeck ter clocken ende sel den rade verghiffenisse bidden ende onser stat te betering geven V^{M} steens.*"

47 HUA 701-1.13: *Raads Dagelijks Boek* 1414–1425, 150v: "*Claes Jans Riderssoen sel voer de clocke comen in hemde ende in broeck ende den rade te beteringe geven V^{M} steens, omdat hij in dronckenscap een glas entwe geworpen heeft bij nacht, Actum swoensdages nae beloken pijnsteren, dat hij weder heeft laten maken...*"; the entry is followed by names of the *borgen* of Claes, i.e. those who would legally guarantee–usually on a certain monetary penalty–that Claes would conform to the punishment decided on.

48 Note that this difference of phrasing can be found in many more instances where a specific occasion is recorded in both the *Buurspraakboek* and the *Raads Dagelijks Boek*. For example: HUA 701-1.13: *Raads Dagelijks Boek* 1402–1408, 18v and HUA 701-1.16: *Buurspraakboek* 1402–1405, 34v; HUA 701-1.13: *Raads Dagelijks Boek* 1408–1414, 15r and HUA 701-1.16: *Buurspraakboek* 1405–1409, 115r; HUA 701-1.13: *Raads Dagelijks Boek* 1414–1425, 158v and HUA 701-1.16: *Buurspraakboek* 1418–1425, 212v.

Council would agree on the procedure of punishment to be followed. This decision and the most relevant details of the case were written down in the *Raads Dagelijks Boek* for future reference. The words *cloc* or *steen* were written in the margins next to the entry if it concerned a publicly performed punishment or one that provided a contribution to the construction of the city wall respectively. Entries with the word "cloc" were copied into the *Buurspraakboek* as part of a list of items that were to be publicly pronounced at the *buurspraak*, including verdicts of different kinds. It is difficult to determine conclusively whether the entries in the *Buurspraakboek* were written down either during or before the actual events themselves. One might imagine the clerk in charge of the *Buurspraakboek* to prepare the entries in advance. The standardization of the language of this kind of records certainly makes this plausible. In any case, regardless of whether these accounts were written down before or during the occasions, their character differs strongly from the texts on which Pössel bases her argument. Instead of being simple recountings of ritual occasions, these texts formed an intricate part of the events themselves. Being read aloud as part of the performance of justice, they were both the script on which the performances were based and claims on the authoritative interpretation of these same events. These texts were normative as well as descriptive, a guideline for the oral, ritualized and symbolic communication during the events as well as these events' textual record.

LEGAL PERFORMANCES AND THE COMMUNICATIVE PROCESS IN LATE MEDIEVAL UTRECHT

The pluralistic functioning of these textual records underscores the role of the judicial performances in late medieval Utrecht as focal points of a multiplicity of communicative devices. Not only were these performances used in a ritual sense to schematize reality, but their staging involved many "tricks and turns" to transmit the message–or messages–potentially inherent in them. The urban space was actively involved as a stage on which the actors of this "play" performed their story of crime, punishment, repentance and forgiveness. Through symbols and signs the public was presented with claims on the essential ordering of society and the norms and values that ought to govern people's behaviour. Furthermore, both the script and the supposed interpretation of the events were made public in a way that combined visual, oral and textual transmission.

Several explanations present themselves for this extensive and in a sense peculiar communicative practice, both in the specific case of Utrecht and, in a broader sense, for other societies and their authorities. On a very practical level, the use of a wide array of communicative devices ensured that the messages intended to be transmitted in the penal process could reach a large audience. One has to realize that by far the majority of the population of cities like Utrecht in this period will have been illiterate[49]. To reach a large audience, different kinds of media were indispensable. These media in their turn did not appear out of thin air. More often than not the means used by authorities to transmit their messages built upon existing frames of communicative behaviour. Orality is of course a case in point, but other forms were equally omnipresent in late medieval societies. Several authors have for example noted the ritualization inherent in feuding practices. By following a set course of actions an avenger could publicly claim the legitimacy of his violent behaviour[50]. Frequently this also involved the public and theatrical performance of certain emotions, most often anger or hatred[51]. In a comparable vein, the more peaceful resolution of disputes regularly comprised the ritual reconstitution of a status quo ante[52]. There is even evidence that the specific practice of ritualized legal performances in Utrecht was not "new" in its use by the civic authorities.

49 Taking, of course, into account the problematic link between the medieval terms *litteratus* and *illiteratus* and modern understandings of literacy and illiteracy, as pointed out in M. Clanchy, *From Memory to Written Record. England 1066–1307*, Chichester, Wiley-Blackwell, 1979/2003 (3rd edition), p. 228–236.

50 P. R. Hyams, *Rancor & Reconciliation in Medieval England*, Ithaca & London, Cornell University Press, 2003, p. 6–11; Netterstrøm, "Introduction", p. 56–59; C. Reinle, "Peasants" feuds in medieval Bavaria (Fourteenth – Fifteenth Century)", Netterstrøm & Poulsen (dir.), *Feud in Medieval and Early Modern Europe*, p. 161–174, esp. 173 argues that this practice was not limited in any way to feuds among nobles.

51 Althoff, *Spielregeln Der Politik*, p. 258–281; S. D. White, "'The politics of anger", *Anger's past. The Social Uses of an Emotion in the Middle Ages*, B. H. Rosenwein (dir.), Ithaca & London, Cornell University Press, 1998, p. 127–152; D. Lord Smail, "Hatred as a Social Institution in Late Medieval Society", *Speculum: a Journal of Medieval Studies* 76, no. 1 (2001), p. 90–126; D.l Lord Smail, *The Consumption of Justice. Emotions, Publicity, and Legal Culture in Marseille, 1264–1423*, Ithaca & London, Cornell University Press, 2003, p. 89–132.

52 Althoff, *Spielregeln Der Politik*, p. 11–17.

The oldest record of this type of ritual practice in Utrecht comes from an entry in the book of Utrecht bylaws entitled the *Liber Albus*. It records a verdict given by the bishop of Utrecht in 1346, in which he condemns a group of rabble-rousers to the act of coming before himself and the Council in a simple garb of linen clothing, bareheaded and barefooted, with a bare sword in hand, and begging, first the bishop and then the Council, for mercy[53]. The specific practice of ritualized legal performances as used by the Council in the late fourteenth and early fifteenth centuries had direct precursors, forming part of earlier political constellations as well. We can confidently state, therefore, that the communicative practice of the Council depended by and large on media that were already embedded in this society's communicative structure.

This also helps us to understand how the particular ritualized nature of legal performances influenced the way in which they were and could be used by a late medieval authority, such as the Council of Utrecht, to communicate its ideas about the proper ordering of society. Following the characterization of ritualized acts as presented by Bell and Humphrey and Laidlaw, we might say that the specific relationship between communicative structures and social agents, as created by the ritualization of actions, gave these performances both augmentative and restrictive qualities for their use in public communication. By presenting its audience with specific schemata of ritual punishment, based on references to socio-political issues varying from an individual's social status to communal responsibilities, the Council claimed legitimacy for its role as legal and political authority. Repeatedly visualized and vocalized through the legal performances, these schemata provided certain answers to the issues at hand, which in turn reflected a specific view on the proper ordering of society. However, the same schemata that provided the Council with these communicative possibilities, were also severely limiting in many ways. Based as they were on existing communicative structures and referential systems, the use of these schemata carried with them the load of previous interpretations and contexts. And it was not only previous interpretations that could hinder

53 Muller I, *De middeleeuwsche rechtsbronnen*, p. 58: "*Voert segghe wi, dat Louwe Stommekiin, …, binnen dreen daghen na desen daghe comen sellen, ten ersten voer ons ende na voer den ghemenen raet vander stat ende voer die clocke, horeliic in enen bloten paer linnen cleder bloetshoefts ende barvoet, ende yeghelic van hem sel een baer swaert in siin hant hebben ende sellen bidden ons voer ende den rade na, also alse gheseghet is, dat wi hoers liifs ghenade hebben willen; …*"

the conveyance of specific intended meanings. Individual readings of the legal performances will have differed markedly, especially in a socially and politically charged context such as late medieval Utrecht. After all, the difference between the curbing of behaviour harmful to society and the repression of people's freedom to act is only a matter of perspective.

It was therefore necessary for the Council to try and restrict the multiplicity of interpretations possible of these legal performances: not only presenting certain issues to its audience, but also leading the audience in its interpretation of the questions and their answers as suggested by the Council. By setting up explicitly scripted performances as well as providing an authoritative interpretation of these occasions, the Council attempted to increase its control of the communicative process. Because late medieval authorities such as the Council of Utrecht were only one of many competitors on the field of public communication, controlling the space of representation in all its facets was a central concern. Not only did this space form a potential arena for dissonant voices, but the political and legal powers claimed by authorities would have been void without the means to communicate their claims to a larger public. It is in this sense that we may understand the vital importance of the practice of legal performances as locus of communicative devices in a late medieval society such as the city of Utrecht.

COMMUNICATIVE PUNISHMENT AND (PRE)MODERNITY

There are larger implications to this kind of understanding of penal practice. One should of course be careful in drawing very broad conclusions from an isolated case like late medieval Utrecht. Therefore, I would present the following ideas merely as provisional afterthought rather than solid conclusions. Nevertheless, they do form a first sketch of a more serious contribution to the larger debate about punishment and (pre)modernity. As noted before, authors like Foucault and Spierenburg see the change from public to private punishment as one of the central differences dividing the "modern" from the "premodern" world. For

Foucault the change signalled an epistemological rupture from one conceptual framework into another. Whereas the physical body had been the central point of reference in the premodern period, the focus of penal thinking now shifted to the soul. Spierenburg places the changing role of public punishment in a longer process, spanning the whole early modern period. In this period, according to him, a generally more humanitarian mentality developed, to which authorities reacted by decreasing the amount and intensity of public punishments. Although both Foucault and Spierenburg signal an important development in penal practice, their accounts lack any real explanation of this change.

Over the last decade, sociologists of law and crime have come to emphasize the role of cultural and discursive factors in the practice of punishment[54]. Philip Smith, for instance, has argued for understanding punishment primarily in relation to "public meaning". According to him, punishment should be seen as a didactic or communicative act in which messages are sent concerning contrasting pairs of concepts, such as order versus disorder, purity versus pollution, and sacred versus evil. In such a conception of the nature of punishment, an individual's or institution's legitimacy depends upon whether it is regarded as being able to promote order over disorder, purity over pollution, etcetera[55]. In order to account for the shift in penal practice as witnessed by Foucault and Spierenburg, I think we should follow the line of reasoning of Smith and similar sociologists and regard punishment–as I have done in this contribution–primarily as a message-sending activity. In this light it forms part of a more general communicative practice, through which the authority imposing said punishment posits its claims not only on the norms and values that members of society are supposed to adhere to, but also, through this, on the essential constitution of society–in which cases does one belong to it and in which cases not–and, furthermore, on its own position within this same society as regulator of social behaviour. I would argue, therefore, that the change described by Foucault and Spierenburg is primarily a change in modes of communication within western-European societies.

54 For example: D. Garland, "Concepts of Culture in the Sociology of Punishment", *Theoretical Criminology*, 10 (2006) 419–447; P. Smith, *Punishment and Culture*, Chicago & London, The University of Chicago Press, 2008.

55 Smith, *Punishment and Culture*, p. 1–15.

An interpretation of this kind gives us the possibility to look for more tangible explanations than the abstract transition of general mentalities or conceptual frameworks. One might for example imagine the effects of the major demographic and social changes during the eighteenth and nineteenth–let alone the twentieth–century to have seriously influenced the ways in which this type of public transmission was handled. The judicial performances described here were held in and for communities which were considerably smaller and far less literate than our current mass societies. Justice was usually handed out in front of people directly associated with the convict in question–relatives, neighbours, acquaintances–who were therefore much more susceptible to the messages sent through his public punishment. At the same time, the small scale of premodern societies increased the effectiveness of the public shaming inherent in performative justice, as it more fundamentally involved the convict's direct social environment. The increase in both the scale of societies and the scope of legal institutions brought with it a growing anonymity in judicial practice, as the chances of directly knowing a convict decreased. Furthermore, rising levels of literacy made textual media an increasingly effective alternative to oral, visual and performative modes of communication, which were–and here I agree with Foucault–less easy to control. So although the essential messages inherent in punishment did not change, the modes of transmitting them did. This in its turn allows for a less omnipotent view of legal authorities than both the models of Foucault and–to a lesser extent–Spierenburg make room for. Rather than writers of the script, these authorities were–and are–themselves actors in the legal play. In order to function effectively and ensure the legitimacy of their claim on legal power, they needed to adapt to changing social and communicative contexts. For in the end it is society that authorizes its authorities.

Frans CAMPHUIJSEN
University of Amsterdam

APPENDIX 1
Constituent acts of the performance of justice in Utrecht between 1400 and 1425

The judicial performances in late medieval Utrecht could comprise many different acts. Not all acts, however, can be found in every entry, and several only appear in very few cases. In the overview below, I have, for the 124 entries in the *Buurspraakboek* and the 174 in the *Raads Dagelijks Boek* describing the practice over the years 1400–1425, noted how many times each individual element appears. Each number gives the amount of mentions of a certain act, not the number of convicts involved (sometimes a group of several people is punished in one entry).

Element	BSB	RDB
Presenting oneself:		
– In "shirt and pants" before the Council	81	54
– Bareheaded before the Council	42	68
– Bareheaded before the victim	0	3
Asking forgiveness:		
– To the Council	121	158 (+1)[56]
– To the Council, after declaring one's life forfeit	1	3
– To the Council, after declaring one's life forfeit with a bare sword in hand	2	2
– To the victim	2	45
– To the elders of the guilds	0	2

56 Several mentions of the asking of forgiveness and the paying of a fine name no recipient. Since it is most likely that the recipients intended were the Council and the city respectively, these mentions are added to the relevant entries between brackets.

Fine/monetary compensation:		
– To the city	50 (+5)	49 (+16)[57]
– To the Council	7	47
– To the victim	12	42
– To the bishop of Utrecht	0	2
Making an official promise:		
– "Willekeur" to atone with a deceased person's relatives before the Council	10	11
– "Willekeur" with a different content	34	43
– "Oorvede"	0	9
Other Elements		
– Imprisonment	99	87
– Loss of citizenship	18	19
– Elements with a religious character[58]	3	7
– Other elements[59]	18	31

57 See note 56.

58 Containing actions like taking part in a procession, asking forgiveness to God and/or a saint and bringing candles to a certain church.

59 Including the withdrawal of certain words, dismissal from the Council, the loss of a profession, and many more. Most of these elements appear only a few times in the records, and are therefore grouped together.

LA VIERGE ET LA LOI, MARIE AVOCATE[1]

Avant même la Création, un jugement précipite les mauvais anges au fond de l'enfer ; même si l'enfer n'est que la privation de la jouissance de contempler Dieu ; même si celui qui y est précipité a eu l'arrogance de se distinguer, de s'individuer en se séparant du tout divin – même si le récit de la chute des anges est bien postérieur aux récits de la genèse[2] – il importe de considérer qu'avant même la création du monde se trouvent mis en place le forfait, le juge, le jugement, le coupable et la sanction. Ce premier jugement annonce évidemment celui qui conclura l'histoire des hommes, et place Dieu du côté de la justice.

Mais cette justice divine est-elle analysable et justifiable en termes de droit ? on pourra constater que dans une telle situation, Dieu est juge et partie, et que le châtiment qu'il inflige ne peut se légitimer en termes strictement juridiques, sauf à invoquer ce que sera plus tard l'autorité naturelle qui, si elle est reconnue d'un père pour ses enfants tant qu'ils sont en bas âge, est conçue pour leur bien, et cesse dès qu'ils sont majeurs[3]. Il n'empêche ; qu'il le veuille ou non, le Malin est bien obligé de se soumettre à Dieu juge et arbitre, garant d'une loi qui ne souffrira pas d'exception jusqu'au Jugement Dernier, moment où celui qui accusait tous les hommes sera enfin condamné :

> Maintenant le salut, la puissance et l'empire sont à notre Dieu, et l'autorité à son Christ ; car il a été précipité, l'accusateur de nos frères, celui qui les accuse jour et nuit devant notre Dieu[4].

---

1 Cette intervention est la première partie d'une étude qui trouve son achèvement dans “Autour de *l'Advocacie Notre Dame*, de la narration à la dramatisation”, *De l'Oral à l'écrit, le dialogue à travers les genres romanesque et théâtral*, C. Denoyelle (éd.), Orléans, Paradigme 2013, p. 141-168.

2 En fait, le récit le plus complet s'en trouve dans Ap 12, 7-9. Les références sont clairsemées dans la Bible, et la doctrine sera formulée au cours du 4e concile de Latran.

3 Du moins selon ce qu'énonce le fameux article « Autorité politique » de l'*Encyclopédie* de Diderot et d'Alembert, t. I, 1751, p. 898.

4 Ap 12, 10.

L'ensemble de la création est donc postérieur à la justice et au droit. La faute de l'homme entraîne légitimement une sanction, comme le crime de Caïn, comme celui de Nemrod. Mais l'homme peut également être puni sans qu'une faute puisse lui être imputée : c'est l'histoire de Job ; on sait la part que Satan prend à cette réflexion sur la justice divine, qui trouve cependant son aboutissement dans une soumission, alors même que Dieu invective Job :

> Veux-tu donc anéantir ma justice, me condamner afin d'avoir droit[5] ?

La justice divine, quelles que soient ses voies, est constante et implacable, elle est littéralement *impensable*, et c'est tout l'enjeu du livre de Job ; en même temps, elle se laisse fléchir, y compris par des marchandages – que l'on pense à ceux d'Abraham cherchant à sauver Sodome[6], ceux de Job intercédant pour ses amis[7]. De même, Michel archange semble avoir une grande fonction auxiliatrice dans la tradition juive, même si ce n'est qu'un passage de Jude qui y fait allusion :

> L'archange Michel lui-même, lorsqu'il contestait avec le diable et lui disputait le corps de Moïse, n'osa pas porter contre lui une sentence d'exécration, mais il se contenta de dire : « Que le Seigneur te punisse[8] ! »

Même s'il est parfois protégé par des figures aimées de Dieu, l'homme, s'il triche ou se rebelle, est toujours rattrapé par une justice qui sanctionne les fautes et répare les iniquités. Cela, jusqu'à la Rédemption, puisque le Christ incarné paie la dette de l'humanité. C'est là que, d'une certaine façon, la justice est battue en brèche, là que l'univers qui avait été mis en place dans l'ancienne alliance vacille sur ses bases : le pardon, la miséricorde font leur entrée, la capacité à ne plus peser, compter et diviser, mais celle à oublier, à pardonner, à « changer le compte » ; toutes choses qui rendent certes l'existence supportable – comment pourrait-on vivre avec l'impitoyable mémoire des fautes commises et des préjudices subis – mais qui bouleversent radicalement non seulement une vision du monde, mais surtout une vision de la justice. La façon dont le Christ, aux portes de l'enfer, organise

5 Job, 40, 3.
6 Gn, 18, 17 *sq.*
7 Job, 42, 7-10.
8 Jud, 1, 9.

l'évasion collective de tous les patriarches de l'Ancien Testament – ou leur libération, selon le point de vue – inaugure un monde où ne règne pas que la justice.

Cet aspect de la bonne nouvelle mettra beaucoup de temps à être intégré, et il faudra bien des siècles avant que la figure tantôt hiératique d'un christ pantocrator, tantôt terrifiante du Dieu du Jugement Dernier ne quitte le portail des cathédrales. Cette bascule, qui se fait, pour l'histoire de l'art, entre la période romane et le premier gothique, entre Moissac et Chartres, coïncide avec un certain nombre d'éléments, dont le premier est évidemment la paix relative dans laquelle se retrouve la population ; la justice des hommes arrive à canaliser les exactions, et en même temps les délits ne sont plus faits de guerre ou de violence, mais faits individuels, pour lesquels on peut recourir à la justice et obtenir réparation, en même temps que le repentir prend en compte non seulement le destin du corps, mais celui de l'âme.

Le deuxième est évidemment le développement de la dévotion mariale en occident. Ce n'est pas le lieu de rappeler les raisons et les modalités de cette dévotion ; ce qui m'intéressera davantage, c'est bien évidemment sa dimension juridique, ou plutôt la relation que la dévotion mariale entretient non seulement avec la justice, mais aussi avec le droit : c'est l'axe de ce travail, qui s'efforcera d'arriver au plus vite sur des questions théâtrales. On le devine, parmi les textes que je vais être amené à travailler se trouvera, de façon privilégiée, *L'Advocacie Notre Dame*[9]. Le texte est embarrassant à plus d'un titre, et il n'est pas étonnant qu'il soit au bout du compte assez peu étudié – regrettons que l'édition préparée par Gérard Gros ait mis si longtemps à être disponible[10]... De plus, si l'on a travaillé sur le rapport de l'*Advocacie* avec le mystère qui porte ce nom[11], il semble que n'aient pas été fouillés les rapports qui lient sa dimension juridique

9 *L'advocacie Nostre-Dame et la Chapelerie Nostre-Dame de Baiex*, poème normand du XIVe siècle imprimé pour la première fois, d'après le manuscrit unique de la Bibliothèque d'Évreux, [éd. Anatole de Montaiglon], Paris, Académie des bibliophiles, 1869.

10 Le texte est maintenant accessible dans l'édition américaine *Our Lady's Lawsuits in « L'Advocacie Nostre Dame » and « La Chapelerie Nostre Dame de Baiex » : Our Lady's Advocacy and The Benefice of Our Lady's Chapel*, trad. J. M. Davis, F. R. P. Akehurst et Gérard Gros, Tempe, Arizona Center for Medieval and Renaissance Studies (Medieval and Renaissance Texts and Studies, 393), 2011.

11 G. A. Runnalls, « The *Mystère de l'Advocasie Nostre Dame* : a recently-discovered fragment », *Zeitschrift für romanische Philologie*, 99, 1983, p. 41-77.

à la théâtralité[12]. Mais je voudrais élargir un peu la question, non seulement en allant en amont – au fait, qu'implique effectivement la notion de Marie avocate ? – mais également en aval, en travaillant sur quelques textes théâtraux palinodiques. Plusieurs aspects seront à mettre en évidence, dont l'évolution de la position de la Vierge, qui est juge parfois, avocate souvent, partie à d'autres moments. Il est évident de même que le milieu, tel qu'on peut le dessiner, aura une incidence sur la façon dont non seulement la Vierge, mais aussi la justice sont appréhendées sur scène.

MARIE AVOCATE ?

Qu'en est-il de Marie avocate ? L'appellation semble remonter au moins au *Salve Regina,*

> *SALVE, Regina, mater misericordiae, [...]*
> *Eia, ergo, advocata nostra, illos tuos misericordes oculos ad nos converte...*

On sait qu'une antienne de ce type était chantée dès 1135 à Cluny, ce qui fait remonter à cette époque au moins la ferveur à Marie Avocate[13], et qu'elle plaisait particulièrement à la vierge, si l'on en croit l'anecdote rapportée par Lacordaire dans sa *Vie de saint Dominique* : à Rome, une nuit, pendant que les frères dorment dans le dortoir, trois femmes passent dans le corridor et bénissent les moines assoupis ; Dominique les interroge, quoique sachant déjà de qui il peut s'agir :

> Je suis celle que vous invoquez tous les soirs ; et lorsque vous dites : *Eia, ergo, advocata nostra*, je me prosterne devant mon Fils pour la conservation de cet ordre[14].

---

12 On consultera avec profit l'article de D. Terkla « A Basochian proto-drama and its mariological contact : *L'Advocacie Nostre Dame* », *Medieval Perspectives*, 6, South-Eastern medieval association, 1991, p. 87-100. Merci à l'auteur de m'avoir fait parvenir ce stimulant travail paru dans une publication confidentielle peu accessible en Europe.

13 La dernière série d'invocations « O clemens, O pia, O dulcis Virgo Maria », a été ajoutée par saint Bernard selon la tradition, ce qui nous mettrait au milieu du XIIe siècle.

14 Lacordaire, *Vie de Saint Dominique*, Paris, Vve Poussielgue, 1860, p. 317-318 ; Lacordaire renvoie pour cet épisode à la relation de sœur Cécile.

S'il est avéré que ce mot est attesté dans le premier tiers du XIIe siècle dans une des plus célèbres oraisons mariales, il semble qu'il ait existé auparavant, puisqu'une des plus insignes reliques de Rome, un des portraits de Marie réputés peints par saint Luc, est mentionnée dès le IXe siècle sous le nom de *Maria advocata*[15], et conservée dans la basilique Santa Maria in Aracœli – endroit que connaissait bien saint Dominique. La tradition attribue évidemment cette représentation de Marie à saint Luc lui-même, l'icône qui est vénérée aujourd'hui étant une copie faite au entre le XIe et le XIIe siècle d'une icône plus ancienne qui serait venue de Byzance au cours du Ve siècle[16]. C'est celle-là même que promenait en procession le pape Grégoire en 590 quant un ange apparut au sommet du Mausolée d'Hadrien pour signifier que la ville serait épargnée par la Peste[17]. La cité de Rome a été consacrée à cette icône en 1948.

Cette icône porte plusieurs noms, *Aghiosoritissa*, puisqu'elle était associée à l'urne où était conservée la ceinture de la Vierge ; mais aussi *Paraklisis*, à cause de son geste d'intercession. La Vierge, représentée de trois-quarts face, regarde l'observateur ; sa main droite est à la verticale, les doigts entrouverts ; la main gauche presque à l'horizontale. L'attitude n'est pas analysée par François Garnier dans son *Langage de l'image au Moyen Âge* ; mais il donne quelques éléments qui permettent d'analyser le double geste ; les deux mains de Marie présentent : « une structure qui correspond assez exactement à celle de l'expression verbale, avec un sujet et deux compléments[18] ». On comprend combien le geste traduit à la fois la prise en compte des fautes de celui qui regarde le tableau et que Marie regarde, et l'intercession vers le ciel, pour une demande de pardon. La représentation est suffisamment marquante – sans même prendre en compte son origine et ses actions miraculeuses – pour qu'elle se diffuse au travers de la chrétienté. C'est au moment où apparaît cette

15 Il en reste encore diverses versions, à Santa Maria in via Lata, Sant'Alessio, San Lorenzo in Damaso, Santa Maria in Campo Marzio et Santa Maria del Rosario à Monte Mario. *Cf.* E. Sendler, *Le icone bizantine della Madre di Dio*, Milano 1995, p. 213.

16 Cette dernière semble se trouver aujourd'hui au Monastère de Monte Mario ; il s'agit d'une des plus anciennes icônes conservées (*cf.* l'article très convaincant sur internet http://fatherdavidbirdosb.blogspot.fr/2010/10/irenikon-oldest-marian-icon-in-rome-and.html, consulté en février 2014).

17 *Cf.* Cl. Bolgia, « The Felici Icon Tabernacle (1372) at S. Maria in Aracoeli, Reconstructed : Lay Patronage, Sculpture and Marian Devotion in Trecento Rome », *Journal of the Warburg and Courtauld Institutes*, Vol. 68, 2005, p. 27-72 ; p. 29.

18 F. Garnier, *Le Langage de l'image au Moyen Âge*, Le Léopard d'or, 1989, t. II, p. 112.

copie de l'icône que l'appellation semble se généraliser ; on a rappelé l'invocation qui figure dans le *Salve Regina*, composé entre le XIe et le XIIe siècle ; mais c'est également dans cette période qu'Adam de Perseigne utilisera cet appellatif :

> Combien heureuse est celle qui est mère et épouse de Dieu, porte du ciel, charme du Paradis, maîtresse des anges, reine du monde, joie des élus, avocate des croyants, force des combattants, rappel des égarés, médecine des souffrances[19]

Marie avocate des croyants, voilà une belle adresse, qui cependant reste elliptique. Saint Bernard ne dit pas vraiment autre chose, et la notion reste ainsi particulièrement floue. Adam de Perseigne précise ailleurs « celui dont Marie voudrait être l'avocate, il triomphera de toutes les hostilités[20] ». Dans la dévotion telle qu'elle est actuellement formulée à la suite du Concile Vatican II, l'appellation est associée à Marie Médiatrice et Auxiliatrice. Dès Ambroise, on avait précisé que Marie reprendrait sur terre la mission de médiation qui lui est attribuée par le Christ sur la Croix[21].

Il faut remonter, semble-t-il, à Irénée pour avoir quelques éclaircissements sur les raisons de cette appellation. Il parle de Marie avocate à deux reprises, et semble fonder une tradition sur laquelle s'appuieront la plupart des auteurs :

> De la même façon qu'Ève a été séduite par l'ange [déchu], pour qu'elle s'écarte de Dieu, détournée de lui par ses paroles, de la même façon celle-ci a été évangélisée par la parole angélique, au point de porter Dieu, obéissant à sa parole. Et en cela elle obéissait à Dieu ; mais parce qu'elle a été persuadée d'obéir à Dieu, ainsi, la Vierge Marie a été faite avocate d'Ève[22].

---

19 « *quam felix est quae Dei est et mater et sponsa, porta coeli, amoenitas paradisi, angelorum domina, regina mundi, sanctorum laetitia, advocata credentium, fortitudo pugnantium, errantium revocatio, poenitentium medicina.* » *Epistola XVI*, *Ad abbatem de Turpiniaco*, Migne, *Patrologia Latina cursus completus* (Dorénavant PL) CCXI, col. 634.

20 « *cui Maria advocata esse voluerit, contra omnes inimicitias praevalebit* » *epistolae*, *PL* CCXI, col. 685.

21 « *Jesus non egebat adjutore ad redemptionem omnium, qui omnes sine adjutore servavit / Unde et dicit :* Factus sum sicut homo sine adjutorio inter mortuos liber (Psal LXXXVII, 5) *suscepit quidem affectum parentis, sed non quaesivit alterius auxilium* » Ambroise, Epist. LXIII, PL. XVI, col 1218.

22 « *Quemadmodum enim illa per angeli sermonem seducta est, ut effugeret Deum, prævaricata verbum ejus ; ita et hæc per angelicum sermonem evangelizata est, ut portaret Deum, obediens ejus*

On comprend dès lors que Marie est *appelée* en remplacement d'Ève ; c'est sans doute cela que signifie au départ le mot : dans un premier temps, il s'agit de tenir la place, puis de conseiller sans forcément plaider (c'est un des sens attesté dans le Gaffiot), puis enfin de tenir la place dans un procès, en plaidant. Marie Conseillère, Marie qui intercède, Marie qui prend la place, voilà des éléments qui apparaissent régulièrement dans les miracles, où l'on voit même la Vierge tenir le rôle d'une nonne séduite ayant quitté le couvent, et cela jusqu'à son retour plein de repentir, des années après[23].

On rencontre chez Hildefonse de Tolède quelques formulations éclairantes :

> *Tu enim es electa a Deo, assumpta a Dei, advocata a Deo*[24]
>
> *Es mediatrix et advocata nostra praecipua apud Deum*[25]

Dans les deux occurrences, où le mot a fonction de participe passé et induit un complément, le mot *advocata* renvoie à cette position intermédiaire qui caractérise Marie : non seulement avocate des hommes, mais aussi avocate *auprès de Dieu*. Ce que l'on peut retenir de cette première enquête, c'est qu'alors même que Marie va être indiscutablement auxiliatrice – et que le fait qu'elle apporte de l'aide au pécheur ne pose en soi aucune difficulté, le nom de Marie *avocate* est plus complexe ; on a tendance à le prendre aujourd'hui dans un sens exclusivement juridique, et il semble que ce n'est pas en ce sens précis qu'il a été compris dans les premiers emplois à son sujet.

---

verbo. Et si ea inobedierat Deo, sed hæc suasa est obedire Deo, uti virginis Evæ Virgo Maria fieret advocata » ; Irénée, *Contra Haereses*, V, XIX, 1, *in* Migne, *Patrologia Graeca*, t. VII/2, col 1175.

23 Adgar, Miracle 40 : de la Nonne et du Chevalier, *Gracial*, ed. C. Neuhaus, Heilbronn, 1886, p. 223. On pourra également consulter l'édition de P. Kunstmann, édition de l'Université d'Ottawa, 1982, p. 305 *sq.*

24 Hildefonse de Tolède, *De perpetua virginitate S. Mariae*, PL XCVI, col 58.

25 Auctor incertus, *De Corona Virginis*, PL XCVI, col 318.

MARIE HORS LA LOI

Si Marie aide et remplace, il est certain que son statut juridique reste assez complexe ; il suffit d'étudier le premier exemple canonique d'intervention mariale, celui du miracle de Théophile ; si l'on prend le récit qu'en fait Fulbert de Chartres, le premier en occident, les choses sont assez claires ; on se souvient que déçu d'être disgracié par l'évêque d'Adana, Théophile finit par entrer en contact avec un juif :

> En parlant avec son intermédiaire (le Juif), il renia la chrétienté avec le diable, adora le diable, et lui transmit sa mancipation écrite de sa main (*chirographum*), signée de son anneau[26].

La *mancipation* – mot qui traduit le latin *mancipatio* – est définie ainsi dans le Gaffiot : « aliénation de la propriété avec certaines formes solennelles ». Le mot renvoie, par sa construction, à l'idée de recevoir de la main : une formule qui semble bien proche de ce que peut être le geste de l'hommage – celui-là même qui est représenté dans le vitrail de Théophile de la cathédrale de Beauvais ; la pérennité du geste, impliqué par le mot dans la première attestation, représenté dans le vitrail, montre qu'il s'agit là de quelque chose d'essentiel ; le terme de *chirographe* qui renvoie non seulement à un manuscrit, mais à une signature autographe, est un terme juridique présent chez Fulbert, et que l'on retrouvera dans la plupart des versions latines. Au moment de son repentir, lorsqu'il obtient le pardon de Marie :

> Que dire de plus ? La mère, encline à la miséricorde le prit en considération, et lui apparaissant dans une vision, elle lui démontra son impiété, l'invitant à se confesser au Christ. Elle consola le malheureux en lui promettant le pardon, et afin qu'il ne doute pas de cette promesse, elle rapporta au captif en gage de libération le pacte déjà mentionné, arraché de force au diable[27].

26 « *Hoc mediatore locutus cum diabolo Christianitatem abnegavit, diabolum adoravit, eique de sua mancipatione chirographum tradidit annulo suo signatum* », Fulbert de Chartres, *epistola X. De Assumptione B. Virginis Mariae*, PL XXX, Col 323.

27 « *Quid multa ? Respexit hunc propitia misericordiae Mater, et per visionem illi apparens de impietate coarguit, ad Christi confessionem excitans. Consolata est dolentem pollicendo veniam, et ne dubitaret de promisso, supradictum chirographum diabolo potenter ereptum captivo reddidit in pignus libertatis.* » *Ibid.*

Ce qui revient à dire que Marie s'est par là-même rendue coupable de voies de fait à l'égard du diable, qu'elle a arraché par la force le bien de celui-ci – il s'agit donc d'un vol – et qu'elle a détruit des documents officiels garantissant la bonne exécution d'un contrat. Le texte de Rutebeuf – enfin un texte théâtral – souligne clairement le cas : la seule protestation de Satan, c'est bien qu'il a rempli sa part du contrat :

> Ja li rendi je sa provande,
> et il me fist de lui offrande
> Sans demorance,
> De cors et d'ame et de sustance[28].

La Vierge, en revanche, le menace de violence physique : « et je te foulerai la pance[29] ! ». Il s'agit évidemment là d'un rappel du verset du protévangile, annonçant que Marie écraserait Sathan de son talon. Mais au-delà du geste symbolique, on ne peut que retenir la violence d'une auxiliatrice, d'une avocate certes, mais au comportement juridiquement peu recevable.

C'est le premier point que je souhaitais préciser ici : Marie avocate n'est pas au départ une juriste attentive, elle est surtout une fidèle auxiliatrice, dont les procédés pas toujours avouables ne sont justifiés que par l'évidence de la « bonne cause » qu'elle défend. Ce qui est ainsi mis en place, et se retrouvera assez longuement dans la suite des textes théâtraux mettant Marie en scène, c'est justement cette capacité à résoudre les solutions insolubles sur le plan juridique.

Deux exemples, assez canoniques ; l'un est la substance même du miracle, puisqu'il s'agit d'évoquer le Miracle de l'enfant que notre dame ressuscita, le quinzième des *Miracles de Notre Dame par personnages*[30]. On se rappelle la situation : après avoir longuement désiré un enfant, après avoir longuement travaillé en couches, une femme s'endort dans le bain qu'on lui prépare après son enfantement ; l'enfant qu'elle tenait dans ses bras se noie. Un prévôt qui se plaignait de ne pas avoir de cause survient à cause du bruit, un « haro de femmes ensemble[31] ». C'est ainsi que se met en marche une machine judiciaire excessive. Une première

28 Éd. M. Zink, « Lettres gothiques », p. 577, v. 581-584.

29 *Ibid.*, v. 585.

30 *Miracles de Nostre Dame par personnages* publiés d'après le manuscrit de la Bibliothèque nationale, G. Paris et U. Robert (éd.), Paris, Firmin Didot pour la Société des anciens textes français, 1876-1893, t. 2, 1877, p. 281 *sq.*

31 V. 704.

audience arrache des larmes à toute l'assistance, et la mère serait graciée par le comte – « mais c'on lui pardoint son meffait, / Car, par ma foy, elle m'a fait / pitié au cuer » (v. 1051-1053) – si n'intervenait un avocat soulignant que le comte risque, en accordant sa grâce, d'être accusé par son souverain de ne pas faire régner la justice. La machine judiciaire poursuit donc implacablement sa route, et la seule façon pour Marie d'arrêter la logique du procès est simplement de supprimer le corps du délit, et de ressusciter l'enfant, à la grande joie de tous.

Dans ce cas précis, on voit combien le droit et son application ont besoin d'une aide pour garder l'esprit de justice. Il s'agit de racheter la faute, en la supprimant purement et simplement ; on comprend mieux, d'ailleurs, pourquoi Marie s'empare du pacte de Théophile : ce n'est ni son orgueil ni sa fatuité qui le damnent, mais bien qu'à un moment il a suffisamment désespéré pour se détourner de Dieu ; son appel au secours en quelque sorte rachète ce moment d'égarement, et rend obsolète le pacte signé alors. Cette démarche se retrouvera dans bien des cas. Symétriquement, on pourra noter le côté extrêmement procédurier de Satan, qui fait toujours les choses le plus strictement qu'il peut. La chartre qu'a rédigée le diable, telle que nous la fait connaître Rutebeuf, commence effectivement comme un document officiel :

> A toz ceuls qui verront ceste lettre commune
> Fet Sathan a savoir que ja torna fortune,
> Que Theophiles ot a l'evesque rancune [...]
> Et lors me fist hommage, si rot sa seignorie
> De l'anel de son doit seela ceste letre,
> De son sanc les escrist, autre enque n'i fist metre[32].

Le deuxième exemple se trouve dans le *Mystère de saint Genis*. Elle a lieu quand Genis reçoit le baptême : au moment de revêtir le vêtement blanc qui symbolise sa vie nouvelle, il fait une prière à Marie pour l'aider dans sa démarche :

> A ton chier filz por moy fay priere,
> Fay que je puisse convertir
> Par tes beaux motz delicïeux
> Donne moy puyssance conre ces mescreans[33].

32 *Op. cit.*, v. 640-642, 651-653.

33 *L'Ystoire et la vie de Saint Genis*, W. Mostert et E. Stengel (éd.), Marburg, 1895, v. 1756-1759.

À cette prière Marie répond, en intercédant auprès de son fils :

> Doux filz pleyse toy regarder [...]
> Et luy pardone son malfait
> Et toux les pechiez qu'il a fait
> La bas en la vïe mondaine[34].

Pendant qu'il revêt ses nouveaux habits, une didascalie nous indique :

> Ici, qu'il mette ses habits ; ensuite, qu'un ange apparaisse devant lui, le livre écrit par le diable ouvert devant lui, et qu'il parle à Genis, en lui montrant cette écriture – que la main du Seigneur soit au dessus de lui[35].

L'ange expliquera qu'ainsi sont effacés « tous les pechiez de cestuy livre[36] » : Genis est un homme nouveau. Pendant qu'il rend grâces, une nouvelle didascalie précise :

> Alors, que l'ange rapporte en secret son livre au diable[37].

Nous pourrons passer, en quelques vers, du sublime du baptême de Genis à une scène comique ; Sathan sait bien que Genis ne peut lui échapper :

> Ja ne toy porras escuser
> Que tu ne sois seulemant nostre
> *hic respiciat librum suum et ostendat alteri Dyabolo, dicendo* :
> Regarde cy quel patre nostre
> Je ly ay fait cy devant escrire !
> *Nunc vertat folia, et cum nichil inveniet scripture, clamet fortiter, dicendo* Haro
> Haro, Haro de dieu mauldite
> Soit ta vïe ribault mendeux !

Devant le livre vide de toute faute – je n'ose écrire *vierge* – les diables ne peuvent masquer leur stupéfaction et leur dépit, évidemment, et vont chercher un coupable :

> [SATHAN]
> Je pance qu'il s'est ja rendu

34 *Ibid.*, v. 1763, 1768-1770.

35 « *Hic induat se ; deinde sit angelus coram eo, libro aperto de scriptura dyaboli, et dicat Genisio, ostendendo sibi scripturam illam – sit super eum manus domini.* », *Ibid.*, p. 72.

36 V. 1788.

37 « *Nunc revertatur angelus secrete librum suum Dyabolo* », *Ibid.*, p. 73.

A ce faulx homme Jhesu crist
Et qu'il n'ayt effacié l'escrit...

ASTAROTH
Celle faulce vierge Marie
Ly aura tout ce yci fait fere,
Car elle est de si faulx affere
Que tous jours nous fait enragier
Et nous ne nous pouvons vengier
D'elle pour ce maulvais Jhesus
Car Dieu le pere de lassus
Luy a donné tant de puissance
Qu'a brief parler et sans dobtance,
Elle fait tout ce qu'elle veult[38].

Dans le récit de la conversion de saint Genis, la Vierge n'apparaît qu'en cette occurrence ; il est révélateur qu'elle intervienne ici, en quelques vers, comme pour souligner qu'il va se passer quelque chose d'exceptionnel et d'inhabituel ; au moment du baptême sur scène, en plus du livre et de Genis, on peut voir, outre la Vierge, l'ange qui tient le livre, et la main du Seigneur. Le sacrement du baptême est connu pour purifier du péché originel, mais aussi de tout péché : « Celui qui croira et sera baptisé sera sauvé, celui qui ne croira pas sera condamné[39] » ; c'est donc *a priori* un abus de langage de décréter que la Vierge est responsable de cette disparition des péchés sur le livre ; et cependant, on aurait pu faire l'économie de cette séquence, souligner que le baptême purifie de soi le pécheur, sans même que Marie ait à intervenir. Si elle est présente, c'est semble-t-il en vertu d'une tradition théâtrale qui la fait présider à tous les moments où le pécheur est sauvé par un acte de bonté et de miséricorde ; elle incarne, sur les *establies*, la mission de d'intercession, de médiation qui lui a été donnée auprès de Dieu ; elle est, dans la tradition d'Irénée, une sorte de prolongement de l'humanité médiatrice de Jésus.

Les diables disent vrai : Marie fait tout ce qu'elle veut, et elle est très exactement au dessus des lois. C'est ce qui, en termes de dévotion, explique sa popularité.

38 *Id.*, 1893-1896, 1899-1908.
39 Mc, 16, 16.

MARIE EN LA LOI

Il est bien probable que le terme d'*advocata* qui avait, au départ un sens presque non juridique, une simple fonction auxiliatrice et on l'a vu médiatrice, a été compris différemment, au cours du XIIIe siècle, à la lumière de la formation juridique qui devient prépondérante chez les clercs, qu'ils soient canonistes ou spécialistes du droit romain. En ce sens, il faut rappeler qu'un ecclésiastique n'a pas le droit d'être avocat en cour séculière, selon le droit canon[40]. La fonction d'avoué est pour elle définie ainsi :

> L'avoué était autrefois l'avocat de l'Église, et l'*avouerie* ou l'*advocatie* la charge ou l'emploi même de l'avocat[41].

Lorsque Marie occupe une place dans le procès, elle le fera dans la stricte observance des règles du droit ; c'est de cela qu'il est question dans le texte qui nous retiendra maintenant, l'*Advocacie Notre Dame.* On sait que cette fiction a donné naissance à deux versions différentes, l'*Advocacie* à proprement parler, qui a été éditée à diverses reprises, et le *Mystère de l'Advocacie*, édité par G. A. Runnalls. Ce récit, qui met en scène un débat céleste entre Dieu, l'homme et le Diable, s'inscrit dans une lignée qui a été bien retracée[42] ; une des premières attestations, qui en donne les linéaments, se trouve chez Hugues de Saint-Victor ; il se trouve dans deux versions presque identiques, d'une part un chapitre du *De Sacramentis*[43], d'autre part, dans un texte isolé, le *De causa litis*

40 « On appelle *avocat* (du latin *advocatus*, appelé auprès, au secours) celui qui est choisi, appelé par une autre personne pour l'assister en justice, exposer ses plaintes ou contredire celles de la partie adverse. Les clercs, constitués dans les ordres sacrés, ne peuvent plaider au for séculier que pour eux-mêmes, pour leurs églises, ou, en cas de nécessité, pour leurs parents... » *Dictionnaire de droit canonique et des sciences en connexion avec le droit canon*, André et Condis, t. 1, H. Walzer (Paris), 1894, p. 185.

41 *Op. cit.*, p. 186.

42 *Cf.* H. Traver, « The four Daughters of God », *PMLA*, Vol. 40, No. 1 (Mar., 1925), p. 44-92. J'ai repris et poursuivi cette enquête dans un article destiné à compléter celui-ci : D. Hüe, « Autour de l'*Advocacie Notre Dame*, de la narration à la dramatisation », *De L'Oral à l'écrit, le dialogue à travers les genres romanesque et théâtral*, colloque de Toronto, Orléans, Paradigme, 2013, p. 140-168.

43 Hugues de Saint-Victor, De Sacramentis, pars octava, *De reparatione hominis*, ch. 4 « de causa hominis adversus Deum et Diabolum ». P.L. 176, col. 307. *sq*.

inter Deum hominem et diabolum. L'essentiel est dit en une sorte d'exposé méthodique, et l'organisation de la discussion est développée en un peu plus de deux colonnes de la *Patrologie* :

> Ils sont trois en cause : le diable, l'homme et Dieu. Le diable est convaincu d'avoir fait injure à Dieu, car son serviteur, c'est-à-dire l'homme, il l'a détourné par fraude et l'a gardé par la violence. L'homme est convaincu d'avoir fait injure à Dieu, parce qu'il a méprisé son commandement, et qu'il s'est damné en s'asservissant sous la main d'autrui. De même, le Diable est convaincu d'avoir fait injure à l'homme, car il l'a trompé tout d'abord en lui promettant de bonnes choses, et ensuite l'a lésé en le mettant dans les souffrances. C'est injustement que le Diable possède l'homme, mais l'homme est justement asservi, car si le diable n'a jamais mérité que l'homme lui soit assujetti, l'homme a mérité par sa faute de lui être soumis. Il est clair en effet qui s'il ignorait que les promesses du diable étaient mensongères, il n'ignorait pas qu'il ne devait pas, même si c'était vrai, désirer quelque chose contre la volonté de son créateur[44]...

Tout le texte suit cette argumentation, dont on voit la rigueur logique, qui aboutit évidemment à la présentation de l'Incarnation comme la solution idéale :

> Le Christ donc, en naissant a payé la dette de l'homme au Père, et en mourant a expié la charge imputée à l'homme, en sorte que comme il a supporté pour l'homme une mort qui ne lui était pas due, il est juste que l'homme soit libéré d'une mort qui lui était due...

Ce qui me retiendra dans ce texte, malgré l'absence de Marie, c'est qu'en quelque sorte tout l'argumentaire des procès de Paradis est mis en place ; c'est autour d'Hugues de Saint-Victor, plus sûrement peut-être qu'autour de la figure de Guillaume de Digulleville, qui en sera assurément le relais, que se met en place la dialectique de cette idée, où les décisions concernant le genre humain sont prises en charge et explicitées par divers protagonistes. La finalité est multiple ; on devine que, chez Hugues de Saint-Victor, la fonction essentielle est de réduire à la logique ce qui est l'occasion d'un émerveillement de la foi et de démontrer ainsi la merveille plus grande encore d'une *nécessité* du Salut ;

---

44 Hugues de Saint-Victor, *Miscellanea*, liber secundus, *Adnotationes elucidatoriae in quosdam psalmos David*, cap. VIII, « De causa litis inter Deum hominem et diabolum ». P.L. 177, col. 591-592. Ma traduction.

mais dès que cette cause est développée et narrée, dès que le canevas établi par le Victorin est amplifié pour donner lieu à un récit, les enjeux sont différents ; il est question alors, organiquement, de théologie et de droit. En ce qu'il préfigure les procès de paradis qui seront développés tout au long des grands mystères du XVe siècle, le texte est évidemment d'ordre théologique et explicite l'économie de la Rédemption ; en même temps, il est aussi la mise à l'épreuve de la notion même de justice. On l'a souligné plus haut, il semble que si Marie triomphe, dans les plus anciennes attestations des miracles, c'est d'une certain façon en trichant, en renversant à son avantage une cause désespérée ; on s'efforce, dès le XIIIe siècle, d'être dans un état plus juste, en tous cas plus juridique : si Marie triomphe, et nous savons qu'elle doit triompher, c'est en termes de droit, ou au moins selon la justice. C'est ici que se situe à mon sens le clivage ; le texte qui nous intéresse est évidemment l'ancêtre de nombreux procès de Paradis où vont s'affronter Justice et Miséricorde ; mais si la miséricorde est d'essence divine, la justice l'est également, et c'est elle qui s'exprime dans les mystères médiévaux, comme pour expliciter le projet du Père.

Reste à *justifier* les interventions mariales, à les inscrire dans l'économie de la Rédemption non pas comme un coup de force, à leur donner un cadre légal : pour cela, Marie va participer au procès, intervenir, pour défendre et soutenir l'homme ; c'est cette fonction qu'elle va occuper, dans un cadre qui n'est plus celui du Procès de Paradis, puisque l'enjeu en est différent, mais celui d'une cour de justice où elle aura à affirmer, devant un Satan fin légaliste, la légitimité de l'ensemble de son action, la légitimité de la démarche du Salut.

C'est cela même que rapporte l'*Advocacie Notre Dame.* Le texte est connu, mais à vrai dire assez peu travaillé, et en dehors des travaux de Gérard Gros, peu a été écrit sur ce texte depuis plus de cinquante ans. Il est révélateur, G. Gros l'a montré, de la perméabilité de certains genres littéraires, qui permettent de faire passer le *dit* vers des dramatisations ; ce qui était dans l'*Advocacie* une sorte de dialogue pourra aisément se mettre en scène, et donner naissance à un texte dramatique, le *Mystère* dont Graham Runnalls avait montré qu'il était réparti en plusieurs protagonistes, toute une série de saints se répartissant le rôle de Marie. Le travail d'amplification, la démultiplication des personnages, tout laisse penser que le *Mystère* est tiré du texte narratif, et non le contraire. On doit raisonnablement penser que ce texte, très technique malgré tout, a été destiné à un public averti : ce qui ne veut pas forcément dire grand' chose : si l'on peut penser à des avocats et membres du Parlement, très à-même d'apprécier cela en connaisseurs – la pièce pourrait en ce cas être jouée par des clercs de basoche – il n'est pas certain que pour être spectateur de ce type de représentation, le niveau d'expertise exigé dépasse celui d'un quidam ayant eu une ou deux expériences judiciaires : ce peut alors être n'importe quel *grand* public, et les acteurs peuvent être ou les troupes de jeunes mentionnées plus haut, ou tout simplement la troupe habituelle d'un mystère.

Il a alors une fonction presque éducative, permettant à de nombreux acteurs de répartir la matière juridique, d'expérimenter sur scène une performance judiciaire, de s'*entraîner* en un mot s'il s'agit d'étudiants. On notera que si les saints se démultiplient pour tenir le rôle que Marie tenait seule dans la version narrative, le Diable reste seul à assumer l'accusation : sans doute parce que son approche est plus prévisible sur le plan juridique, sans doute surtout que personne ne souhaitait endosser un tel rôle.

Un texte dramatique donc, et un texte juridique, qui s'appuie non seulement sur une procédure précise, mais aussi sur des détails de jurisprudence qui ont été relevés par les premiers commentateurs ; Chassant souligne « son habileté en chicane, comme un madré praticien[45] ». Il semble cependant que, si on a souligné la dimension juridique du texte, si on a éventuellement évoqué la source, elle n'a pas été particulièrement étudiée :

> L'*Advocacie Notre-Dame*, qui est une adaptation amplifiée d'un ouvrage latin, le *processus Sathanae*, attribué à tort au jurisconsulte Bartolo (1313-1356), se rattache au thème des procès de paradis[46].

Il était nécessaire, à partir de cette simple mention, de revenir aux sources indiquées du texte qui nous intéresse. Le travail remarquable de Carmen Cardelle de Hartmann permet de voir clair dans un texte et une tradition rhétorique qui nous sont largement conservés, sous de nombreuses versions et avec des titres variables, dans de nombreux

45 *L'advocacie Notre-Dame ou la Vierge Marie plaisant contre le diable, poème du* XIVe *siècle [...] extrait du mnauscrit de la Bibliothèque d'Évreux*, par A. Chassant, Paris, Auguste Aubry, 1855, p. 22.

46 G. Grente, *Dictionnaire des Lettres Françaises*, 2e édition revue et mise à jour sous la direction de G. Hasenohr et M. Zink, « La Pochothèque », 1992, p. 795 a.

états et dérivations[47]. Deux auteurs sont mis en avant, responsables de deux versions parentes mais distinctes ; on attribue à Bartole le texte du *Processus Satanas*, et à Guy de Colmieu une version dite *Advocacie*, mais aucune de ces attributions n'est assurée ; de même, la datation est floue, et se situe entre le deuxième quart du XIIIe siècle et le début du XIVe siècle. Le texte s'inscrit dans une tradition plus large de débats où Jésus argumente avec le diable, soit lorsqu'il est sur la croix, soit lorsqu'il se trouve devant la porte des enfers. Ce motif se trouve déjà dans la tradition byzantine.

Le nom le plus communément reçu est *Processus Satanae*, et le texte est accessible grâce à deux éditions, une récente mais assez difficile d'accès en France[48], l'autre procurée par L. B. Hauréau dans les *Notices et extraits*[49], et maintenant disponible sur Gallica. J'ai pu pour ma part retrouver les références d'une édition anglaise[50], mais qui peut aussi bien renvoyer au texte qui nous intéresse qu'au *Miracle Play* anglais. Le texte peut se trouver également avec facilité dans les œuvres de Bartole[51], sous le nom de *Tractatus quaestionis ventilate coram domino nostro Jesu Cristo inter virginem Mariam ex una parte et Diabolus ex altera parte.* Il figure également dans des éditions anciennes, comme le volume intitulé *Processus juris joco-serius*[52], qui contient outre le texte qui nous intéresse le *Processus Belial* ou *Processus Luciferi* de Jacobus de Teramo, et une version latine des *Arrêts d'amour* de Martial d'Auvergne. Cette dernière attestation me semble révélatrice de deux éléments : il existe

47 *Cf.* C. Cardelle de Hartmann, *Lateinische Dialogue 1200-1400, Literaturhistorische Studie une Repertorium*, Leiden-Boston, Brill, 2007. On se reportera principalement au ch. 6 : « Streitgespräche über das Heilsfeschehen und Satansprozesse », p. 233-241, ainsi qu'au répertoire qui recense diverses versions R5, a, b, c, p. 305-320.

48 I. Friedlander, « *Processus Satanae contra genus humanum.* En förbisedd litterär text i en formulärbok från Vadstena kloster », *Archivistica et medievistica Ernesto Nygren oblata*, Stockholm, Norstedt, 1956, p. 123-157.

49 L. B. Hauréau, *Notices et extraits des manuscrits de la Bibliothèque nationale*, t. VI, Paris, Klincksieck, 1893, p. 92-105.

50 *Processus Sathanae*, Walter Wilson Greg, Oxford UP, 1931.

51 Bartolus de Saxoferrato, *Consilia, disputationes necnon tractatus*, J. Siber (Lyon) – 1498, accessible sur Gallica.

52 Processus iuris ioco-serius, tam lectu festiuus et iucundus, quam ad usum fori & praxeos moralis cognitionem utilis ac necessarius : in quo continentur, I. Bartoli a Saxoferrato ... Processus Sathanae ... II. Iacobide de Ancharano ... Processus Luciferi ... III. Martialis Aruerini ... Aresta ... Éd. Villerianis, impens. Conr. Biermanni & cons., 1611, 964 pages.

une tradition ludique, un exercice du droit *joco-serius*, et le texte attribué à Barthole n'est pas isolé, loin de là.

Il faudrait faire une analyse détaillée de ce texte, et montrer à quel point il constitue le canevas détaillé de l'*Advocacie* ; les situations se répondent terme à terme et le détail des argumentations juridiques est suivi. Mais davantage, certaines éditions du *Processus* ajoutent à ce texte une série d'annotations directement insérées dans le texte, et qui renvoient aussi bien à des passages bibliques qu'à des textes juridiques. Ainsi, alors que le texte donné par le manuscrit Paris, BnF, lat 18216 (édité par L. B. Hauréau) porte simplement :

> *Qua die sancta adveniente, cogitans daemon quod major erat contumacia actoris quam rei, quodque nullos in regno caelorum habebat amicos, comparuit tempestive (ut loquamur more humano) in loco scilicet in quo Dominus pro tribunali sedere consueverat ; quia in domo domini mansiones multae sunt*[53].

Celui de l'édition des *Opera* de Bartole porte :

> *Qua die sancta adveniente, cogitans demon quod major erat contumacia actoris quam rei,* C. de judi. l properandum.§. si quidem et .§. se, *et quodque in regno caelorum habebat inimicos, comparuit tempestive ut loquamur more humano in loco ubi seu in quo pro tribunali Jesus stare consueverat ut* ff. de justu. *Et jure* .l. omnes populi et alia, et ff. quos or in bon pos. serve. l. .ij. *quare in domo Dei mansiones multe sunt.* Facit per hoc glo. notabiliter lxxxiij. dic. ad b. in glo super verbo et potiores et cum tex. de pe. di. iiij. §[54]...

L'abondance des incises renvoyant à des passages juridiques autant qu'à des références bibliques montre combien ce texte a pu évoluer des linéaments narratifs à une sorte de *vademecum* juridico-théologique. On doit en conclure cependant que si le texte du *Processus* fonctionne comme une sorte d'objet parodique, traitant avec le plus grand sérieux une question fictive, il convoque pour chacun des arguments l'ensemble de la tradition juridique, dont il va constamment donner les références : le lecteur de ce *processus* est à la fois en train de s'amuser du détournement ou de l'utilisation habile d'un texte de loi, de le découvrir ou le redécouvrir peut-être, de voir enfin jouer devant lui la dramatique divine,

---

53 *Op. cit.*, p. 94.

54 Bartolus de Saxoferrato, *Consilia, disputationes necnon tractatus*, J. Siber (Lyon) – 1498 (non paginé).

en des termes qu'il comprend du mieux qu'il peut, assorties à chaque fois de références précises à tel ou tel chapitre du Digeste ou d'autres textes de référence[55].

Marie avocate l'est donc maintenant selon les règles ; au lieu de tenir la place de Dieu et d'être en quelque sorte un prolongement de sa bienveillance, elle devient un acteur au milieu d'autres, un acteur privilégié certes, mais qui va respecter un rituel juridique auquel dorénavant même la Vierge Marie ne peut échapper. De la quasi-divinité toute puissante qui lui était attribuée dans les premières occurrences de mon enquête – et qui s'étendra dans la durée, comme une tradition populaire – elle est passée à un statut où tout en étant mère, fille et épouse du Seigneur, elle se soumet à une tradition juridique dont Dieu seul est le garant. Ici, elle y participe, intégrée dans l'ordre divin comme avocate, experte non seulement sur le plan juridique, mais également sur celui des artifices de la plaidoirie[56].

Les hasards de la tradition manuscrite font qu'après avoir été toute puissante au XIIIe siècle dans le *Théophile* et prépondérante au XIVe siècle – mais il est vrai que la relative unicité des *Miracles de Notre Dame par personnages* brouille la perception – Marie s'estompe dans la tradition théâtrale et occupe une place moins centrale au cours du XVe siècle. Figure essentielle des mystères – rares sont ceux où elle ne figure pas, comme protagoniste quand on rappelle l'Incarnation ou la Passion, comme intercesseur dans les vies de saints – elle n'a cependant plus la place de premier plan que lui accordaient les premières pièces. Davantage, au cours du XVIe siècle, alors que le monde urbain s'empare du théâtre, elle change de rôle et devient, d'avocate, justiciable. La controverse qui enflamme les ordres mendiants autour de la Conception de Marie va faire d'elle l'enjeu d'âpres joutes oratoires, qui trouvent leur aboutissement dans la tradition théâtrale du Puy des palinods. J'ai développé ce point ailleurs[57] et mentionnerai simplement un élément emblématique de cette évolution où Marie n'est pas actrice, mais enjeu.

55 Il n'est pas étonnant qu'une bonne analyse de ce *Processus* puisse se trouver dans un petit volume de David Murray, *Lawier's Merriment*, publié en 1912 : il s'agit effectivement d'un divertissement de juriste, dont l'*Advocacie* n'est que la partie la plus populaire.

56 Je développe cet aspect dans ma communication au colloque de Toronto qui fait suite à cette enquête, *cf.* note 42.

57 « Politique et polémique dans deux moralités du Puy de Rouen », *Le Théâtre polémique français*, M. Bouhaïk-Gironès, J. Koopmans, K. Lavéant (dir.), Rennes, PUR, 2008, p. 139-160.

Dans la *Moralité à dix personnages* de Jacques Le Lieur[58] se met en place un simulacre de procès où Ignorance nie le privilège marial devant Sapience divine. Celle-ci convie les Arts Libéraux et la Vierge à une confrontation qui n'est pas exactement un procès, dans la mesure où il n'y a pas de juge, et où Ignorance finira par rendre les armes. Mais ce qui me retiendra ici, c'est la modestie de Marie, sa crainte à se présenter devant une assemblée qui la jugera. Marie est accusée, Marie pourrait être coupable (coupable d'avoir la faute originelle), et c'est sur ce paradoxe que se met en place le récit ; on appréciera la distance qui sépare l'arrogance de Marie chez Rutebeuf de l'humilité excessive de Marie chez Jacques Le Lieur.

Appelée par Sapience, Marie répond :

> Treshaulte dame et comme se peult faire
> Ung tel affaire,
> Veu les mechantz des villes et des champs
> Qui mon honneur s'efforcent de deffaire ? [...]
>
> SAP[IENCE]
> Fille, non, non ne craignez la poincture
> Des mesdisantz, ilz n'ont sur vous povoir.
>
> MARIE
> Comment ? Yrai ge en humaine vesture,
> Sans couverture
> Et sans la force avoir,
> Pour eviter la perverse nature
> De leur lecture
> Et oblique sçavoir[59] ?

On le voit, nous sommes ici dans un monde où Marie est déchue de sa toute puissance, déchue même de sa maîtrise du droit. C'est son double, Sapience Divine, née comme elle avant tous les siècles, qui prend le relais pour la protéger. Attaquée par les Dominicains, elle a besoin d'un tiers pour assurer sa défense. On comprend mieux le scandale qu'a

58 Manuscrit B. M. Rouen, Y 17, inédit. On pourra consulter D. Hüe, *La Poésie palinodique à Rouen*...Champion 2002, p. 405-416, ainsi que J. E. Moore, « *La Morale de Sapience* et la question de l'Immaculée Conception », *Première Poésie française de la Renaissance, autour des Puys poétiques normands*... J.-C. Arnould et Th. Mantovani (dir.), Paris, Champion, 2003, p. 37-50.

59 Ms B. M. Rouen, Y 17, f. 192-193.

pu provoquer la position dominicaine, qui prétendait condamner la protectrice même de l'homme auprès de la justice divine. Il est révélateur, somme toute, que la dernière moralité du Puy de Rouen qui nous soit conservée ne choisisse pas d'organiser un procès en bonne et due forme – alors que les poètes du Puy connaissaient admirablement la matière juridique, familiers qu'ils étaient pour la plupart du Parlement de Rouen – mais préfère organiser une controverse entre Sapience et Ignorance, convoquant l'ensemble des Arts Libéraux plus que la Justice : c'est qu'en dehors des arguties juridiques, Marie reste indiscutable. À mesure que s'organise la loi des hommes, elle se distingue de la justice divine : c'est le message que semble nous donner l'itinéraire que nous suivons aujourd'hui.

Denis HÜE
Université Rennes 2 –
Haute Bretagne

LA FIGURE DE L'INQUISITEUR ET LE VISAGE DE L'ACCUSÉ DANS LE *MYSTÈRE DE LA SAINTE HOSTIE*

Une femme de pauvre condition laisse, en échange de trente sols, son manteau en gage chez Jacob Mousse, un usurier juif de la rue des Jardins. Le jour de Pâques arrive et la femme, ne s'imaginant pas autrement que dignement vêtue pour les solennités pascales, retourne chez son prêteur avec l'espoir de récupérer son bien. L'usurier accepte de lui restituer son vêtement à condition qu'elle s'engage à lui apporter l'hostie consacrée qu'elle recevra ce jour en communion. La femme accepte et revient quelques temps plus tard de l'église Saint-Merri en possession de l'hostie dérobée.

Après le départ de celle que le texte appellera désormais la *mauvaise femme*, le Juif réunit sa femme, son fils et sa fille autour du Saint-Sacrement. Voulant vérifier « ce que les Crestiens mallois dient et maintiennent estre tel », le Juif commence à dépecer l'hostie avec un petit couteau. Effrayés de voir que celle-ci se met à saigner, la femme et les deux enfants supplient le Juif d'interrompre son geste. Ce dernier refuse et s'obstine. Il coupe, cloue, brûle, transperce et hache l'hostie qui ne cesse de saigner et virevolter à travers la pièce. Désemparé face à ce redoutable adversaire, le Juif finit par le jeter dans la chaudière remplie d'eau bouillante. Dans l'eau devenue sanguinolente, la fille prétend voir le corps de Dieu jouer comme un enfant quand tous s'ébahissent devant l'apparition d'un crucifix au-dessus de la chaudière. Le Juif terrifié se réfugie sur son lit, alors que le reste de la famille, converti à la vue d'un tel miracle, quitte le foyer.

Un peu plus tard dans la journée, le fils du Juif révèle innocemment les faits à une voisine chrétienne. Alertée par ces dires inquiétants, la voisine s'aventure dans la maison de l'usurier avec le prétexte de venir chercher quelques braises. En découvrant l'intérieur dévasté, elle se signe de la croix et voit l'hostie miraculeuse se poser dans l'écuelle qu'elle tient à la main. Elle s'empresse de la confier au prêtre de Saint-Jean en Grève, qui charge alors deux bourgeois d'aller prévenir le prévôt et l'évêque de Paris. À l'annonce de la nouvelle, le prévôt et son escorte, guidés par le fils du Juif, se rendent immédiatement à la maison de la rue des Jardins. Ils y arrêtent le Juif, sa femme et ses deux enfants avant de faire l'état des lieux. Ils commentent ainsi l'eau toute sanguine et la demie lance ensanglantée jusqu'au manche, puis s'emparent de la chaudière, du trépied, du couteau et du lavement, d'autant de reliques marquées du précieux sang. De son côté, l'évêque commande à l'official de constituer une assemblée de clercs pour partir à la rencontre du prévôt. Les deux cortèges se retrouvent à l'hôtel de ville où le Juif est appelé à livrer sa version des faits. Il reconnaît ses actes et demande le baptême. Offusqué d'une telle doléance, le prévôt requiert qu'il soit mis à mort sur le champ. L'évêque souhaite, en revanche, un procès de raison à la fin des fêtes pascales et demande à ce que l'accusé soit emprisonné jusque-là. Dans le même temps, la femme et les enfants du Juif sont, quant à eux, reconnus convertis et l'évêque leur administre le baptême.

L'épisode qui fait suite, intitulé *La condamnation du faux Juif, comment il fut ars et bruslé hors Paris au marché aux pourceaux*, s'ouvre sur les préparatifs du procès. L'évêque demande au sergent de la cour de Paris de faire assembler des personnalités de haute autorité pour juger le profanateur. Sorti de prison, le Juif comparaît devant l'inquisiteur, le recteur d'université, le prévôt et l'évêque. L'accusé refuse de se repentir et le procès tourne court. Le prévôt prononce la peine capitale et, sans plus attendre, le Juif est brûlé vif sous les yeux de ses juges.

Inquiétée, la mauvaise femme quitte Paris pour trouver refuge à Senlis. Alors qu'elle travaille depuis sept ans dans une hôtellerie, elle se retrouve enceinte de ses frasques avec le valet. Pour cacher sa faute, elle fait périr le nouveau-né sous un tas de fumier. Sa maîtresse découvre l'infanticide et la dénonce aux autorités. Après avoir confessé tous ses crimes au bailli de Senlis, la femme est condamnée à mort. Elle meurt sur le bûcher en exprimant son profond repentir.

L'histoire sordide que conte *Le Mystère de la sainte hostie*[1] ne trouve probablement plus d'écho dans l'esprit du lecteur d'aujourd'hui. Pourtant,

1 On compte trois éditions imprimées de ce texte : *Le Mistere de la saincte hostie*, imprimé à Paris chez la veuve Trepperel, approximativement entre 1512 et 1519 (Bnf Réserve p Yf 564) ; *Le Mistere de la saincte hostie nouvellement imprimée à Paris*, entre 1530 et 1537

ce texte devenu si discret dans la vaste bibliothèque des mystères français de la fin du Moyen Âge est l'adaptation dramatique d'un thème autrefois très populaire. À l'image de Philippe de Vigneulles qui s'enthousiasmait des afflux de sang inondant le parc lors d'une représentation se tenant à Metz en 1513[2], les spectateurs connaissaient sans nul doute le célèbre miracle parisien dit des *Billettes* alors mis en scène[3].

Depuis 1290, date prétendue des faits, la légende du Juif profanant une hostie aux propriétés miraculeuses a connu une diffusion exceptionnelle. Célébré chaque semaine lors d'offices parisiens, relaté dans les chroniques comme l'un des événements notables de l'histoire de Paris mais surtout, sculpté et peint sur bon nombre de pièces ornant les églises, le miracle parisien se répandit largement et durablement en France[4], et même à l'étranger, puisque l'on recense deux œuvres italiennes du XVe siècle directement inspirées des faits[5]. Dans cette nébuleuse de textes et d'images, le jeu de *la sainte hostie* n'est alors qu'une énième version du miracle probablement rédigée par un anonyme au milieu du XVe siècle[6]. C'est donc en tant que tel que ce jeu est évoqué dans

par Jean II Trepperel ou Alain Lotrian (Bibliothèque Méjanes d'Aix-en-Provence Rés. S. 60) ; *Le jeu et mystere de la saincte hostie par personnages. A Paris par Jehan Bonfons, libraire demourant en la rue Neufve Nostre Dame a l'enseigne sainct Nicolas*, probablement entre 1547 et 1566 (Bnf Réserve Yf 2915).

2 L. Petit de Julleville, *Les Mystères*, Paris, 1880, t. II, p. 103.

3 Sur ce miracle : *Cf.* Théodoric de Saint-René (père), *Remarques historiques, à l'occasion de la sainte Hostie miraculeuse conservée pendant plus de quatre cents ans dans l'église paroissiale de Saint-Jean-en-Grève à Paris*, Paris, Antonin Des Hayes libraire, 1725 ; V. PAGET, « Le miracle des Billettes à Paris (1290) », *L'Eucharistie*, Paris, Maison de la Bonne Presse, 1912, t. 3, p. 281-293, p. 378-390, p. 424-437 ; G. Dahan, « Il y a sept cents ans à Paris (1290), L'affaire des Billettes », *Communauté Nouvelle*, décembre 1991, n° 58, p. 72-84.

4 Les principaux foyers français de diffusion du miracle (Paris, Troyes, Metz) se situent dans les régions où se développa tout particulièrement la dévotion au Saint-Sacrement (*Cf.* M. Rubin, *Corpus Christi : The Eucharist in Late Medieval Culture*, Cambridge, Cambridge University Press, 1991, chapitre III et IV, notamment p. 164-287). La Révolution française et la disparition de l'hostie miraculée, jusque-là conservée et exposée à la vénération des fidèles dans l'église de Saint-Jean-en-Grève, atténueront le souvenir.

5 Il s'agit d'une prédelle de Paolo Uccello (P. Uccello, « Le Miracle de l'hostie » ou « Miracle de l'hostie profanée », 1467-1469, prédelle sur bois, 42x361, conservée au palais ducal d'Urbino, Italie) et d'une pièce de théâtre toscane intitulée *La Rapresentatione d'uno miracolo del Corpo di Cristo*. J.-L. Schefer évoque six éditions imprimées datant du XVIe siècle. Il propose une traduction de l'incunable, non daté, édité par Bartolomeo dei Libri à Florence, actuellement conservé sous la côte INC. C. 269 à la Biblioteca Trivulziana de Milan (J.-L. Schefer, *L'hostie profanée, histoire d'une fiction théologique*, Paris, P.O.L., 2007, p. 63-88).

6 Le texte, si l'on en croit l'état de la langue des trois versions imprimées aujourd'hui conservées, est caractéristique du milieu du XVe siècle. Les frères Parfaict, M. de Beauchamps

quelques ouvrages de théologiens ou d'historiens de l'art. En 1725, le Père Théodoric de Saint-René le mentionne comme étant une « pièce justificative » du miracle, au même titre que les bulles, sermons et diverses représentations iconographiques ; en 2007, Jean-Louis Schefer l'incorpore à sa somme de documents amoncelés en vue d'illustrer la « fiction théologique » qu'est l'histoire de l'hostie profanée[7]. Toujours collationné comme un récit du miracle, jamais étudié en tant qu'œuvre dramatique, le jeu s'est souvent vu laissé pour compte.

Il va sans dire que les récits et représentations qui se succèdent jusqu'au milieu du XVIe siècle ne présentent pas de variations notables. Néanmoins, J.-L. Schefer nuance à juste titre cette constatation hâtive en rappelant que cela n'est vrai qu'en ce qui concerne l'épisode de la profanation. Le sacrilège étant, dans la croyance populaire, une pratique rituelle calquée sur la Passion du Christ, il se résume, par définition, à une série d'actes, immuables et peu flexibles. L'épilogue judiciaire de cette affaire n'est, en revanche, pas soumis à la même rigueur. Les chroniqueurs ne s'entendent pas toujours sur l'issue du procès[8]. Converti pour l'un, mis à mort pour les autres, les intentions prêtées à l'accusé comme le devenir que lui réserve la justice, varient curieusement. À partir de la deuxième moitié du XVe siècle, la tradition semble toutefois

---

ou encore J. de Douhet s'entendent sur la date de 1444. *Le Journal d'un Bourgeois de Paris* évoque dans sa description de la grande procession parisienne du 15 mai 1444 un Mystère du Juif en précisant que le cortège des personnages suivait les reliques en monstrances. Certains veulent y voir les prémices du jeu, d'autres un mimodrame sur chariots ; une curiosité que de vouloir trancher alors que les deux formes purent parfaitement coexister. En effet, ce type de *continuum*, où se fondent spectacle, procession et messe était déjà pratiqué à la fin du XIVe siècle. Ce fut le cas, par exemple, lors de *La présentation de la Vierge au temple* que Philippe de Mézières fit représenter le 21 novembre 1385 à Avignon. Après le jeu, *stricto senso*, la Vierge-enfant et les autres acteurs assistent à la messe et entrent en procession parmi les fidèles. Sans certitude, on peut imaginer que le texte dramatique de *la sainte hostie* fut joué à Paris, en mai 1444, et que par la suite les personnages intégrèrent la procession (*Journal d'un bourgeois de Paris de 1405 à 1449*, C. Beaune (éd.), Paris, « Lettres Gothiques », Livre de Poche, 1990, p. 47 et 48 ; P. L'Hermite-Leclercq, « Les Juifs et Synagogue chez Philippe de Mézières », G. Dahan (dir.), *L'expulsion des Juifs de France 1394*, Paris, Éditions du Cerf, 2004, p. 135-174, p. 157).

7 Théodoric de Saint-René (père), *op. cit.* ; J.-L. Schefer, *op. cit.*

8 Dans la *Chronique de Jean Thilrode*, le Juif « se convertit à la foi, avec toute sa famille » (*Iohannis de Thilrode Chronicon*, *MGH Scriptores* XXV, Hanovre, 1880, repr. Stuttgart-New-York, 1964, p. 578) alors que dans *Ly Myreur des Histors de Jean de Preis*, dit d'Outremeuse, le Juif « fut arse à Paris en le plache à porcheaux, si com faux tirans, et la femme enssi qui li avoit vendut fut arses » (*Recueil des historiens des Gaules et de la France*, M. Dom Bouquet (dir.), Paris, Victor Palmé, 1869, t. XXII, p. 32).

mieux établie. Les représentations iconographiques illustrant l'épisode judiciaire nous montrent un Juif condamné, le plus souvent mené au bûcher sur une charrette[9]. Quoiqu'il en soit, entre les chroniques qui ne passent qu'en quelques phrases sur le devenir du Juif et les œuvres iconographiques des peintres et verriers qui n'en font pas un motif indispensable, la séquence est soumise à une fluctuation évidente.

La peine capitale étant plus ou moins une issue convenue de la légende courant XVe siècle, c'est sans grand étonnement que la version théâtrale condamne le Juif au bûcher. Plus surprenante est l'importance que l'auteur accorde au règlement judiciaire de cette affaire : arrestation du Juif et de sa famille par le bras séculier, perquisition des pièces à conviction par quelques bourgeois venus constater les faits, comparution devant l'évêque, procès, condamnation et exécution du Juif, sans oublier la condamnation de la femme à l'origine du sacrilège, retrouvée sept ans plus tard et jugée à mort par le bailli de Senlis pour avoir enfoui son nouveau-né sous un tas de fumier. Notre auteur ne lésine pas sur les dispositions prises après l'acte de profanation, au point d'y consacrer près des deux tiers de son texte, reléguant inévitablement le miracle eucharistique au second plan. L'anonyme qui se livra à cet exercice de transposition théâtrale a vraisemblablement repris la trame de la relation primitive datant du premier tiers du XIVe siècle[10]. Néanmoins, en même

9 Il s'agit le plus souvent de vitraux de chœur en l'honneur de l'Eucharistie qui accordent une place visuelle à l'hostie bien plus qu'aux différents protagonistes du miracle. Dans son article, Jackie Provence dresse l'inventaire des vitraux du miracle recensés en Champagne méridionale. Sur les six verrières datant approximativement de la seconde moitié du XVIe siècle, quatre présentent la scène de conduite du Juif en chariot (J. Provence, « Le miracle de la sainte hostie dans les vitraux de Champagne », *La Vie en Champagne*, n° 25, janv.-mars 2001, p. 31-40, p. 35).

10 Cette relation dite ici primitive constitue la plus ancienne relation connue du miracle. Il s'agit d'un récit latin en prose composé par un anonyme sous Charles IV Le Bel, entre 1322 et 1328. Ce texte de neuf chapitres relatant prolixement les faits, était lu lors des différentes célébrations commémoratives du miracle. Jusqu'à la Révolution, trois versions manuscrites de cette narration existaient encore. Aujourd'hui, il ne reste de celles-ci que quelques pages du Livre d'Office de l'église Saint-Jean en Grève, conservées aux Archives Nationales (Manuscrits : Section historique, IIe carton, L. 664). Il existe, par ailleurs, une version imprimée de ce texte. En 1604, J. Séguier, conseiller d'État et marguillier d'honneur de l'église Saint-Jean en Grève, le fait imprimer en latin et en français (*Tractatus miraculi Biletani super sacratissimo Corpore Christi a Judeo confixo. An 1290. Lutetiae. Apud Federicum Morellum Architypographum Regium.* 1604. La partie française a pour titre : *Histoire Miraculeuse de la Saincte Hostie gardée en l'Église de Saint-Jean en Grève, ensemble quelques Hymnes au Saint Sacrement de l'Autel.* De la traduction de H.S.P.A. Paris

temps qu'il adaptait à la scène cette relation vieille de plus d'un siècle, il remaniait par petites touches le dispositif judicaire jusque-là érigé en modèle. Ainsi, le théâtre propose des figures de justiciers démultipliées condamnant un accusé au profil assombri, et l'exagération judiciaire devient d'une certaine manière la spécificité de ce texte parmi les nombreuses œuvres célébrant la légende parisienne. L'originalité théâtrale est encore de mise et cette fois-ci bien au-delà de l'extrapolation et de l'amplification propre à la forme dramatique, si l'on considère la présence d'un inquisiteur parmi le rang des juges chrétiens. Noyé dans le flot des figures d'autorité et n'ayant de voix que pour quelques menues répliques, ce personnage n'a de toute évidence pas marqué les esprits de ceux qui se penchèrent sur ce texte[11].

Pourtant, cette intrusion n'est pas aussi fortuite et donc dénuée de sens qu'il y paraît. Dans l'arsenal juridique que propose la scène du XVe siècle, la figure de l'inquisiteur est intéressante car proprement nouvelle. En même temps que cette figure ecclésiastique participe de l'image rêvée d'une société chrétienne unifiée et répressive à l'encontre de tous les détracteurs de la foi, elle se donne en réponse au nouveau visage de l'accusé. Assailli par les accusations, le personnage du Juif offre à présent tout de la caricature du prosélyte hérétique. Toutefois, cette affaire inquisitoriale n'a peut-être pas encore la portée allégorique très claire qu'elle aura dans les représentations du début du XVIe siècle. Au moment où le théâtre adapte le miracle eucharistique, il semble qu'il ne soit pas encore question de déposséder entièrement le coupable de son identité religieuse. Au contraire, l'intervention de l'inquisiteur pourrait servir à dénoncer une subsistance juive grandement redoutée en cette fin de Moyen Âge. L'étude de ce discret personnage ouvre alors le texte de *la sainte hostie* à des visées nouvelles qui font définitivement sortir l'objet dramatique de son carcan commémoratif.

---

chez Frédéric Morel, Imprimeur ordinaire du Roy .M.D.C.IV.) On retrouvera la version française retranscrite dans son intégralité dans l'ouvrage du père Théodoric de Saint-René. Notons cependant qu'il en modernise l'orthographe pour le rendre accessible à ses lecteurs du XVIIIe siècle (Théodoric de Saint René (père), *op. cit.* ; J.-L. Schefer, *op. cit.* J.-L. Schefer reproduit également la relation primitive dans la version française du père Théodoric de Saint-René).

11 Seul J.-L. Schefer se contente de relever l'apparition exceptionnelle du personnage sur la scène (J.-L. Schefer, *op. cit.*, p. 36).

L'INQUISITEUR : UN MEMBRE DE L'ARSENAL JURIDIQUE SPECTACULAIRE

À la fin du XIIIe siècle, les récits de miracles eucharistiques liés à une profanation d'hostie par un ou des Juifs sont en pleine expansion. Comme le rappelle Gilbert Dahan, cette forme de procès s'inscrit directement dans la filiation des accusations de meurtres rituels que l'on impute aux Juifs depuis la deuxième moitié du XIIe siècle[12]. Au XIIIe siècle, on accuse désormais ces « ennemis de la Chrétienté » de répéter la Passion non plus sur un homme, image de Dieu, mais sur une hostie, chair même de Dieu. Alors que la dévotion au Saint-Sacrement est en plein essor suite à la rigoureuse définition du dogme chrétien de la transsubstantiation formulée en 1215 lors du Concile de Latran IV, cette nouvelle accusation, encore plus grave, finit d'isoler un peu plus les Juifs au sein de la société chrétienne, soit seize ans avant leur première expulsion en 1306 par Philippe Le Bel. Néanmoins, la mise à mal d'une hostie par un Juif n'est pas complètement nouvelle dans l'imaginaire médiéval[13]. En revanche, la nouveauté qui s'illustre dans la vague de récits de profanations en cette fin de siècle, c'est la thématique précise et limitée de Juifs usuriers qui se procurent une hostie par ruse pour lui infliger divers outrages calqués sur la Passion et qui, une fois révélés aux autorités seront le plus souvent massacrés, rarement convertis. Fleurissent ainsi des miracles montés en série, véritable fruit d'une « piété populaire » alimentée par des enjeux politiques, symboliques et évidemment théologiques (ou plus exactement doctrinaux), nous situant bien loin de toute véracité[14].

---

12 Si les Juifs sont accusés de commettre des meurtres à des fins rituelles depuis l'Antiquité, G. Dahan rappelle que c'est avec l'affaire de William de Norwich en 1144 que ce type d'accusation se développe considérablement pour devenir commune par la suite (G. Dahan, *Les intellectuels chrétiens et les juifs au Moyen Âge*, Paris, Les Éditions du Cerf, 1999, p. 27).

13 Joshua Trachtenberg rappelle qu'au Xe siècle, un Juif, cherchant à insulter le Christ, réussit à communier parmi la foule. Au moment de mettre l'hostie dans sa poche, il fut incapable de fermer la bouche, révélant ainsi son sacrilège à la vue de tous les Chrétiens alentour (J. Trachtenberg, *The Devil and The Jews, The Medieval Conception of the Jews and its relation to Modern Anti-Semitism*, Yale, University Press, 1943).

14 J.-L. Schefer conçoit que ces récits se « prouvent mutuellement par concaténation » (J.-L. Schefer, *op. cit.*, p. 113). Rappelons seulement que l'expression de « piété populaire » telle qu'elle

À une époque où les dévotions et croyances populaires avoisinent le monde du savoir, le cas récent de la profanation d'hostie par des Juifs ne laisse pas indifférents les théologiens qui s'interrogent sur la procédure à suivre à l'égard de ces nouveaux profanateurs. La source exacte du débat nous est révélée par la question que pose Henri de Gand, sous la forme d'un *casus*, à l'occasion d'une dispute quodlibétique pendant la session de l'Avent 1290. Sans se référer à une quelconque réalité, Henri de Gand discute un cas d'école pour lequel se pose un problème de juridiction évident : « Un Juif qui poignarde une hostie consacrée, et qui, voyant qu'elle rougit du sang jaillissant de ses plaies, se convertit et se fait baptiser à la vue de ce miracle, doit-il être puni pour ce délit par la justice publique[15] ? », il précise que : « Si ce Juif n'était pas puni pour ce délit par la justice publique selon la loi chrétienne, alors ce méfait resterait impuni, parce que les Juifs ne le puniraient pas selon leur loi[16] » . Le point de départ de cette singulière préoccupation est le statut complexe que les Juifs occupent dans la société médiévale. En cherchant à définir l'attitude de l'Église à l'égard des Juifs, G. Dahan revient sur le caractère exceptionnel de leur situation et cherche à savoir « en quoi l'Église a quelque chose à dire sur les Juifs ? » Toute la difficulté lorsqu'il s'agit de traiter juridiquement des affaires impliquant les « ennemis de la croix du Christ » tient au fait qu'ils sont « dans la société (contrairement à tous les autres non-chrétiens), mais hors de l'Église (contrairement aux hérétiques)[17] ». Le cas si particulier de la profanation d'hostie pose dès lors un problème d'ordre juridique : comment l'Église a-t-elle pu prétendre punir un Juif qui, par définition, n'est pas soumis à la législation des Chrétiens ?

Alors que le miracle, qui restera assurément le plus mémorable du genre, venait de se donner à voir rue des Jardins, la vie intellectuelle parisienne débat sur le sort du Juif profanateur. Le casus universitaire révélerait ainsi, en 1290, un miracle des Billettes à l'issue encore discutable et non fixée. Le fait divers tel qu'il est décrit dans la relation

---

employée par J.-L. Schefer a été l'objet de controverses. Initié par Étienne Delaruelle, ce concept fut vigoureusement contesté par Jean-Claude Schmitt, Francis Rapp ou André Vauchez qui lui préfèreront l'expression de « religion populaire ».

15 E. Marmursztejn, « Du récit exemplaire au casus universitaire : une variation théologique sur le thème de la profanation d'hosties par les Juifs (1290) », *Médiévales* 41, automne 2001, p. 37-64, p. 38.

16 *Ibid.*, p. 45.

17 G. Dahan, *op. cit.*, p. 104 et 113.

primitive rédigée au début du XIVe siècle propose un épilogue judiciaire parfaitement ficelé où se précise l'alternative de la conversion et de la condamnation à mort. Après que la voisine, le curé de Saint-Jean et quelques badauds sont allés faire le récit de cet accident à l'évêque puis au prévôt, il est écrit :

> *on va en diligence en la maison du Juif, & sans autre forme de procès il est mis dans une étroite prison, avec sa femme & toute sa famille. L'Evêque de sa part fait assembler en peu de tems les plus graves Ecclesiastiques de son Diocese, les Docteurs en Theologie, les Prédicateurs, les Ordres Mendiants, & plusieurs autres venerables personnes, & devant une telle assemblée, on fait venir le malheureux Juif* [...] *A tant il est mis es main de la Justice, & condamné par le jugement de personnes notables à être brûlé vif. L'exécution n'en est pas long-tems differée ; il est aussi-tôt livré au Prévôt de Paris*[18].

Dans ce récit, on ne trouve plus la moindre réflexion théologique quant au devenir des coupables, encore moins l'évocation d'un quelconque problème juridictionnel, mais une justice chrétienne répressive et imminente qui scelle sans tergiverser le destin du Juif. Le procès s'achève à présent par une mise à mort, celle du Juif profanateur et réfractaire au repentir, et trois conversions, celles des membres de la famille révélés à la foi chrétienne dans la contemplation du miracle. Au demeurant, pour rendre une justice vraisemblable, le récit du début du XIVe siècle fait état d'un dispositif conforme à la juridiction ecclésiastique en pratique à cette époque[19].

Elsa Marmursztejn s'étonne de l'écart qui se creuse entre le *casus* théologique, qui « consistait dans l'exposé d'un problème lié à une situation particulière, dont la solution devait servir de modèle dans toutes les situations analogues », et les récits de miracle postérieurs à son exposition publique. Alors que le cas exposé au cours de la dispute quodlibétique faisait explicitement mention de la conversion du Juif parce qu'on considérait la mise à l'épreuve du Saint-Sacrement comme

18 J.-L. Schefer, *op. cit.*, p. 46 et 47. Rappelons que J.-L. Schefer reproduit la relation primitive en son entier telle que le père Théodoric de saint-René l'avait retranscrite dans une orthographe modernisée du XVIIIe siècle.

19 À cette époque, les cours d'Église occupent de larges compétences et celles-ci sont exclusives en ce qui concerne les crimes contre la religion tels que le sacrilège, l'hérésie ou la sorcellerie. Toutefois, le juge d'Église devra recourir au bras séculier pour le prononcé et l'application de la peine de mort, l'Église ne pouvant prononcer cette peine en vertu de l'adage *Ecclesia abhorret a sanguine*.

une « expérience » et non un « outrage », ce récit de peu ultérieur, comme tous ceux qui s'ensuivent, « insistent au contraire sur l'opiniâtreté dont le profanateur avait fait preuve » et témoignent « d'un endurcissement dans l'erreur que confirme le refus de la conversion[20] ». Revenu dans le monde de l'imaginaire collectif, et donc loin des cadres de pensée de la scolastique, le récit de miracle se radicalise, et l'obstination du profanateur se heurte à une justice sans appel. Il va sans dire que le blanc juridique qui prêtait à discussion dans l'enceinte de l'université, se voit ici comblé par une juridiction proprement irréelle. Ainsi, à la « juridiction intellectuelle » du théologien qui s'évertuait à faire entrer le Juif dans les cadres normatifs de la justice chrétienne, se substitue ce que J.-L. Schefer nomme une « justice de parabole[21] ».

Une juridiction qui fait défaut, et c'est la brèche où s'engouffre l'imagination populaire. Le fait divers de 1290 ainsi achevé, diffuse désormais un message pluriel : si le miracle atteste de la présence réelle sous les espèces de l'hostie, l'épisode judiciaire, lui, grossièrement élaboré, sert à mettre en garde tous les détracteurs de la foi chrétienne. La sanction pénale doit bien évidemment susciter la peur chez celui qui oserait porter atteinte au Saint-Sacrement mais plus certainement mettre en garde celui qui se permettrait de remettre en question le dogme eucharistique fraîchement promulgué. Rappelons que le Juif est ici condamné non pas pour avoir profané une hostie mais parce qu'il refuse de se convertir à la suite du miracle qui s'est offert à lui. C'est donc bien le refus de croire qui le conduit à la mort. Mais, J.-L. Schefer qui analyse le miracle des Billettes dans sa diffusion ultérieure, pousse plus loin la dimension parabolique de la légende. Considérant la contradiction juridique soulevée par Henri de Gand, mais prenant également en compte le fait que les diverses versions ne cessent de complexifier le dispositif apte à juger le profanateur, il conçoit l'aspect judiciaire comme démonstratif de l'importance mystique de l'Eucharistie. Derrière l'exagération judiciaire se dessine, selon lui, l'image médiévale du Corps Mystique. Dans la théologie chrétienne, le Corps du Christ, dit Corps Mystique, désigne l'ensemble de la communauté des fidèles. L'Église, et donc l'ensemble de la chrétienté, forme un corps harmonieux et hiérarchiquement ordonné. Le roi est à la tête de ce corps et chaque membre de la communauté correspond à un organe essentiel,

20 E. Marmursztejn, *op. cit.*, p. 42 et 43.
21 J.-L. Schefer, *op. cit.*, p. 38.

l'ensemble étant placé sous le regard de Dieu. Dans cette conception sacrée du royaume, on comprendra sans mal que l'Eucharistie représente « le symbole fondateur de l'État chrétien[22] ». Recevoir l'hostie c'est participer au grand corps mystique, *a contrario* profaner l'hostie c'est nuire à sa cohésion. Toute atteinte au Saint-Sacrement engage ainsi l'essence même de l'État chrétien. Dans cette perspective, le regroupement des personnages appelés à juger dans les différents récits relatant l'affaire des Billettes ne se justifient que dans l'idéologie du Corps Mystique et leur nombre n'a d'égal que l'importance que revêt le Saint-Sacrement.

Quand le théâtre adapte cette légende à la scène, nous sommes vraisemblablement au milieu du XVe siècle. L'anonyme qui se livra à cet exercice de transposition théâtrale semble avoir travaillé à partir de la relation primitive du XIVe siècle. Que le membre de la confrérie des Billettes ou le fatiste professionnel auquel cette même confrérie aurait communiqué le matériau, ait pu avoir connaissance de cette version narrative près d'un siècle et demi plus tard n'est pas étonnant. La relation primitive ayant été lue lors des offices hebdomadaires et des commémorations annuelles, et ce jusqu'à la Révolution française, il ne pouvait en être autrement. Qu'il ait clairement adapté ce texte à la scène est plus incertain, même si certains recoupements invitent à le penser[23]. Quoiqu'il en soit, alors que la piété eucharistique est à son comble et que l'idée de *faire corps* est largement répandue[24], le jeu propose un dispositif judiciaire élargi de la présence d'un inquisiteur. Au-delà du fait que cette amplification touche à la théâtralité de cette version (la démultiplication des personnages n'est *a priori* pas surprenante dans ce registre : c'est avant toute chose, faire du temps de représentation,

---

22 *Ibid.*, p. 37.

23 Tout d'abord, cette relation primitive constitue la version la plus développée et la plus accessible de la légende parisienne. Ensuite, le texte dramatique représente deux scènes inexistantes dans les autres versions connues du miracle : celles des anges invisibles empêchant la femme ayant recueillie l'hostie de s'enfuir de l'église et celle du Juif réclamant qu'on aille lui quérir le Talmud. Quoi qu'il en soit, comme les nombreux récits de la légende, le texte dramatique reprend vraisemblablement la procédure juridique que lui impose le récit du XIVe siècle, c'est-à dire, une procédure en deux temps, celui du jugement par l'évêque, juge d'Église, en charge d'examiner la vérité des faits, puis, celui de la proclamation de la peine et de son exécution par le juge royal, le prévôt de Paris. La bascule des pouvoirs s'effectuant par ces mots prononcés par l'évêque : « L'Église a plein se demet » (v.1229).

24 *Cf.* C. De Pisan, *Le livre du corps de policie*, Édition critique par R.-H. Lucas., Genève, Librairie Droz, 1967.

du temps de délectation pour les spectateurs, du temps de rentabilité pour tous les agents qui se sont investis dans cette production unique), J.-L. Schefer conçoit l'introduction de ce personnage comme une façon habile d'augmenter l'appareil judiciaire[25]. Évêque, prévôt, sergents, recteur, inquisiteur, bailli, bourgeois, enfants de la rue, les visages des juges transposés au théâtre n'auraient que peu d'importance dans le cours de ce procès proprement irréel. Cet ensemble de personnages aux fonctions et statuts sociaux très divers seraient simplement des figurants juxtaposés en vue d'incarner ce corps unifié, qui brocarde le Saint-Sacrement comme le garant de son intégrité. À la suite de son probable modèle et des différentes versions du miracle, le théâtre expose une société, unie derrière le Corps Mystique, qui prononce un verdict sans appel pour éradiquer ce Juif profanateur, perçu comme « le membre putride » nuisible à la cohésion de l'État chrétien[26].

Au cœur de cette farandole mise au service d'une « justice de parabole », l'inquisiteur n'est assurément qu'un personnage discret et de peu de consistance. Mais sorti de cette vision globale, où les récits s'enchaînent au fil du temps pour louer la sainte Eucharistie, le personnage ne semble pas à ce point dépourvu d'intérêt. Son apparition en scène, qui répond à un choix délibéré de l'auteur, se comprend d'autant mieux lorsque l'on quitte le clan des juges pour observer avec attention le nouveau visage de l'accusé. En se penchant sur le profil métamorphosé de l'inculpé juif, la place de l'inquisiteur se justifie d'elle-même.

UNE AFFAIRE INQUISITORIALE : MISE EN SCÈNE DU TOPIQUE JUIF

L'accusé pour lequel la judaïté posait justement, à la fin du XIIIe siècle, un problème de législation, se voit au XVe siècle accablé sous le poids de nouvelles accusations. Au théâtre, le sacrilège sur l'hostie consacrée n'est donc plus la seule cause de sa comparution en justice. Le Juif est à

25 J.-L. Schefer, *op. cit.*, p. 36.

26 La métaphore évangélique du membre putride est reprise par Henri de Gand (*Cf.* E. Marmursztejn, *op. cit.*).

présent qualifié d'hérétique par ses juges, une dénomination *a priori* bien curieuse pour celui qui, se tient hors de l'Église et qui par définition ne peut être assimilé à un dissident chrétien. Il est pourtant interpelé de la sorte ; tout juste averti des faits, le prévôt déclare « Allons prendre ce faux hereticque » (v. 766). Il est également traité en tant que tel. Les bourgeois venus le chercher à son domicile se saisissent des preuves du miracle en vue d'en faire des reliques, mais aussi de tous ses biens matériels, ce que l'on comprend lorsque le propriétaire de ces effets s'exclame : « Vous emportez mes biens tres tout, / Ma chaudiere et mon tripié ! / Di ge donc estre pillé ? » (v. 857-859). Une perte sur laquelle il reviendra encore plus clairement lors de son procès : « Pour ce que certainement scay / Que me voulay desheritez » (v. 940-941)[27].

En outre, le texte dramatique fait mention de deux phénomènes merveilleux, qui, faisant suite aux prodiges chrétiens, passent de fait relativement inaperçus. Alors que le Juif s'apprête à vider l'eau de sa chaudière, il constate fort étonné « Dieu qu'esse cy ? De quel matière ? / Elle est blanche, rouge et noire ! / Et ma maison vert comme poire ! Vecy bien pour yssir du sens » (v. 644-647). Si ces changements de couleurs, soulignent l'apparence versatile du Juif, caractère propre aux créatures diaboliques, elles lui imputent aussi un autre crime, celui de sorcellerie. Le procès prend alors en compte cet aspect de l'affaire. L'évêque déclare le premier : « Puisqu'il est en son art magique » (v. 1228), un constat que le prêtre s'empresse de corroborer à sa suite en s'exclamant : « Esprouvons ce magicien ! Cest enchanteur soit esprouvé ! » (v. 1284-1285). Le texte ne s'en tient pas là. Sur le bûcher, alors qu'il réalise qu'il prend feu, il invoque les diables : « O Deable, il semble qu'j'arde ! / Deables, deables ! Brusle et ars ! » (v. 1309-1310), avant de les appeler à son secours : « Deables, venez hastivement / Et m'emportez a ce besoin ! » (v. 1315-1316).

De confession juive, profanateur et désormais hérétique, sorcier et diabolique, les accusations nouvelles pleuvent contre l'accusé. Est-ce à dire que l'auteur du XVe siècle a cherché à rendre l'accusé justiciable et ainsi se démarquer d'une version du miracle juridiquement peu

27 « Certaines décrétales affirment que n'importe qui pourra se saisir librement des hérétiques et de leurs biens meubles qui appartiendront en toute propriété à ceux qui s'en seront emparés. Les magistrats ou responsables municipaux désignés pour arrêter les hérétiques toucheront de la commune le tiers des biens confisqués à ceux qu'ils auront fait incarcérer » (J. Labrot, *Affairistes et usuriers au Moyen Âge*, Cahors, La Louve, t. 1, p. 38).

probante en s'inspirant d'un débat théologique vieux de plus d'un siècle ? L'hypothèse n'est pas à rejeter mais reste peu concluante. En revanche, qu'il ait souhaité assombrir le profil de l'accusé en vue d'en faire un personnage détestable paraît plus vraisemblable. Ce personnage d'usurier dont seule la judaïté expliquait son acte profanateur dans la version narrative, devient au théâtre un personnage cumulant les travers. L'auteur propose aux spectateurs un accusé présentant tous les torts, et pour qui l'acte sacrilège a finalement permis de le révéler aux autorités. Ces amplifications théâtrales s'inscrivent entre autre dans une démarche qui est celle de la composition d'un personnage, qui parce qu'il est chargé négativement, accentue la dimension manichéenne du récit, si chère aux auteurs de Mystères. Mais une fois encore, l'approche générique est réductrice. En réalité, depuis le XIIIe siècle, la représentation du Juif s'est considérablement dégradée et la justice qui prête à leur cas une attention croissante est, la plupart du temps, de teneur inquisitoriale. Ainsi, le théâtre ne fait que figurer le topique juif, dans tout ce qu'il a de complexe et de fantasmagorique, à la fin du Moyen Âge.

Alors que cette assimilation aurait été inconcevable à la fin du XIIIe siècle, au cœur du XVe siècle, le Juif est ouvertement décrété hérétique. Avec bon sens, Jacques Le Goff rappelle qu'en matière d'hérésie, l'historien ne peut se prononcer étant donné qu'« il ne lui appartient pas de dire si telle ou telle hérésie est, oui ou non, fondamentalement en désaccord avec le message chrétien ». Il ne peut alors que constater que « l'Église a décrété hérétique telles ou telles personnes », et chercher « ensuite à comprendre ce qui se passe[28] ». Et effectivement, à y regarder d'un peu plus près, l'ensemble des inculpations portées à l'encontre du Juif au théâtre est en adéquation avec l'idée que l'on s'en fait à l'époque. La « tolérance » dont l'Église avait longtemps fait preuve envers les Juifs n'a duré qu'un temps[29]. Dès le XIIe siècle, les commentateurs chrétiens commencent déjà à débattre de la légitimité du culte juif. Certains en arrivent à conclure que le judaïsme est une idolâtrie ou un athéisme. Toutefois, jusqu'au XIVe siècle, l'assimilation du judaïsme à l'hérésie n'est qu'exceptionnelle. À aucun moment, les théologiens, tel qu'Henri

28 J. Le Goff, *À la recherche du Moyen Âge*, Paris, Louis Audibert, 2003, p. 128 et 129.

29 « La présence des Juifs au XIIIe siècle, par exemple, ne paraissait en rien extraordinaire ; ils n'étaient pas voué à la destruction ; on voyait en eux un élément constitutif de la société. C'est plutôt leur disparition qui eut été une anomalie » (R. Anchel, *Les Juifs de France*, Paris, J. B. Janin, 1946, p. 94).

de Gand, n'ont pu faire la confusion entre hérétiques et Juifs. Seuls quelques manuels de l'Inquisition nomment de la sorte les apostats et les relaps, et de façon très isolé, Guy Terré, dans sa *Summa de heresibus*, considère les Juifs comme hérétiques uniquement dans leur rapport à l'Ancien Testament[30]. Avec la bulle *Turbato Corde* de Clément IV, du 26 juillet 1267, les Juifs entrent pourtant dans le champ d'action de l'Inquisition. Néanmoins, les rapports entre Inquisition et Juifs sont encore relativement bons au XIIIe et au début du XIVe siècle, l'institution se montre encore légaliste et soucieuse de les protéger et ne s'intéresse qu'aux Chrétiens convertis au judaïsme et aux Juifs qui se seraient rendus complices de ces conversions. Avec le XIVe siècle commence une période sombre où s'enchaînent les persécutions et les accusations : empoisonnement des puits, collusion avec les lépreux[31], profanations, meurtres rituels, et comme les Chrétiens, la communauté juive est décimée par la terrible épidémie de peste qui s'abat sur la France entre 1348 et 1350. Dans cette ère d'incrimination, les Juifs sont tenus pour responsables, recevant alors pleinement la fonction de bouc-émissaires[32]. Les esprits s'échauffent et les mentalités populaires repoussent le Juif, étranger mais présent dans la cité encore au XIVe siècle, du côté du diable[33]. À mesure que l'image du Juif se dégrade aux yeux des Chrétiens, et que l'Inquisition entre dans un système de vaste répression, les Juifs vont être rattachés à la polémique antihérétique. Selon G. Dahan, l'assimilation du judaïsme à l'hérésie prend de l'importance à une période où, parce que le christianisme se referme sur soi et se veut mieux délimité, l'Église est amenée à lutter indistinctement contre tous ses ennemis. L'imprécation contre les ennemis de la chrétienté, Juifs et hérétiques réunis, prend, à la fin du Moyen Âge, la forme d'« un *topos*, les uns et les autres étant beaucoup plus des entités abstraites que des réalités identifiables[34] ». Après cette lente et longue dégradation, celui sur lequel se cristallisent

30 G. Dahan, *op. cit.*, p. 558.

31 C. Ginzburg, *Le Sabbat des sorcières*, Paris, Gallimard, 1992, p. 43-69.

32 R. Girard, *Le Bouc-émissaire*, Paris, Grasset, 1982. L'ouvrage commence par le texte de Guillaume de Machaut accusant les Juifs d'avoir propagé la peste.

33 Le lien entre le Juif et le diable trouve son origine dans un verset de l'Évangile selon saint Jean : « Vous avez pour père le diable et ce sont les désirs de votre père que vous voulez accomplir » (*Jean*, VIII, 44) et dans l'évocation du motif de la Synagogue de Satan dans *L'Apocalyse* (*Apocalypse*, III, 9). Les miracles de Notre-Dame et notamment l'histoire de Théophile contribueront grandement à diffuser l'image du Juif diabolique.

34 G. Dahan, *op. cit.*, p. 365.

toutes les peurs d'une société est finalement expulsé du Royaume de France par Charles VI en 1394, laissant derrière lui une image pour longtemps ternie[35]. À la vue d'une telle curée, on comprend qu'en cette fin de Moyen Âge, le nouveau visage du Juif est inextricablement lié à la figure de l'inquisiteur et que le choix théâtral de mettre en scène un tel face à face se justifie aisément.

Or, dans une France réputée sans Juif, on peut penser que le fait d'exposer, même subrepticement, la figure de l'inquisiteur sert à inscrire clairement le personnage du Juif dans un rôle allégorique. En face de ce juge, l'accusé devient une caricature du prosélyte hérétique et est en mesure d'incarner tout ennemi de la chrétienté, qui, parce qu'il a fait le *mauvais choix*, contrarie les dogmes de l'Église catholique. Notons qu'à chacune de ses apparitions, le personnage de l'inquisiteur n'est pas seul, il se trouve en compagnie du recteur d'université. À aucun moment les deux personnages ne seront séparés, le théâtre les fait jouer ensemble, constituant une espèce de binôme indissociable et complémentaire. Si la figure du recteur est bien évidemment une manière de donner un corps aux « Docteurs en théologie » tels que nous les annonçait l'anonyme des Chartes dans la version primitive, elle rappelle surtout que les universitaires se trouvaient parfois impliqués dans des affaires qui excédaient les limites de leurs domaines. Sur scène, le fonctionnement de ce duo est alors simple et efficace : l'inquisiteur par sa présence suffit à qualifier le délit, à savoir l'hérésie doublé de sorcellerie ; une fois le délit qualifié, le recteur par sa présence apporte la caution théologique en même temps qu'il confère une dimension théorique au débat. Il n'est alors plus question de débattre d'un Juif mais de discuter d'un « cas », terme que les protagonistes de la justice que sont l'évêque, le recteur et l'inquisiteur, réitèrent pas moins de cinq fois dans les vers qui précèdent l'ouverture du procès. Le Juif, sur scène, se voit, en quelque sorte, dépossédé de son identité pour incarner un « cas » d'hérésie au sens large. Le théâtre à travers ce personnage « gabarit » s'offre la possibilité de dénoncer indifféremment tout ennemi de la chrétienté.

La dimension allégorique du jeu est bien incontestable. Cependant, il semble qu'il faille être prudent sur le sujet en commençant par éviter l'écueil de l'anachronisme. Certes, les impressions et les représentations du *Mystère de la sainte hostie* qui datent du début du XVIe siècle sont

35 B. Blumenkranz, *Le Juif médiéval au miroir de l'art chrétien*, Paris, Études Augustiniennes, 1966 ; *L'expulsion des Juifs de France 1394*, G. Dahan (dir.), *op. cit.*

indéniablement une forme « allégorisée » de la légende dès lors qu'elles dénoncent l'hérésie des reformés bousculant le dogme eucharistique, mais le texte de théâtre antérieur à celles-ci de quelques décennies campe un décor qui n'est pas encore celui de la Réforme. Or, l'écart qui sépare l'acte d'écriture des représentations connues a pu susciter la confusion. Par conséquent, l'idée de faire disparaître totalement le visage du Juif derrière les traits d'un *Autre* nuisible, si elle est évidente au début du XVIe siècle, pourrait bien être encore un peu prématurée au milieu du XVe siècle. En effet, la possibilité d'un référent Juif au cœur de la société reste encore recevable au milieu du XVe siècle. Certains détails laissent ainsi penser que le jeu fait écho à une préoccupation contemporaine de l'acte d'écriture, la peur des judaïsants, aussi appelés les faussement convertis.

LA PEUR DU JUDAÏSANT ?

Lors de la première comparution du Juif devant ses juges, là où la narration primitive montrait un Juif réfractaire à toute repentance face à un tribunal soucieux de le voir se convertir, le texte de théâtre présente un Juif repenti, admettant les faits et réclamant le baptême en invoquant les Écritures : « Mais j'ay pieça ouy compter / Que on trouve dedans vos escris / Nolo mortem peccatoris / Sed ut convertatur et vivat / S'ainsi est bien, veu mon estat, / Voulentiers me baptiseray » (v. 942-947). L'évêque puis le prévôt le lui refusent de peur qu'il ne veuille être baptisé que par crainte de la mort. En effet, le Juif finit par trahir ses réelles intentions en s'offusquant de voir que les siens renoncent à la loi judaïque (v. 979-981). L'évêque comme le prévôt avaient vu juste, ce soudain désir de conversion n'était qu'une « échappatoire ». Suite à cette requête frauduleuse, heureusement démasquée par les accusateurs instruits et coutumiers de la pratique, est annoncé le procès auquel sera convié l'inquisiteur. Durant la séance, l'inquisiteur et le recteur qui l'accompagne cherchent au travers de leurs questions à amener le Juif à la conversion. Une vaine entreprise puisque le Juif refuse avec obstination. Derrière les préoccupations des juges transparaît donc le souci de la conversion et plus encore de la conversion vraie.

La peur d'une conversion par intérêt réapparaît ailleurs dans le texte. L'évêque, en baptisant les trois autres membres de la famille, insiste sur leurs engagements en tant que nouveaux Chrétiens. Lorsqu'il confie aux deux bourgeois de Paris la charge de leur enseignement, il précise : « Et qu'ils soient endoctrinez / En la foy tout premierement / Sur peine d'excommuniement » (v. 1035-1036). Le texte fait ainsi état d'une pratique religieuse bien gardée et vante les mérites d'une justice chrétienne qui débusque la parole frauduleuse et reconnaît les sincères demandes d'accession à la chrétienté. De son côté, le spectateur peut témoigner de la justesse de ce jugement. La version théâtrale a pris le soin de montrer en amont, lors de la profanation, les observances religieuses des différents membres de la famille juive. Face à l'hostie puis à la vue de ses tourments, la femme et les deux enfants accèdent incontestablement à la foi chrétienne. Leurs invocations et leurs pratiques se modifient au cours de la scène, ils renoncent par exemple au nom de Mahe pour honorer le « tres glorieux Pere puissent » ou encore se mettent à genoux pour prier « a joinctes mains » (v. 425)[36]. Par la suite, l'évêque croit, sur paroles, en leur conversion et leur accorde le baptême sans aucune hésitation. *A contrario*, soupçonnant la ruse, l'évêque le refuse au père qui, le spectateur le sait, n'avait pas failli devant l'ampleur du saccage, maudissant sans mesure l'hostie et la loi des Chrétiens.

Dans son *quodlibet*, Henri de Gand évoquait déjà cette feinte du coupable comme un possible dans le cours du procès. Il faisait allusion à ce risque du baptême fallacieux en assurant que si le Juif avait voulu « être baptisé que par crainte de la mort et pour la fuir [...] alors il n'aura fallu l'admettre en aucun cas au baptême, à moins qu'il ne soit apparu, par des indices probables, qu'il se fut lui-même vraiment converti et qu'il n'eut pas demandé le baptême par crainte de la mort. Autrement, il fallait le considérer comme un imposteur, et ne pas l'admettre au baptême, mais plutôt le châtier[37] ». L'intransigeance d'Henri de Gand à l'encontre de la possibilité d'un Juif faussement converti témoigne d'une peur bien réelle et largement répandue chez les Chrétiens du Moyen Âge et plus encore à sa fin. Elle renvoie à la doctrine de l'Église chrétienne à l'égard de la communauté juive. Selon les Pères de l'Église, la présence

36 G. Dahan, « La prière juive au regard des chrétiens », *Revue des études juives* n° 154, 1995, p. 437-448.

37 E. Marmursztejn, *op. cit.*, p. 59.

des Juifs parmi les Chrétiens trouve son origine dans les propos de saint Paul : ils seront les derniers à se convertir avant le retour du Christ[38], leur conversion sera l'annonce de la venue du rédempteur sur terre. Cette attente implique, en tous cas jusqu'à leur expulsion au XIVe siècle, de les accepter, de les « tolérer » autant que de leur assurer protection, car « l'Église entend qu'ils vivent, qu'ils se perpétuent comme une preuve de la vraie foi et pour l'édification des fidèles[39] », mais, parallèlement, de les convaincre pour leur éviter la damnation. La communauté des Chrétiens se doit de souhaiter et d'encourager leurs conversions tout en veillant à ce que celles-ci ne soient pas frauduleuses et de fait nuisibles à la cohésion de la chrétienté. Une menace de taille, qui renoue avec la métaphore évangélique du membre gangréné pourrissant le corps.

Du reste, il ne faut pas que les rôles s'inversent et que le judaïsme entraîne des conversions chez les Chrétiens, là aussi une des craintes permanentes de tout l'Occident du Moyen Âge. Ces inquiétudes générées par la promiscuité ont donc très tôt suscité l'attention des autorités. Les inquisiteurs ont eu à charge de traiter ces cas particuliers, ces sortes de conversions illicites (relaps, judaïsant, apostat), pour lesquelles ils se montrent très incisifs. Pour preuve, Bernard Gui, dans la cinquième partie de son traité à l'usage des inquisiteurs, intitulée « De la perfidie des Juifs », condamne les Juifs qui s'efforcent de ramener les nouveaux Chrétiens à « la perfidie judaïque » et demande à ce que l'on traite comme des hérétiques, les Juifs convertis au christianisme qui retourneraient « au vomissement du judaïsme[40] ».

Les affaires de ce type se répètent, la vigilance perdure, les mesures se durcissent, et c'est finalement autour de l'histoire d'un Juif converti au christianisme que se solde leur destin sur les terres du Royaume de France. Dans l'ordonnance datée du 17 septembre 1394, Charles VI s'indigne, entre autres, des récentes affaires « dans lesquelles il apparaissait que manifestement des Juifs et des Juives *"avaient commis et perpétré plusieurs*

38 *Épître aux Romains* (XI, 25-26). Cette attente est présentée durant tout le Moyen Âge comme l'une des raisons de leur présence parmi les Chrétiens. Dans *La présentation de la Vierge au temple*, Philippe de Mézières fait dire les quatre raisons au personnage de Vérité : 1. Grâce aux Juifs les Chrétiens n'oublient pas la Passion ; 2. il est dit qu'ils se convertiront un jour ; 3. parce que les Juifs prêtent de l'argent aux Chrétiens ; 4. ce qui évite aux Chrétiens de pécher en prêtant à intérêt qui est chose aux « Chrestiens deffendue et abominable à Dieu » (P. L'Hermite-Leclercq, *op. cit.*, p. 146).

39 R. Anchel, *op. cit.*, p. 95.

40 B. Gui, *Le manuel de l'Inquisiteur*, Paris, Les Belles Lettres, 1964, tome II, p. 7.

crimes et délits, spécialement contre la foi chrétienne et les privilèges[41]" », avant d'exiger du prévôt de Paris, des autres justiciers, officiers et lieutenants qu'ils « vident » prestement le Royaume de sa population juive de la manière qui leur conviendra. L'allusion à certains crimes contre la foi chrétienne serait, selon Roger Kohn, une référence à la conversion de Denis Machaut, disparu et prétendu tué par ses anciens coreligionnaires qui avaient vainement tenté de le ramener au judaïsme[42]. Cause réelle ou simple prétexte, la France ne devait plus compter de Juifs sur son territoire le 4 janvier 1395. La plupart se réfugia dans les territoires limitrophes, tels que la Provence, le Comtat Venaissin ou la Lorraine, d'autres purent se convertir, s'ils ne l'avaient déjà fait un an plus tôt, suite à l'ordonnance prise en Grand Conseil le 4 avril 1393 qui annulait la confiscation des biens des Juifs qui se convertissaient au christianisme[43].

Mais comment imaginer que la peur du « fauteur », ainsi que le nommait Bernard Gui, ait pu disparaître à cette période où l'on assiste à une vague de conversions massives assurément motivée par les promulgations royales ? Officiellement, les Juifs ne sont plus présents, il s'agit d'un état de fait que l'ordonnance de 1394, l'expulsion qui s'ensuit et l'absence de documents les concernant jusqu'au milieu du XVIe siècle, ne peuvent remettre en question. Mais qu'en est-il du Juif masqué, du judaïsme latent jugé plus redoutable par cet État chrétien en phase d'unification ?

Robert Anchel est l'un des rares à émettre malgré tout l'hypothèse d'une présence juive durant cette période. Il tient compte de ceux qu'ils nomment marranes ou judaïsants, « qui pressés par la persécution, se sont convertis au christianisme et en ont, eux et leurs descendants, ouvertement pratiqués tous les rites, cependant que, dans leur cœur, ils restaient Juifs et qu'ils continuaient à observer secrètement certaines prescriptions religieuses du judaïsme. Parmi les familles marranes, les unes ont fini par adhérer sincèrement au christianisme, les autres ont conservé leur foi primitive en la dissimulant très longtemps et l'ont révélée quand elle n'a plus été un danger pour elles[44] ». Par conséquent, il imagine qu'il y ait

41 E. Nicolas, « Typologie des sources chrétiennes », *L'expulsion des Juifs de France 1394*, *op. cit.*, p. 97.

42 R. Kohn, « Les Juifs en France du nord », *L'expulsion des Juifs de France 1394*, *op. cit.*, et, *Les Juifs de la France du nord dans la seconde moitié du XIVe siècle*, Louvain-Paris, 1988, p. 253-258.

43 E. Nicolas, *op. cit.*, p. 108.

44 R. Anchel, *op. cit.*, p. 125.

pu avoir des Juifs en France après l'expulsion de 1394 qui, soit auraient dissimulé leur qualité, soit se seraient « convertis extérieurement au christianisme », les uns et les autres étant de toute façon condamnés à vivre dans le secret. Les faits sont évidemment hypothétiques et les documents d'archive du XVe siècle laissant apparaître des noms aux résonnances israélites, ou les quelques registres sur lesquels sont inscrits des recommandations suggérant une présence juive, ne constituent, comme le déclare lui-même R. Anchel, que de minces présomptions[45].

Toutefois, on peut penser que la peur d'une présence juive dissimulée à l'intérieur du Royaume était bien réelle au cours du XVe siècle. La peur est d'autant plus forte que le Juif faussement converti terrorise aux portes du Royaume et ce, tout au long du siècle. Par exemple, en 1409, Alexandre V adresse à l'inquisiteur d'Avignon, Ponce-Feugeyron, une bulle au contenu révélateur du climat général de suspicion. Il s'agit de cinq articles dirigés contre les Juifs, en particuliers contre les judaïsants et les récents retournés au judaïsme. À plusieurs reprises, les Chrétiens sont associés aux Juifs pour l'usure, les pratiques magiques ou la sorcellerie mais surtout pour l'invention de nouvelles sectes et rites prohibés, considérés comme du prosélytisme contre la foi chrétienne. Le pape et l'inquisiteur redoutent apparemment l'excessive promiscuité engendrée par l'arrivée en nombre de Juifs chassés du Royaume de France[46]. La bulle traduit ainsi des peurs fantasmatiques ou légitimes.

La peur à l'encontre des Juifs convertis gagne de l'ampleur et trouve son héraut en la personne du franciscain castillan, Alphonse De Spina. Son œuvre intitulée *Fortalicum Fidei*, achevée entre 1461 et 1465, connaît une incroyable diffusion entre 1475 et 1525. Il consacre la plus grande partie de son ouvrage aux Juifs, mais concentre ses attaques sur les *judeoconversos*, qui sont selon lui en tête des ennemis de la foi chrétienne et de ses fidèles. Il devient alors le pourfendeur de ces faux Chrétiens qu'il accuse de poursuivre la destruction intestine de la société chrétienne entreprise par les Juifs. Face à ce qu'il perçoit comme un fléau national, il prône une inquisition qui examine avec minutie les pratiques religieuses des convertis au christianisme et réclame, à l'image de la France, leur expulsion définitive. Il est finalement entendu en 1478 quand Sixte IV

45 *Ibid.*, p. 126 et 127.

46 M. Ostorero, « Itinéraire d'un inquisiteur gâté : Ponce-Feugeyron, les Juifs et le sabbat des sorciers », *Médiévales* 43, 2002, p. 103-117, p. 108.

instaure l'Inquisition dans la péninsule ibérique. Les pays limitrophes sont concernés par ces délocalisations forcées et la France redoute les flux se dirigeant vers ses frontières.

Les quelques extraits mentionnés précédemment résonnent comme des allusions à cet arrière-plan historique particulier. On peut alors se demander si le Juif Mousse, tel qu'il est mis en scène, n'est pas en partie une peinture du redouté judaïsant. Il est impossible d'affirmer que ce panorama inquiété par « les Juifs espandus *déguisez* en plusieurs lieux de cestuy [...] royaume[47] » ait pu être à l'origine de l'adaptation théâtrale de la légende, même si les protagonistes juifs de l'affaire des Billettes se prêtent parfaitement à l'illustration de cette cause nationale. En revanche, il est presque certain que celui qui travailla à la transposition dramatique de la légende ne pouvait concevoir de mettre en scène un Juif sans s'inspirer de l'image du faux converti.

Dans le vaste épisode judicaire que le théâtre met en scène pour dénouer la célèbre affaire parisienne de profanation d'hostie, le personnage de l'inquisiteur passerait volontiers inaperçu, si celui-ci n'avait pas comme principale caractéristique d'être l'une des originalités de cette version dramatique adaptée vraisemblablement au milieu du XVe siècle. En effet, le théâtre est bien le seul *medium* diffusant la légende à octroyer au juge de l'Inquisition, une place, si petite soit-elle, dans le cours du procès. Tout l'intérêt de l'apparition du personnage réside donc dans le fait qu'il est non historique mais proprement dramatique.

D'emblée, l'introduction du personnage permet une amplification de la matière judiciaire et spectaculaire. Le juge intègre un ensemble de personnages aux fonctions et statuts sociaux très divers rassemblés sur la scène afin de constituer un dispositif judiciaire visuellement imposant et dissuasif. La procédure est alors irréelle mais l'image recherchée par la mise en scène est célèbre et forte de sens. Sans aucun doute, le spectateur reconnaîtra derrière cette cohorte de Chrétiens, qui brocarde le Saint-Sacrement comme le garant de son intégrité, une représentation allégorique de l'État chrétien, celle du Corps Mystique, hiérarchisé et solidaire, tel que le louait Christine de Pisan dans son *corps de policie*, au début du siècle.

Par ailleurs, compte tenu de ses compétences, la simple convocation de l'inquisiteur au procès sous-entend un profond changement de la

47 Lettre patente du 23 avril 1615 citée dans R. Anchel, *op. cit.*, p. 128.

condition de l'accusé. Le juge d'Église se fait alors le miroir d'un Juif au profil noirci par le temps et les événements, l'indicateur d'une image au combien dégradée et dégradante. Contrairement aux versions narratives antérieures, le théâtre ne se contente plus d'exposer un usurier juif désireux d'éprouver le Dieu des Chrétiens à travers les espèces de l'hostie. Il campe un personnage qui saborde la société des Chrétiens bien au-delà de son expérience profanatrice : l'homme se livre à la sorcellerie, invoque le diable, et ses juges ne voient plus en lui qu'un hérétique. Tout se passe alors comme si l'entrée en scène de ce nouveau juge installait définitivement le personnage du Juif dans un rôle allégorique. Face à ce traqueur d'opposants à la religion chrétienne, le Juif n'est plus qu'un « cas » d'hérésie, il devient l'*Autre*, le « membre putride » qu'il faut éradiquer pour préserver la cohésion de l'État chrétien symbolisé par le précieux Corps du Christ.

Néanmoins, la lecture allégorique dans laquelle le condamné à mort se voit totalement dépourvu de sa judaïté, si elle est parfaitement envisageable dans les représentations du début du XVIe siècle, ne peut pas être exclusive au XVe siècle. Dans une France qui se veut sans Juif, la peur que quelques-uns aient pu se livrer à de fausses conversions pour échapper à l'exil est bien présente dans ce Royaume, qui, après cent ans de guerre et de luttes intestines, ne rêve que de puissance et d'unification. Tout porte alors à croire que l'inquisiteur, convoqué juste après la fausse demande de conversion de l'accusé, est le digne représentant de cette Inquisition qui traque sans relâche ceux qu'elle dit être *sicut canis revertitur ad vomitum*. Le texte dramatique dénoncerait bien un Juif en cette fin de Moyen Âge et le jeu ferait référence à un arrière-plan historique précis.

Que le réveil de la légende au théâtre ait été allégorique ou qu'il y ait eu la volonté de dénoncer une situation historique particulière, le jeu de *la sainte hostie*, tel qu'il a été mis en scène au milieu du XVe siècle, se présente non seulement comme un objet de commémoration et de piété populaire mais comme une véritable arme de propagande arborant le Saint-Sacrement pour nourrir un sentiment national.

Camille SALATKO-PETRYSZCZE
Université Rennes 2 –
Haute Bretagne

DAME JUSTICE ET SES SUPPÔTS,

un personnel dramatique sur la scène des moralités et sotties (XVe-XVIe siècle)

Ce que nous nommons théâtre est un objet pluridimensionnel. D'une part, le texte écrit, tel qu'il nous parvient après la représentation et tel, peut-être, qu'il lui préexistait, est troué, à l'instar d'une partition, par une performance qui lui donne chair[1]. Il se livre donc aujourd'hui au lecteur entre transparence et opacité. D'autre part, ni ce texte qui demeure ni la performance disparue pour nous n'épuisent le sens du fait théâtral. Le geste qu'est la représentation s'étoffe des réactions immédiates ou différées d'une réception mouvante, spectateurs puis lecteurs. Une communication sociale se tisse, mettant en jeu des intentions et des interprétations, celles des auteurs, des joueurs, du public ; mettant aussi en relation des modes de pensée, pensée du monde, pensée de la scène. Il a été remarqué, en effet, que les structures du théâtre reflètent et mettent à distance les dispositifs relationnels qui régissent le réel[2]. Si l'enjeu semble bien pour l'historien, comme l'a indiqué Christian Biet, de cerner l'invention, provisoire et collective, d'un sens à travers la reconstruction du phénomène qu'est la *séance* – notion qui subsume texte et représentation –, il semble que la tâche dépasse une analyse ancrée dans la *littera*, dans le fonctionnement rhétorique et actantiel d'un texte. Pour autant, celle-ci peut avoir son importance dans la reconstitution de ce processus dynamique.

La présente étude n'envisagera pas le droit qui se constitue historiquement autour de la pratique théâtrale, et par là l'éventuelle conceptualisation

1 Cette définition de la nature du texte théâtral est inspirée des nombreux travaux de la critique contemporaine, synthétisés dans Ch. Biet et Ch. Triau, *Qu'est-ce que le théâtre ?*, Paris, Gallimard, 2005.

2 C'est en particulier le cas d'E. Goffman, montrant dans *La Mise en scène de la vie quotidienne* (Paris, Minuit, 1973, 2 volumes), que la représentation tire son efficacité de la duplication des dispositifs du réel, actions, contractions, répliques, médiatisés par la fiction de la scène.

juridique de cette dernière au cours des XVe et XVIe siècles. On s'interrogera plutôt sur la façon dont interagissent, au sein de textes, les modes de pensée évoqués plus haut. Notre hypothèse est qu'en représentant la loi, la permission ou la sanction par des personnages, la scène interroge la possibilité de son propre discours. La question est de savoir si – et comment – l'autorisation d'une prise de parole publique comme le théâtre peut se construire en prenant appui sur certains éléments du système dramatique lui-même.

Les études critiques préoccupées d'explorer les intersections entre droit et littérature dans les œuvres de fiction s'arrêtent souvent sur le fonctionnement du discours judiciaire, tel que l'ont défini les arts rhétoriques depuis Aristote[3]. Impliquant l'affrontement contradictoire du juste et de l'injuste, à la source donc de *l'âgon* qui forme fréquemment le nœud des intrigues, la rhétorique judiciaire tire une grande partie de son efficacité du fait qu'elle n'est pratiquement jamais employée seule. Elle permet en effet d'introduire les discours délibératifs et démonstratifs, engageant les notions de *fama* et d'opinion[4]. Cependant, en particulier au théâtre, un élément permet de préciser cette approche : le personnage, dont le statut est souvent lié à l'utilisation de divers modes rhétoriques[5]. *Persona* : selon l'étymologie communément admise, l'essence du personnage serait en effet de porter au loin une voix (*personare*, faire retentir), et de figurer, non pas un être particulier, mais un type ou un statut, sous une forme à la fois révélatrice et cachée (*persona*, le masque). C'est à partir de cette définition que nous choisissons de considérer comme personnages des rôles auxquels ce nom est parfois refusé, comme les personnifications allégoriques[6].

3 Aristote, *Rhétorique*, I, 3.

4 La fonction encadrante de la rhétorique judiciaire est familière aux écrivains du XVe siècle, qui savent en user en virtuoses. Sur ce point, nous nous permettons de renvoyer à E. Doudet, « *Les Droitz Nouveaux de Rhétorique* : structures judiciaires et efficacité épidictique dans les œuvres des Grands Rhétoriqueurs » dans *Littérature et droit, du Moyen Âge à la période baroque : le procès exemplaire*, Paris, Champion, « Colloques sur la Renaissance européenne » n° 58, 2008, p. 217-232.

5 On peut renvoyer sur ce point aux analyses de M. Fumaroli, « Rhétorique et dramaturgie : le statut du personnage dans la tragédie cornélienne », dans *Héros et orateurs*, Genève, Droz, 1990.

6 Quoique l'ouvrage porte sur la période moderne, cette question est abordée par R. Abirached, *La crise du personnage dans le théâtre moderne*, Paris, Gallimard, Tel, 1994, notamment dans « La *mimésis*, esquisse d'une théorie du personnage », p. 15-93.

Comment les scènes des XVe et XVIe siècles représentent-elles les acteurs du droit ? Dans une perspective traditionnelle, deux types de personnages semblent se distinguer. D'une part existent ceux qui assument un rôle social faisant référence à une pratique professionnelle réelle (juge, avocat, procureur), dans une intrigue de caractère « historique ». Ainsi Caïphe dans une *Passion* assume un rôle dans la mise en scène judiciaire contre le Christ, en même temps que son nom et son comportement réfèrent à une réalité intertextuelle. Miracles et mystères seraient donc, pour la majorité de leurs scènes, des écritures à dimension historique. Les moralités et sotties, en revanche, montrent souvent des personnages qui incarnent une idée générale (Justice, Injustice, Droit, Abus), dans une diégèse « fictionnelle », c'est-à-dire une intrigue dépourvue d'épaisseur référentielle et historique. En réalité, de pareilles distinctions s'avèrent rapidement caricaturales si on les utilise dans la classification générique élaborée par la critique du XIXe siècle, comme l'a montré A. Knight[7]. Les scènes liminaires de nombreuses *Passions* proposent des allégories engagées dans des pratiques judiciaires, au premier chef Justice dans les Procès de Paradis. Les farces, scènes fictionnelles par excellence, ne se peuplent que très rarement d'allégories. Ce qui est à prendre en compte semble moins le *mythos* ou nature de l'intrigue, que *l'éthos* du personnage et l'évaluation de son fonctionnement comme rôle (social, historique) ou comme statut (conceptuel, général). Mais même dans cette perspective, distinguer et classer n'est pas chose aisée.

À cela s'ajoute que les désignations des pièces n'ont rien de stable dans les documents qui nous sont parvenus. Fréquemment les textes théâtraux de cette période sont accompagnés, dans les archives qui en parlent ou le support qui les diffusent, d'une désignation double, « sottie et moralité », « farce et moralité », ou d'une titulature complexe, « farce moralisée » ou « moralité mystère ». Une certaine prudence est de mise. D'une façon générale, on envisagera ici les personnages dont la principale fonction est d'incarner un statut idéel, sous le masque de noms allégoriques : Dame Justice et ses suppôts. Ils interviennent le plus souvent dans des pièces mettant en scène un *âgon*, et dont la perspective morale subsume d'autres messages politiques, sociaux ou spirituels. On se contentera de nommer ces pièces en fonction de leur titre originel, « moralités » ou « sotties », sans tendre vers une systématisation générique des analyses.

7 A. Knight, *Aspects of genre in Late Medieval French Drama*, Manchester, Manchester University Press, 1983.

La présence de Dame Justice sur une scène allégorique dite de moralité est fréquente, comme en témoignent les sept moralités du *Recueil Trepperel*[8]. Ce recueil étant une anthologie du début du XVIe siècle où il est difficile de démêler le choix d'un imprimeur d'un possible répertoire de troupe, il offre un spectre intéressant de la diversité herméneutique et statutaire du personnage. Presque toutes ces pièces proposent une mise en scène judiciaire explicite, procès ou tribunal, et font apparaître Justice ou l'une de ses figurations. Le rôle fondamental joué par la rhétorique judiciaire dans leurs cadres discursifs est évident. Il est donc possible de prendre appui sur ce *Recueil* pour affronter une première question : qui est Justice et qu'incarne-t-elle en scène ?

La première moralité compilée dans le *Recueil Trepperel*, *La Moralité du Sacrifice d'Abraham*, s'inscrit dans un récit biblique qui l'apparente à la mise en scène « historique » des mystères. On y trouve un procès de Paradis, faisant s'affronter devant Dieu Miséricorde et Justice. Si Miséricorde déploie un discours *piteux*, Justice, quasi silencieuse, finit par se confondre avec la voix de Dieu. Miséricorde le souligne en jouant sur la double référence du nom de son adversaire – un personnage et un concept : *Ce sera terrible justice*, dit-elle en parlant au Seigneur (v. 361). L'assimilation de Justice et de Dieu est également présente dans la *Moralité des Quatre Élements*. Dieu y organise un tribunal dont il est le juge, afin de départager les droits et les devoirs des Éléments face à la conservation d'un homme défunt. La question « qui doit prendre en charge le corps du mort ? » est déplacée de la propriété à la spiritualité : c'est à la Terre que les corps vont, les âmes à Dieu. Terre, bien que peu satisfaite du jugement, ne peut que s'incliner devant la double *auctoritas* incarnée par la figure du Dieu Juge.

Dans les pièces à dimension spirituelle, Justice, par sa capacité à se confondre avec la voix de Dieu, à en être au sens propre la *per-sona* – ce qui la porte aux oreilles des hommes – ne semble donc pas incarner le

---

8 *Le Recueil Trepperel*, l'une des sources de notre connaissance du théâtre français dans les premières décennies du XVIe siècle, a été édité partiellement, les sotties par E. Droz, puis les farces par cette éditrice et H. Lewicka. De cette entreprise, les moralités ont été les parents pauvres. En attendant leur édition chez Garnier, on peut les consulter à partir du fac-similé du *Recueil* (*Le Recueil Trepperel, fac-similé des trente-cinq pièces de l'original*, introduction E. Droz, Genève, Slatkine, 1974) ou de l'imprimé de Paris, BnF Rés. M – Yf 149. On en trouve également une transcription dans la thèse inédite de W. E. Walton, *Les sept moralités du Recueil Trepperel*, sous la direction d'A. Knight, Pennsylvania State University, 1978.

droit tel qu'il se pratique, ni même tel qu'il se pense en tant que réalité. Elle est la *Justitia*, définie par E. Kantorowicz comme « la prémisse extra-juridique de la pensée juridique[9]. » Il est remarquable que la faiblesse de son statut diégétique dans ces deux pièces (elle apparaît peu ou indirectement) soit compensée par son importance sémantique, puisqu'elle oriente toute la compréhension du message.

Lorsque Justice figure une *auctoritas* confondue avec celle de Dieu, elle court le risque de disparaître et d'effacer ainsi l'une de ses fonctions les plus importantes : celle de la *mediatrix*. Les moralités de *Nature et Loy de Rigueur* et de *L'Homme fragile* abordent ce problème, mettant toutes deux en scène le personnage ambigu de Loy. Dans *L'Homme Fragile*, Loy porte les tables mosaïques et incarne la rigueur punitive de Yahvé, alors que Dame Foy, fille du Nouveau Testament, prend les traits reconnaissables d'Équité. Dans *Nature et Loy de Rigueur*, le personnage se scinde en Loy de Rigueur et Loy de Grace, Rigueur finissant par reculer devant la naissance de l'avocate par excellence, la Vierge. Dans les deux cas, le dédoublement actoriel qui accompagne Loy insiste à la fois sur la tension interne de cette notion et sur la nécessité d'assimiler Justice à une médiation. Médiation entre raison (Loy de Rigueur ou Loy) et équité (Loy de Grace, Foy), entre loi de Nature et loi des hommes, Justice peut alors se masquer sous des traits qui ne sont plus ceux de Dieu, mais de la Vierge.

Parole d'autorité, parole de médiation, Justice est donc loin d'être un personnage stable, à la fois dans ses incarnations scéniques et dans ses discours. Ce qui la rend difficile à saisir est que ses apparitions en chair et en os sur la scène alternent avec son aptitude à transformer d'autres actants en *pers-sona* d'elle-même. Ainsi du bon prince, que les théories des juristes ont érigé, au fil du Moyen Âge tardif, en *justitia animata*[10]. *Si le prince tend à être idéalement lex incarnata*, c'est parce que sa parole n'est pas seulement privée mais publique, comme l'est la parole de Justice (et comme l'est, nous y reviendrons, la parole théâtrale). La scène des moralités peut donc aisément glisser d'une représentation

9 E. Kantorowicz, *Les deux corps du roi*, trad. J-P. et N. Genet, 1re édition 1957, Paris, Gallimard, 1989, p. 95.

10 Inconnus du droit romain et haut-médiéval, *lex animata* et *justitia animata* sont les termes-clefs de la doctrine politique et juridique du bon prince, idéologie puissante à l'époque des pièces envisagées. Elle est élaborée en particulier par les juristes de l'école de Bologne au cours du XIIIe siècle, *cf.* E. Kantorowicz, *ibid.*, p. 104-108.

allégorique à une fiction dont la référence est apparemment historique. Dans le *Recueil Trepperel*, *L'empereur qui tua son neveu* est ce qu'en moyen français on nomme une histoire romaine. L'intrigue antique sert surtout à soutenir une réflexion éthique, justifiant qu'on puisse l'inclure dans la présente analyse. L'empereur lègue la couronne à son neveu, en lui indiquant les droits et devoirs impliqués par le statut d'héritier. Mais celui-ci commet aussitôt une grave entorse aux préceptes de son oncle en violant une jeune fille. Le prince, sur la demande de la famille de la victime, accepte de se constituer en juge, condamne son héritier et l'exécute. Il est ensuite tourmenté par son action. Avait-il le droit d'exercer la justice ? La punition ne le rend-elle pas coupable de crime ? Un miracle divin, une hostie se plaçant dans la bouche du vieil homme, le rassure : il a bien été, le temps du jugement, *Justitia animata*. La fille violée et sa mère les assimilaient déjà dans leurs exhortations : *priant que justice me faciés* (v. 620) ; *faictes moy justice* (v. 635). L'empereur, s'étant au sens propre fait Justice, se tourne ensuite vers la figure médiatrice pour trouver la justification de son geste : « *Justice ay je pour tout pesché ?* » (v. 1029[11]). L'intervention divine démontre la validité morale et spirituelle du choix princier. L'hostie, métaphore de l'Incarnation christique, exprime la réussite de l'Incarnation de justice dans l'empereur. Grâce à lui, le droit des hommes a retrouvé la loi de Dieu. La consolation miraculeuse, ouvrant sa bouche tout en venant clore celles des critiques légalistes, souligne que les deux questions essentielles dans cette pièce sont celle de l'autorité discursive (à qui est-il permis de porter un jugement ?) et celle de la médiation (qui représente Justice et qui Justice représente-t-elle ?).

Deux autres moralités du *Recueil Trepperel*, *Langue Envenimée* et *Les Trois Etatz*, déplacent enfin Justice vers un registre plus polémique. Elle y est montrée comme une régulatrice de la parole publique, en butte à de nombreux abus. Dans *Les Trois Etatz*, elle apparaît sous les traits transparents de Raison qui *loix et coustumes ordonnait* (*Trois Etatz*, v. 4), assimilation assez habituelle des deux personnages[12]. Elle est la gardienne d'un ordre social menacé par des paroles déchaînées. S'il est

11 La ponctuation de ce vers est épineuse et nous préférons laisser la possibilité de diverses interprétations en n'ajoutant pas de virgule au texte original.

12 Montrée dans les textes doctrinaux et les œuvres qui s'en inspirent depuis le XIIIe siècle comme une *mediatrix* entre Raison (ou *Sapientia*) et Équité, Justice tend à transformer ces personnages en avatars d'elle-même, notamment sur les scènes théâtrales où cette ventriloquie est particulièrement efficace.

licite, dans les discours d'une allégorie juridique, que la rhétorique du juste et de l'injuste tende vers le mode épidiptique, l'autorisant à louer ou blâmer, le blâme est, hors de ce contexte, en péril de devenir diffamation ou *mesdisance*. De même, dans une société politique troublée, les *langues envenimées* contournent la loi, mettent en danger la *renommée*, parlent sans contrôle. Le rôle de Justice est alors de les affronter et de tenter de les contrôler.

Comme la plupart des personnages scéniques, la personnification allégorique Justice peut être définie comme un nœud diégétique, sémantique et syntaxique des pièces où elle apparaît[13]. Les exemples précédents ont montré que ces trois dimensions ne sont pas nécessairement équilibrées, une présence discrète de Justice dans l'intrigue lui ôtant rarement son importance sémantique pour le spectateur et son rôle dans l'articulation des scènes. Du point de vue sémantique, la force du personnage repose sur la liaison étroite de trois dimensions : spirituelle, éthique, judiciaire. La capacité de Justice de passer d'une dimension à une autre explique que la présence sur scène de cette allégorie puisse être variable, transformant d'autres figures en masques d'elle-même. De la même façon, Justice se fait aussi masque d'autorités qui la dominent, comme Dieu, ou qui lui sont inférieures, comme le prince. Son statut de *mediatrix*, élaboré dans la doctrine politico-juridique du temps et réinvesti dans le jeu théâtral, permet à ce système de se complexifier à souhait.

En tant qu'élément central dans la syntaxe du discours dramatique, Justice tire aussi sa puissance du fait qu'elle incarne une parole publique, permettant ou sanctionnant d'autres paroles. Son combat en scène est discursif, non seulement par ce que c'est la nature du théâtre que les affrontements entre personnages soient essentiellement langagiers, mais parce que son essence est langage – et contrôle du langage – public. Aussi lorsque Justice prend la parole, est-il attendu qu'elle parle autant à ses interlocuteurs qu'aux spectateurs, se définissant par le caractère ostensif de ses interventions. Le « quatrième mur », en admettant que cette notion anachronique puisse être employée en parlant du théâtre des XVe et XVIe siècles, serait réduit en poussière par les fougueux monologues de Dame Justice. Cette capacité à maintenir avec le public une

13 *Cf.* A. Lascombes, « Le personnage des cycles et des moralités : éléments de la problématique », dans *The problematics of Texte and Character, Tudor Theatre*, vol. 1, Tables Rondes 1-3, Peter Lang S.A, 1994, p. 127-144, notamment p. 128.

relation à la fois intime – Justice en appelle à la morale des spectateurs – et différée – Justice affronte d'autres personnages dans la fiction – est un trait général du théâtre allégorique. La fable montrée y toujours moins importante que la communication d'un message. Dans le cas de Justice, le discours projeté du personnage fait du spectateur modèle, construit comme horizon des pièces, le juge ultime de ce qui se joue. Ainsi la médiation assumée par Justice dans la fiction, entre Dieu et le prince ou entre le prince et les hommes, fonctionne-t-elle également dans la communication théâtrale, entre la scène (tribunal fictif) et la salle (tribunal réel), entre spectateur modèle et spectateur empirique.

Loin d'être transparent, le caractère de *per-sona* que possède une personnification allégorique permet donc d'élaborer des figures polysémiques, caractérisées par un feuilletage référentiel qu'il n'est pas toujours facile aujourd'hui de saisir. Il est donc temps d'en venir à la question : à quoi sert Justice sur une scène ? Quels problèmes permet-elle d'affronter pour les dramaturges et leurs publics ?

La Moralité de Mars et Justice, pièce polémique parisienne, a été datée par ses éditeurs modernes de 1564[14]. L'époque supposée de la représentation, paramètre essentiel d'une compréhension de la *séance* mais souvent difficile à saisir dans ce type d'écriture dramatique par manque d'indices externes et internes, n'est ici pas insignifiante. Les années 1560, comme l'ont montré J. Koopmans et K. Lavéant, voient un durcissement sensible des institutions politiques face au théâtre. La crispation est reflétée par la législation qui accompagne la plupart des expressions publiques. Ceci n'est pas sans conséquences sur la construction des personnages théâtraux dans des pièces faisant allusion à l'actualité. Le texte de la moralité, dont les éditeurs hésitent à faire une sottie et à qui ils donnent une origine basochienne qui reste difficile à prouver, s'inscrit dans un double contexte qui fait fonctionner la polysémie allégorique. En 1563, la guerre qui fait rage entre Catholiques et Huguenots a été suspendue par la Paix d'Amboise. Mais les passions restent vives dans les milieux anti-protestants, notamment à Paris. La création récente de tribunaux de commerce confiés à un consulat bourgeois suscite aussi l'inquiétude du Parlement, peu enclin à se laisser arracher ses prérogatives juridiques.

14 *Deux moralités de la fin du Moyen Âge et du temps des Guerres de Religion*, J-C. Aubailly et B. Roy (éd.), Genève, Droz, TLF, 1990, *Mars et Justice*, p. 73-125.

La scène s'ouvre sur l'arrivée du belliqueux Mars qui rencontre un Ministre protestant. Il s'abouche avec lui et lui garantit, en échange d'argent, la possibilité de nouveaux prêches, expression fortement réglementée par le récent édit de tolérance. Les désordres civils promis par l'allégorie guerrière permettront ainsi de renverser les lois qui règlent la parole publique. Mars s'entretient ensuite avec un Marchand et le pousse à déséquilibrer le pouvoir civil de Justice. Le caractère pernicieux de la parole du Marchand tient à ce qu'elle se pare d'une autorité usurpée, les nouveaux tribunaux de commerce, bloquant le fonctionnement habituel du système judiciaire.

Dame Justice, qui apparaît alors, se trouve en butte à une double attaque, venue de prises de parole apparemment différentes, mais également non autorisées dans le domaine public : deux *langues envenimées* qui menacent d'éteindre à la fois la bonne parole religieuse (le prêche catholique), le discours légal (les arrêts du Parlement) et la défense de la morale, représentée ici par la parole dramatique. *Faire taire* est donc l'enjeu de la pièce.

LE MINISTRE À MARS
Justice taire fais : les lois et les status
De tous ces justiciers sont par toy abbatus (v. 53-54)

C'est dans ce contexte que la polysémie de l'allégorie joue. Justice, attaquée par une parole religieuse montrée comme subversive, fonctionne dans une référentialité spirituelle : elle est la voix de Dieu, la juge des discours et des actes. La dimension généralisante de l'allégorie conceptuelle permet ainsi d'assimiler le discours catholique au paradigme du juste. L'attaque de Mars porte également sur un référent professionnel précis, le Parlement de 1564. Représenté par la Dame et ses suppôts, le milieu des juristes défend ses droits, ceux de la légitimité savante, face à l'agression des tribunaux de commerce, parés d'une fausse autorité légale.

ROUGE AFFINÉ, SUPPÔT DE JUSTICE
Mais depuis quelque temps, aulcuns mal advisez
Pour justice tollir ce sont autorisez
D'ung siege de lectrez, qui en leur ignorance,
Sans avoir des deux droicts aulcune congnoissance
Arrest deffinittif et sans aulcun appel
Ont baillé tellement quellement… (v. 197-202)

Le lien entre les deux agressions peut paraître un peu ténu et le Marchand lui-même se défend d'une assimilation de ses revendications avec les actions des Protestants : *Cil qui change de loy*, change-t-il aussi de *foy* ? (v. 129). La polysémie possible de *loi*, sens religieux, moral, juridique, amplement utilisée par la tradition dramatique des moralités spirituelles, balaie ces timides réserves. Des querelles internes au système judiciaire entrent ici dans une relation d'équivalence avec les craintes religieuses.

Or, malgré la vaillance de ses suppôts et son épaisseur référentielle fort bien construite, Justice ne triomphe pas. C'est peut-être l'un des traits qui permet de distinguer les différentes dynamiques scéniques de ce personnage. Lorsque son statut idéel soutient un message moral général, il est rare que son *auctoritas* soit discutée. Mais, dans des pièces à dimension polémique où le feuilletage des références cache une réflexion sur l'actualité, Justice est souvent bafouée, trahie. Terrible spectacle qui doit inspirer au spectateur modèle une vertueuse indignation et un rôle actif d'adjuvant face à la menace de l'injustice. Dans la moralité de *Mars et Justice*, et malgré l'intervention de Bon Droit au secours de la malheureuse, Mars reste maître du jeu. Il chasse Justice de l'espace scénique, la dépouille de son costume et lui arrache sa puissance discursive. Appelé à donner la paix à son adversaire, il ne lui présente par dérision qu'un os rongé, *la paix d'une espaulle* : dévoration de la guerre et allusion ironique au bras fracassé de Justice. Il ne reste à la dame que le *planctus* et à ses *suppôts* le blâme pour répondre à ces agressions. Face à la fausse autorité de ceux qui usurpent la loi et s'emparent de la rhétorique judiciaire, face aux discours religieux qui menacent l'équilibre du royaume en brouillant les notions de vrai et de faux, socles du mode délibératif, il demeure une rhétorique, celle de l'éloge et du blâme, et une parole autorisée, celle du théâtre.

C'est à partir de l'apparence extérieure d'un personnage que le spectateur construit sa relation avec la fiction dramatique. La personnification allégorique, transformation d'une abstraction en chair, est définie par un certain nombre de traits anthropomorphiques qui ont tous une valeur métaphorique. Il est intéressant de noter que les accessoires qui permettent de reconnaître Justice sont peu repérables dans les pièces qui privilégient une référentialité générale de l'allégorie. Sans doute existent-ils en scène, mais les indices internes aux textes sont peu nombreux[15]. En revanche, plus

15 Les indices externes sont quasiment inexistants.

Justice s'actualise, plus elle peine à s'imposer face à ses adversaires, plus son corps et ses accessoires s'exhibent, avant de disparaître, brisés ou tournés en dérision par les forces du mal. Dans la moralité parisienne évoquée plus haut, Mars rompt sa *main* (v. 314, *rompu de Justice la main ;* v. 327, *Tu m'as rompu le bras*), puis la dépouille de ses principaux attributs, le *sceau* et le *manteau* (v. 342). Le jeu de scène avec le manteau, déchiré par Mars qui promet de le vendre, est assez élaboré. Visuellement Mars remotive l'intertexte biblique de Joseph et ses frères en même temps que son geste fait surgir une image évangélique très efficace, celle de la tunique du Crucifié. Le manteau arraché et mis en pièces traduit l'imbrication des interprétations, sociale, politique, spirituelle, que les spectateurs sont invités à déchiffrer : la rapacité des marchands, la déchirure du royaume, le désordre diabolique.

Il arrive que l'abstraction qu'est la personnification se nuance de métaphores corporelles ou spatiales moins spectaculaires. *La Moralité du Bien Public*[16] permet à Justice, à la fin de la pièce, d'expliquer sa curieuse apparence : elle entre les yeux bandés. Justice aveugle, image qui nous est familière, semble être un motif relativement récent, qui se répand à la fin du XVe siècle. Or ce détail est ambigu : est-il signe que Dame Justice – entendons le système judiciaire réel – est loin de l'omniscience supposée de l'idéale *Justitia* ? Le personnage rassure ici Bien Public : son bandeau symbolise l'impartialité qu'elle met dans ses jugements[17].

JUSTICE
Et par les yeux je fuz bandéz
Dont raison diray convenable :
Justice suis pour dire voir
Qui egalement juger doy (v. 935-938)

---

16 Le texte est daté par son éditeur actuel, J. Blanchard, de 1468, ce qui est une hypothèse possible, mais, comme presque toujours pour ce type de pièce, difficile à certifier de façon absolue. *Cf. La Moralité du Bien Public*, musée Condé ms. 685, J. Blanchard (éd.), *Bibliothèque d'Humanisme et de Renaissance*, t. 70, 2008, n° 3, p. 615-661.

17 Au cours du XIVe siècle, ni à la chapelle Scrovegni de Padoue ni au Palais communal de Sienne, sous les pinceaux de Giotto et Lorenzetti, l'allégorie n'apparaît les yeux bandés. En revanche, les témoignages de la fin du XVe siècle abondent. Un bois célèbre illustrant la traduction française de *Das Narrenschiff* de Sébastian Brant, en 1497, montre un fou bandant les yeux de Justice. La *Moralité du Bien Public*, comme d'autres textes un peu plus tardifs, s'oppose à cette interprétation satirique et donne un sens moral à la représentation. L'origine du motif et sa datation (chez Brant vers 1495 ? auparavant ?) pose problème. On peut consulter, sur l'iconographie judiciaire, l'étude de Jean Hilaire (Académie des Sciences morales et politiques) http://www.asmp.fr/travaux/communications/2008/hilaire.htm.

Justice est aussi créatrice d'un espace métaphorique. Acceptant la demande du malheureux Bien Public affaibli par divers déboires politiques, elle lui offre un lit pour se reposer :

JUSTICE
Or sus ! or faison diligence
De l'asseoir sur ce beau lit (v. 995-996)

Sur le « lit de Justice » et à l'ombre du pouvoir royal, Bien Public retrouvera santé et force. Le lit, objet concret dont la signification première est transformée au contact de Justice, fonctionne comme une médiation entre l'espace de la scène et l'espace extra-scénique, où il réfère à une forme de la justice royale et peut-être à un évènement de l'actualité[18].

Il est fréquent que les locutions attachées à notre personnage, trône de justice, fontaine de justice, lit de justice, soient à la source d'un espace scénique, ponctuel comme dans la *Moralité du Bien Public*, ou encadrant toute l'action. Il semble d'ailleurs que, pour un public habitué à la gymnastique herméneutique de l'allégorisation, la mise en scène d'une fontaine suffise, par exemple, à faire signe vers la présence implicite de Justice et vers l'autorité éthique qu'elle donne à la parole théâtrale.

C'est du moins l'une des hypothèses que l'on peut proposer à la lecture du témoignage d'Henri Baude sur la moralité qui l'a envoyé en prison en 1486. Comme on le sait, la pièce est perdue, mais Henri Baude s'est expliqué sur sa portée et sur ses principaux éléments rhétoriques dans deux épîtres adressées à Jean II de Bourbon pour lui demander protection[19]. Baude dit avoir voulu montrer que *droict est souvent interdict*, en d'autres termes que la parole de Justice est dérivée, éteinte par les mauvais conseillers, les menteurs, toutes les *langues envenimées*. Il semble avoir mis en scène une *fontaine vive*, dont le cours

18 L'exemple de la métaphore dramatique « lit de justice » illustre la puissance que prend, sur une scène allégorique, la tension entre ce que Peirce appelait identité iconique et iconicité. *Cf.* U. Eco, « Paramètres de la sémiologie théâtrale », *Sémiologie de la représentation*, A. Helbo (éd.), Bruxelles, Complexes, 1975, p. 33-41.

19 J. Quicherat, dans *Les vers de maître Henri Baude, poète du 15e siècle*, Paris, 1856, rassemble les documents ayant trait à cette affaire (p. 113-120) ; leur analyse a été menée par M. Bouhaïk-Gironès, *Les clercs de la Basoche et le théâtre comique (Paris, 1420-1550)*, Paris, Champion, 2007, p. 143-149.

est arrêté par des *graviers*[20]. L'argumentation de l'écrivain paraît avoir reposé sur les liens habituels tissés entre Dame Justice, sous la métaphore transparente de la fontaine, le Parlement auquel certains joueurs de la pièce étaient attachés et la situation politique contemporaine. La dénonciation par le blâme devait ainsi s'autoriser et se protéger grâce à la polysémie allégorique de Justice. Pour paraphraser une sentence d'Expérience, juge de Banquet dans la *Condamnation de Banquet*[21], il était en quelque sorte présupposé que *Justement parle qui met en scène Justice.* Malheureusement pour Henri Baude, sa stratégie ne fonctionne pas. Certains s'étant reconnus dans les *graviers* qui *le droit court de Justice empeschent* ont mal pris l'allusion et envoyé toute la troupe au *petit chastellet.* Si le théâtre des moralités parie souvent sur la légitimité morale de son personnel allégorique pour autoriser sa prise de parole, il se heurte à une réalité : le système judiciaire réel n'est pas toujours du côté de Dame Justice et des tréteaux.

Qui parle en effet lorsque Justice discourt en scène : le personnage, ce qu'il représente, l'auteur, l'acteur ? Le questionnement sur la fiction et son message agite le monde intellectuel français depuis la fin du XIIIe siècle. Les différences que Jean de Meun faisait jouer de façon retorse entre intention d'auteur et discours des personnages dans *Le Roman de la Rose* ont complexifié la responsabilité discursive. La *Querelle sur le Roman de la Rose* qui oppose en 1401-1402 les défenseurs du livre, comme Pierre Col ou Jean de Montreuil, et ses détracteurs, Christine de Pizan et Jean Gerson, y trouve l'un de ses moteurs[22]. Un auteur n'a-t-il pas *licence*, pour employer un terme de Pierre Col, de mettre en scène la nécessaire congruence entre une allégorie et son discours, même s'il n'en fait pas son porte-parole ? Il est naturel que Médisance parle mal ou Justice justement. Mais ce sont des personnages de fiction, que seule une lecture coupablement naïve peut confondre avec une *intentio auctoris.* À cet

20 Cette interprétation repose sur l'idée que l'allégorie proposée par Baude dans sa seconde épître en vers reproduit la mise en scène de sa moralité. Il dit en effet que d'aucuns *se veullent applicquer / a herbes, autres a gravois*, faisant sans doute référence aux éléments scéniques de la représentation. On ignore, au-delà des métaphores incriminées, quels rôles animaient la *briefve moralité* de Baude.

21 Expérience : *Justement vit qui exerce Justice*, dans Nicolas de la Chesnaye (?), *La Condamnation de Banquet*, J. Koopmans et P. Verhuyck (éd.), Genève, Droz, TLF, 1991, p. 183, v. 1771.

22 *Le débat sur le Roman de la Rose. Christine de Pizan, Jean Gerson, Jean de Montreuil, Gontier et Pierre Col*, Eric Hicks (éd.), Genève, Slatkine, 1996.

argument, Gerson répond que la différence entre intention et discours prononcé est biaisée, en particulier dans le cas du personnage allégorique. Ce n'est qu'une manière d'échapper à la responsabilité que l'auteur doit endosser lorsqu'il donne un caractère public à sa parole. Si l'on montre des personnages proférant des menaces contre le roi en pleine guerre de Cent Ans, dit Gerson, pourra-t-on excuser les auteurs, sous prétexte qu'ils faisaient parler des fictions[23] ? L'autorité que l'allégorie tire de son sens éthique et de la tautologie attendue entre ce qu'elle est et ce qu'elle dit est donc à double tranchant : elle donne certes du poids à sa parole, mais ne dédouane pas ceux qui la mettent en scène. D'ailleurs, dévoiler que Justice n'est qu'un personnage fictif, n'est-ce pas mettre en danger la dimension herméneutique qu'elle donne aux pièces ?

Le problème ne semble pas avoir échappé aux dramaturges des XVe et XVIe siècles. Certaines sotties et moralités polémiques explorent à la fois la perte des identités habituelles – les figures centrales s'y nomment Chascun, Tout-le-Monde ou demeurent anonymes – et la déstabilisation des allégories conceptuelles. Justice se fait souvent discrète ou se dévoile trop humaine sur ce type de tréteaux. Ses suppôts, quittant sa proximité immédiate, questionnent son autorité ou se parent de ses oripeaux.

Dame Justice tire une partie de sa force d'un entourage de personnages secondaires, qu'elle nomme ses *suppôts*. Le terme n'est pas indifférent. Le *suppositus* en effet désigne celui qui est attaché à une institution ou à une compagnie. Subordonné à une autorité qui lui donne son identité, le suppôt a la conscience d'appartenir à un corps constitué dont il défend les droits. Ce sont des personnages sémantiquement faibles, souvent privés de noms propres et qui fonctionnent collectivement, en quelque sorte comme les fractions d'un rôle. Pourquoi Vérité ou Miséricorde n'ont-elles pas de suppôts, alors que Justice en a ? Il semble que ce fait s'explique par la riche référentialité de la personnification. Certes, Justice n'apparaît pas toujours entourée de ses *famuli*. Ils sont d'autant plus discrets que le statut idéel et général du personnage est fort. Mais lorsque Justice fait référence au système judiciaire, les suppôts sont rarement absents. Leur appellation collective, qu'ils n'hésitent pas à proclamer à leur entrée en scène, leur permet

23 *Je vous demende : se aucun se nommoit adversaire du roy de France et sus ce nom et come tel li faisoit guerre, ce non garderoit il d'estre traytre et a la mort ?* (J. Gerson à P. Col, éd. citée p. 71).

de se définir, au sein de la diégèse, comme les adjuvants privilégiés de Justice, leur mère. Figures souvent sans grande responsabilité actantielle, ils représentent les hommes de loi, petits clercs, avocats, juges, fonctionnaires du Parlement. Accompagnant Justice, ils apparaissent comme les défenseurs d'un discours juste, sur laquelle l'ordre du monde et la paix civile reposent.

> BEC AFFILÉ, SUPPÔT DE JUSTICE
> Justice a tel pouvoir
> Que jusques a la mort je feray mon debvoir.
> Affin qu'on vive en paix convient la guerre faire
> Pour domter le meschant et, si on peult, deffaire.
> L'ennemy est vaincu de parolles, par quoy
> Les armes porteray pour maintenir la loy[24].

Il arrive pourtant que, dans l'univers théâtral des sotties par exemple, le lien entre Dame Justice et les suppôts se distende. *L'esbahissement, la merancolie* dont sont saisis les suppôts dans la *Sottie des Esbahis* vient de ce que leur monde est devenu opaque. Justice ne leur dévoile pas le sens des faits et des êtres, qu'elle-même ne connaît pas, et peine à répondre à leurs questions[25]. Le lien peut même se rompre et Justice disparaître des tréteaux. Les suppôts continuent à y vivre, perdant cependant le statut qui faisait leur identité auprès de l'allégorie. « Personnes en défaut » non de « loi commune », mais de « loi » tout court, ils passent souvent – presque toujours ! – sous la coupe des représentants d'Injustice, tel que Abus dans la *Sotise à huit personnages*, à qui Sot Corrompu, représentant les gens de loi, déclare allégeance[26] :

> SOT CORROMPU
> O maistre de qui crëature
> Je suis, Dieu gard, et tes consors ! (v. 193-192)

Sot Corrompu se donne à une autre puissance, l'argent. À l'allégorie conceptuelle se substitue la transaction matérielle, vidant de leur sens spirituel et civique les procédures judiciaires :

---

24 *Mars et Justice*, éd. citée, v. 234-238, notre ponctuation.

25 J. Koopmans, *Le Recueil de Florence. 53 farces imprimées à Paris vers 1515*, Orléans, paradigme, 2011, p. 73-81.

26 *Sotise à huit personnages*, O. Duhl (éd.), Genève, Droz, TLF, 2005.

SOT CORROMPU
Procureurs, advocatz ! Procureurs, advocatz !
Par nostre arrest, briefve sentence,
Nous disons, sans que homme s'en tence,
Que cellluy qui plus baille argent
A le droict si cler et se gent. (v. 182-187)

La collusion des ex-suppôts et de l'argent est un thème habituel des pièces polémiques, qu'elles soient intitulées moralités ou sotties. Sa puissance repose sur l'inversion des valeurs dont se rendent coupables ceux qui sont censés les protéger, à l'instar des boulangers affameurs ou de la police fauteuse de troubles. Le scandale est aussi dans le fait que l'action des suppôts était originellement liée à la défense d'une parole publique garante de l'ordre du monde. Que cette parole se défasse et tout est renversé : la rhétorique judiciaire se met au service de l'injustice, la mise en scène des procès montre le triomphe de la fausseté, les personnifications vertueuses disparaissent ou sont acculées à la défensive. L'unique instance capable de leur résister est le spectateur modèle, dont la position de juge face aux dérives de la société contemporaine est alors renforcée. Dans la *Moralité des Quatre Âges*, la décadence présente est incarnée par Âge de Fer. Il annonce un empire du faux discours, symbolisé par la multiplication des procès iniques :

ÂGE DE FER
Je me delecte en proces,
Je faicts plaider le fils a pere
Et le frere contre le frere
Et la fille contre la mere[27].

La *Moralité à six personnages (Heresie, Simonie, Force, Scandale, Proces et l'Eglise)*, qui exploite un thème similaire dans une perspective anti-protestante, donne à tous les opposants d'Église une clef allégorique avec laquelle chacun essaie de forcer ses portes[28]. À tous sauf à Procès, qui semble n'avoir d'abord pour arme que sa parole déviante. Église lui déclare : *Je te congnoys en ta parolle* (v. 97). On ne tardera pas à s'apercevoir

27 *La Moralité des quatre Âges*, dans *Recueil de farces, moralités et sermons joyeux, publié d'après le manuscrit de la Bibliothèque royale*, A. Leroux de Lincy et F. Michel (éd.), Paris, 1831-1838, 3 volumes, vol. 2, p. 21.

28 Pièce du Recueil La Vallière éditée par J. Beck dans *Théâtre et propagande aux débuts de la Réforme*, Genève, Slatkine, 1986, p. 181-203.

que *l'accessoire* de Procès (v. 33) est l'argent, dissimulé dans le *saq* qu'il exhibe à la fin de la pièce. L'attribut professionnel du clerc de justice est ici détourné par homophonie (*en saq* / à sac) vers le pillage de l'Église : *Sus Proces, qu'on la mecte en saq* (rondeau, v. 294-302).

Retrouver une identité professionnelle loin de l'allégorie et de son système de valeurs transforme l'ancien suppôt en un être dégradé et vil. Pire, il dégrade son rôle au point d'en faire un masque que n'importe qui, c'est-à-dire Tout le Monde, peut endosser. La *Moralité à quatre personnages de Chascun, Plusieurs, le Temps qui court et le Monde* est l'un des nombreux exemples de cette réduction spectaculaire du personnage à une *per-sona* vide. Le Temps qui court se fait tour à tour homme d'Église, d'arme et de loi devant les yeux mi-admiratifs, mi-étonnés de Chacun et Plusieurs. Il endosse le costume de l'avocat, cornette et robe, et adopte aussitôt son comportement vicieux, appât du gain et tromperie du langage par inversion (*travers*) du juste et de l'injuste :

LE TEMPS
Par ma cornete & ma grand robe
Gras & menus par toult desrobe
Prenant mon entiere & accetz
Sur brouillerye & gros proces. [...]
Du droict faictz tort & du tort droict
J'en prens de travers & a droict[29].

Même jeu dans *Le Moral de Tout le Monde*, qu'Émile Picot a recueilli parmi les sotties[30]. La pièce met en scène trois compagnons hantés par le désir d'un pouvoir non précisé (*Par toult vouldroys estre maistre*, v. 7), ce que *Faulte d'Argent* rend impossible. Ils se mettent à la recherche de Tout le Monde. Celui-ci apparaît dans un équipage burlesque qui superpose les accessoires traditionnels des états : *Y porte l'estat de Noblesse, / de Marchant, Labeur et Eglise.* Cette mascarade est expliquée par le commun dénominateur des *estatz*, l'argent bien entendu, puissance capable de troubler l'ordre du monde en brouillant les qualités propres à chaque groupe social. Puis Tout le Monde révèle de nouveaux accessoires : *l'escriptoire et le chaperon de Justice* (v. 152-153, p. 37). Mais ces objets ne

29 *Recueil de farces, moralités et sermons joyeux, publié d'après le manuscrit de la Bibliothèque royale*, A. Leroux de Lincy et F. Michel (éd.), Paris, 1831-1838, vol. 3, p. 17.

30 *Moral de Tout le Monde à quatre personnages*, dans *Recueil général des sotties*, E. Picot (éd.), Paris, SATF, 1902-1912, 3 volumes, t. 3, p. 25-43.

s'ajoutent pas aux autres ; ils changent la relation entre les personnages, transformant le regard critique des compagnons en complicité. Ce sont alors eux qui vont, tour à tour, affubler Tout le Monde de différents costumes, lui proposant diverses identités, mais sans réussir à vaincre son irrésolution.

La petite scène du *chaperon de Justice*, qui sert de charnière syntaxique à l'action, est curieuse. Tout le Monde ne révèle pas clairement ce que ces accessoires signifient, d'autant qu'ils s'ajoutent à un *rolle*, des *lettres closes*

> Qui ne seront par vous descloses
> Car vous estes trop peu discres
> Pour voir mon rolle et mes segres (v. 166-170)

L'effet sur les compagnons est saisissant. Comme on l'a dit, ils modifient leur attitude, après avoir indiqué qu'il faut *changer de parolle.*

> LE PREMIER
> Le parler en est dangereulx
> Et pourtant changeons de parole (v. 160-161)

Il semble possible d'interpréter ce jeu de scène comme l'indice que l'on redoute un contrôle judiciaire sur les propos échangés et des sanctions prévisibles contre les acteurs. Ce trait est fréquent dans les sotties, qui mettent en scène à travers des accessoires[31] le péril guettant la parole dramatique. Le costume de l'homme de loi est ici signe de la dissociation entre l'expression théâtrale et une légalité considérée comme répressive. On ne peut mieux faire voler en éclats la cohérence allégorique que les moralités postulaient en Dame Justice : une puissance spirituelle et civique, une autorité légale et politique, un discours public reposant sur le processus de sa propre légitimation.

Étrange parole que la parole théâtrale. Elle se construit entre performance et trace écrite. Elle se tisse d'autres discours : évaluations qui l'encadrent pour l'autoriser ou l'interdire ; commentaires qui en naissent. Il n'y a donc pas, au-delà de la variance ponctuelle des œuvres dramatiques qui nous sont parvenues des XVe et XVIe siècles, un texte mais des textes, archives, témoignages, documents judiciaires ; non

31 On songe aux bonnets sans oreilles des sots dans la *Sottie des Béguins*, entre autres.

une parole, mais des paroles bruissant sur et autour des tréteaux. Or l'articulation et la circulation de ces paroles font signe vers des questions de droit : qui est autorisé à dire ou à ne pas dire ? Les statuts de l'acteur, de l'écrivain, du spectateur sont ainsi mis en jeu. Mais il nous semble qu'est aussi abordé par ce biais le statut du personnage. Au tournant des XVᵉ et XVIᵉ siècles, la question n'est ni nouvelle ni propre au théâtre, comme en témoignent les discussions du *Débat sur le Roman de la Rose*. Cependant, l'écriture théâtrale n'étant qu'un interstice que la performance complète, l'interrogation sur la nature du personnage allégorique (fiction ? masque ?) conduit à y penser d'une façon plus complexe les idées de représentation et de médiation. Ce sont ces trois notions, autorité, médiation, représentation, qui nous ont conduit à nous intéresser au personnage de Justice. Lorsqu'apparaît sur la scène un tel personnage, imaginaires de la loi et réflexions sur le discours théâtral se croisent-ils et comment ?

Alors que de nombreuses pièces dites « farces » s'amusent de la mise en question du droit familial (la femme et le mari, les parents et les héritiers) et explorent les identités juridiques instables que Ch. Biet a étudiées sous le nom de « personnages en défaut de loi commune[32] », moralités et sotties élaborent des systèmes actantiels dominés par une identification éthique de la *persona*[33]. De ce fait la question de la justice y est centrale. Dame Justice y joue au centre d'une distribution apparemment simple : entourée d'ennemis – injustes, il va sans dire –, elle entraîne avec elle une petite troupe d'adjuvants, ses suppôts. D'un point de vue rhétorique, même transparence apparente : Justice est juste et parle justement. Mais regarder de plus près le corpus théâtral des moralités et sotties conduit à penser que le personnage est loin de se réduire à ces tautologies.

Justice peut d'abord apparaître comme une figure de l'autorisation, particulièrement importante pour un théâtre en quête de légitimité.

32 Il s'agit en particulier des bâtards, cadets et veuves ; *cf.* Ch. Biet, *Droit et littérature sous l'Ancien Régime. Le Jeu de la valeur et de la loi*, Paris, Champion, 2002, « Les personnages en défaut de loi commune », p. 225-284.

33 La majorité des moralités et sotties se construisent à travers l'interrogation de la légalité des actions et des paroles. Le fait semble aveuglant au point qu'Olga Duhl dans son étude sur la sottie (*Folie et rhétorique dans la sottie*, Genève, Droz, 1994) a omis de consacrer un chapitre à la rhétorique judiciaire qu'elles utilisent massivement, alors qu'elle se penche sur les liens entre discours délibératif et épidictique.

Celle-ci vient de son *auctoritas* quasi divine, puisqu'elle tend souvent à se confondre, dans les moralités spirituelles, avec la voix du Dieu Juge. Maîtresse en scène du discours judiciaire, et par là des deux autres modes rhétoriques (le vrai et le faux dans le délibératif, l'éloge et le blâme dans l'épidictique), elle est une instance de contrôle du langage, punissant la médisance, assurant le triomphe du juste. Sa puissance discursive rejaillit naturellement sur la scène qui la montre, assimilant les tréteaux à un tribunal et ce tribunal à une comparution céleste. Les liens bien connus entre rituel religieux, rite judiciaire et mise en scène théâtrale fonctionnent à travers elle avec une grande efficacité. Il a été indiqué au cours du propos que la puissance de Justice nous semblait reposer sur sa triple référentialité possible, touchant aux domaines spirituel, moral et politique, à travers l'institution judiciaire réelle qu'elle peut figurer. On pourrait ajouter à cela le domaine de la communication, Justice donnant force et autorisation à la parole théâtrale.

Justice est aussi figure de médiatrice, puisqu'elle tend toujours à représenter autre chose qu'elle-même, comme toute allégorie : en tant qu'incarnation d'un concept, son statut idéel la pousse à se projeter dans des incarnations terrestres, prince, prêtre, juge[34]. Il arrive donc assez fréquemment que sa présence en scène soit variable ou masquée, ce qui n'enlève rien à l'importance sémantique du personnage. La fonction de la *mediatrix* est également importante pour la qualité de son discours, projeté vers un spectateur modèle constitué en juge ultime de ce qui est montré.

Cependant, contrairement à ce que l'on pourrait croire, ce prestige ne lui assure pas toujours le triomphe, ce qui ne laisse pas de problématiser le fonctionnement des pièces. Le personnage est beaucoup moins stable qu'il y paraît et sa riche référentialité peut devenir ambiguë. Il participe alors à différentes dynamiques communicationnelles qu'il ne faut sans doute pas réduire à une simple classification de « genres ». Si elle est en général victorieuse sur des scènes qui privilégient son statut idéel, elle est très souvent bafouée, défaillante, voire absente d'autres textes qui lui offrent une mission plus terrestre. Au fur et à mesure qu'elle est gagnée par les références au réel, Justice vacille, tout en se

34 L'assimilation statutaire entre le gouvernant, médiateur de la Justice, les juristes et les prêtres, serviteurs des lois divines et humaines, est l'un des traits essentiels de la doctrine de l'école de Bologne au XIIIe siècle. On la retrouve exposée avec la même force sous la plume de Guillaume Budé trois siècles plus tard. *Cf.* E. Kantorowicz, *ibid.*, p. 100-101.

parant de signes dramatiques plus précis, accessoires, adjuvants comme les suppôts. Les uns et les autres peuvent se détacher d'elle, démontrant que la Loi et la loi, la vertu et les hommes, le personnage et le masque sont dissociés. La parole théâtrale joue alors à la marge de règlements judiciaires qui peuvent la réduire au silence.

Qu'il soit triomphant ou déstabilisé, central ou étouffé sur la scène, le discours de Justice semble donc généralement soutenir, non sans quelques paradoxes, la communication théâtrale. Reposant elle aussi sur l'autorité et la médiation, interrogeant la représentation qui la fonde, la scène se donne pour apte à remplacer Justice dans l'espace public réel, si y est trahi ce que l'allégorie incarne – ou plutôt ce que auteurs, acteurs et spectateurs souhaitent déchiffrer en elle. À l'image de la corde qui, dans la fresque siennoise d'Ambrogio Lorenzetti, passe des mains de l'allégorie à celles des citoyens qui la portent à Bien Commun[35], le personnage de Justice sur les scènes dramatiques permet de tisser une réflexion, de la *littera* à la *séance*, sur la circulation de la parole publique.

Estelle DOUDET
Université Grenoble Alpes
Institut universitaire de France

35 A. Lorenzetti, fresque dite du *Bon Gouvernement*, Sienne, Palazzo Communale, vers 1340.

CINQUIÈME PARTIE

POUR UNE THÉORIE JURIDIQUE ET HISTORIQUE DU THÉÂTRE SOUS L'ANCIEN RÉGIME

SÉANCE, ASSEMBLÉE, MÉDIATION SPECTACULAIRE ET COMPARUTION THÉÂTRALE[1]

Ce que nous proposons ici est une réflexion inachevée qui consiste à faire le lien entre l'histoire du théâtre, l'histoire des théories juridiques sous l'Ancien Régime, la dramaturgie de ce temps et son rapport aux spectateurs. « Pour une théorie juridique et historique du théâtre sous l'Ancien Régime », ou « pour une histoire du théâtre juridico-théorique », ce pourraient être nos sous-titres.

Toutefois, avant de formuler l'irruption du théâtre sous une forme d'abord métaphoriquement judiciaire puis principiellement juridique, il convient de dire quelques mots de ce qu'il est comme phénomène en tension et comme événement complexe.

HYPER-PRÉSENCE, MÉDIATION, TENSION

Le théâtre se joue au présent, à partir d'un dispositif matériel et « réel ». Des présences diverses s'intègrant dans un présent éphémère et dans un lieu particulier donnent ainsi lieu à un événement. Ce faisant, le théâtre exprime, à un moment donné, l'être là des regardés, leur performance, et l'être là des regardants qui contribuent à produire l'événement ou la performance. Le théâtre s'intègre donc dans un « hyper-présent » hyper-éphémère qui se donne et se montre tel.

Cependant, le théâtre, comme tout art, est une expérience de médiation. En l'occurrence, il est l'expérimentation, donc présente et éphémère,

1 Voir Ch. Biet et Ch. Triau, « La comparution théâtrale. Pour une définition esthétique et politique de la séance », *Tangence*, n° 88, mars 2009.

dans un lieu particulier, d'un système différé qui permet de dire indirectement, grâce à une médiation artistique, ici particulièrement complexe, ce qu'il en est du monde, *de la médiation elle-même et de son effectuation dans le champ d'une assemblée*. En cela, le théâtre est à même de parler de la cité, de la représenter à blanc, et d'en montrer ostensiblement et en toute conscience les contradictions et les horreurs, tout en les jouant, tout en montrant qu'il les figure (« *showing doing*[2] »). C'est cette médiation qui permet de vivre dans un monde civilisé, et, dans le même temps, c'est elle que le théâtre tente, par moments, d'effacer lorsqu'il entend frôler le réel, quand il cherche à faire semblant d'être le réel, ou à s'appuyer sur le fait qu'il est aussi du réel présent.

Ainsi, lorsque le spectacle théatralisé, ou théâtral, se met en place, on peut observer deux faits simultanés : la médiation qui met le monde en distance et la réalité de la performance qui jamais ne disparaît. En effet, si le théâtre est bien, par fonction, médiation, système différé, ou représentation, il est aussi un art qui joue, par la performance, à supprimer la différence, à réduire ou annihiler la médiation, à ne pas oublier que des corps réels sont présents, à mettre de côté la représentation. Le spectacle, ainsi, oscille entre ces deux pôles, ce qui a pour effet de mettre les spectateurs dans une attitude ambiguë d'hésitation sur ce qu'ils voient et sur ce qu'ils entendent. Sans médiation, le monde n'est plus que corps, objets, littéralité et/ou violence extrême, mais sans médiation et sans différence, on peut aussi dire que ce qui est là est « vrai ». Alors qu'en intégrant la médiation dans son principe, le théâtre peut produire des conduites et des jugements à blanc qui permettent, *justement*, en se dégageant du « réel », du « vrai » et de sa violence immédiate, de penser et de juger ce monde ainsi représenté et dévoilé grâce à la distance de la représentation.

On pourrait alors affirmer que le théâtre est double : il est *présence réelle* (terme sur lequel il serait intéressant de se pencher, principalement au Moyen âge et durant les XVIe et XVIIe siècles), en tant qu'il est conscience forte de cette présence, autrement dit performance (performative ?), d'une part, et, simultanément, il est médiation de cette présence. Et c'est cette tension qui permet un constant questionnnement du théâtre sur lui-même en même temps qu'il s'accomplit, un questionnement

2 Voir R. Schechner, *Performance studies, An introduction*, Londres / New York, Routledge, 2003.

« en actes » de la présence réelle, de l'extension de sa définition, de son effectivité, de sa qualité, et de son impact.

Et la réfléxivité, le questionnement du théâtre sur sa présence même et sur ce que sont ces corps qui se meuvent et qui jouent à ce moment là et dans ce lieu là, est une fois de plus redoublé et mis en perspective par le fait qu'il s'agit d'un jeu éphémère, au présent, et opéré devant plusieurs. Qu'on soit comédien, praticien, performer ou spectateur, on est ainsi en état d'« éprouver » (dans les deux sens du terme, en ressentant et en expérimentant) l'événement spectaculaire, la séance, alors qu'il s'agit bien d'un événement complexe puisqu'il contient d'autres événements, dont le jeu théâtral proprement dit, niché dans la somme des événements, et la fiction dramatique, elle-même incluse dans la réalité événementielle.

Si bien que l'événement *et* les cas (re-)présentés, sont pris dans une sorte de porosité entre la matérialité des « réels » de la séance et de la performance, et le virtuel de la figuration ou de la représentation. Le théâtre pense et figure ainsi simultanément, dans son effectuation même, la question de savoir s'il peut rester une médiation, ou comment il peut être une médiation dans un lieu de parole différé (par la mimésis, la représentation, l'emblématique, le symbolique, ou par tout autre mode de fonctionnement), tout en étant matériel et présent, tout en cherchant systématiquement à frôler le réel, à *être* le réel en faisant en sorte que s'expriment les corps, le sang, les humeurs, etc.

Inspiration et intériorisation du monde pour le penser en distance, pour le figurer par la mise en fiction, la dramatisation, la virtualisation du monde. Expiration et expression en actes et en action de la dynamique corporelle, par la performance présente et « réelle », le mouvement du théâtre est bien une suite de tensions. Inspiration/expiration, le mouvement est naturel, corporel, esthétique et théâtral.

Mais il est une autre tension qui tient cette fois à ce que le théâtre entend être sur la scène du monde, sur sa fonction. Car si le théâtre est d'abord un lieu éphémère dans lequel viennent sans contrainte (autre que de mode, ou de convention sociale, donc une contrainte de faible degré, c'est donc un *loisir*), sans convocation (contrairement à la pratique religieuse ou à la convocation judiciaire) et sans obligation (sauf hélas pour les scolaires, de nos jours), des hommes et des femmes de toutes sortes pourvu qu'ils puissent payer leur place, il doit s'affirmer comme ayant une fonction dans la société : il doit nommer le lieu qu'il est et lui donner une action possible sur la cité. C'est là qu'il est pris entre une fonction de lien social, *via* le divertissement, le loisir, la puissance de cohésion et l'émotion esthétique commune, et une fonction de décalage, qui donne à ce lieu une autre valeur, une valeur de diffraction, de contradiction et de critique, de *savoir dialectique critique*, et qui induit, ou provoque, le phénomène du jugement.

Le premier cas de figure montre en effet que le spectacle théâtral a pour objet la production d'un lien social et esthétique et, pour ce faire, suppose qu'il possède une puissance cohésive efficiente et effervescente, énergique et homogénéisante qui met en conformité avec les autres chaque participant à l'événement. Ce type de théâtre vise donc à l'homogénéité des participants, ou même à leur harmonie, en tâchant d'effacer d'abord une séparation, ou une opposition entre les regardants et, parfois même, en cherchant à réunir dans une même expérience pratique les regardants et les regardés. Dès lors, le spectacle peut revêtir des allures si unificatrices qu'elles deviennent ritualisantes ou, dans le cas du spectacle de propagande, peut s'arroger une fonction de réunion de tous autour d'une idée et de valeurs communes que la représentation produit au même titre que l'ensemble de l'événement. Ceux qui, alors, ne participeraient pas à l'harmonie ou en contesteraient la fonction de cohésion, s'excluraient d'eux-mêmes ou seraient exclus.

On distinguera cependant les spectacles qui tendent directement à la cohésion du public en vue d'une action au sortir du théâtre, qui s'acharnent à persuader ou qui s'intègrent à un travail de propagande, des spectacles qui cultivent une esthétique propre à émouvoir les spectateurs autour d'une performance, pour qu'en même temps cette émotion réfléchisse, dans les deux sens du terme, à des valeurs communes et positives. Il s'agit là d'un type de spectacle qui parfois distingue les regardants et les regardés, parfois les unit (avant, pendant ou après la « représentation »), et qui tente aussi de réunir l'ensemble des présents dans une effusion afin que tous soient, en cours ou à la fin de la séance, convaincus qu'il est nécessaire de ressentir du lien social et humain, d'éprouver des valeurs communes, et de tenter de vivre au dehors cette effusion qu'on a connu à l'intérieur du spectacle. C'est semble-t-il le fonctionnement et la fonction des dernières mises en scène du Théâtre du Soleil.

Enfin, il y a les spectacles qui se donnent comme de simples divertissements et qui revendiquent n'être que cela même. Ils sont aussi censés produire le même effet : réunir l'assistance et les praticiens autour d'une même fonction, celle d'un public (au singulier donc) en cohésion sociale et qui partage pleinement, ici tout le temps du spectacle, les figurations du monde que la représentation véhicule. De là (donc des Romains...) vient le sens des applaudissements qui réunissent les regardants et les regardés autour de la célébration d'une performance qui vient d'avoir lieu et qui se poursuit encore, tandis que les spectateurs évaluent en commun le plaisir qu'ils ont eu à voir les regardés et qu'ils ont encore à le montrer.

Toutefois, de même que les applaudissements peuvent être plus ou moins nourris, ou striés par des sifflets, l'expérience de l'événement démontre que l'unité visée toujours s'échappe, et qu'elle est en quelque sorte déniée par le fait que le spectacle réunit des individus isolés parmi tous les autres et qu'expérimenter l'union de soi et du groupe renvoie le plus souvent à l'expérience d'une séparation d'avec le groupe et d'avec autrui. Le second cas de figure, ainsi, repose sur un système de médiation qui ne lie pas les participants entre eux, excite des passions individuelles et collectives contradictoires, peut aller jusqu'à les rendre immaîtrisables, et surtout se présente comme le lieu critique spécifique de la cité. C'est alors de ce lieu, placé au sein la cité, qu'il devient possible de regarder le pouvoir, la ville et la société, d'en dévoiler les « vérités », les apparences et les travers, d'en proposer *hic et nunc* une figuration et une série d'interrogations à même d'être différemment jugées par l'ensemble des partenaires du spectacle. Ici, l'hyper-présence et l'éphémère se rejoignent, au sein d'un mouvement ambigu, paradoxal et réversible qui propose dans le temps et l'espace de l'événement une figuration qu'il s'agit de juger en examinant les certitudes et les incertitudes des questions qui y sont posées. Partant du cadre codé et conventionnel de la loi commune, l'événement théâtral le dépasse alors en laissant une grande place à l'exceptionnel et à la surprise.

Si bien que cet événement *en tensions* dont on a déjà dit qu'il était pris entre sa fonction esthétique de médiation et son appétence à vouloir frôler, sans médiation, le réel, ne cesse aussi d'osciller entre deux pôles : le lien et le lieu. D'un côté le théâtre tente sans cesse de réaliser une cité unie, harmonieuse, conforme, en tout cas engagée dans un seul mouvement, déploratoire, fervent, ou heureux, prise dans une sorte de célébration du lien, de « l'être-ensemble », de l'unité dans le plaisir et le divertissement, la fierté ou le déplaisir et le deuil *partagés*, la pensée cohésive et l'acceptation de valeurs communes. D'autre part il est la figuration de la disparité, de la scission, des contradictions : dans ce second ordre là, les individualités, les petites solidarités et les autonomies de toutes sortes jouent leur rôle critique, font exploser l'union et la cohésion du premier pôle et empêchent, au nom des contradictions qui s'expriment, qu'un lien, qu'une cérémonie ou qu'une sorte de rituel social communs aient lieu. Ce qui, en l'espèce, reste commun, c'est alors non plus « l'être-ensemble » mais le fait d'être ensemble pour voir et co-produire un événement dans un temps et un lieu donnés. C'est le fait de ressentir, de jouir et de réfléchir ensemble mais pas forcément dans la même direction, ni en éprouvant les mêmes sensations, ni en épousant les mêmes valeurs, ni en proposant des solutions et des jugements partagées par tous.

Ce sont ces deux tensions qui, semble-t-il, marquent par exemple l'évolution du théâtre médiéval : médiation et frôlement du réel, fonction de lien social (et religieux) et fonction du lieu de jeu, orientée vers l'expérience critique des contradictions.

Enfin, et même lorsqu'on considère que le théâtre parvient à réunir dans l'effusion, le partage de valeurs communes et la pensée d'un devenir commun, la complexité de cet événement et, on l'a dit, son incapacité à être maîtrisé par personne (sauf en excluant une partie des spectateurs ou une partie des praticiens) font que le théâtre est sans cesse un lieu de porosité et de perturbation notionnelle (qu'en est-il du réel ? qu'en est-il du virtuel ?) et sociale (que faire de cette société libre, hétérogène et marginale ?). Au cours de la longue histoire du théâtre, on peut alors observer toutes sortes de tentatives et de moyens inventés pour contrôler l'événement théâtral au nom du fait qu'il est, ou peut être, potientiellement dangereux. Il peut en effet devenir irrespectueux et blasphémateur, par exemple, non par destination mais par sa réception : le libertin Saint-Evremond, à la fin du XVIIe siècle, affirme ainsi qu'il ne faut pas représenter des tragédies religieuses puisqu'on ne sait jamais qui, d'une loge, peut faire rire à ses dépens en se moquant, par exemple, qu'on puisse arrêter une armée ennemie avec une mâchoire d'âne ! Les pouvoirs politiques auront beau multiplier les ordonnances, et les « partis » moraux et religieux auront beau imaginer toutes sortes d'interdictions, rien n'y fera. En outre, il est toujours difficile d'intervenir pendant la séance, ou de surveiller les débats et les effets qu'elle produit, car la séance est une catastrophe pour toute tentative de contrôle. Et, à côté des contraintes externes, les partisans d'un théâtre épuré auront beau produire toute sorte de contraintes dramaturgiques internes à l'écriture ou à la mise en scène, le contrôle des performances et de l'événement social mêlant la présence des corps et des voix échappera à l'ordre. Ainsi, le spectacle pourra être supportable, voir encouragé, s'il trie et maîtrise son public (contraintes externes) et si ce qu'il représente s'accorde aux règles esthétiques conventionnelles (contraintes internes) telles qu'elles sont tolérées par le pouvoir et admises par ce qu'il est convenu d'appeler « la réception ». Toutes ces tentatives plus ou moins fondées en droit, mais toujours faites au nom d'une esthétique revendiquée comme celle du « beau », ont donc tenté un dressage social du théâtre en amont (par la censure ou l'auto-censure des textes et l'affichage des projets de mise en scène) et en aval (par la répression en cas de transgression ou de désordre) des événements. Régulation, censure, interdictions, peuvent alors être efficaces à partir du moment où le pouvoir est homogène, ou se conduit comme tel, à partir d'une doctrine et de lois unies pratiquement et théoriquement. Or, fort souvent, ce n'est pas le cas puisque le pouvoir est composé de différentes instances : politiques, religieuses, policières, esthétiques, de corps, ou de métiers qui empêchent un contrôle homogène et laissent le désordre s'installer dans l'interstice de leurs oppositions. Le contrôle est donc lui-même généralement hétérogène puisque les pouvoirs n'ont que très rarement eu, ensemble, les mêmes évaluations des transgressions.

C'est dans ce jeu entre les pouvoirs hétérogènes qui produisent, souvent malgré eux, des contraintes juridiques et esthétiques hétérogènes, et l'événement lui-même, immaîtrisable pendant la séance et parfois après, en tout cas difficilement maîtrisable malgré les contraintes et les pressions de toutes sortes, qu'on peut penser la place du théâtre.

Ainsi, lorsqu'il ne fonctionne pas dans le cadre d'une cérémonie pure et simple où chaque spectateur, par sa ferveur, est impliqué dans une réception qui est ou qui devient, *en principe*, commune, le théatre est un objet formellement et socialement hétérogène, pris dans un espace hétéronome et hétérodoxe. C'est encore, à proprement parler, une hétérotopie, un « espace autre » qui dit simultanément l'ailleurs (ou l'autrefois) et le présent dans un dispositif expérimental qui vise l'imagination et l'entendement des spectateurs à l'intérieur d'un lieu où se réunit une assemblée.

Or cette assemblée est marquée par le champ de forces contradictoires et opposées que déterminent ses instances (comédiens, praticiens, auteurs, spectateurs, et maintenant metteur en scène et/ou plasticien). Et l'on peut alors affirmer que, dans le présent éphémère de l'expérience théâtrale se joue ainsi une *relation* et une série de *tensions* fondamentalement caractérisées par les contradictions, l'hétérogénéité, la multiplicité des points de vue. C'est là que s'effectuent une mise en place et une autre mise en jeu du commun, le fait que le commun soit mis et sans cesse remis en jeu dans le monde du théâtre et dans le monde extérieur, et un jeu de l'individuel par rapport à ce commun[3]. Et même lorsque le théâtre revendique une action homogène, réunifiante, ou de mise en commun partagé du monde à travers un système d'apparence ritualisée, autrement dit lorsqu'il se donne pour objet une action à la fois esthétique, sociale, voire morale et politique, en tout cas positive et transitive de réunification et de partage, quelque chose résiste, qui est la structure même de l'action théâtrale, son hétérogénéité, sa discontinuité, son hétérotopie structurelles, ainsi que sa manière, ou plutôt sa forme, judiciaire oppositionnelle, tendue et contradictoire.

La question qui se pose alors au critique, devant cet état des lieux on ne peut plus parcellarisé et mis en *tensions*, est de savoir non seulement comment observer le fait théâtral, mais surtout quel objet, quel fait il devient alors possible d'observer. La mise en scène ? la « représentation théâtrale » ? ou plus simplement ce qu'il convient d'appeler « la séance théâtrale[4] ».

---

3 On ajoutera qu'un certain type de théâtre formel, fort prisé de nos jours, ne cesse de revendiquer ce jeu et ce commun, au risque parfois de l'autoréférentialité tautologique, d'une part, et d'une conception de la communauté théâtrale qui ne renverrait qu'à un seul « partage » du même (la théâtralité), voire à un « partage » harmonieux du monde, de valeurs morales données comme humaines, et de l'esthétique entre les spectateurs et l'objet vivant qu'ils regardent ou qu'ils produisent.

4 Ce qui peut être gênant dans le mot de *séance* (qui étymologiquement suppose que l'on soit assis, mais qu'on conservera néanmoins parce qu'il est moins problématique que le mot *événement* ou, en anglais, *event*), l'anglais en gomme la difficulté par le mot de *session*.

SÉANCE THÉÂTRALE, RELATION ESTHÉTIQUE : CONTRADICTION ET SIMULTANÉITÉ

La méthode serait alors la suivante. Outre l'amont de l'événement (le texte s'il y en a un, les conditions de production esthétiques, politiques, économiques, etc., les répétitions, la préparation de l'événement, etc.), il s'agit donc de noter, théoriquement, si possible historiquement, c'est-à-dire à partir de documents précis (témoignages, rapports de police, paratextes, etc.) les phénomènes qui participent à cette *séance*, c'est-à-dire ce que des spectateurs informés et actifs, en position de divertissement et de réflexion, peuvent exprimer, seuls et à plusieurs, seuls parmi plusieurs, à partir des questions que le spectacle, dans son entier, leur pose, et à partir des questions qu'ils se posent lors de leur réception, à un moment donné de l'histoire et dans un lieu particulier. Il s'agit donc, par la notion de *séance*, de réunir au sein de notre observation l'ensemble des phénomènes constituants du spectacle (en amont, dans son effectuation, et en aval).

Cela ne va certes pas sans grands obstacles, car si la question de la recherche et de l'interprétation du document est une première difficulté, la seconde tient en cela que le point de vue critique adopté varie selon le type de réception auquel il s'applique, et l'on sait encore que le théâtre, objet éphémère et réitéré, est produit par différentes instances et différents métiers, composé à partir d'un champ de forces contradictoires, que chaque instance (spectateurs inclus) et chaque métier revendiquent à juste titre, et chacun de leur point de vue, pour sien. De même, à l'intérieur de chaque instance, les points de vue et les intérêts s'étoilent ; les spectateurs par exemple, qui composent l'instance du public, ne peuvent être essentialisés puisqu'ils forment un ensemble hétérogène, et leur observation, qu'ils soient ou non avertis, qu'ils soient ou non critiques, ne peut qu'être partielle. De même, un point de vue qui se situerait au sein des instances productrices, elles aussi hétérogènes, devra assumer le fait qu'il ne compose qu'une partie du spectacle, et que son action est située dans un rapport de forces (qui peut être dominant, harmonieux, contradictoire, etc.) vis-à-vis des autres instances de production. L'action du moderne metteur en scène, par exemple, sera alors à saisir par rapport au responsable du texte (auteur, dramaturge, traducteur, par exemple), par rapport aux autres responsables de la mise en œuvre matérielle du spectacle (comédiens, décorateur ou scénographe, éclairagiste, costumier, techniciens, etc.) et par rapport à des spectateurs, autrement dit par rapport à un public composé d'entités distinctes et hétérogènes dans un lieu donné et à un moment donné.

L'intervention critique descriptive et interprétative que nous postulons tient donc dans une attitude simultanément historique, esthétique et politique qui peut être présentée en deux assertions majeures. 1. Le théâtre est cet objet formellement et socialement hétéronome : une sorte d'hétérotopie particulière marquée par le champ de forces que déterminent ses instances elles-mêmes striées par des mouvements structurels contradictoires qui, d'une certaine manière, assurent une dynamique de production de l'événement. 2. Ce champ de forces est à la fois extérieur et intérieur aux processus sociaux, donnant à voir et à partager, ou plutôt à produire en commun et individuellement des formes qui, de manière différée, construisent un rapport entre des figurations humaines (individuelles et/ou collectives) prises dans l'histoire, les lieux et les temps dans lesquels le spectacle prend place.

Cette attitude, nécessairement imparfaite puisqu'elle ne peut tendre ni prétendre à l'exhaustivité, a pour nous l'avantage d'éliminer la question de l'essence, donc celle d'une sorte de métaphysique, ou de sacré qui tiendrait à la cérémonie et qui supposerait la recherche et la présence potentielle d'un idéal absolu, capable de fédérer toutes les interventions des participants à ce qui, il faut le rappeler, n'est quand même qu'un loisir et un divertissement (politique et esthétique, certes, mais un divertissement). Et si les praticiens (auteurs, comédiens, metteurs en scène, etc.), si les praticiens et les spectateurs ont parfois besoin, ou ont eu besoin, pour légitimer leur mode d'intervention, d'une revendication métaphysique, sacralisante, ou cérémonielle (ou encore cérémoniale) supposant un idéal absolu, nous ne le dénirons pas mais nous l'observerons comme une légitimation possible de leur activité qui, pour chaque cas, s'appuie sur et donne lieu à une forme particulière, historicisée, de proposition, d'événement, de tentative de définition et de contrôle de la séance, voire de publication.

En outre, et justement parce que nous postulons l'absence d'une essence et donc de toute an-historicité, il nous semble capital, nous l'avons dit, d'en revenir, avant toute chose, à la description diachronique et formalisée des événements spectaculaires, en ne faisant pas seulement appel aux « intentions » des praticiens – écrivains, dramaturges, metteurs en scène, comédiens, techniciens, etc. – mais aussi à ceux qui composent, majoritairement, la « séance théâtrale », autrement dit les spectateurs, ceux qui sont présents *aussi et en majorité* lors de l'événement. En d'autres termes, nous ne situons pas seulement l'esthétique théâtrale en amont, dans les principes – prescriptifs – de réalisation du texte ou du spectacle tels que les scènes seraient chargées de les appliquer et les publics de les accepter, mais dans l'événement même et dans l'aval, dans la résultante – ou la réception au sens large – diachronique de l'événement, qu'il soit spectaculaire (présence au spectacle) ou éditorial (publication et lecture, le cas échéant).

Plus précisément, il s'agit tout simplement de saisir le fait théâtral – comme tout fait esthétique – en tant que *relation*. Une relation qui ne se résout pas dans le seul objet proposé (l'œuvre, le spectacle construit par les praticiens), mais bien dans ce qui se joue *entre* le spectacle représenté et ses récepteurs, en une dialectique active, jamais résolutive, et « tendue » (qui ne se résoudrait donc pas non plus, à l'inverse, dans la seule appropriation imaginaire ou le seul jugement de goût du spectateur : une relation forte et contradictoire, presque agonistique, même si elle peut avoir lieu pacifiquement, entre ces instances, à l'intérieur de ce champ de forces).

Elle suppose donc d'un côté l'étude de l'identité de cet objet esthétique offert au regard, assumée par un ensemble polyphonique de praticiens. En cela, elle implique la prise en compte d'une analyse de l'objet-spectacle en tant que tel, comme construction ayant sa cohérence et ses lignes de forces tout autant que sa complexité et ses points aveugles. Cette approche sera alors celle de l'esthétique induite par telle ou telle « œuvre » théâtrale, et par extension la possibilité de l'étude de l'esthétique récurrente de tel ou tel praticien[5], ou de telle ou telle équipe de praticiens (de nos jours plus ou moins réunie, mais non forcément harmonisée ou harmonieuse, sous la signature de la fonction « mise en scène », souvent mais pas forcément articulée sur un matériau textuel). Mais, puisqu'il s'agit d'une œuvre dont la nature même est d'être mise en jeu dans une

5 Un peu selon ce que l'on appelait à une époque, pour le cinéma, une « politique des auteurs ».

relation esthétique, puisque tout dispositif théâtral, et plus largement artistique, est une présence offerte à la saisie intellectuelle et sensitive et constitue en creux une/des place(s) potentielle(s) pour son récepteur, on devra noter que le fait théâtral ne se fige jamais dans une supposée « autonomie » de cet objet. Au contraire, « l'œuvre » implique, dans sa propre organicité, la pensée de la relation qu'elle prétend instaurer : ce que l'on désignera comme le mode d'*adresse* qu'elle aspire à instituer, en sachant que ce sont finalement les spectateurs eux-mêmes qui sont maîtres du choix de leur(s) réceptions(s), et que celle(s)-ci est une part essentielle du fait théâtral.

Il ne s'agit donc pas d'ignorer les tentatives principielles des praticiens, de refuser d'observer leur mise en œuvre, mais de les *mettre en perspective* et d'évaluer le rapport qu'elles entretiennent – au-delà de leurs seules prétentions – sur toute leur étendue temporelle avec leurs réceptions (lieux, temps, publics, types de mise en scène, etc.). On prendra donc fondamentalement en compte l'autre pôle de la dialectique, c'est-à-dire, pour le théâtre, le pôle *des* récepteurs, dans sa multiplicité simultanée, lui-même jamais essentialisable mais toujours pris dans un contexte historique, culturel, social, circonstanciel, etc.

Notre travail consistera donc à privilégier *l'événement, la séance*, ou *l'événement de la séance autant* que la prestation, la représentation ou la performance, afin de tenir compte des publics, de leur présence et de leur aptitude à co-produire un spectacle à un moment précis ; rappeler, également, la diachronie en réévaluant par exemple les formes de théâtre anciennes, afin de ne pas prendre pour une singularité ou une invention moderne les reprises, conscientes ou non, de processus déjà expérimentés ; évaluer la distance entre les esthétiques proclamées ou revendiquées et leur application à l'intérieur des séances et devant des publics non nécessairement captifs ou acquis ; comprendre les champs de forces, les luttes et les résistances… C'est, après tout, enfoncer des portes ouvertes puisqu'il s'agit, à chaque fois, de poser à l'objet les mêmes questions : comment est-on *et avec qui* est-on, à ce moment *et* en ce lieu, « un parmi plusieurs », pris par le spectacle *et* néanmoins en distance, diverti *et* à même de penser, en butte au pathos et à l'émotion, *mais aussi* aux discours tenus (au logos), *et simultanément* capable de réflexion pour penser une sorte d'*ethos*, ou de conduite individuelle et sociale ? Comment cerner cet événement, comment le décrire et l'apprécier (ou l'évaluer) à partir des questions clefs de la rhétorique, en particulier de la rhétorique juridique des cas : *quis* ? (qui le produit ?) ; *quid* ? (quoi ? qu'est-ce qui est produit ?) ; *ubi* ? (où ?) ; *quibus auxiliis* ? (avec quelles aides (témoins) ? retour au *quis* pour la séance : de quel ensemble de producteurs ou de témoins est-il question ?) ; *quomodo* ? (comment ?) ; *quando* ? (quand ?) ; enfin *cur* ? (pourquoi (le mobile) ?, pouquoi produire cet événement théâtral ?). Mais aussi, comment, pourquoi et dans quel(s) but(s) est-on guidé, contrôlé, aidé, *et, parallèlement*, pourquoi, comment et grâce à quel dispositif inscrit dans le spectacle et son effectuation en séance résiste-t-on à cette fonction d'encadrement et de régie ? Comment découvre-t-on ou pourquoi pense-t-on découvrir ce que l'histoire, la tradition, ou soi-même, ont oublié pour à nouveau le considérer comme neuf et le juger en conséquence ? Et surtout, comment et pourquoi a-t-on le plaisir divertissant d'être là, *seul et ensemble*, dans cette assemblée qui entretient un rapport décalé avec le monde et se livre, sur ce monde donné comme extérieur à la séance, à des jugements complexes et hétérogènes *a priori* à blanc, mais qui peuvent avoir des conséquences modélisantes, ou le plus souvent perturbantes, quant à l'action sociale, politique, religieuse ou morale qu'on aura en sortant ?

On le voit, ces questions, formellement, tiennent sur deux dispositifs abstraits producteurs de questions ouvertes : le *paradoxe contradictoire* et la *simultanéité*, si bien que ces deux figures structurantes, toujours présentes sur quelque aspect qu'on se penche, seront aussi structurantes du travail esthético-critique, qu'il soit formel, dramaturgique, historique ou axiologique.

SÉANCE ET COMPARUTION THÉÂTRALE

Dès lors, poser et reposer ces mêmes questions à chaque cas, ré-enfoncer les portes ouvertes en passant par l'histoire des représentations, peut avoir un impact et déterminer des sortes de constantes : par exemple, faire ressortir des évidences recouvertes par les fictions et les *topoï* esthétiques dont on pense qu'ils fonctionnent ou qu'ils ont fonctionné pour constater que le spectacle oublie, mais reprend avec ou sans conscience, et souvent en pensant rompre avec une idée essentialiste du théâtre traditionnel, des formes pratiques et esthétiques en fonction du temps, des lieux et des publics dans lesquels il est. Mieux, il ne se contente pas d'être une sorte de miroir, il expérimente sans cesse, au contraire, les dispositifs possibles pour engager un divertissement et une réflexion sur le dispositif, sur le monde qu'il inclut et sur le monde auquel, qu'il le veuille ou non, il réfère.

On n'a ainsi, par exemple, pas attendu les acquis des années 60-70 pour donner aux publics, de gré ou de force, un rôle dans la production de la séance. Le spectacle a toujours été un lieu et un moment de tension entre toutes les forces qui le constituent et qui ne sont pas toutes à inclure dans la revendication d'un processus esthétique, mais dans l'effectuation d'un processus social, d'assemblée. Autrement dit, le théâtre n'est pas à aborder en termes d'autonomie de l'œuvre d'art, même lorsqu'il aspire à l'être, parce qu'il est composé de corps vivants et sociaux qui amènent avec eux, le temps de la séance, ce monde dans lequel, ou face auquel, il s'agit de prendre parti ou auquel il est nécessaire et urgent de poser des questions difficiles, ne serait-ce que pour passer un bon moment.

S'agissant alors de la notion d'esthétique théâtrale, on constatera que les deux dimensions de prescription et d'ordre, d'un côté – et ce côté est plutôt celui des théoriciens de l'esthétique et des écrivains de théâtre –, et de résistance à la prescription doxique de l'autre – ce que font très généralement les spectateurs et, d'une certaine manière les comédiens –, semblent innerver l'ensemble de l'histoire du théâtre, *simultanément, paradoxalement, contradictoirement.* La structure de la séance elle-même, son hétérogénéité, fait qu'il y a résistance à la mise en œuvre d'un ordre univoque (ce qui permet évidemment de distinguer le spectacle de théâtre, tel qu'on l'envisage ici, des cérémonies ritualisées, religieuses et politiques).

C'est donc à partir de ce fait, la contradiction, l'hétérogénéité, le champ de forces des instances, la multiplicité des points de vue, et en même temps leur présence éphémère et la présence éphémère d'une assemblée se divertissant et pensant, en un seul lieu et en un seul temps, qu'il faut bien réfléchir ; et s'interroger sur le fait qu'il y a alors, dans le présent éphémère de l'expérience théâtrale, dans la performance et dans la séance, une sorte de *mise en place et de mise en jeu du commun*, d'un *jeu de l'individuel par rapport à ce commun* : un phénomène de lien, et un jeu avec ce lien, à l'intérieur du lieu de spectacle et de son institutionnalisation en théâtre.

Comment alors décrire et nommer cet ensemble à partir de l'unité d'observation qu'est la séance mais cette fois en s'interrogeant sur la dynamique qui l'occupe ? Comment en formuler le mouvement sans recourir à l'idée problématique de « partage », pour mieux conserver les idées du champ de forces, de la contradiction nécessaire à l'effectuation du théâtre, tout en tenant compte de la co-présence éphémère des instances et de leur *rapport* ? Peut-être en revenant, une fois du plus, au phénomène qui s'élabore dans la séance et qui, selon nous, pourrait être nommé la « comparution[6] ».

On dira donc que, lors d'une séance théâtrale *comparaissent*, les uns devant les autres et à travers des figurations hétérogènes et des postures différentes, les acteurs, les spectateurs, les praticiens, mais aussi les personnages et les *performers* entre eux et devant les publics, enfin, devant les praticiens (intermédiaires alors) et devant des spectateurs, les productions de fiction ou de performance proposées par des auteurs individuels ou collectifs. Comparutions multiples qui figurent et induisent des jugements multiples, mettant à nu dans le lieu théâtral la nécessité du lien social en même temps que la nécessité, en en prenant conscience, de le perturber, ou de le questionner. Il ne s'agit donc ici, au sens où l'entend Lyotard dans *Au juste*[7], ni d'une simple « exposition » (c'est la définition qu'il donne du théâtre ancien)[8], ni d'une « donation » (définition du théâtre moderne), mais d'une mise en pratique et en jeu des instances et des individus à l'intérieur d'un même lieu alors qu'ils ont conscience de leur(s) présence(s) et de leur co-présence afin qu'ils s'interrogent sur cette présence même. Comparution immédiate, parce que faite dans l'instant, dans l'éphémère de la séance, avec tous les risques que l'hétérogénéité des relations inscrites dans la séance suppose. Comparution médiate ou médiatisée, parce qu'à l'intérieur de la séance il y a performance et/ou représentation d'un autre événement que le simple événement de rassemblement, parce qu'il y a « art ».

6 C'est dans un tout autre contexte que Jean-Christophe Bailly et Jean-Luc Nancy emploient cette notion, que nous reprenons ici en l'adaptant à notre propos. Voir J.-Ch. Bailly et J.-L. Nancy, *La comparution : politique à venir*, Paris, Christian Bourgois, 1991.

7 J.-Fr. Lyotard et J.-L. Thébaud, *Au juste : conversations*, Paris, Christian Bourgois, 1979.

8 Ni même exactement au sens, pourtant non dépourvu d'intérêt pour la réflexion esthétique théâtrale, où peut l'employer Jean-Luc Nancy.

C'est pourquoi la *comparution théâtrale*, définie ici, n'est pas seulement la mise en jugement d'un seul individu, ou d'un groupe d'individus représentant une notion ou une entité, devant d'autres individus ou groupe d'individus chargés de le/les juger (ce qui peut être un des ressorts du théâtre, mais seulement l'un des ressorts), mais une relation réciproque, diffractée et hétérogène, autour d'une proposition (formelle et donc forcément sémantique) consciente, incluse dans un rapport de forces isolé dans un moment et un lieu dans la cité (la séance théâtrale) et qui, nécessairement, n'est pas là pour déterminer une position ou une solution unique. Car la question n'est pas celle de l'établissement d'une résolution absolue, finale ou idéale, mais, à partir d'une proposition esthétique, la comparution elle-même en ce qu'elle produit *simultanément, contradictoirement et paradoxalement* l'hétérogénéité des jugements – cette hétérogénéité que l'on craint tant. Et c'est en cela qu'en même temps qu'il s'agit bien d'une opération esthétique pratique et figurée par des corps en mouvement, des objets et des sons et des souffles qui souvent portent un texte, il s'agit aussi d'une opération politique spécifique au lieu dans lequel elle prend place.

La comparution théâtrale[9] sera donc cette opération esthético-politique en ce qu'elle figure pour tous les présents un événement social qui relève du rassemblement et qui s'inscrit nécessairement dans le politique. L'*opération* politique, ainsi, ne veut pas nécessairement dire que le théâtre est ostensiblement un acte politique, une action politique, mais qu'il est une opération du politique, une façon d'accomplir ou d'actualiser le politique par sa présence même dans la cité. Il ne s'agit pas pour le théâtre de véhiculer tel ou tel message mais de réaliser avant tout une assemblée d'individus qui se voient, se rencontrent et échangent (à des degrés plus ou moins intenses), liée, ou non, par des valeurs et des références communes tout en étant traversée de contradictions et de tensions.

Pour mieux dire, le théâtre fait entrer les représentations qu'il propose et surtout sa représentation même dans le politique, dans la cité en figurant les zones et les questions sur lesquelles, par exemple, *la* politique et

9 L'anglais, ici aussi, peut avoir son intérêt dans la mesure où la *comparution judiciaire* peut se traduire par *judicial appearance*. Si bien que l'anglais insistant à la fois sur l'apparition, sur le fait d'être là et sur le fait d'être là au sein du processus judiciaire, permet, comme en français mais autrement, qu'on garde cet ensemble en le transposant au théâtre par *theatrical appearance*.

le droit achoppent ou qu'elles ignorent. Et l'on ajoutera que le problème du *politique* au théâtre ou du théâtre comme jeu politique désignant et figurant la comparution de tous devant tous n'induit donc pas le fait que le théâtre, seulement, *témoigne*, car, en tant que jeu ou performance, il ne fait pas que témoigner : il ajoute pratiquement, il fait *quelque chose* au (dans le) monde par la co-présence de ses instances, à l'intérieur même des propositions et des productions esthético-politiques présentes, *quelque chose* qui est de l'ordre du processus du jugement. Ainsi, il complexifie, dans ce processus même, des données qu'il introduit dans du présent éphémère pour les faire comparaître devant et avec des individus co-présents. Ce faisant, il fait exister ces jugements, il leur donne un corps, une chair autre que celle des images.

C'est dans l'optique d'une observation historicisée des phénomènes liés à la séance théâtrale que nous avons souhaité ressaisir quelques évidences bonnes à rappeler, et les articuler : que le théâtre est marqué par la simultanéité présente, le jeu des paradoxes et des contradictions, la nécessité d'expérimenter des questions capables d'intéresser les participants (en les divertissant et en les mettant, seuls et en groupe, en état de penser), pour en arriver à forger une sorte de notion, la comparution théâtrale, qui permettrait de rendre compte du fait spectaculaire.

DE LA LIBRE INCERTITUDE AU JUGEMENT-VALEUR THÉÂTRALE

C'est donc aux creux des tensions et des contradictions, au sein de ce dispositif tel que nous venons de le décrire, au sein du phénomène de la séance qui rend ostensiblement possible l'indéfinie relation réciproque de comparution théâtrale que le spectacle mime le droit et le dépasse, y renvoie, se glisse dans ses interstices et ses failles. Car la séance suit le mouvement du droit, calque le processus juridique ou judiciaire pour le perturber[10] : si le droit, en effet, ou plutôt si le

10 On ne rappellera pas ici la manière dont la dramaturgie semblablement fonctionne (voir Ch. Biet, *Droit et littérature sous l'Ancien régime, le jeu de la valeur et de la loi*, Paris, Champion, 2002).

processus judiciaire, cherche à aller du moins connu au plus connu, de l'incertain au certain, l'art, et plus particulièrement le phénomène théâtral dans le présent de sa performance, poursuit (dans tous les sens du terme, y compris juridique) ce processus d'examen et d'élucidation pour le mettre en doute et le dépasser, pour rendre incertain le certain et mettre en doute l'élucidation même, voire pour proposer d'autres certitudes, en tout cas d'autres jugements concurrents aux jugements autorisés. Le théâtre, en principe *incapable* sur la scène juridique et sociale, parce que divertissement, parce qu'art, se donne, à côté du droit, comme le lieu de revendication d'une autonomie de jugement, d'un rejet de tutelle, d'une volonté d'affranchissement. Si bien qu'en se saisissant du droit et en le débordant par l'étoilement des jugements, le théâtre peut revendiquer une manière de produire une légitimité, voire un champ, rivalisant, par les conduites qu'il crée, avec le droit lui-même.

La séance théâtrale, ainsi, semble mimer, ou réaliser à côté, dans une hétérotopie, les moments où le droit, dans son processus d'élucidation et de passage à la certitude (relative mais efficace), hésite, n'a pas les moyens véritablement de trancher, s'obscurcit, est frappé d'ambiguïté. Et comme, lors de cette pluralité de tentatives d'élucidations et d'interprétations qui caractérise le processus de la séance, les partenaires présents ont bien conscience qu'ils s'expriment dans l'incertitude et l'inconfort, ils deviennent à leur tour des juges dont le jugement n'a d'autre exercice que celui d'être à blanc, mais qui pourtant sont en droit de juger : des juges de l'incertitude, des cultivateurs de cette incertitude, des juges en état de douter. C'est là que le théâtre, ou plutôt la séance théâtrale prend toute sa place, par son dispositif même, en montrant que, dans le présent de l'événement, toute loi peut être jugée et que tous les jugements peuvent être *interprétables* et jugés par tous. Ce faisant, lors de cette incertitude perturbante le théâtre produit un doute spéculatif, critique, sur le « juste », ou sur un « juste » qui ne se limite pas aux frontières que le droit détermine. C'est ainsi un système alternatif, substitutif, ou en tout cas décalé et critique, que la séance théâtrale propose au droit et au monde en dégageant une liberté générale de juger. Dès lors, la valeur de la séance, et partant du théâtre, devient celle du jugement, de mettre en place l'idée et la fonction de juger, comme valeur commune que chaque partenaire de la séance, en effet, possède. Le théâtre contradictoire, phénomène d'oppositions et de tensions multiples, produirait ainsi non une valeur morale, politique, qu'il s'agirait d'appliquer, mais une valeur définie par un processus, par une dynamique d'interrogation capable d'animer, à la fois à blanc, comme divertissement, et avec un impact sur le monde, l'ensemble des partenaires en les mettant en état de juger. Le jugement comme valeur, comme production et exercice de savoir critique : là serait la valeur que la séance théâtrale figure lors de son effectuation, procure à chaque partenaire, enfin transmet au dehors du théâtre, et insère dans le monde.

Le théâtre, ainsi, pourrait être défini comme une figuration-performance du jugement, un événement de jeu, ou un *événement-jeu*, un lieu d'interaction esthétique et sociale qui explore le danger du jeu lui-même et du jugement généralisé de chacun : un *jeu de figuration du jugement*, dont la fonction et le fonctionnement individuels et collectifs consistent à figurer du jugement dans une interaction constante, une comparution, organisée dans le cadre d'un événement présent.

Dès lors, ce jeu complexe pourra être pensé, non seulement comme un procédé fondé sur l'acceptation de codes, sur de la connivence, ou sur la transgression de cette connivence, mais plutôt comme un processus de comparution de tous devant tous à partir de la figuration de conduites exceptionnelles à travers des bouffées excessives de violence dans les actions, comme à travers le discours. C'est ainsi qu'il deviendra un art profondément social et politique complexe, et non une didactique, ou son contraire, une donation esthétique en regard sur elle-même. Car le théâtre utilise l'ensemble des formes de questionnement (images, parole, gestes, actions violentes, etc.) à même d'être jugées à la fois dans le cadre des protocoles esthétiques qu'il installe et dans le cadre de la cité qu'il convoque. À l'aune du théâtre, la justice rencontre le juste tel qu'il peut être contradictoirement ou paradoxalement défini par la somme hétérogène des spectateurs et des praticiens. À l'aune de performances de toutes sortes, qu'elles soient dramatiques ou épiques, il crée des événements de jeu, des espaces de sensation et de pensée qui donnent la possibilité à ceux qui partagent la co-présence de cet événement de produire un jugement, applicable ou non au monde dont ils viennent et dans lequel, après la séance, ils reviennent plus ou moins changés. Le théâtre, ainsi, *s'adresse*. Mais cette adresse est réciproque, partagée, conflictuelle et contradictoire, elle fonctionne comme un champ de forces hétérogènes et répercute en son centre, la séance, et dans le centre du centre, la scène, l'hétérogénéité problématique du monde qui est à sa périphérie[11].

Christian BIET
Université Paris-Nanterre

11 Ce texte, prononcé à Amsterdam en 2009, fait état de recherches qui, depuis, ont été formulées ailleurs et autrement : « Pour une extension du domaine de la performance (XVIIe-XXIe siècles) », in *Communications*, numéro spécial « Performance », direction Christian Biet et Sylvie Roques, N° 92, Seuil, 2013 ; « Séance, performance, assemblée et représentation : les jeux de regards au théâtre (XVIIe-XXIe siècle) » in *Littératures classiques*, dir. Sylvaine Guyot et Tom Conley, « L'Œil classique », n° 82, Armand Colin, 2013 ; « Voices of Spectators and Audience Power », Polemos, volume 9, Issue 2, p. 249-263, août 2015 ; « Émotions expérimentales : théâtre et tragédie au XVIIe siècle français, affects, sens, passions », chapitre 21 de l'*Histoire des émotions*, I. De l'Antiquité aux Lumières, volume dirigé par Georges Vigarello, Seuil, 2016.

INDEX DES NOMS

INDEX DES LIEUX

INDEX DES ŒUVRES

RÉSUMÉS

Arjan VAN DIXHOORN, « The Law, Justice, Governance, and Theatrical Knowledge in the Sixteenth-Century Dutch-speaking Low Countries »

Afin d'être efficaces, les autorités de la première modernité durent prendre en compte la nature des phénomènes théâtraux qu'elles voulaient réguler. Par suite d'une censure croissante, les agents du gouvernement acquirent et créèrent plus de savoir sur le monde de la rhétorique et du théâtre ; ce savoir fut universalisé dans des lois, des ordonnances et dans la littérature juridique du XVIe siècle. Ainsi, les autorités se firent agents de changement dans le monde théâtral de cette région.

Anne-Laure VAN BRUAENE, « Le théâtre des rhétoriciens et les ambiguïtés de la censure dans les Pays-Bas pré-modernes (XVe-XVIIe siècle) »

Cet article analyse la question de la censure du théâtre urbain des rhétoriciens dans les Pays-Bas de la période pré-moderne. L'argument central est que, même si les rhétoriciens eux-mêmes, tout comme les autorités qui les sanctionnaient, étaient convaincus du besoin de poser des limites au discours et à la performance publics, ces limites sont toujours restées fluides et ont même créé de nouvelles opportunités pour une pratique littéraire riche.

Alessandra RIZZI, « Discipline in Play-related Activities in Communal Italy »

Entre le XIIIe et le XVIe siècle, les villes-états italiennes évoluèrent en principautés ou en républiques oligarchiques. Le jeu donna lieu à des régulations largement répandues, laïques et religieuses. Les différentes autorités publiques coopéraient plutôt qu'elles ne s'affrontaient dans des conflits de juridictions. Cependant, à partir de la fin du XVe siècle, on constate une séparation des activités et célébrations ludiques promues par les autorités laïques, et celles contrôlées par des membres du clergé.

Mathieu FERRAND, « “Et de ne jouer n’en peut venir que bien.” L’interdiction et le contrôle du théâtre universitaire à Paris (1450-1550) »

L’article parcourt les archives de l’Université et du Parlement de Paris pour faire apprécier la façon dont les autorités ont tenté de contrôler le théâtre des étudiants parisiens. Ces tentatives s’inscrivent dans un double contexte d’affirmation de l’autorité royale et parlementaire et de développement du système collégial. Au théâtre des étudiants, souvent insaisissable, s’oppose ainsi un théâtre signé et situé, c’est-à-dire un théâtre de collègue, placé sous l’autorité des maîtres.

Heidy GRECO-KAUFMANN, « Curbing carnival activities by staging carnival plays? Renward Cysat’s ambigous resolution of jurisdictional conflicts »

Le carnaval médiéval se terminait par un dépassement des limites mettant en danger la loi et l’ordre. À partir du Moyen Âge, les autorités de Lucerne luttèrent pour canaliser ces festivités. La mise en scène du *Convivii Process* de Cysat en 1593 marque le point culminant du conflit entre les défenseurs du plaisir et les promoteurs de la morale. Ce spectacle tragi-comique portait le message de la réforme catholique : les incorrigibles fêtards du carnaval devaient en subir les terribles conséquences dans l’au-delà.

Olivier SPINA, « Suivre la loi ou concourir au bien commun ? Les fabriques de paroisse et les lieux de spectacles dans Londres à la fin du XVIe siècle »

Cet article étudie la construction des amphithéâtres londoniens à la fin du XVIe siècle et la façon dont les fabriques de paroisse ont accueilli ces implantations dramatiques. Il n’existe pas de politique élisabéthaine des spectacles centralisée et formalisée dans un cadre juridique rigide. Les institutions urbaines à l’autonomie grandissante peuvent largement interpréter le droit édicté par la monarchie. La politique des spectacles du Londres élisabéthain apparaît comme un champ de forces dynamique et complexe.

Walter PREVENIER, « Quand un honorable bourgeois de Malines, “marié avec une bonne et honeste femme”, s’encanaille dans une troupe de théâtre en marge de la bonne société (1475) »

La lettre de pardon pour Mathieu Cricke nous renseigne sur les activités d’une compagnie de théâtre itinérante, et sur un conflit autour d’une prostituée et actrice, Maria van der Hoeven. C'est la première apparition documentée d'une actrice sous contrat dans les anciens Pays-Bas. Le cas souligne le mélange des publics cultivés et populaires dans les représentations en espaces fermés, et permet de mieux cerner le parcours d'une troupe d'acteurs professionnels, ainsi que leurs démêlés avec la justice.

Dylan REID, « *"Chevauchees, mascarades et jeux acoustumez"*. Jurisdiction over carnival in sixteenth-century Rouen »

L'Abbaye des Conards, l'association qui organisait les festivités du carnaval à Rouen au XVIe siècle, revendiquait une juridiction facétieuse sur ces fêtes. Les autorités judiciaires rouennaises, au contraire, intervenaient dans le carnaval suite à leurs inquiétudes concernant le respect de l'ordre public (notamment sur le port de masques ou la musique). Grâce à une interaction complexe entre ces organisations, les Conards obtinrent une juridiction réelle sur le carnaval, accordée par les autorités de la ville.

Antonio SÁNCHEZ JIMÉNEZ, « Conflicts of Jurisdiction in Golden Age Spanish Theater. A Panoramic Overview and Enquiry into Antonio de Soria's 1644 Trial vs. the Villa de Madrid Regarding the Ban on the *Comedia* »

Afin d'examiner les conflits de juridiction dans le théâtre du Siècle d'Or espagnol, cet article analyse une étude de cas à partir d'une procédure juridique en 1644-1645, mettant en cause Antonio de Soria, exploitant des *corrales* de Madrid. Après avoir décrit les pratiques qui touchent aux *corrales*, l'article se concentre sur des exemples de conflit légal entre institutions civiles. L'analyse du procès de Soria montre ensuite comment le système espagnol cherchait à prévenir et résoudre les conflits de juridiction.

Frans CAMPHUIJSEN, « *"In hemde ende in broeck"*. The performance of justice in late medieval Utrecht »

À partir de l'étude d'un procès à Utrecht à la fin du Moyen Âge, et en s'appuyant sur les théories anthropologiques du rituel, cet article propose une interprétation socio-communicative de l'histoire des punitions en public. Parce qu'elles combinaient des aspects textuels, oraux, visuels, symboliques et performatifs dans des événements ritualisés spécifiques, les performances pénales à Utrecht n'étaient pas de simples éléments de répression, mais formaient un espace ouvert aux revendications de vérité sociale.

Denis HÜE, « La Vierge et la loi, Marie Avocate »

Si la figure de Marie avocate des croyants est présente dans l'iconographie dès le haut Moyen Âge, c'est dans le cadre d'une réflexion théologique sur la faute originelle et son rachat qu'elle prendra sa dimension exemplaire. Le personnage de Marie interviendra dès lors dans une situation dialectique où à la justice et au droit, s'oppose la miséricorde qui les dépasse et transcende. Le théâtre médiéval sera le lieu privilégié de ces procès où Marie illustre droit et miséricorde.

Camille SALATKO-PETRYSZCZE, « La figure de l'inquisiteur et le visage de l'accusé dans le *Mystère de la sainte Hostie* »

Quand le théâtre du XVe siècle s'approprie le miracle du Juif parisien profanateur d'hostie, il choisit d'introduire sur la scène la figure de l'inquisiteur. Bien que fort discrète, cette originalité dramatique invite à ouvrir le texte du *Mystère de la sainte Hostie* à des visées nouvelles. Face à ce nouveau juge, le personnage du Juif pourrait servir à dénoncer le judaïsant grandement redouté à la fin du Moyen Âge.

Estelle DOUDET, « Dame Justice et ses suppôts, un personnel dramatique sur la scène des moralités et sotties (XVe-XVIe siècle) »

Cette contribution étudie les figurations de Justice sur les scènes allégoriques des XVe et XVIe siècles, en particulier moralités et sotties, à partir de l'hypothèse que les mises en scène de la loi interagissent avec le statut que les pièces donnent à la notion. Autorité régulatrice du monde dans les moralités, Justice prend des traits d'une institution sociale discutée dans les sotties, son corps théâtral s'entourant d'accessoires et de commentateurs à mesure que sa force s'affaiblit.

Christian BIET, « Séance, assemblée, médiation spectaculaire et comparution théâtrale »

Cet article est une réflexion inachevée qui fait le lien entre l'histoire du théâtre, l'histoire des théories juridiques sous l'Ancien Régime, la dramaturgie de cette époque et son rapport aux spectateurs. Avant de formuler l'irruption du théâtre sous une forme d'abord métaphoriquement judiciaire puis principalement juridique, l'étude le décrit en quelques mots comme phénomène en tension et comme événement complexe.

TABLE DES MATIÈRES

DEUXIÈME PARTIE

CONTRÔLER LES SPECTACLES DANS LA VILLE

TROISIÈME PARTIE

CONFLITS ET PROCÈS

ÉTUDES DE CAS

QUATRIÈME PARTIE

JUSTICE EN SCÈNE

CINQUIÈME PARTIE

POUR UNE THÉORIE JURIDIQUE ET HISTORIQUE DU THÉÂTRE SOUS L'ANCIEN RÉGIME

IMPRIM'VERT®

Achevé d'imprimer par Corlet Numérique,
à Condé-sur-Noireau (Calvados). N° d'impression : 143263
Imprimé en France